ESSAYS IN THE HISTORY OF MAINSTREAM POLITICAL ECONOMY

Also by Warren J. Samuels and published by New York University Press

ESSAYS ON THE ECONOMIC ROLE OF GOVERNMENT
Volume 1: Fundamentals
Volume 2: Applications

ESSAYS IN THE HISTORY OF HETERODOX POLITICAL ECONOMY

ESSAYS ON THE METHODOLOGY AND DISCOURSE OF ECONOMICS

Essays in the History of Mainstream Political Economy

Warren J. Samuels
Professor of Economics
Michigan State University

NEW YORK UNIVERSITY PRESS
Washington Square, New York

First published in the U.S.A. in 1992 by
NEW YORK UNIVERSITY PRESS
Washington Square
New York, N.Y. 10003

Printed in Hong Kong

Library of Congress Cataloging-in-Publication Data
Samuels, Warren J., 1933–
Essays in the history of mainstream political economy/Warren J. Samuels.
p. cm.
Collection of previously published essays by the author.
Contents: Includes bibliographical references and index.
ISBN 0–8147–7945–X
1. Economics. 2. Economic policy. I. Title.
HB171.S25 1992
338.9—dc20 91–39105
CIP

To those under whom I studied the history of economic thought: Brooks Johnson, George J. Malanos, Gerald Franklin, Grover A. J. Noetzel, James S. Early, Martin Bronfenbrenner, Martin Glaeser, Eugene Rotwein, Hans Gerth

Contents

Acknowledgements ix

Introduction 1

1 The Physiocratic Theory of Property and State 12

2 The Physiocratic Theory of Economic Policy 28

3 Adam Smith and the Economy as a System of Power 47

4 The Political Economy of Adam Smith 65

5 The Classical Theory of Economic Policy: Non-Legal Social Control 86

6 Introduction to Thomas Robert Malthus, 'An Essay on the Principle of Population', 1798 (*with John P. Henderson*) 140

7 Introduction to Thomas Robert Malthus, *Principles of Political Economy*, 1820 (*with John P. Henderson*) 151

8 Edgeworth's *Mathematical Psychics*: A Centennial Notice 167

9 Ashley's and Taussig's Lectures on the History of Economic Thought at Harvard, 1896–7 176

10 The Teaching of Business Cycles in 1905–6: Insight into the Development of Macroeconomic Theory 203

11 The Teaching of Monetary Economics in the Early 1900s: Insight into the Development of Monetary Theory (*with Andrew Gray*) 223

12 Preface, 'Friedrich von Wieser in the History of Economic Thought' 239

13 Taussig on the Psychology of Economic Policy 245

14 Introduction, Frank W. Taussig, *Inventors and Money-Makers* 258

15 The Influence of Friedrich von Wieser on Joseph A. Schumpeter 267

16 Introduction, William H. Hutt, *Economists and the Public* 284

Name Index 291

Subject Index 292

Acknowledgements

The author and publishers wish to thank the following publishers, editors and co-authors for permission to reprint material:

'The Physiocratic Theory of Property and States', *Quarterly Journal of Economics*, vol. 75 (February 1961), pp. 96–111, and 'The Physiocratic Theory of Economic Policy', *Quarterly Journal of Economics*, vol. 76 (February 1962), pp. 145–62. Reprinted by permission of John Wiley & Sons, Inc., All Rights Reserved.

'Adam Smith and the Economy as a System of Power', *Review of Social Economy*, vol. 31 (October 1973), pp. 123–37, and *Indian Economic Journal*, vol. 20 (January–March 1973), pp. 363–81, by permission of the *Review of Social Economy*.

'The Political Economy of Adam Smith', *Nebraska Journal of Economics and Business*, vol. 15 (Summer 1976), pp. 3–24, by permission of *Quarterly Journal of Economics and Business*, formerly, *Nebraska Journal of Economics and Business*.

'The Classical Theory of Economic Policy: Non-Legal Social Control', I–II, *Southern Economic Journal*, vol. 31 (July, October 1964), pp. 1–20, 87–100, by permission of the *Southern Economic Journal*.

With John P. Henderson, Zu Malthus' 'Essay über die Entwicklung der Bevolkerung', first published in German language in Engels, Hax, Hayek and Recktenwald (eds), *Klassiker der Nationalökonomie* (Dusseldorf/ Darnstadt: Verlag Wirtschaft und Finanzen GmbH, 1986), pp. 11–28.

With John P. Henderson, 'Malthus als Theoretiker', in *Uber Malthus' Principles of Political Economy*, first published in German language in Engels, Hax, Hayek and Recktenwald (eds), *Klassiker der Nationalökonomie* (Dusseldorf: Verlag Wirtschaft und Finanzen GmbH, 1989), pp. 35–9.

'Edgeworth's *Mathematical Psychics*: A Centennial Notice', *Eastern Economic Journal*, vol. 7 (July–October 1981), pp. 193–8, by permission of *Eastern Economic Journal*.

'Ashley's and Taussig's Lectures on the History of Economic Thought at Harvard, 1896–7', *History of Political Economy*, vol. 9 (Fall 1977), pp. 384–411; 'The Teaching of Business Cycles in 1905–6: Insight into the Development of Macroeconomic Theory', *History of Political Economy*, vol. 4 (Spring 1972), pp. 140–162; with Andrew Gray, 'The Teaching of Monetary Economics in the Early 1900s: Insight into the Development of Monetary Theory', *History of Political Economy*, vol. 8 (Fall 1976), pp. 324–40, by permission of Duke University Press.

Preface, 'Friedrich von Wieser in the History of Economic Thought', in Friedrich von Wieser, *Gesammelte Abhandlungen* (Vienna: Hermann Bohlaus, 1991), by permission of Institut für Soziologie, Karl-Franzens Universität.

'Taussig on the Psychology of Economic Policy', *Indian Economic Journal*, vol. 15 (July–September 1967), pp. 1–13.

'Introduction', Frank W. Taussig, *Inventors and Money-makers* (New Brunswick: Transaction, 1989), pp. xi–xxxiv, by permission of Transaction Publishers.

'The Influence of Friedrich von Wieser on Joseph A. Schumpeter', Presidential Address, *History of Economics Society Bulletin*, vol. 4 (Winter 1983), pp. 5–19, by permission of the History of Economics Society and *Journal of the History of Economic Thought*, successor to *History of Economics Society Bulletin*.

Introduction, William H. Hutt, *Economists and the Public* (New Brunswick: Transaction Books, 1991), by permission of Transaction Publishers.

Note: the reprinted materials appear as in the original publications except that minor alterations have been made to the style and presentation for the purpose of publishing this collection of readings in book form.

Introduction

The following selected essays explore aspects of the history of mainstream economics, or, as I prefer to call it, for reasons to be made clear, political economy. The study of the history of economic thought has at least one characteristic in common with the economy *per se*, namely, *scarcity*. Scarcity is one of the – perhaps the very most important – foundation concepts of economics, and one of its implications is the idea of opportunity cost. Scarcity necessitates choice and the inexorable incurrence of foregone alternatives. The connections between scarcity and opportunity cost are complex but include the following chain: scarcity implies choice, which implies conflict over the choices to be made, the bases of choice, and the nature of the choosing process and its structure. Choices, and corresponding opportunity costs, are therefore specific to the structure of the choosing process. Choices and costs are necessarily political, meaning by political having to do with the exercise of power.

In matters of technical economic theory, one would say that Pareto-optimal solutions (choices due to the agreement of decision makers, perhaps traders, each capable of withholding consent) are specific to the power structure and decision-making process which have given rise to them; and the opportunity cost generated by each would depend on the choices produced by the decision-making structure and process. There is accordingly a political element in the development of both the economy and economic theory: in each case, the results are due in no small degree to the operation of the actual or the assumed power structure, that is, definition and assignment of rights and institutions.

In the history of economic thought, the picture which we have of the past depends to no small degree on the present state of economics. The past is often interpreted and evaluated on the basis of the present (to which practice the names 'presentism' and 'Whiggism' are typically given), and the opportunity costs of such history are, first, the materials of the past which the present view of the discipline more or less conveniently forgets, and second, the factors and forces which operated in the past to select, out of an *ex ante* array of possible lines of development, that which in fact developed and which constitutes, *ex post*, the present state of the discipline. The story is further complicated because at all times the discipline has been, and remains, heterogenous, comprised of a mainstream which is itself heterogenous and an array of heterodoxies. The history of economics, accordingly, is a history of (1) what did develop, typically understood on the terms solely of what developed, especially the mainstream or predominant school; (2) what might have further developed but did not, yet nonetheless existed and perhaps still exists but not in the mainstream; and (3) something of an invention, from the point of view of the present (that which did develop), of how and why it developed as it did. The history of economics, like the history of nations, is a history generally written from the point of view of the victors. But, whereas history written from the point of view of the present tends to interpret that past as an inexorable path to the present, something given in the nature of things, that history manifests both a structure and process of choice and is, in that respect at least, a political phenomenon. Scarcity in the form or sense that only one school of thought has come to predominate, means that the opportunity costs of the development of economic thought comprises both the alternative avenues hitherto foregone and the materials of the past which are either excluded from or denigrated in the history of the discipline to the extent that its history is written from the point of view of the presently predominating school (presentism). To the extent that its history of the past written from the perspective of the present involves, first, the omission of the complex processes by which the present did in fact emerge from the past, and second, deliberate and/or unintentional obscurantism as to the political premises of elements in modern economic theory, then these too constitute the opportunity cost of the development of the field.

There is an important sense in which we are necessarily presentist: each present-day historian of economic thought can inspect the past only on the basis of his or her contemporary perspective. In a post-Kantian and post-Wittgensteinian world, we are self-consciously aware that our perceptions of reality and our language do not necessarily refer to a hypothesized independently given and unequivocally approachable reality, and our study of the objects of inquiry are mediated by the human mind. Historians of economic thought can deal with the ideas of the past only with minds mediated by the present state of their discipline, the state into which they have been inculcated and socialized. We cannot completely transcend our own mind set or milieu. This means not that we cannot study either reality (whatever that term is taken to mean) or the past but that we must do so with some degree of diffidence and caution. This also means (as I shall discuss below) that in analysing past thought on the economic role of government one has to adjust for ideological preconceptions which the historian may, or may not, share with the original authors.

The history of economic thought is therefore richer than one might contemplate on the basis of the perspective of the present, richer in regard to content and to interpretation. It is richer in regard to *content*, for example, inasmuch as there is more to the history of eco-nomics than the history of value and price theory and of markets. It is a history of certain very large issues in which the history of value and price theory is nested. These issues constitute the typically obscured penumbra of intellectual considerations from which the theory of markets has emerged, the issues are raised inevitably raised by the theory of markets. Not the least of these subjects is the nature, origins, and evolution of the economic system *qua* system. It is also the history of some very great intellects, intellects which often focused on value, price, and markets but which understood that more than these were involved in the study of economic system *qua* system. And it is also, *inter alia*, the history of the filtration process through which the theories of value, price, and markets came to take central position in the discipline, thereby incurring the opportunity costs of the other subjects so largely foregone, at least within the mainstream of neoclassical theory.

The history of economic thought is richer in regard to *interpretation*, for example, in regard to the enormous heterogeneity of each school of thought, each of which is more complex and diverse in its methodology, central tenets, and implications than its typical convenient caricaturist summary permits. It is also a history in which the work of leading writers – such as Adam Smith, David Ricardo, Karl Marx, and John Maynard Keynes – can be given dramatically different and fundamentally conflicting interpretations, so that answers to questions like, 'what did Smith really mean?', are subject to the problem of the hermeneutic circle. Answers are based on the prior assumption of positions which respectively privilege one or another answer and which do not derive solely from the recondite text constituting the object of inquiry but which, rather, add to and superimpose upon that text the chosen perspective of the interpreter.

The history of economics also in a history of both 'historical reconstructions' and 'rational reconstructions', to use Mark Blaug's felicitous distinction. By historical reconstruction Blaug refers to 'attempts to give an account of past thinkers' systems of thought 'in their own terms,' that is, in terms these thinkers would have accepted as a correct description of what they had done'. By rational reconstruction is meant efforts to 'treat the great dead thinkers of the past as contemporaries with whom we can exchange views . . . [and] analyze their ideals in *our* terms in order to locate their "mistakes" and to verify that there has been rational progress in the course of intellectual inquiry'. It may well be that the latter is highly presumptuous, in part for the reason that we cannot conclusively know, even in our own terms, what the earlier system really amounted to, and in part because the notions of 'mistakes' and 'rational progress' give effect to selective substantive, presentist, and Whiggish assumptions. But Blaug is certainly unequivocally correct when he notes that while 'there is a genuine distinction to be made between these two styles in the historiography of economics, they tend invariably to shade into one another: what is in principle separable is in practice almost inseparable'.[1]

The foregoing means that the serious and self-critical historian of economics must appreciate the tension between a belief that one's own analysis is in some sense 'correct' and an understanding that that analysis, whatever else it may be, is an exercise in a mode of discourse, telling one story among many.

What has driven, or motivated, the development of economic thought, say, from the eighteenth century to the present? This is not an easy question and any reasonably complete answer must have disparate elements, with different ones stressed by different interpreters. 'The quest for truth' is one answer but is obviously incomplete given the variety of what people believe constitutes both the epistemological basis and substantive content of 'truth'. One approach, with several possible variations, would stress three functions of economics: that it has been an attempt at knowledge, increasingly of 'scientific' knowledge, of the economy as it 'really' is; that it has been, as both a supplement to and substitute for religion, an institution of social control; and that it has been, in an effort to counter existential uncertainty due to radical indeterminacy, psychic balm. Another approach would emphasize the operation, especially (but by no means solely) since the late nineteenth century, of such motivations as the desire for scientific status; the desire for the social role of the knowledgeable expert; and the (not unrelated) role of someone who has something important and possibly conclusively dispositive about the details of the economic role of government. Still another would emphasize subtle efforts to affect the distributions of income and wealth and to control, perhaps ultimately for that very purpose, the economic role of government. This would also be the case to the extent that economic thought was unknowingly guided by ideological preconceptions. Pervading all these and other approaches would be the at least implicit but often enough explicit effort to influence the definition of reality and values in order to control policy governing the social (re)construction of economic reality through controlling economic theory. Central, therefore, to both the economy and the history of economic thought are considerations of the economic role of government – and such considerations have been a principal focus of my work as a historian of economic thought, in which my overriding objective has been to identify what actually seems to have constituted the treatment of the economic role of government in earlier economic thought. This has involved the need somehow to transcend the limits of conventional ideology and language, to overcome the distinctive but limiting epigrammatic formulations of the spirit of the modern age without losing their distinctive orientation.

The first five articles reprinted below (the fifth of which is in two parts) address several important and deep considerations resident in the ideas of the Physiocrats and the English classical economists. These ideas have to do with the fundamental institutions which make the economy what it is; with the power structure which helps form the economy and to which the economy gives effect; and the economic role of both government and other, non-legal forces of social control. These considerations are readily and frequently lost sight of when analytic attention is focused on the mechanics of price and resource allocation (and even macroeconomic questions). They are also arguably either distorted or ignored when the work of these writers on the economic role of government is treated as '*laissez-faire*' or 'non-interventionist'. Here the methodologically individualist and mechanistic tendencies of economic theory are reinforced by the normatively individualistic and mechanistic mindset of modern society (which may also have generated the characteristics of economic theory) so as to posit the existence of a transcendentally given, self-subsistent economic order independent of government.

The two chapters on the Physiocrats constitute a reconstruction of what François Quesnay and his disciples had to say on the topics of property, state, and the economic role of government. These articles attempt to do so on the basis of what the Physiocrats themselves had to say on these topics, their naturalistic metaphysics and exhortative rhetoric notwithstanding. They therefore comprise a blend of rational and historical reconstruction. One sees here the fundamental importance of the selective uses to which government would have been put should the Physiocrats have come to dominate policy making, uses no less equivocal for the Physiocrats' belief that they derived from nothing less than the natural order of things. One also sees here Quesnay's concerns about economic instability, in which regard he was one of the first, if not the first, macroeconomists. One sees also the importance for both the Physiocrats' economic theory and their theory of economic policy of their fundamental assumptions as to social structure: so much depends on their assumption of the premier economic and political status of the land-owning class. Notwithstanding their evident practice of equating their conception of the ideal economic order with the 'natural order', in the work of the Physiocrats neither property nor state was effectively given; both were a matter of human (re)construction.

The chapter on Adam Smith and the economy as a system of power attempts to show that the *Wealth of Nations* contains both a theory of the market process and a study of the power process through which it is determined whose interests will count. This latter process is one of power and a contest for the control of markets and therefore also of government in order to control the formation, operation, and performance of markets. It is pointed out that the subsequent combination of the narrowing of economic categories and models, the felt demands of ideological purity, and scientific convenience (which itself is likely not uninfluenced by the foregoing two factors) have tended to emphasize the former and to obscure the latter process. Implicit in the article is the belief that Smith did not posit in detail a particular power structure but left the matter to be worked out by economic actors, not specified in advance in accordance with some ideological system.

The chapter on the political economy of Adam Smith incorporates but goes beyond the foregoing combination of market and power. It presents an interpretation of Smith as having formulated something like a complete theory of human society, polity, and economy – a synoptic and synthetic system of society encompassing both deliberative and non-deliberative processes of social control and the operation of markets within their constraints. In his *Theory of Moral Sentiments* Smith addressed the processes of human interaction – consequent to the operation of the principles of approbation and disapprobation – leading to the formation of moral rules and thereby the socialization of individuals in the ways of the society into which they have been born and in whose mores they have been raised. In his *Lectures on Jurisprudence* (and in an intended volume on law and government) Smith addressed the parallel operation of governmental (judicial, legislative, and administrative) processes in the determination and assignment of rights. In the *Wealth of Nations* Smith addressed the operation of markets giving effect to the division of labour in the production of the goods constituting the wealth of nations. The three books combined present the possibility of conflicts between the spheres of morality and law, morality and market, and law and market; between sympathy and self-interest; and between individualism and social control; but they especially constitute a general theory of society as a whole. Smith emerges, with John Locke, as a preeminent philosopher of the modern economic system. But he was a philosopher who, for all the limitations of language (which he also addressed in other writings), was able to emphasize the manifest complexities and openendedness of the society, polity, and economy about which he was writing. He was an advocate of the modern market economy, of modern liberal society (in the nineteenth- if not also twentieth-century sense), but he was no ideologue. Not only do the details of such a society remain to be (re)worked out but they necessarily include elements of both freedom and control, and of deliberative as well as non-deliberative social control and social change, thereby rendering the frequent allegation of Smith as 'non-interventionist' highly suspect if not manifestly wrong.

If government was important as social control to Smith and the other classical economists' analysis of the economic system, so also were religion, custom, morals, and education. The two-part article on the classical theory of non-legal social control argues that for the classical economists (not solely Smith) the concept 'theory of economic policy' involved the economic role of both legal and non-legal social control and social change,[2] and therefore, once again, that the 'non-interventionist' and '*laissez-faire*' characterization of their policy orientation is highly misleading.

The basic argument of these essays on the Physiocrats and the English classical economists, including Smith, has to do with the treatment of the economic role of government in their writings and the significance therefore for later thought on that topic. These earlier writers, some or all of whom comprised the founders of the discipline, treated government within naturalist, individualist, and *laissez-faire* non-interventionist modes of discourse. In this view, government appears to be so secondary or tertiary in importance that it can meaningfully be minimized. Yet when one penetrates beneath the discursive surface of their analyses, one can perceive the very important roles attributed by them to government. The conventional failure to recognize the actual roles which these writers effectively envisioned for government, a failure due in part to the dominance of the modern mind by much the same ideology as theirs, gives effect to, perpetuates, and both fails to correct for and yet underwrites the selective application of that ideology.

The next two essays were prepared, jointly with John P. Henderson, for publication in German, as introductions to facsimile reproductions of the first editions of Thomas Robert Malthus's principal works. The *Essay on the Principle of Population* (1798), while by no means entirely original in argument, turned out to be a landmark of human intellectual history. It provided not only a major premise for classical economics but an articulation of a major concern for human society near the beginning of the modern population explosion. The *Principles of Political Economy* (1820) represents a significant alternative formulation of classical economics to that of David Ricardo. The introductions indicate that the two books, while concerned with the theoretical examination of very practical questions, raised serious questions concerning such matters as the metaphysical–theological framework within which social science is to be undertaken (a matter also germane to the understanding of Smith's work) and the role of structural assumptions (as to whose interest is to count and of what interests consist) in the deployment of a theory – here regarding the role of class structure in the use of the theory of rent for policy purposes.

The *Principles of Political Economy* is in part important for, first, an understanding of the relationship of Ricardo's theory of value in relation to modern price theory, at least as the former is understood by Malthus; and, second, its author's understanding of the nature and origins of macroeconomic instability, a matter not fully appreciated until the work of John Maynard Keynes in the 1930s. For all of Malthus's identification with the land-owning establishment, his demand-and-supply theory of prices and his emphasis on the sufficiency of investment for effective demand, mark him as a very modern, and also a very perceptive, economist. Apropos of Malthus's objection to what has been called Say's Law of the Market, to which James Mill perhaps had a prior claim of originality, it is noteworthy that Say wrote in response to Quesnay, and that Malthus was therefore writing, in opposition to Mill and Say, in what amounts to the Quesnayian tradition, though apparently unknowingly.

Chapter 8 is a centenary view of Francis Ysidro Edgeworth's *Mathematical Psychics*, an important early contribution to what eventually became the marked mathematical formalization of economic theory. The article focuses on Edgeworth's case for axiomatization, the question of whether his economics is a corpus of description or a set of tools, the important relationship between the assumption of competition and the reaching of determinate solutions, and the complexities of utilitarian welfare maximization analysis. Among other things, it is seen that the use of formalized techniques, is unobtrusively accompanied by important limiting assumptions about the nature and operation of the economic order, thereby rendering economic theory *political economic* theory.

The next three chapters report on archival materials consisting of student notes emanating from courses given at Harvard University during 1896/7, 1902, and 1905/6. The earliest notes were taken as a student by A. Piatt Andrew in courses given by William James Ashley and Frank William Taussig, and the later sets of notes were taken by Robert Lee Hale in courses later taught by Andrew as a young faculty member. The earliest notes were from courses on the history of economic thought and the later were from courses on monetary theory and what eventually became macroeconomics. My co-author, Andrew Gray, is the grand-nephew of A. Piatt Andrew, who first learned of my interest in these subjects when he read the article on the teaching of business cycles based on the Hale notes. Altogether, the articles suggest the richness of turn-of-the-century economic thought.

Chapter 9 is of interest to the specialist in the history of economic thought for both the similarities and dissimilarities of coverage and thematic development relative to such courses as taught today, at least with regard to the periods common to both. The dissimilarities are perhaps most significant in the treatment of Ricardo and Alfred Marshall but there are numerous incidental matters of interest involving differences of interpretation. The article suggests that the history of the discipline is more complex, and subject to more varied interpretation, than is conventionally appreciated, raising the important possibility of using archival materials to inquire into the filtration process by which certain interpretations survive and others pass into oblivion.

The same is true of the two chapters on monetary and macroeconomic topics in the courses taught by Andrew. The notes indicate the richness of monetary and macroeconomic theory in a period in respect to which it is so easy simply to maintain that Say's law dominated professional opinion and analysis. Crises and cycles *were* widely written about and discussed in classes devoted to the subject, despite the evident facts that Say's law would seem to have rendered them impossible, and that Say's law was later considered to have then been dominant. Paul Samuelson has seemingly correctly identified the schizophrenia of pre-Keynesian macroeconomic thought. Clearly the thinking of early twentieth century economists was very complex, yet much of the complexity has not been fully registered in overgeneralizing histories of economic thought. This is true both of their thought on economic instability, possibly inevitably seen against the subsequent Keynesian revolution, and their analyses of money and banking topics, both theoretical and institutional.

The next selection is again an introduction, also to a German republication, to a work of Friedrich von Wieser, a leader of the second generation of the Austrian school. The introduction points out that Wieser was a splendid example of two ironic tensions within Austrian political economy: between its advocates' narrow formal definition of economics and their natural broad analyses of the political economy, and between their normative libertarian orientation and their positive analysis which focuses so much on social control and collective action and processes. So that one can say that Wieser was a brilliant theorist in both the theory of value and the theory of social economic organization.[3]

The two chapters on Frank William Taussig identify the respects in which his work went beyond mainstream price theory. Taussig was one of the leading American economists for almost half a century; indeed, he was called 'the American Marshall' by Joseph Schumpeter, an attempt to establish for him an importance in the USA comparable to that of Alfred Marshall in England. As a major theorist, Taussig attempted to reformulate the wages fund theory, although his most important work was in the theory of international trade and the practice of protectionism. The materials reprinted here demonstrate, however, that Taussig dealt, in a characteristically candid way, with deep questions of economic order that have normally been finessed by price theory. These included the complex psychology of economic actors and the role of structural variables, especially power and class – in both respects what Taussig called (using the terminology of his day) the instinct of domination. Taussig's analysis of the economy went well beyond the pure mechanics of the price system. The mainstream of the discipline was for Taussig, as with the Physiocratic and the English classical writers, political economy, nor economics.

The penultimate chapter, my 1982 presidential address to the History of Economics Society, concerns the putative influence of Friedrich von Wieser upon Joseph A. Schumpeter. Schumpeter has always been recognized as a brilliant, idiosyncratic, magisterial, and broad-ranging theorist and interpreter of the history of economic thought. Wieser has been appreciated in somewhat similar terms, especially as regards his combination of Austrian fundamentalism and idiosyncratic considerations of power (see also the earlier selection on Wieser). Here I suggest that certain substantive themes common to both writers may well suggest the influence of Wieser the professor on Schumpeter his student. These themes deal, in part, with leadership and the leadership selection process, and the role of discipline and historical education. Both themes are important and suggestive dimensions of political economy that have been excluded from mainstream theory and economics – and from histories of economic thought which seek only or principally to establish the percursive origins of modern theory, that is, history of the past in accordance with the selective, narrow interests of the present.

The final selection is again an introduction, to the republication of a 1936 book by William Harold Hutt. Not unlike Taussig, Hutt was interested in both the defence of capitalism and the resuscitation of classical political economy. The book, *Economists and the Public*, is significant in a number of respects, not the least of which is its attention to three modes of thought found in economics: power thought, custom thought, and rational thought; in which respect it is a major precursor of contemporary work in the rhetoric of economics, or the study of economics as discourse.

The reader will perceive that among the tasks of historians of economic thought are (1) the rescuing of bodies of analysis hitherto largely ignored by modern mainstream economic theory, not because the earlier work is wrong but because it does not comport with contemporary interests, which may or may not be permanent; (2) the reconstruction of earlier bodies of work, based in part on the application of subsequent more sophisticated understandings and in part on the isolation of metaphysical and ideological elements; and, *inter alia*, (3) the analysis of what it is that economists are doing when they do economics, especially of its philosophical, political, and discursive facets. As stressed earlier, however, work in the history of economic thought is, given the problem of the hermeneutic circle, not likely to be conclusively dispositive of the issues treated by historians of economic thought. For historians of economic thought, as readily as economists studying the economy, can superimpose their own views on their objects of study. The reader of work in the history of economics is therefore in the same position as is the historian of economics with respect to the works of economists which are the objects of their study, which is to possess the inexorable burden of analysis and interpretation.

In the view of the present author, however, among the themes which the foregoing materials seem to reasonably conclusively demonstrate are, first, the viability of the claim for political economy against a narrow, technical economics; second, the importance of government as both a dependent and independent variable in the economy; third, the importance of the discipline as both a dependent and independent variable in regard to the dominant ideology and public opinion; fourth, the great sophistication on fundamental questions (questions beyond the pure theory of price and markets) to be found in the annals of mainstream political economy; and fifth, the brilliance of the intellects who have contributed to the history of the discipline.

Notes

1. Mark Blaug, 'On the Historiography of Economics', *Journal of the History of Economic Thought*, vol. 12 (Spring 1990), pp. 27–37. The quotes are from pp. 28 and 29.
2. My comprehensive reconstruction and analysis of the classical economists' writings on both legal and non-legal social control is presented in *The Classical Theory of Economic Policy* (Cleveland: World, 1966).
3. See also my introduction to Friedrich von Wieser, *The Law of Power*, W. E. Kuhn, Translator (Lincoln: Bureau of Business Research, University of Nebraska, 1983).

1 The Physiocratic Theory of Property and State*

Economists have long interpreted the Physiocratic concept of the relation of the state to property as essentially the protection of private property. The thesis of this article is that the Physiocratic theory of property *de facto* valid, however doctrinal its advocacy of private property, is a theory of malleable property rights premised upon an utilitarian understanding of the social function of private property and necessarily involving the state in the continuing reconstitution of property rights.

There is no question that the 'protection of property' interpretation is amply supported by the Physiocrats' own statements. Their affection for private property as the dominant institutional form is clear: 'Respect for property', wrote Quesnay, 'is the primary element of the power of society'.[1] Schlatter paraphrases la Rivière:

> It is from the right of property, maintained in all its natural and primitive fullness, that all the institutions which make up the essential form of society *necessarily* flow: you can think of the right of property as a tree, and all the institutions of society are the branches which it shoots forth, which it nourishes, and which perish when they are detached from it.[2]

The fourth of Quesnay's *Maximes Générales* thus declares:

> That the ownership of the landed properties and the mobile wealth be assured to those who are their legitimate possessors; for *the security of property is the essential fundamental of the economic order of society*.[3]

Possessed of this view toward private property the Physiocrats were often equally explicit as to a desirable property–state relationship. Having also held that 'The social laws established by the Supreme Being prescribe only the preservation of the right of property, and of that liberty which is inseparable from it',[4] du Port inferred that, 'No order of any kind is possible in society unless the right of possession is guaranteed to the members of

* Originally published in *Quarterly Journal of Economics*, vol. 75 (February 1961), pp. 96–111. The author would like to acknowledge the assistance provided by the Bureau of Business and Economic Research at Georgia State College of Business Administration, and in particular by Dr Willys R. Knight, Director.

the society by the force of a sovereign authority.'[5] This reflects the dictum of Quesnay that 'There is only the sovereign power which assures the proprietorship of the subjects.'[6]

The 'protection of private property' would thus seem demonstrated as the distinctive component of the Physiocratic theory of property–state relations. *Private* property would appear upheld as inviolable and indivisible, something not to be infringed. The Physiocrats were aware that interpersonal property claims are always in a process of adjudication, the state reconciling conflicts between private litigants, with a concomitant expansion of the law of property.[7] But what of the property–state relationship as it involved, not the conflicting claims of private interests, but *conflicting private and public, or social, interests*? Does the Physiocratic theory of property maintain or imply that the social interest is best served when, perhaps without substantial exception, private property rights are unrestrained and unabridged? Or does the Physiocratic theory of property encompass – and if so to what extent and by what criteria – an element of restriction on behalf of some definition of the social interest? We know that the Physiocrats 'accepted' private property, but was the state to be only a *gendarme* in its protection?

ON THE ORIGIN AND JUSTIFICATION OF PROPERTY

Three explanations of private property are recognized in the literature on Physiocracy: private property as (a) an object of divine will, (b) a manifestation of the natural order, and (c) derived from the application of labour. In each case private property is postulated as given and independent of the volition of man.

Yet a fourth, less absolutist, justification of private property is also present. This may be called the 'instrumental', for it maintains that private property is not only *right* but also *expedient*. Emphasis upon private property as a means rather than as something given or ordained pervades the Physiocrats' writings in two contexts.

First, it is contended that the harmony of interests is to be effectuated through the institution of private property. The logic involves an equation of individual and social interests, the social interest being consonant with the sum total of individual interests when, *ceteris paribus*, individual interests are effectuated and secured with private property. Private property rights are defended as instrumental in securing private interests and in attaining the harmony of interests – 'the unity of social interests and its conformity with the law of justice' (Letrosne).[8] Hence the proposition that 'Individual interest is the primary bond of society, which will be the more solid in proportion as private interest is secure',[9] is the basis for holding that 'freedom in exchange, an absolutely unshackled use of the wealth of individuals, could not be dissociated from the full enjoyment of the rights of private property'.[10]

Second, private property rights are justified on the equally utilitarian ground that private property stimulates and facilitates the production and accumulation of wealth, i.e., economic welfare. Private property becomes the foundation of the natural order 'most essential' and 'most advantageous' to the human race because it is so functional.'[11] When Quesnay argues that 'the security of property is the fundamental essential of the economic order of society', the reason he advances for its necessity is that,

> Without the certainty of ownership, the territory would rest uncultivated. There would be neither proprietors nor tenants responsible for making the necessary expenditures to develop and cultivate it, if the preservation of the land and produce were not assured to those who advance these expenditures. It is the security of permanent possession which induces the work and the employment of wealth to the improvement and to the cultivation of land and to the enterprises of commerce and industry.[12]

La Rivière is equally explicit in propounding this instrumental justification of private property:

> The greatest possible happiness of the community as a whole consists in the greatest possible abundance of useful goods and in the greatest possible liberty to make use of these goods. I have made it clear that this maximum of enjoyment is the necessary consequence of the establishment of the right of property and that it is only by establishing this right that we are able to attain happiness.[13]

In contrast, then, with the three conventionally recognized theories, the instrumental theory is utilitarian in its appeal for acceptance; for private property is functional in use and its benevolent efficacy – given the ends defined above – serves as its own justification. Private property as an institution becomes a *means* subject to discretionary value criteria. The former theories serve as mandatory criteria for the state, which would have to 'maintain' or 'protect' private property. Other than the adjudicatory function, nothing further can be inferred. The instrumental theory, however, suggests that the *substance* of private property rights, nominally the essence of the property–state relationship, may be malleable. Private property as an institution is advanced as desirable on functional grounds; it seems reasonable to infer that the state would have justification for altering the dimensions or substance of property rights should the harmony of interests for some reason not be achieved or should there be some obstacle to the attainment of the wealth and happiness of the populace and the nation. While private property would be the desired form of property arrangement, the actual construction of the institution would seem subject to the same criterion as applied to the adoption of private property itself, namely, a strictly utilitarian one, and as such subject to change.

The recognition of the instrumental role of private property would warrant the question: what was the *social claim* on private property? If the state does not merely 'protect' private property, what are the other dimensions to the property–state relationship?

THE SOCIAL CLAIM ON PRIVATE PROPERTY – SOME EVIDENCE

Private ownership was to be *de jure* the accepted form of property rights, and the duty of the state was here to protect property. But Physiocratic property theory also encompassed the reasoned modification–reconstitution of such rights as necessary to maintain and strengthen the same social interest by which private property itself was sanctioned. The evidence recorded below suggests that the Physiocratic theory of property rights is more nearly a theory of 'social utility' than a theory of exclusive or absolute private *dominium*. Such a view was propounded by de Tocqueville, when he observed that the Physiocrats had neither concern nor respect for contractual and proprietary rights. Such claims are minor, compared with the social interest: 'there are no longer private rights, but only a public utility'.[14] With respect to property, the role of the state was thus seen as an active manipulator, rather than a passive securer.[15]

1. *Foundations*. The two administrations of public office by Turgot, together with the large body of his writings both public and private, provide us with much serious insight into the social character of private property as understood by an important member of the Physiocratic group.[16] One of the most striking examples concerns Turgot's attitude towards 'foundations', an attitude comparable to the Anglo-Saxon law of perpetuities. Turgot argues that the government has an 'incontestable right . . . to dispose of old foundations, to extend their funds to new objects, or, better still, to suppress them altogether. Public utility is the supreme law, and it ought not to be nullified by any superstitious respect for what we call the *intention of the founder* – as if ignorant and short-sighted individuals had the right to chain

to their capricious wills the generations that had still to be borne'.[17] When private right or private interest is not coincident with social interest, then 'public utility is the supreme law'.

2. *Famine Relief.* Another notable example relates to Turgot's pragmatic program for the relief of the depression engendered by the severe famines of 1769 and 1770, during his Intendency in the Generality of Limoges. Turgot was responsible for (a) the imposition of a voluntary charitable assessment, which was supplemented by (b) a compulsory tax, to finance (c) a system of useful public works. Furthermore he required (d) the compulsory maintenance and provision of the cultivators and their families by the employer-landlords, and (e) even went so far as to regulate and recalculate the grain rents, and (f) abrogate the privileges of the bakers of Limoges.

That Turgot employed his powers of governance to modify the rights of privilege and property is clear. Turgot wrote in his report that 'It has been necessary for the public authority to require the proprietors and inhabitants in better circumstances in each parish to assess themselves for the relief of the poor.' Anticipating the principle of 'social fault yet private responsibility' of present-day unemployment compensation, he argued that 'The labourers must find resources in the advances from, or in the gratuitous assistance of, their *masters*, who owe to them this support not less on the score of charity than on that of justice, and as landlords, for their own interest, rightly understood.' Thus by ordinance he proclaimed:

> For these causes we order that the proprietors of domains, of whatever quality or condition they may be, privileged or not privileged, shall be held to keep and to maintain, until the next harvest, the labourers whom they had on October 1 last, as well as their families, men, women, and children.[18]

Moreover, when the landlords demanded payment of the métayers' rent in grain, as originally contracted, or the money value thereof at the existing market famine-price, Turgot intervened. Although 'The landlords were requiring no more than their legal right, and they upheld the principle of the inviolability of contract',[19] Turgot persuaded the Parliament of Bordeaux to sanction a recalculation of the grain rents in terms of an earlier, somewhat lower, price. In a letter to the Chancellor, Turgot justified his course of action:

> In times of scarcity it is humane, and even just, to bring the law to the assistance of the overburdened tenant. The proprietor whom the scarcity

enriches cannot, without showing most odious greed, attempt to draw, from the cruel circumstances in which his tenant is now placed, a profit still more exorbitant than before.[20]

3. *Guilds*. Turgot's Edict suppressing the guilds – consonant with the general Physiocratic program of reform – is well-known as part of Turgot's endeavour to rid commerce of the burden of the many restrictions then imposed upon it. But the significance of the Edict for the Physiocratic theory of property is less well appreciated.

Seguier, challenging the principle of the Edict before the Parliament of Paris, 'contended, and with much force, that the masterships were items of property which had been purchased; that to abolish the guilds, rather than to reform them, meant nothing less than to confiscate the property of innocent purchasers'.[21] Furthermore, said Seguier, 'To give to all your subjects indiscriminately the right to hold a store or to open a shop is to violate the property of the *masters*, who compose the communities.'[22] Turgot's response is characterized by Shepherd as that of a 'minister who saw not tradition but the future; who felt that justice to the many demanded injustice to the few who exploited the many'.[23] Hence valuable property rights were, by the Edict, to be done away with, or at least seriously modified. This was the case and it was recognized as such.

4. *Economic Stability*. It is now well recognized in the literature that several of the Physiocrats were solicitous lest an improper pattern or an inadequate volume of spending impede the maximization of the net product and thereby national prosperity.[24] Of the specific policies proposed by Quesnay, the regulation of interest rates for the purpose of insuring an adequate flow of capital to agriculture is also well-known, as is also the strenuous objection raised by Turgot, du Pont and Letrosne (*vis-à-vis* Mirabeau, who concurred with Quesnay). But the fact nonetheless remains that Quesnay was not alone in accepting such restriction of property rights as is involved in interest-rate regulation. Even more striking are several other proposals by Quesnay having as their purpose the modification of property rights for the objective of protecting the social interest in the processes of circulation and reproduction.

Du Pont, in a letter to Turgot, urged the view that 'the formation of capitals arises much less from saving out of the expenditure of revenues than from the wise employment of the expenditures'.[25] Thus Quesnay devoted two *Maximes* to public policy both compensatory and promotional toward the proper pattern and magnitude of expenditures:

> That the government be less occupied with economies than with the operations necessary for the prosperity of the kingdom; . . . .
>
> That the economic government occupy itself only in favoring the productive outlays and the commerce of agricultural commodities, and that it leave alone the sterile outlays.[26]

Both fiscal and monetary policies are contemplated by Quesnay. Immediately after stating and reiterating the need to emphasize agricultural (*vis-à-vis* manufacturing and luxury) production as the foundation of a prosperous economy, Quesnay offers, in italics no less, two rather astounding but concrete restrictions on the use of property, restrictions suggestive no doubt of how he would further minimize the problem of 'sterile hoarding'. Says Quesnay:

> That a part of the sum of incomes not pass to a foreign country without returning, in money or in merchandise.
>
> That they prevent [*évite*] the desertion of inhabitants who would carry their wealth out of the kingdom.[27]

As with hoarding, 'Money', it would seem, 'is strictly speaking, a public utility', as Rogin has postulated;[28] or, in Schumpeter's words, unspent saving is 'a sort of public enemy'.[29]

Nor is that all, for Quesnay's often-cited maxim on 'the complete freedom of commerce' is preceded by two maxims which modify such freedom by requiring, in effect, that there be no social loss in foreign trade – perhaps another reversion to currency and, also, to import–export controls.[30]

It is clear that these controls, having as their objective the promotion of the social interest in national economic prosperity, would have necessarily involved to some direct and indirect extent (as do their modern counterparts) the modification of the rights of private property. Individually and in their totality these modifications would have constituted a social claim on private property. Conversely, it is again evident that the uninterfered-with use of private property was, in the minds of the Physiocrats, contingent upon the consonance of that use with the requirements of justice and the prosperity of the system, as defined by them.[31]

5. *Taxation. A priori* it would be expected that any theory of property–state relations characterized by the 'protection of property' formulation would have as concomitant views that (a) taxes are intrinsically inimical to private property, (b) spending is generally best when done by private hands, and (c) taxes (and the cost of government), being essentially sterile, should

therefore be minimized. One would expect an attitude thoroughly condescending and repugnant to taxation, in which the necessity for some compulsory contribution to government would be but grudgingly acknowledged. It will be found, however, that for a group presumably holding private property sacred and inviolable, the Physiocrats are not unduly hostile to taxation *per se*; rather they attribute to taxation (and government) considerable positive social significance.

The *impôt unique* was proposed by Quesnay as a means of protecting the agricultural advances and thereby the prosperity of the nation. Quesnay also warns 'That taxation not be destructive, or disproportionate to the total income of the nation . . . otherwise the tax degenerates into spoilation and causes a dwindling away which quickly ruins a state'.[32] This emphasis upon the destructive potential of taxation is reiterated throughout the writings of the Physiocrats. But concentration upon such destructive potential would be, however, a demonstrably inadequate characterization of the Physiocratic attitude toward taxation. Beyond this manifest concern over the proper magnitude and form of taxation, the Physiocrats had a pervasive solicitude for what may be called the *constructive* facet of taxation and public expenditures. Taxation becomes less of a nemesis and more of an instrument of social utility. Indeed, L. Einaudi expresses as a principle of Physiocratic tax theory that:

> Tax, if kept within its rational limits, is not a burden at all. On the contrary, is a condition toward the maximization of the national dividend.

The object of taxation is 'that part of the national dividend which is the necessary remuneration of the political class'. '[i]n an orderly, progressive society the national dividend reaches a maximum when a sufficient quota is devoted to the maintenance of the political governing class', for 'we see that tax is born out of its very utility'. There is no burden, 'because it is the fruit of the work done by the political class, acting either individually or collectively, through the agency of the State'. According to L. Einaudi, then, taxation for the Physiocrats was 'a problem not of a burden laid on individual producer's shoulders for the sake of keeping the consumptive governmental machine going, but . . . a problem of distribution between productive agents – the State being counted among them according to his (its) proper nature – of a total national dividend produced by the same agents'.[33]

This interpretation of L. Einaudi is supported not only by la Rivière and du Pont, both of whom are cited by him, but also by Baudeau,[34] Quesnay and Turgot. Maxim XXVII reads in full:

> That the government be less occupied with economies than with the operations necessary for the prosperity of the kingdom; for very great expenses can cease to be excessive by the augmentation of wealth. But it must not confound the excesses with the simple expenses; for the excesses would be able to swallow up all the wealth of the nation and sovereign.[35]

So also says Turgot:

> If the realm becomes generally more wealthy, if there is more money, more capital, and greater activity in industry and trade, all the king's expenses will increase proportionately. Everything is dearer in France than in Poland, everything in England and in Holland than in France. If France, in proportion to its extent, were as wealthy as Holland, the people would surely be in position to pay taxes in proportion to the expenses which the increase of that wealth made necessary, and no one would have cause for complaint.[36]

Also relevant is Quesnay's dictum that 'the sovereign power which assures the proprietorship of the subjects . . . has a primitive right in the division of the fruits of the land'.[37]

It is also clear that the reconstruction of the tax system proposed by the Physiocrats would have necessarily involved the abrogation of valuable and privileged property rights of long standing. The *impôt unique* is proposed not only on grounds of efficiency but also 'Because (indirect taxation) is a disproportionate burden on the poor consumer', a rich man's consumption not being proportionate to his greater wealth.[38] Moreover, 'The expenses of the government having for their object the interests of all, all ought to contribute to them; and the more one enjoys the advantages of the society, the more ought it to be held a matter of honor to participate in these charges.'[39] Taxation being subject to considerations of public utility, privilege would have to give way to a rational tax administration. That such a reconstruction involved a concomitant reconstitution of property rights[40] goes without saying. As with the *impôt unique*, so with the *corvée*: the rights of privilege and exemption were to be abrogated. Such a revolution was involved in Turgot's plan to replace the *corvée* with a direct money tax on the real beneficiaries ('It is then the class of proprietors of land which receives the fruit of the construction of roads; it is that class which ought alone to make the necessary advances, since they finally secure the benefits.')[41] That the Parliament of Paris refused to register the Edict for the suppression of the *corvée* because, in its own words,

> . . . this suppression would be against justice. The first rule of justice is to preserve to every one what belongs to him: this rule consists, not only in preserving the rights of property, but still more in preserving those belonging to the person, which arise from the prerogative of birth and positions.[42]

In the later development of American economic policy the same issue was to be formulated in terms of a juxtaposition of the two due process clauses to the national commerce and tax powers and the state police power. For the Physiocrats, with respect to both guild and *corvée* reform, a change in policy and of the system involved what was correctly considered a reconstitution of the rights of property, differences of opinion arising over what best served the 'social interest'. A similar position was taken, it should be noted, by Quesnay with respect to 'abolishing or moderating the excessive rights of rivers and tolls . . . those to whom these rights belong will be sufficiently compensated by their part of the general increase in the incomes from the lands of the kingdom'.[43] Privileges, vested interests, and property rights disturbed by reform in the public interest were thus to be compensated only by the resultant general prosperity.

While it was intrinsic, then, to Physiocratic thought that taxation not be destructive and uneconomical, it is also characteristic of Physiocratic thought that taxation (and therefore tax reform) is a matter of public utility not to be subjugated to any priority of private property rights. Taxation and private property itself were envisioned as instruments of social utility.

THE PHYSIOCRATIC THEORY OF PROPERTY–STATE RELATIONS

To the Physiocrats, private property was the accepted, indeed cherished, form of institutionalized ownership. They frequently couched their justification of private property in mandatory, superhuman sanctions, embodied in a theory of apparently absolute individual *dominium*. Viewed thus, the Physiocratic theory would appear to involve the state in the simple protection of private property.

The foregoing analysis reveals, however, that the Physiocrats also endeavoured to justify the institution on functional grounds, reducing the institutionalization of ownership to the domain of human volition and to the service of discretionary ends and values. Physiocratic thought both theoretically and practically, implicitly and explicitly, evidences a departure from the theory of individual *dominium*. While the *dominium* theory served as doctrine, Physiocratic thought and programme belies the adoption *de facto* of a 'bundle-of-rights' theory of property.

The character of property, as operationally understood by the Physiocrats, was such that the positive parameters and composition of all property, and of the dimensions of the rights of any given property, were all determined by and through the state and reworked in accordance with their conception of the social interest. Property rights thus took the form of a summation or bundle of rights, which did not exist in a vacuum in some predetermined absolute form, but were extant in reference to the functional requirements of their proposed *Royaume Agricole*. There was no rights independent of state law; there was no operationally definable quantum of rights extant in the Physiocratic literature that persists beyond the scope of law-making by the state. In a word, property rights are malleable, and the social claim on private property is manifest through changes in the bundle of rights, such changes presumably justified by the public interest – the law of social utility.

The Physiocratic social claim on private property has the following major dimensions: the application of the *police power* as conventionally understood, and the implementation of the Physiocratic programmes of *social construction, economic development* and *economic stability*. The ultimate sources of such property–state relationship include: (a) the vestiges of a feudal conception of property, with the sovereign conceived as co-proprietor of property and economy, coupled with the Physiocratic theory of a paternal, absolute (albeit benign) sovereign; (b) more important, operationally at least, their equating of the natural order not with the status quo but with the ideal with the consequent programme of social change and reconstruction along the lines of the ideal through the agency of the sovereign, i.e., the state; and (c) the recognition that the presumed harmony of interests, if it was to be realized, had to be attained (and disharmonies and obstacles precluded) through the agency of the state, especially (but not only) for the maximization of the *produit net* and the proper functioning of the processes of circulation and reproduction.

All these considerations support the recognition of the *de facto* alteration of the fabric of property rights. There is no question but that the divesting of property rights (vested interests) through the focusing and refocusing of economic activity through state action is tantamount not to the protection of property in the abstract but to the material remaking of property and property rights. For the Physiocrats it was axiomatic that the state was responsible for the development of property, that it was through the agency of the state that property was to be reconstructed continuously in the social interest. The role of the state was thus to manipulate property law, thereby manipulating the bundle of rights that constituted property. From the perspective of the individual holder of property, the uninterfered-with use of private property was contingent upon the consonance of that use with the public interest as defined by the state. The concept of social function was thus correlative to that of private right, and for practical purposes the former would govern the latter.[44]

Notes

1. Quoted in George John Malanos, *The Evolution of the General Theory* (unpublished doctoral dissertion, Harvard, 1946), p. 45.
2. Richard Schlatter, *Private Property: The History of an Idea* (New Brunswick: Rutgers University Press, 1951), p. 217.
3. Auguste Oncken (ed.), *Oeuvres Economiques et Philosophiques de F. Quesnay* (Paris: Joseph Baer, 1888), p. 331.
4. Quoted in John Herman Randall, Jr, *The Making of the Modern Mind* (Boston: Houghton Mifflin, 1926), p. 324.
5. Quoted in Charles Gide and Charles Rist, *A History of Economic Doctrines* (Boston: Heath, n.d.), p. 37.
6. Oncken, *Oeuvres Economiques*, p. 332.
7. 'All property', reads du Pont's *necrologue*, 'is bound by the surrounding properties as all liberty by other liberties. They press together but are still separate as the cells of a honeycomb.' Further, 'Yet the respect for liberty and proprietorship requires that men and capitalists live completely [free] from any masters in the usage of their advances and their time, provided that the results of it neither hinder liberty nor damage the proprietorship of anyone' (ibid., pp. 803, 804).
8. R. H. Palgrave (ed.), *Dictionary of Political Economy* (London: Macmillan, 1908), vol. II, p. 598.
9. Ibid., vol. III, p. 105.
10. Ibid., vol. II, p. 148.
11. Taken from the title of la Rivière's *L'Ordre naturel et essential des sociétés politiques* and the sub-title of du Pont's *Physiocracy*, 'The Natural Constitution of That Form of Government Most Advantageous to the Human Race'. Quesnay's utilitarian tenor is also evident in his definition of natural law: 'We shall understand by physical law *the regular course of any physical occurrence in the natural order obviously most advantageous to mankind.* We shall understand by moral law *the pattern of all human action in the moral order which conforms to the physical order obviously most advantageous to mankind.*'

    'Positive legislation consists, then,' says Quesnay, 'in the enunciation of the natural laws which make up the order obviously the most advantageous possible for men in society' (K. W. Kapp and L. L. Kapp, *Readings in Economics* (New York: Barnes and Noble, 1949), pp. 100, 101). See also Nicolas Baudeau, *Première Introduction à la Philosophie Economique* (Paris: Librairie Paul Geuthner, 1910), p. 31.

12. Oncken, *Oeuvres Economiques*, pp. 331–2.
13. P. C. Newman, A. D. Gayer, and M. H. Spencer, *Source Readings in Economic Thought* (New York: Norton, 1954), p. 103.
14. Alexis de Tocqueville, *The Old Regime and the French Revolution* (Garden City: Doubleday Anchor, 1955), p. 159. (See also the French edition, published by Librairie Gallimard, 1952, vol. I, p. 210.) Mario Einaudi, *The Physiocratic Doctrine of Judicial Control* (Cambridge: Harvard University Press, 1938), p. 3.
15. Schlatter cites Baudeau's view that, 'It is a common error to attribute property to the civil law' (*Private Property*, p. 217). The inference that private property exists prior and preeminent to civil law reflects Lord Acton's dictum that, 'Society secures rights; it neither bestows nor restricts them' (quoted in Paschal Larkin, *Property in the Eighteenth Century* (Dublin: Cork University Press, 1930) p. 198). Turgot, however, agreeing 'that labour gave a natural title to property', added, says Schlatter, that 'in the state of nature property in land lasted only so long as the appropriator continued to occupy and cultivate: permanent property in land was a creation of the civil law' (p. 217; see below, n. 31). Larkin found another qualification by the Physiocrats, that 'Every individual has a natural right to at least those things which are necessary for his welfare' (p. 200). Quesnay also qualified the general rule by noting that 'the strong can unjustly employ violence upon the weak', by 'the condition that he injure neither himself nor others', and by recognizing differential 'circumstances' (Kapp and Kapp, *Readings in Economics*, pp. 97, 99).

    (These are the same qualifications propounded by Locke himself. Locke qualifies his explanation of property in the natural state (*On Civil Government*, paragraphs 26, 27, 28, 29, 32, 33) by assuming abundance (paragraphs 33, 36) and the use of the qualifying phrase, 'As much as anyone can make use of' (paragraphs 31, 36). Civil society is also differentiated from the state of nature. See Larkin, *Property in the Eighteenth Century*, pp. 59–64, and Huntington Cairns, *Legal Philosophy from Plato to Hegel* (Baltimore: The Johns Hopkins Press, 1949), pp. 335–61.)

    Schlatter concludes that: 'These civil extensions of the right of property were justified by their general utility, but they should be revised whenever they conflict with the original right of nature' (p. 217). 'Thus the privileges of the aristocracy, he advised the king, are civil rights which deprive others of their natural right to enjoy the produce of their own industry: these privileges ought, consequently, to be suppressed.' On the distinction between feudal rights as privileges or legitimate property, see Larkin, pp. 213 ff.
16. While not a Physiocrat in every doctrinal respect, Turgot's association with the group is reasonably close; moreover, his attitude towards governmentally induced social change and social reconstruction does parallel the general Physiocratic view in almost every respect. Turgot may have been 'more of a fellow-traveler . . . than a Physiocrat *pur*', but he is also the only major Physiocrat providing the historical analyst with practical experience as a source of insight (Ronald L. Meek, 'The Physiocratic Concept of Profit', *Economica*, n.s. XXVI (Feb. 1959), p. 52).
17. W. Walker Stephens (ed.), *The Life and Writings of Turgot* (New York: Longmans, Green, 1895), pp. 227–8.
18. Ibid., pp. 50, 53, 54.

19. Ibid., p. 51.
20. Ibid., p. 54.
21. R. P. Shepherd, *Turgot and the Six Edicts*, Columbia University, Series in History, Economics and Public Law (New York, 1903), vol. XVIII, p. 131.
22. Stephens, *Life and Writings of Turgot*, p. 134.
23. Shepherd, *Turgot and the Six Edicts*, p. 131.
24. J. J. Spengler, 'The Physiocrats and Say's Law of Markets', I–II, *Journal of Political Economy*, vol. LIII (Sept. and Dec. 1945), pp. 193–211, 317–47, esp. pp. 204–11, 317–29, 345–7; Henri Woog, *The Tableau Economique of François Quesnay* (Bern: A. Francke, 1950), pp. 22–5, 82–98 ('The "Tableau Economique" in Disequilibrium'); Leo Rogin, *The Meaning and Validity of Economic Theory* (New York: Harper, 1956), pp. 23–4, 29; Joseph A. Schumpeter, *History of Economic Analysis* (New York: Oxford University Press, 1954), p. 287; A. R. J. Turgot, *Reflections on the Formation and the Distribution of Riches* (New York: Macmillan, 1922), p. ix; Edmund Whittaker, *Schools and Streams of Economic Thought* (Chicago: Rand McNally, 1960), p. 95.
25. Turgot, *Reflections*, p. ix.
26. Oncken, *Oeuvres Economiques*, pp. 336, 333.
27. Ibid., p. 333.
28. Rogin, *The Meaning and Validity of Economic Theory*, p. 23.
29. Schumpeter, *History of Economic Analysis*, p. 287.
30. Oncken, *Oeuvres Economiques*, p. 336.
31. Spengler points out that 'Among the economic principles to which the physiocrats subscribed were these three: (a) the institution of private property is essential, at all times and in all places, to the well-being and development of societies; (b) complete economic liberty – freedom of exchange, of entry, and of competition – is prerequisite to the maximization of effort and conducive to the private and the public interest; (c) activity and policy directed to the maximization of the net product are necessary to, and consistent with, the maximization of the collective welfare'. He notes that critics 'have pointed out that principle *c* is not universally consistent with principle *b*; that pursuit of principle *c* must eventually involve conflict with, and sacrifice of, principle *b* and its corollary, principle *a*'. 'Were the pursuit of principle *b* to run counter to that of principle *c*, it is said, Quesnay would have sacrificed principle *b* to principle *c*, even to the extent of supporting state intervention in favour of agriculture.' But, the critics agree, Quesnay's disciples 'other than Mirabeau, who subscribed without qualification to Quesnay's views, assigned primacy to principles *a* and *b*. These disciples of Quesnay, in event of conflict between principles *c* and *b*, would have subordinated the pursuit of principle *c* to that of the overriding principle *b*, it is inferred'. This characterization of Quesnay's position is consonant with the position taken here. Spengler's final comment also supports the present thesis: 'At most, supposing principle *b* were subordinated to principle *c*, consumer sovereignty would be more restricted' ('The Physiocrats and Say's Law of Markets', pp. 328, 329). Restricted, that is, in the use of their property: Quesnay is quite clear in proscribing unproductive consumption (manufacturing and luxury expenditures) and hoarding. See Oncken, *Oeuvres Economiques*, maxims VII, VIII, IX, XXI, XXII, pp. 332–5.

A related point concerns the accountability of the landlords for the use of their property, primarily the lands capable of cultivation, as stewards of society. Quesnay accepted a feudal class structure, but he had his reservations and doubts over the efficacy of 'the dependence of the current process of production on the financial resources of the landed class' (Woog, 'The Tableau Economique, p. 19). Says James Bonar:

> the land should be allowed to become property not only because men have worked on it, but in order that they may have the motive to go on working upon it. [But he continued] This tacitly implies that, if they do not work upon it, their title is *pro tanto* insecure, and the State would not be bound to treat them as absolute masters of their land. But the existence of proprietorship without work is certainly tolerated by the Physiocrats. (*Philosophy and Political Economy* (New York: Macmillan, 1909), p. 143.)

Spengler also concludes that the Physiocrats held the proprietors and cultivators *should* maintain the annual reproduction and net product, as well as 'the *continued augmentation* of advances until net product has been raised to the attainable maximum', i.e., that they were 'morally responsible, each within his own sphere' and that such conduct was considered 'meritorious'; but that such behaviour was not 'obligatory' ('The Physiocrats and Say's Law of Markets', pp. 208–9). Whether a Physiocratic regime would have imposed sanctions towards such a goal is speculative and unanswerable. It must be remembered, however, that under the *ancien régime* there was 'confiscated the whole local property of an owner who left his land derelict' (Woog, 'The Tableau Economique', p. 13). There would no doubt have been a schism of opinion among the Physiocrats.

32. Oncken, *Oeuvres Economiques*, p. 332; see also pp. 337–41.
33. Luigi Einaudi, 'The Physiocratic Theory of Taxation', in *Economic Essays in Honour of Gustav Cassel* (London: George Allen & Unwin, 1933), pp. 131–5.
34. Baudeau, *loc. cit.*
35. Oncken, *Oeuvres Economiques*, p. 336.
36. Shepherd, *Turgot and the Six Edicts*, p. 99. 'As for government expenditures', says Shepherd, 'Turgot held that there was a direct connection between governmental expenses and public prosperity. He did not question that as the economic development of the state required enlarged expenditure by the government, the taxes to meet growing needs would be more and more easily borne by the people. He had public and private expenditure so closely allied that he could consider no increase of the budget allowable, except in case of dire necessity, until the indebtedness of the state was in process of liquidation' (p. 138).
37. Oncken, *Oeuvres Economiques*, p. 332. See also Gide and Rist: 'the Physiocrats argued that taxes ought to be paid liberally, and not grudgingly' (*A History of Economic Doctrines*, p. 38). The fact that 'the public authority must also incur some expense, which might be designated *avances souveraines*' (Baudeau), is one justification. (*Loc. cit.*) As Spengler notes, the sovereign becomes 'a co-proprietor'. 'What was transferred to the sovereign, consist-

ently with the principles of the natural order, was not really a tax, therefore, but only his share. Moreover, this share had not really been the possession of the existing land-owning class; it had not been bequeathed or sold' ('The Physiocrats and Say's Law of Markets', p. 211). Said du Pont: 'The tax is a kind of inalienable common property. When proprietors buy or sell land they do not buy and sell the tax. They can only dispose of that portion of the land which really belongs to them, after deducting the amount of the tax. This tax is no more a charge upon property than is the right of fellow proprietors a burden upon one's property. And so the public revenue is not burdensome to anyone, costs nothing, and is paid by no one. Hence, it in no way curtails the amount of property which a person has' (quoted in Gide and Rist, *A History of Economic Doctrines*, p. 40). This can only be the case if, as L. Einaudi argues, the state is one of the 'agents' of production. Thus Baudeau 'recognized the advisability of periodical revaluations "in order that the sovereign power should always share in both the profits and the losses of the producer". And he addresses this important caution to the proprietors: "Take no credit to yourselves for the increase in the revenue of land. The thanks are really due to the growing efficiency of the sovereign authority"' (Gide and Rist, *A History of Economic Doctrines*, p. 40).

As Gide and Rist note, the percentage limitation 'affords a barrier against the autocracy of the sovereign – a barrier that is much more effective than a parliamentary vote' (p. 44). But – and this is very important for property theory – they also state that, 'There is no mention of representation as a corollary of taxation. This form of guarantee, which marks the beginnings of parliamentary government', and which involves the doctrines of *consent* (or at least implied consent) so intrinsic to conservative property theory, 'could have no real significance for the Physiocrats' (p. 35). Said du Pont in a letter to Say: 'It is a narrow and churlish English idea which decrees that an annual sum should be annually voted to the Government, and that Parliament should reserve to itself the right of refusing this tax' (p. 38).

38. Stephens, *The Life and Writings of Turgot*, p. 320.
39. Quoted in Shepherd, *Turgot and the Six Edicts*, p. 103
40. For example, the right of exemption from taxes was an object of purchase and sale, a valuable property right indeed. Ibid., pp. 108–9.
41. Ibid., p. 152.
42. Stephens, *The Life and Writings of Turgot*, p. 132–3.
43. Oncken, *Oeuvres Economiques*, p. 241.
44. Compare R. H. Tawney, *The Acquisitive Society* (New York: Harcourt, Brace, 1920), chs II and III. Given the recognition of these manipulations, 'their philosophies would have permitted and would even have compelled them to regard' them 'as ordained by Nature' (O. H. Taylor, *Economics and Liberalism* (Cambridge: Harvard University Press, 1955), p. 99). As Spengler notes, even 'Dubois admits that if it could have been proved to Quesnay that legislation (e.g., tariffs) would increase the net product, he might have found such intervention to conform to the natural order' ('The Physiocrats and Say's Law of Markets', p. 328).

2 The Physiocratic Theory of Economic Policy*

The conventionally accepted interpretation of the Physiocratic theory of economic policy[1] is that of *laissez-faire*. While partial dissents have been registered, the *laissez-faire* view has persisted substantially unchallenged. The purpose of this article is to restate the theory of economic policy to which Physiocratic doctrine can be meaningfully and operationally reduced, including a delineation of the role of *laissez-faire*.

In an earlier article, this writer has shown that the Physiocratic theory of property–state relations encompassed an activist role of the state in the utilitarian and continuing modification of property rights.[2] Developing the inference implicit therein, the author will show here that *laissez-faire* is an inadequate characterization of the Physiocratic theory of economic policy. While the Physiocrats ostensibly advocated the principle of non-intervention (thereby reflecting 'the spirit of an age or the truth of an idea so great that it moved a generation'),[3] a valid statement of their theory of policy has to depart significantly from such an interpretation. As one writer has put it, '*Laissez-faire* was a leaf out of their book, but not enough to be the title of what they had to say.'[4]

The author will demonstrate that *laissez-faire* has a place only within the broader dimensions of the Physiocratic theory of economic policy, the latter deriving its basic character from its activism as a theory and programme of social change and social control. These activist dimensions encompass programmes of (a) social reconstruction, (b) economic development, and (c) economic stability, and comprise the fundamental economic functions of Physiocratic government.

As with the Physiocratic theory of property and state, the traditional interpretation finds support in certain of the Physiocrats' own statements. In his article 'Grains', Quesnay argued: 'all commerce must be free. . . . It suffices in the government . . . to not hinder the activity at all'. In the *Maximes Générales* is found the clearest and most frequently cited statement giving doctrinal credence to the *laissez-faire* view:

* Originally published in *Quarterly Journal of Economics*, vol. 76 (February 1962), pp. 145–62.

> That there be maintained the complete freedom of commerce; for *the policy of interior and exterior commerce the most sure, the most exact, the most profitable to the nation and the state, consists in the full freedom of competition.*[5]

Quesnay's advice to the Dauphin is well-known, as is that of la Rivière to Catherine the Great. La Rivière also wrote that:

> The movements of society are spontaneous and not artificial, and the desire for joy which manifests itself in all its activities unwittingly derives it towards the realization of the ideal type of State.

As Gide and Rist comment, 'This is *laissez-faire* pure and simple.' The view is reflected in Baudeau's declaration: 'Remove all useless, unjust, contradictory, and absurd laws, and there will not be much legislative machinery left after that',[6] and in Turgot's letter to Terray:

> Whatever sophisms the self-interests of some commercial classes may heap up, the truth is that *all* branches of commerce ought to be free, equally free, *entirely free*;[7]

The Physiocrats also emphasized naturalism to denigrate government and government policy: 'Legislation, if conformable to nature, was unnecessary, and if in violation of it, certain of defeat, for in the long run nature was the strongest.'[8] Man did not make the laws of the natural order, he only executed them;[9] and, what is more, attempts to direct the course of nature were futile, for 'the result would only be to let things go precisely as they would have gone of themselves'.[10]

Thus wrote the Physiocrats of non-intervention. While they did not use the term themselves,[11] they often wrote, and perhaps largely understood, in the manner of the doctrine of *laissez-faire*. It must be said then that the Physiocrats, perhaps because of their preoccupations, did not fully appreciate the significance of many of their own ideas.[12] Or perhaps they did, and for that reason avoided the phrase. In either case, their general statements are at odds with both broad and particular aspects of their own scheme of policy, and neither exhaust nor characterize the Physiocratic theory of economic policy.

GOVERNMENT AND SOCIAL CHANGE

For the purposes of policy analysis the essence of Physiocracy is its involvement in and proposal of change. Comprising a programme for the reconstitution of the fabric of society, and for the redirection of the path of social development, Physiocracy *is* policy: for the proposal of *change* is a matter of *choice*, which is in every respect (given the realm of possibilities capable of being acted upon and their probable achievement) a matter of *policy*. Fundamental, then, to the Physiocratic theory of economic policy is the recognition of Physiocracy as a system of social reconstruction and redirection, the substance of the Physiocratic answer to the question of choice becoming the primary object of policy.

Considered as a programme for social change, it is evident that the Physiocratic system was of considerable breadth, 'a social philosophy embracing what today would be included in economics, politics, sociology and ethics',[13] which, however, 'places economics considerations into the foreground'.[14] It may be argued that recognition of the breadth of Physiocratic thought is responsible for the inclusion of socioeconomic change as a dimension of Physiocratic policy and further that such is unnecessary or undesirable. The counter-argument may be advanced, however, that economic policy for the Physiocrats did *in fact* comprise a programme of change, and to ignore such is to make sterile the scope of economic policy.

The crucial matter, however, is not the breadth of Physiocratic thought but its *activism*.[15] The Physiocrats were primarily concerned with the question of how the economy should be organized and controlled, and this preoccupation governed the nature of their theory. Physiocracy was not just a system of theory, meaning by 'theory' either the identification and explanation of assumed preexistent phenomena, or the systematic analysis of the employment of means given an hierarchy of ends already extant. Rather than being Aristotelian in their theory (i.e., theory as explanation: what is the phenomenon, and how and why did it come about?), the Physiocrats were essentially proposing what *should be* the case, and in their writings both justifying the rationale of their system and describing how it *would* work. The Physiocrats were thus promulgators of theory as a *constructive proposal*, ergo Platonic and normative. Since they did not accept the economic status quo, their analysis involved an ends–means model reaching back to the basic foundations of society, and their theory was accordingly activist rather than predictive. As Myrdal has pointed out, the radicalism of their ideas as to economic reorganization was tempered by the conservatism of other facets of their thought,[16] but this does not vitiate the real character of their economic policy, namely, a theory of how the economy should be organized and controlled, and how such should be brought about. Moreover, their naturalism can be reduced to the hypothesis and advocacy of a particular system in terms of the ethical 'ought', the 'ideal' becoming in their system the 'natural', the acceptance of which was argued on both mandatory and utilitarian grounds.[17]

Physiocracy was not only Platonic in its theory of knowledge as applied to action and change, but further would have directed the accomplishment of such change *through the agency of the political state*. So far from calling for abstinence on the part of the state, and a departure from Colbertism, the Physiocrats would have used the state to accomplish their own particular reorganization and redirection of the economy. It is one thing to denigrate the present system, call for its cessation through voluntary abdication by government from past policies and the abstinence from adopting any new state programme save abstinence itself, and at the same time seek the free, voluntary and uncontrolled reorganization of the economy through a spontaneous emergence. But it is quite something else to call for the substitution of one system of activist policy for another, and moreover, as will be seen, one also involving continuing supervision by the state. What Physiocracy would have accomplished was the *substitution* of their own programme of agriculturalism for that of Colbertism; i.e., of their aims, their policies and their organization of the economy, for the aims, policies and organization of the economy of the *ancien régime*. Smith, notwithstanding his praise, also recognized that Physiocracy was a *system* no less than was mercantilism, that Physiocracy simply would have changed the structure and orientation of state policy rather than adopting the principle of having *no* state policy of restraint and promotion, or what Smith called 'the simple and obvious system of natural liberty'.[18]

The first function, then, of the Physiocratic theory of economic policy is the enactment of the Physiocratic programme of reconstruction of an agricultural kingdom by the political state.

The Physiocratic theory of economic policy is thus founded upon not only a theory of socioeconomic change but also a theory of the exercise of social control by the state. The Physiocrats recognized that the fact of social existence, of society itself, required a system of social control; that, further, the state is an instrument of social control; and that the practice of social control by the state extends over the domain of the choice, organization and control of the economy. Moreover, the Physiocrats recognized that since the economy is or may be controlled by the state, the theory of economic policy employed by the state governs the organization of the economy. Thus aware that to control the state is to control economic policy, the Physiocrats' aim was to secure adoption of their particular theory of policy and programme by the sovereign, to whom their programme of change was directed and through whom its realization was to be effectuated.

The Physiocrats tacitly rejected what generally came to be a central tenet of nineteenth-century economic liberalism, namely, that the state is an actual and potential nemesis to the individual, that economic policy was to proceed from the maxim, 'the least government the better'. On the contrary, the Physiocrats readily envisioned the utilization of the political state for the accomplishment of positive good, so that 'From this point of view they would have rejected the ridiculous paradox of Bastiat that the State does harm even when it does good.'[19] The Physiocrats saw that taxes were born out of their 'very utility', that the state itself constituted an agent of production,[20] and that since the state was axiomatically engaged in social control it was to be used as an agency for the realization of the national economy deemed most naturally essential and advantageous to political society. In thus regarding the state as a necessary and useful institution, the Physiocrats were at one with both the conservative Burke and later apostles of democratic reformism.

The Construction of an Agricultural Kingdom

The construction of an economy and society founded upon agriculture, a *Royaume Agricole*, thus became the basis of all public policy for the Physiocrats.[21] Their argument can be reduced to a simple syllogism, the phrases of which may be taken from Quesnay's *Maximes Générales du Gouvernement Economique d'un Royaume Agricole*, the title of which is itself instructive. The reasoning postulates:

> That the sovereign and the nation never forget that the land is the only source of wealth, and that it is agriculture which multiplies it. . . . From this plentiful source depends the success of all parts of the government of the Kingdom.
>
> That the economic government occupy itself only in favoring the productive outlays and the commerce of agricultural commodities, and that it leave alone the sterile outlays.

Thus,

> the order of the government of an agricultural kingdom . . . must unite all interests to a main object, to the prosperity of agriculture, which is the source of all the wealth of the state and all its citizens.[22]

Since agriculture is assumed as the source of prosperity (founded upon productivity), and since it is also assumed that the state is to promote prosperity (concentrating logically upon productivity), it follows that the state must promote agriculture and thus an agricultural kingdom.

It perhaps needs to be made clear that it would be erroneous to reduce Physiocratic policy to the simple formulation, 'promote agriculture', though such was in fact required. What is involved is much broader, for the reconstruction necessary to effectuate the agricultural kingdom would have extended to the basic institutional foundations of the greater society itself. But it does follow that to argue the adoption of an agricultural society is to elevate the interests of the agricultural classes (those deriving their income and status from agriculture and land), which must mean, given the system advocated by Quesnay, the promotion of the interests of the landowner, 'for, in preference to all, *the kingdom must be well peopled by rich farmers*'.[23]

The Reorganization and Redirection of the State

The construction of the agricultural kingdom through the agency of the state required, in the minds of the Physiocrats, the reorganization and redirection of the state itself so as to facilitate the realization of their objective. This alteration of state power involved a reconstitution of the decision-making structure of the state and a change in the focus and conduct of state affairs. In both respects the changes Physiocracy would have wrought would have have been a substantial departure from the hierarchy of policy criteria governing the organization and conduct of such policy under the *ancien régime*. The specific changes are the Physiocrats' solutions to problems then contemporary in France. What is necessary here is to relate the problems to the solutions advocated by the Physiocrats, establishing the identity of those solutions as basic elements of the activist Physiocratic theory of economic policy.

The problems of contemporary France as perceived by the Physiocrats included: (a) the practice of Colbertism, meaning Colbertism *pur*, whereby agriculture was disadvantaged in the interests of the development of national industry in the pursuit of favourable trade balances; two prostitutions of Colbertism *pur*, namely, (b) the refocusing of national economic policy from the objective of a favourable trade balance (and thereby economic development and national strength) to the support of the treasury (i.e., the profligate monarch's imperial and courtly expenditures), and (c) the exploitation and manipulation of government policy for the private pecuniary advantage of those in and out of public office;[24] (d) the internal protection system, resulting from the dual policies of local governments to secure and protect both the locally produced necessities for the local population and the local market for locally produced goods and services; and (e) the social and political division of the French nation, coupled with and manifest in the juridical diversity of the several parts of the nation, and the resultant mutual distrust and hostility.

To the Physiocrats, all of the foregoing was anathema, and for each the Physiocrats had a solution. In the article 'Grains', Quesnay laid down a basic principle of policy: 'The government of the incomes of the nation must not be abandoned to the discretion or authority of the minor administration and private individuals.' Internal protectionism and Colbertism, both pure and impure, were to be abrogated. Physiocratic economic policy would assume the tasks of:

> suppressing the prohibition and prejudicial impediments to the internal commerce and reciprocal external commerce.
>
> abolishing or moderating the excessive rights of rivers and tolls which destroy the incomes of the distant provinces where the commodities can be commercial only by long transports;
>
> It is no less necessary to abolish the special privileges of the provinces, towns and communities for their particular advantages.
>
> It is important also to facilitate everywhere the communications and the transports of merchandise by repairing roads and navigation of rivers.
>
> It is moreover essential not to subjugate the commerce of the commodities of the provinces in the prohibition and permissions shortlived and arbitrary which ruin the countryside under the heady pretext of assuring the abundance in the towns . . .
>
> One must not restrict at all the exportation of grains to some particular provinces because they become exhausted before the other provinces can regarnish them; and the inhabitants can be exposed, during many months, to a scarcity which they attribute with reason to exportation.
>
> But when the freedom of exportation is general, the raising of grains is not susceptible because the merchants draw from all parts of the kingdom, above all from the provinces where the price of grain is low.

The basic ideas are reiterated in the *Maximes Générales.*

A second basic principle was placed at the beginning of the *Maximes Générales*:

> That the sovereign authority be single and superior to all the individuals of society and to all the unjust enterprises of special interests; for the

> object of rule and obedience is the security of all and the lawful interest of all. The system of checks and balances (counterforces) in government is a harmful one which only produces discord among the great and the oppression of the weak. The division of society into various orders of citizens, whereof some exercise sovereign authority over others, is detrimental to the general interest and introduces the dissention of special interests among the various classes of citizens: this division reverses the order of the government of an agricultural kingdom which must unite all interests to a main object, to the prosperity of agriculture, which is the source of all the wealth of the state and all its citizens.[25]

In the words of Turgot, there should be 'a paternal government, based on a national constitution whereby the monarchy is raised above all in order to assure the welfare of all'. Thus, 'The edicts were calculated partly to restore the monarchy to the *de facto* head of the State, re-exalted the hearts of the people, and made free the parasites which were fattening from its already over-weakened vitality, and set forward to impartial government of all the subjects.'[26] The 'liberty of the king's subjects', as Turgot put it, was not to be sacrified 'to the exactions and caprices of private interests'.[27] Quesnay thus devotes the final three *Maximes* to the subject of financial reform.[28]

These Physiocratic solutions in their entirety would have reconstructed the political economy of France so as to (a) centralize, (b) concentrate, and (c) rationalize the power of the state. By the *centralization of power* is meant the abrogation of internal protectionism and the concomitant unification of the nation, involving the transfer of the economic powers of governance from the towns and provinces to the national government. (In this respect the Physiocrats would have done for France what the American Constitution and the commerce clause did for the United States.) By the *concentration of power* is meant the collectivization of power on the national or central level in the hands of the sovereign. Thus the 'sovereign authority', as Quesnay wrote of the Crown, was to be 'single and superior', elevated above the caprices of localities and the quests of clergy and nobility.[29] And by the *rationalization of power* is meant the elimination of the two prostitutions of Colbertism: government was to be made autonomous, independent of those who would seek to capture the policy and machinery of government for private benefit; and government was to conduct its own affairs (monetary, fiscal and debt policies writ large) in such a manner as to be consonant with the agricultural system. These three facets of practical policy derive from the essence of the Physiocratic system, whereby it was necessary (1) for the state *to be able to* adopt and carry out the Physiocratic programme, and (2) that government affairs be so conducted as to contribute to the economic prosperity of the nation through the consonance of all policies with the interests of the agricultural system.

It is clear, then, that 'The physiocrats . . . do not call forth a contrast between state and society; they inquire into the reasons which cause the flourishing or the decadence of both at the same time. The celebrated words of Dupont are the most fitting that can be given of the physiocratic doctrine: " . . . Pauvres paysans; pauvre royaume. Pauvre royaume; pauvre souverain"'.[30] Like the Marxists of a century later the Physiocrats were convinced of the validity of their ideas and programme. What was necessary then was to secure an *efficient* system of political economy capable of effectuating their programme. 'Monarchy justified by expedience'[31] served the purpose well. Yet, in a broader context, the Physiocrats reflect the ascendancy of the nation-state as the dominant formal institution for social control and social change.

GOVERNMENT AND ECONOMIC DEVELOPMENT

As part of their general economic theory, the Physiocrats had a systematic model of economic development the central focus of which was the flow of adequate resources to agriculture. The securing of economic development (defined in terms of agriculture) thus became the second major function of government in the Physiocratic theory of economic policy.

The promotion or protection of adequate agricultural resources may be defined in terms of the *bon prix*: 'The principal function of adequate trade consists in the encouragement of profitable agricultural activity by providing a large salesmarket and a high and stable price for its products.'[32] Or it may be thought of in terms of a proper pattern of spending: 'It is . . . upon the continuity of this circulation and upon the pattern of national expenditure or consumption (i.e., distribution of expenditures between the sterile and productive classes) that, in physiocratic theory, economic health, prosperity, and progress depend.' 'Consumption and expenditure must be according to pattern.'[33] In either case, the Physiocratic theory of economic policy included as a basic proposition that:

> The government's efforts must be directed towards the encouragement of all the expenditures which tend to maintain the high price of agricultural products and ensure a sufficient effective demand to cover the supply of these goods.[34]

One has but to cite *Maxime* VIII and the validity of the present function is clear:

> That the economic government occupy itself only in favoring the productive outlays and the commerce of agricultural commodities, and that it leave alone the sterile outlays.

And two other *Maximes* deal with the same principle.[35]

The matter is even clearer when the negative side is examined. If it is true that 'Prudent or "productive" consumption is one of the major prescriptions for policy',[36] then it is also true that unproductive consumption is one of the major proscriptions of policy. Witness, then, *Maximes* IX and XXII:

> That a nation which has a large territory to cultivate and the facility of exercising a large commerce in agricultural commodities not extend too much employment of money and men to manufactures and luxury commerce, to the detriment of the work and outlays of agriculture; for, in preference to all, *the kingdom must be well peopled by rich farmers*.

> That one not promote the luxury of ornamentation to the detriment of the expenses of the exploitation and improvement of agriculture and the expenses of consumption of subsistence, which maintains the good price and the sale of local agricultural commodities and the reproduction of the nation's income.[37]

But of all the facets of public policy relating to the promotion and protection of economic development, 'the strategic one to Quesnay was the protection of the funds (in real terms) properly destined for replacement and accumulation of fixed and working capital'.[38] To this matter Quesnay devoted no less than three *Maximes*.[39]

In the present age, when agricultural economic policy has apparently reached its zenith (or nadir), the meaning of all this is quite clear, notwithstanding the fact that the Physiocrats (save for Turgot) had no opportunity in France to spell out the particulars of the various general policy prescriptions. But it has long been clear that Physiocratic proposals for tax and monetary reform had as one of their objectives the reduction of burdens upon the advances and thus upon productivity. And it is also true that the purpose of interest rate regulation for several of the Physiocrats was to facilitate the movement of capital to agriculture. Moreover, not only was government to promote and protect the flow of capital to agriculture, but government was also specifically to promote the *grande culture*. Thus the government should help promote 'That the children of wealthy farmers establish themselves in the country for perpetuating the labor supply there', but primarily because 'it is less men than wealth that one must attract into the country' to establish the *grande culture*. While 'One ought not favor the monopoly of the cultivation of landed properties for it is detrimental to the general income of the nation', said Quesnay, it is nonetheless incumbent upon government to provide 'That the lands employed in the cultivation of grains be combined, as much as possible into large farms exploited by rich farmers'.[40] Government participation, promotion and supervision was thus included by the Physiocrats in their theory of economic development.

But it is here also that the principle of the freedom of commercial intercourse belongs, though as a practical maxim postulating substantial freedom to the particulars of economic life and not as dogma or doctrine. As with Adam Smith, so also with the Physiocrats: economic development – the maximization of the net product – was in part contingent upon substantial economic liberty.

> That one not hinder at all the foreign commerce in local commodities; for *such is the sale, such is the reproduction*.[41]

But what 'substantial economic liberty' meant for the Physiocrats is clearly no blanket prescription against any positive and activist role of government in the economy, but rather freedom in the sundry particulars of economic life, and these only given (a) the consonance thereof with the economic development of the agricultural kingdom and (b) the exercise of government authority promotive of the agricultural kingdom.

What 'substantial economic liberty' must be taken to mean, then, are the down-to-earth particulars of (a) substantial freedom in the utilization of privately owned resources, including the freedom of cultivation and the employment of capital, 'the easiness and choice of expenditure',[42] and the freedom of occupations;[43] and (b) substantial freedom in the buying and selling and transport of commodities. These were the matters that were impeded, prohibited or regulated by both Colbertism, pure and impure, and local protectionism; these were the matters in which the Physiocrats generally would have let spontaneity govern – and they involve substantial freedom for the individual in his economic pursuits. It is *laissez-faire*, *laissez-passer*, meaning thereby freedom to do, or freedom to make, and freedom to pass; or, as Marshall put it, 'let people make whatever they like and move wherever they like'. But, as Marshall pointed out:

> *Laissez faire* did not imply that Government should abstain inertly from constructive work: it meant simply that anyone who thought that he could make anything with advantage, whether on old lines or by a new method, should be at liberty to do so. *Laissez passer* had its chief application to difficulties that did not exist in England. It meant that all the various obstacles to the free passage of goods between the various Provinces should be removed.[44]

Such constructive work would take the form of the several functions attributed to government as developed in these pages. Moreover, Quesnay's twenty-fifth *Maxime*, 'That there be maintained the complete freedom of commerce', did not preclude the principle that all behaviour would have to be consonant with the operation of the agricultural system. Thus the 'complete freedom of commerce' is modified by such *Maximes* as those which provide:

> That a part of the sum of incomes not pass to a foreign country without returning, in *money* or in merchandise.
>
> That they prevent [évite] the desertion of habitants who would carry their wealth out of the kingdom.

and that there be no social loss in foreign trade.[45] The exercise of private freedom was contingent upon the essentially collectivist criterion of the effect upon the agricultural system. Private vices were not always public virtues, nor were private virtues always public virtues.

Laissez-faire, laissez-passer thus had an important role in the Physiocratic theory of economic policy: what the neoclassical economist calls resource allocation was to be achieved substantially through the operation of substantial economic liberty, *given* the caveats noted above, namely, the consonance thereof with the agricultural system, and government policy demonstrably activist in other respects. But *laissez-faire, laissez-passer* is not the sum total of the Physiocratic theory of economic policy; for clearly the Physiocratic concept of the role of government in the economy was not one of sitting back and relaxing and letting the world and the economy go by on its own. Individuals were to have greater latitude of action than under the *ancien régime*, but they were still to operate within the social controls of a *Royaume Agricole*. Nor, as Smith himself pointed out, is the Physiocratic theory of economy policy, interpreted as *laissez-faire*, that of Adam Smith. It is now well recognized that Smith's theory of economic policy has no insignificant place for government, though such was not emphasized. In comparison therewith, however, the position here is that in the Physiocratic theory of economic policy, (1) government had a more thorough and activist role, being given specific positive tasks and ends, and (2) *laissez-faire*, as defined above, had a restricted scope. Smith would rely *largely* upon the free market for the direction and course of economic development; the Physiocrats would have adopted some form of what now would be called target planning (and balance planning – see the following section) to govern the form of economic organization and economic behaviour in general. The Physiocrats would have influenced the allocation of resources directly, as they deemed necessary; and, moreover, pervasively, by controlling the particular institutional environment within which resource allocation takes place, to wit, so as to direct resources to agriculture – neither of which is Smithian. The free market of Smith was relatively spontaneous, autonomous and viable; that of the Physiocrats would not be the opposite but it would be a manipulated economy. To Smith, government had positive tasks but was to be relatively passive insofar as resource allocation and economic development were concerned; to the Physiocrats, government was to supervise actively the performance of the economy (thus antedating contemporary programmes of economic development).

GOVERNMENT AND ECONOMIC STABILITY

Correlative to the role of government in securing economic development was a solicitude shared by several Physiocrats over the *stability* of growth. These writers were concerned over obstacles that might impede the process of expansion once the agricultural system had already become a *fait accompli*. As Spengler put it, Quesnay discovered 'that economic relations are resolvable into a circular flow, whose continuity is contingent upon the presence of certain conditions'.[46] Interruption might result from two types of circumstances: first, the proper pattern of spending might not be achieved, with an adverse effect upon the sale of agricultural commodities and agricultural income and investment, the total volume of spending, *ceteris paribus*, remaining unchanged; the second, the maximization of the net product might not be realized due to an inadequate volume of spending *per se*, with a similar contracting effect.[47]

Since growth could be impeded whenever there did not exist the required pattern or volume of expenditures, the Physiocratic theory of economic policy therefore also was concerned with promoting and protecting those necessary conditions. Since 'they did infer, in consequence of their peculiar theory of production, that an economy might be in equilibrium either at a prosperity or at a depression level',[48] several Physiocrats contemplated the exercise of government policy (monetary, fiscal and trade) *vis-à-vis* conditions of instability. While once again the particulars of policy never had occasion to be fully developed, and while there is some question as to how far several of the Physiocrats would have gone,[49] there is ample explicit evidence, as indicated in the author's earlier article, to indicate that Quesnay and several other Physiocrats would have clearly favoured governmental supervision of the performance of the economy in this respect as in others.

The securing of the stability of economic development thus becomes the third general function of government in the Physiocratic system.

CONCLUSIONS

The reformulation of the Physiocratic theory of economic policy that forms the thesis of this article cannot be proven: for all the passage either esoteric or mundane extolling the glories of the abstinence of civil government, of the pervasive existence of *liberté*, there are equally strong exclamations in support of what the Physiocrats called *autorité tutelaire*. The positivist position has been taken here that what counts is what their policy really amounted to, rather than the doctrinaire statements one way or the other. But fundamentally the matter cannot be settled with any great finality because no Physiocratic *régime* came to pass in France. One relies, then, only upon words – and the administrations of Turgot – plus insight. What is important, then, is not the specific utterances or even the specific particulars of policy – to regulate or not to regulate interest rates – but the philosophy and the values of the men involved. Furthermore, once one has penetrated below the level of mere utterances and style of language, what is so clear for their theory of economic policy is that all of the Physiocrats shared basically the same policy perspective. Differences as to detail there were, but they were only to be expected; and in time doctrine overshadowed complications. What counts is that which makes them all Physiocrats, pure or impure, master and ally or over-zealous disciple; and that is their attitude towards social change and the creation (and supervision) of a new society through the medium of the political state.

Moreover, the supposed paradox of economic freedom and political absolutism cannot be resolved by stating that, 'What they wanted to see was the minimum of legislation with a maximum of authority.' After all, the relevant index is not the length or weight of the statute book but rather the character and extent of the role of government, i.e., the realm and exercise of its authority. The paradox is only a paradox as long as the Physiocrats are defined as nineteenth-century economic liberals – which they were not, though *laissez-faire* had a place in their theory of economic policy. Nor can it be argued that, 'It was just the sovereignty of the "natural order" – nothing more.'[50] There seems to be a choice of proffered natural orders, the selection and adoption of which is a matter of discretion, i.e., of policy. The fact of the language of naturalism does not preclude the foregoing analysis from being *policy*; in spite of all their naturalism, the Physiocrats were essentially Platonic. The naturalist interpretation 'fails to grasp the fundamentally reformist character of their teacher and does injustice to their doctrine of economic policy'.[51]

Whitehead has stated that, 'The conduct of human affairs is entirely dominated by our recognition of foresight determining purpose, and purpose issuing in conduct.'[52] The Physiocrats did not achieve the level of 'conduct'; but they had 'purpose', and their purpose may be crystallized in terms of what they would have done had the opportunity for conduct arisen. That part of 'what they would have done' relevant to the organization and control of the economy becomes their theory of economic policy. It is the effective basis of this programme for the realization of purpose that this article has endeavoured to delineate.

The Physiocratic theory of economic policy is fundamentally related to a theory of property–state relations in which private property is the dominant institutional form but wherein the public interest is manifest in the continuing modification or reconstitution of the bundle of rights that comprise private property at any given time.

The theory of economic policy operationally extant in the writings and beliefs of the Physiocrats encompassed the three paramount functions[53] of government defined above: (a) the conduct of socioeconomic change, i.e., the construction of the institutions of an agricultural system; (b) the support of economic development under the new system; and (c) the protection against obstacles to stability of growth. The Physiocratic theory of economic policy is thus far more complex than can be summarized by the term *laissez-faire* (or *laissez-faire, laissez-passer*). If the term be defined broadly – as proscribing or minimizing government activity writ large – then it is patently fallacious and invalid. If it be defined narrowly – substantial freedom for resource allocation, involving wide personal latitude in economic affairs – then it is an incomplete statement of Physiocratic economic policy, for government had positive roles to play over and above – though not independent of – private behaviour.[54] As Randall put it, 'This dual demand for protection in fundamentals and freedom in all else is the controlling principle in the development of the science of political economy.'[55] Doctrine should not obscure the exercise of social control by the Physiocratic state, nor their coming to grips with the problem of securing change in an orderly manner. Nor is it tenable that such social control was of the 'minimal' variety, meaning a real modicum of government authority and activity; minimal 'given the system' is logically correct, but takes rather much for granted, begging the question of 'the system'. To paraphrase J. M. Clark, 'we must take some pains to avoid the implication that economy exists first and is then controlled. Control is rather an integral part of economy, without which it could not be economy at all. The one implies the other, and the two have grown together'.[56] Thus did the Physiocrats implicitly recognize that the basic economic institutions (the organization of economy) are legal in character; that law is an instrument for the attainment of economic objectives and that economy is an object of legal control.

Notes

1. Meaning thereby the 'general body of principles of government action or inaction – the *agenda* or *non-agenda* of the state as Bentham called them – in regard to economic activity' (Lionel Robbins, *The Theory of Economic Policy in English Classical Political Economy* (London: Macmillan, 1953), p. 2).
2. Warren J. Samuels, 'The Physiocratic Theory of Property and State', Quarterly Journal of Economics, vol. 75 (February 1961), pp. 96–111.
3. Henry Carter Adams, quoted in Introductory Essay by Joseph Dorfman (ed.), in Adams, *Relation of the State to Industrial Action and Economics and Jurisprudence* (New York: Columbia University Press, 1954), p. 8.
4. D. H. MacGregor, *Economic Thought and Policy* (New York: Oxford University Press, 1949), p. 66.
5. Auguste Oncken (ed.), *Oeuvres Economiques et Philosophiques de F. Quesnay* (Paris: Joseph Baer, 1888), pp. 240–1, 336; see also pp. 359–77, 747–58.
6. Charles Gide and Charles Rist, *A History of Economic Doctrines* (Boston: Heath, n.d.), pp. 11, 33.
7. W. Walker Stephens (ed.), *The Life and Writings of Turgot* (New York: Longmans, Green & Co., 1895), p. 252, see also pp. 293, 235, 249, 250.
8. O. F. Boucke, *The Development of Economics* (New York: Macmillan, 1921), p. 67.
9. Oncken, *Oeuvres Economiques*, p. 802.
10. Turgot quoted in Stephens, *The Life and Writings of Turgot*, pp. 254–5.
11. See MacGregor, *Economic Thought and Policy*, pp. 54–67; Gide and Rist, *A History of Economic Doctrines*, p. 11; also Oncken, *Oeuvres Economiques*, p. 804.
12. Haney, for example, calls attention to 'the crisp, sweeping exaggerations of the Physiocratic system' (Lewis H. Haney, *History of Economic Thought* 4th edn (New York: Macmillan, 1949), p. 205). A. P. Usher argues that, 'The more critical writers were, perhaps, not without some mental reservations, but in the highly abstract generalizations with which they were primarily concerned, the exceptions did not seem important' (A. P. Usher, 'Laissez Faire and the Rise of Liberalism', in *Explorations in Economics: Notes and Essays Contributed in Honor of F. W. Taussig* (New York: McGraw-Hill, 1936), p. 406). See also Gide and Rist, *A History of Economic Doctrines*, p. 30.
13. Thomas P. Neill, 'Quesnay and Physiocracy', *Journal of the History of Ideas*, vol. 9 (January 1948), p. 164.

14. Joseph A. Schumpeter, *Economic Doctrine and Method* (New York: Oxford University Press, 1954), p. 46.
15. Ibid., p. 61; see also Schumpeter, *History of Economic Analysis* (New York: Oxford University Press, 1954), p. 230.
16. Gunnar Myrdal, *The Political Element in the Development of Economic Theory* (Cambridge: Harvard University Press, 1955), p. 31 '[T]he formulation of normative rules was for them one of the central functions of theoretical analysis. This explains why they attempted no demarcation of their science from rational politics' (p. 6).
17. While 'The philosophy of the natural order presumed that the economic institutions essential to society existed from the beginning as given data or developed spontaneously without the exertion of pressure by the state'. Usher argues that this position 'was due to concentration of attention upon the ultimate fact of economic adjustment rather than to any failure to recognize the magnitude of the obstacles encountered in the development of the institutional mechanisms of social life'. 'Thus liberal economists made substantial contributions to state policy designed to develop or modify private institutions essential to economic activity' (*The Political Element in the Development of Economic Theory*, p. 407). Hence 'their *ordre naturel* was no more than a directive principle for the regulation of industry and agriculture by a supposedly all-powerful and omniscient government. Quesnay's *Maximes* were intended to provide such a government with the viewpoints needed to translate into practical policy the principles of the *Tableau* on the basis of statistical data which he offered to have furnished periodically. The idea of a self-perpetuating system of markets had never as much as entered his mind' (Karl Polanyi, *The Great Transformation* (New York: Rinehart, 1944), p. 135).

    For similar interpretations of the significance of naturalism for the Physiocratic system see: Myrdal, *The Political Element in the Development of Economic Theory*, especially pp. 28–9, 5–6, 115; Schumpeter, *Economic Doctrine and Method*, pp. 47–59; MacGregor, *Economic Thought and Policy*, p. 66; O. H. Taylor, *Economics and Liberalism* (Cambridge: Harvard University Press, 1955), pp. 37–99, in particular pp. 47, 51, 85–6, 98–9; John R. Commons, *Legal Foundations of Capitalism* (New York: Macmillan, 1924), pp. 241–2, and *Institutional Economics* (New York: Macmillan, 1934), pp. 136–7; Neill, 'Quesnay and Physiocracy', pp. 162, 166–73, and 'The Physiocrats' Concept of Economics', *Quarterly Journal of Economics*, vol. 63 (Nov. 1949), in particular pp. 551–3; James Bonar, *Philosophy and Political Economy* (New York: Macmillan, 1909), p. 194; John A. Mourant, 'Mr. Neill and Physiocracy', *Journal of the History of Ideas*, vol. 10 (Jan. 1949), p. 113; and H. W. Peck, *Economic Thought and its Institutional Background* (New York: Farrar and Rinehart, 1935), p. 65.
18. Adam Smith, *An Inquiry into the Nature and Causes of the Wealth of Nations* (New York: Modern Library, 1937), pp. 650–1.
19. Henry Higgs, *The Physiocrats* (New York: Langland Press, 1952), pp. 143–4.
20. Luigi Einaudi, 'The Physiocratic Theory of Taxation', in *Economic Essays in Honor of Gustave Cassel* (London: Allen and Unwin, 1933), pp. 129–42;

discussed in Samuels, 'The Physiocratic Theory of Property and State', pp. 106–7.

21. Except for Turgot, for whom the foundations of the new order would have been broader based, as that of Quesnay might have become had he the opportunity to formulate actual public policy.
22. Oncken, *Oeuvres Economiques*, pp. 330, 333.
23. Ibid., p. 333.
24. Max Weber described as 'political capitalism' or 'fiscal capitalism' the economy wherein profit opportunities accrue from the exploitation of political prerogatives (*From Max Weber: Essays in Sociology*, H. H. Gerth and C. Wright Mills (eds) (New York: Oxford University Press, 1946), pp. 66–7); see also *Max Weber: The Theory of Social and Economic Organization*, ed. Talcott Parsons (New York: Oxford University Press, 1947), pp. 278–80.
25. Oncken, *Oeuvres Economiques*, pp. 241–2, 331; see also *Maximes* XVI, XVII, XXV.
26. R. P. Shepherd, *Turgot and the Six Edicts* (New York: Columbia University, Series in History, Economics and Public Law, Vol. XVIII, No. 2, 1903), pp. 103, 61; see also pp. 138, 37–42, and Stephens, *The Life and Writings of Turgot*, pp. 267–8, 245–6, 240–1.
27. Stephens, *The Life and Writings of Turgot*, p. 45.
28. Oncken, *Oeuvres Economiques*, pp. 337–8.
29. Physiocratic political theory incorporated several checks, or 'guarantees', upon the sovereign power; see Mario Einaudi, *The Physiocratic Doctrine of Judicial Control* (Cambridge: Harvard University Press, 1938).
30. Ibid., p. 25.
31. C. Northcote Parkinson, *The Evolution of Political Thought* (Boston: Houghton Mifflin, 1958). See also Alexis de Tocqueville, *The Old Regime and the French Revolution* (Garden City: Doubleday Anchor, 1955), pp. 164–5.
32. Henry Woog, *The Tableau Economique of François Quesnay* (Bern: A. Francke, 1950), p. 28; see also p. 86.
33. J. J. Spengler, 'The Physiocrats and Say's Law of Markets', I–II, *Journal of Political Economy*, vol. 53 (Sept. and Dec. 1945), pp. 204, 205.
34. Woog, *The Tableau Economique*, pp. 89.
35. Oncken, *Oeuvres Economiques*, pp. 335, 336, *Maximes* XX and XXVII.
36. Harold G. Vatter, 'The Physiocrats and the Growth of Underdeveloped Economies', *Current Economic Comment*, vol. 18 (Nov. 1956), p. 40.
37. Oncken, *Oeuvres Economiques*, pp. 333, 335; see also Vatter, 'The Physiocrats and Underdeveloped Economics', pp. 39–40; Woog, *The Tableau Economique*, pp. 84 ff.; Spengler, 'The Physiocrats and Say's Law of Markets', pp. 208 ff.; and Leo Rogin, *The Meaning and Validity of Economic Theory* (New York: Harper, 1956), p. 32.
38. Vatter, 'The Physiocrats and Underdeveloped Economics', p. 39.
39. Oncken, *Oeuvres Economiques*, pp. 332, 333, *Maximes* V, VI and XII. See also Woog, *The Tableau Economique*, p. 92; and Spengler, 'The Physiocrats and Say's Law of Markets'.
40. Oncken, *Oeuvres Economiques*, pp. 333, 334.
41. Ibid., p. 334.
42. Ibid., pp. 240–1; see also *Maxime* XIII (p. 333).

43. Shepherd, *Turgot and the Six Edicts*, p. 119.
44. Alfred Marshall, *Industry and Trade* 3rd edn (London: Macmillan, 1932), p. 742; see also his *Principles of Economics* 8th edn (New York: Macmillan, 1953) p. 757. See Nicolas Baudeau, *Première Introduction à la Philosophie Economique* (Paris: Librairie Paul Geuthner, 1910), p. 77.
45. Oncken, *Oeuvres Economiques*, pp. 333, 336.
46. Spengler, 'The Physiocrats and Say's Law of Markets', p. 347.
47. Spengler, ibid.; see also Woog, *The Tableau Economique*, p. 83 ff., and Ronald L. Meek, 'The Interpretation of the Tableau Economique'; *Economica*, n.s. XXVII (Nov. 1960), pp. 336–47.
48. Spengler, ibid., p. 327; see also p. 326.
49. Spengler, ibid., pp. 328–9; Samuels, 'The Physiocratic Theory of Property and State', p. 104, n. 4.
50. Gide and Rist, *A History of Economic Doctrines*, pp. 34, 35.
51. George J. Malanos, 'The Evolution of the General Theory', unpublished Ph.D. thesis, Harvard University, 1946, p. 43; see also p. 77. See also n. 17 above.
52. Alfred North Whitehead, *The Foundation of Reason* (Boston: Beacon Press, 1958), p. 13.
53. Two other functions may also be identified, functions mundane but hardly unimportant. These may be called the protective and welfare functions. Both may be clarified as derivative of the police power as conventionally understood. The protective function relates to the securing of person and property against domestic and foreign sources of illegal infringement (see Samuels, 'The Physiocratic Theory of Property and State', pp. 96–7). While all Physiocratic theory and each function of government relates to welfare, the welfare function narrowly defined is basically remedial, as indicated by Turgot's program for famine relief (Samuels, 'The Physiocratic Theory of Property and State', pp. 101–2).
54. Thus if one defines *laissez-faire* 'to embrace the arguments of those who accepted government as a necessity but nevertheless wished to see its functions reduced to the narrowest possible limits', and of those who 'recognized that government must protect life and property and must provide a few common services, such as education, but essentially . . . viewed the state in negative terms and were loath to have it assume positive duties in the interest of the general welfare', then the Physiocrats would appear to belong more properly among 'The theorists of the general-welfare state . . . [who] believed that the state could benefit society by a positive exertion of its powers and that it should therefore act whenever its interposition seemed likely to promote the common well-being' (Sidney Fine, *Laissez Faire and the General-Welfare State* (Ann Arbor: The University of Michigan Press, 1956), p. vii).
55. J. H. Randall, Jr, *The Making of the Modern Mind* (Boston: Houghton Mifflin, 1926), p. 322.
56. J. M. Clark, *Social Control of Business* (New York: McGraw-Hill, 1939), p. 12.

3 Adam Smith and the Economy as a System of Power*

The wisdom of Adam Smith has as its preeminent monument the fundamental paradigm of modern economic theory. The Smithian view, as it has come to be articulated as the conventional paradigm of economics, encompasses the play of spontaneous economic activity, the allocation of resources through market forces, efficiency comprehended in terms of self-interest or personal maximization of well-being, and the regulatory hand of competition. While it is recognized that such harmony as is achieved in this system is very rough indeed and that the operation of the market takes place only within and as structured by the social control forces of morals, religion, custom, education, and the law,[1] the Smithian world, as perceived through modern economics, is constituted by the interplay of individual economic actors engaged in voluntary exchange through the mechanism of a competitive market. Smithian economics is thus seen as the economics of a spontaneous, generally beneficent, powerfully productive economic system, analysed in terms of the impersonal forces of the market; it is the economics of individuals voluntarily choosing from among the opportunities available to them in such a way as to achieve a constrained maximization of their welfare.

In a recent article,[2] I have suggested an alternative paradigm which would make prominent the forces and factors governing the *structure* of economic decision making, just as the conventional Smithian–neoclassical paradigm focuses upon resource allocation through the market mechanism. This is a model of the economy as a system of mutual coercion based on relative power (with the terms defined in the note),[3] in which resource allocation is seen as a function of coercive power in the market which in turn is partially a function of the legal definition and assignment–distribution of rights. It is a model in which resource allocation is a function of mutual coercion operating through the market, and in which both resource allocation and economic power are analysed as facets of the

* Originally published in Review of Social Economy, vol. 31 (October 1973), pp. 123–37; and *Indian Economic Journal*, vol. 20 (January–March 1973), pp. 363–81. Reprinted in J. C. Wood (ed.), Adam Smith: Critical Assessments (London: Croom Helm, 1984), vol. 1.

problem of order, the balancing of freedom and control, continuity and change, and hierarchy and equality.[4] In this model, the interrelation of legal and market processes has profound influence upon the resolution of the basic economic problems. In another paper,[5] I have attempted a revision of the central paradigm of neoclassical microeconomics and welfare economics in terms of a broader and more complex model of choice and power along the foregoing lines. Voluntary market exchange is seen as both a dependent and independent variable in the context of a broad general equilibrium model in which the primary variables are individual choice, power structure, opportunity set structure, working rules, mutual coercion, resource allocation, and income distribution. Instead of a model of choice between alternatives from within opportunity sets, this alternative model emphasizes the factors and forces governing the structure and composition of opportunity sets and thus the attainment and distribution of welfare, all in terms of power and mutual coercion.

In this chapter I would like to suggest that the wisdom of Adam Smith is more profound than has been yet realized. Quite aside from (though an important part of) the broader vision of the economy and society manifest in the *Theory of Moral Sentiments*, the *Wealth of Nations*, and the *Lectures*, there is, I am suggesting, in the *Wealth of Nations*, the elements of a second and broader paradigm of choice and power, a model not just of economic actors allocating their limited resources so as to maximize their welfare but a model also of a struggle for command of resources and market position and thus of welfare maximizing through power and mutual coercion. In this chapter I am going to sketch the model of the economy as a system of mutual coercion and power as found in the *Wealth of Nations*. I shall show that Smith had a deep and powerful understanding of the broader forces and factors at work in the economic system in the determination and distribution of welfare, and that he was very much a realist in appreciating that market forces and the invisible hand work out only in the context of interacting social powers operating through the market. This analysis should provide further insight into, first, the sophistication and subtleties of Smith's underlying approach to the problem of order and, second, his approach to government as an economic phenomenon. We shall see that Smith very much understood the necessity and role of government in economic affairs; that Smith realistically understood how the government operates in practice; and that the critical analytical and policy question is not government versus no government (nor that of minimum government) but rather which interests government is to promote or who uses government for what ends; all of which is to say, that Smith understood the economy as a system of mutual coercion with the state as both a dependent and independent variable insofar as power players and economics are concerned. To existential scarcity (and efficiency) is added the perception of existential choice and the power play which transcend and channel market allocation of resources. Smith was very much aware that (what modern economists call) efficiency requires an antecedent and continuing determination of whose preferences shall count and that the very structuring of the economic system involves an ubiquitous jockeying for positions of preference.

I

I propose to show the fact and substance of Smith's paradigm of mutual coercion and power by examining in some detail his treatment of certain topics in the *Wealth of Nations*.[6] Let us begin with Smith's discussion of the bargain between masters and workers.

Smith begins his chapter 'Of the Wages of Labour' with the explicit assumption of a wage system, a system in which most real incomes are earned by working for others through jobs secured in a labour market, the others being the owners of capital, the masters, as he calls, them. Now what is initially interesting is that Smith's basic understanding of the wage system as a system is predicated upon power relationships: indeed, he just stops short of an exploitation theory of labour, wages, and capitalism. Stating first that 'The produce of labour constitutes the natural recompense or wages of labour', and second that 'In that original state of things, which precedes both the appropriation of land and the accumulation of stock, the whole produce of labour belongs to the labourer. He has neither landlord nor master to share with him', Smith then reasons 'But this original state of things, in which the labourer enjoyed the whole produce of his own labour, could not last beyond the first introduction of the appropriation of land and the accumulation of stock' (pp. 64, 65). That Smith seems to lead up to an exploitation theory is beside the point, as is the quality of this analysis as distribution theory. What is important is that Smith points to the significance of the institutional organization of land and capital, specifically to the impact thereof upon the opportunity structure open to the workers. Wage labour, land ownership, and stock (capital goods) ownership are institutions involving power relations which channel the market within which labour and all other incomes are determined. Further, as we shall see below, the power structure that is involved in this set of institutional arrangements is fundamentally related to the existence and role of government. In sum, the wage system involves a process of mutual coercion and power.

Given the wage system, then, Smith continues:

> What are the common wages of labour, depends everywhere upon the contract usually made between those two parties, whose interests are by no means the same. The workmen desire to get as much, the masters to give as little as possible. The former are disposed to combine in order to raise, the latter in order to lower the wages of labour. (p. 66)

So in his initial statement of the problem, Smith posits a system of jockeying for positions of advantage from which to coerce the opposite party, indeed, even aside from such manoeuvring there is a structure of power and process of mutual coercion, involving, as will be seen below, asymmetry of inequality of power. Then, in two long, revealing paragraphs, Smith elaborates on the labour market as a system of mutual coercion; on relative power as function of law, skewed in one direction depending upon who uses or influences government; on wages as a function of relative withholding power; on manipulation by concentrated private power able to call upon the law; differential identification and publicity given to different coercive actions – all components of a general paradigm of mutual coercion:

> It is not, however, difficult to foresee which of the two parties must, upon all ordinary occasions, have the advantage in the dispute, and force the other into a compliance with their terms. The masters, being fewer in number, can combine much more easily [here note the concept of differential organizability, so important in modern theories of collective action and power] and the law, besides, authorises, or at least does not prohibit their combinations, while it prohibits those of the workmen. We have no acts of parliament against combining to lower the price of work; but many against combining to raise it. [Note here the evident recognition of how opportunity sets, relative advantage and disadvantage, are a partial function of law, i.e., the influence of legal rights upon bargaining position and *pro tanto* upon wages.]
>
> In all such disputes the masters can hold out much longer. A landlord, a farmer, a master manufacturer, or merchant, though they did not employ a single workman, could generally live a year or two upon the stocks which they have already acquired. Many workmen could not subsist a week, few could subsist a month, and scarce any a year without employment. In the long run the workman may be as necessary to his master as his master is to him, but the necessity is not so immediate. [Note here that Smith posits a system of mutual coercion in the market

characterized by an asymmetry or inequality of withholding capacity, an important element in power.] (p. 66)

Smith then proceeds with a well-known but under-appreciated discussion:

> We rarely hear, it has been said, of the combination of masters, though frequently of those of workmen. But whoever imagines, upon this account, that masters rarely combine, is as ignorant of the world as of the subject. Masters are always and every where in a sort of tacit, but constant and uniform combination, not to raise the wages of labour above their actual rate. To violate this combination is every where a most unpopular action, and a sort of reproach to a master among his neighbours and equals. [Note here the subtle nuances of the sociology of power and class as well as the continuation of the discussion of mutual coercion (however skewed).]
>
> We seldom, indeed, hear of this combination, because it is the usual, and one may say, the natural state of things which nobody ever hears of. Masters too sometimes enter into particular combinations to sink the wages of labour even below this rate. These are always conducted with the utmost silence and secrecy, till the moment of execution, and when the workmen yield, as they sometimes do, without resistance, though severely felt by them, they are never heard of by other people. Such combinations, however, are frequently resisted by a contrary defensive combination of the workmen; who sometimes too, without any provocation of this kind, combine of their own accord to raise the price of their labour. Their usual pretences are, sometimes the high price of provisions, sometimes the great profit which their masters make by their work. But whether their combinations be offensive or defensive, they are always abundantly heard of. In order to bring the point to a speedy decision, they have always recourse to the loudest clamour, and sometimes to the most shocking violence and outrage. They are desperate, and act with the folly and extravagance of desperate men, who must either starve, or frighten their masters into an immediate compliance with their demands. The masters upon these occasions are just as clamorous upon the other side, and never cease to call aloud for the assistance of the civil magistrate, and the rigorous execution of those laws which have been enacted with so much severity against the combinations of servants, labourers, and journeymen. [Note on whose terms law and order is defined; note too the beautiful description of how private mutual coercion is conducted in labour markets and of the invocation of the state to enforce rights which the masters earlier secured in their favour.]

> The workmen, accordingly, very seldom derive any advantage from the violence of those tumultuous combinations, which, partly from the interposition of the civil magistrate, partly from the superior steadiness of the masters, partly from the necessity which the greater part of the workmen are under of submitting for the sake of present subsistence, generally end in nothing, but the punishment or ruin of the ring-leaders. (pp. 66–7)

Smith then points out a major principle of his formal wage theory:

> But though in disputes with their workmen, masters must generally have the advantage, there is however a certain rate below which it seems impossible to reduce, for any considerable time, the ordinary wages even of the lowest species of labour. (p. 67)

Without going more deeply into Smith's wage theory, it is obvious that regardless of the minimum of subsistence, the wage rate is a function of the relative power positions from which the parties mutually coerce each other, that *pro tanto* income distribution is a function of power structure and mutual coercion, and that the state enters into both the structuring of power and the exercise of mutual coercion through its recognition and enforcement of rights providing coercive advantage or exposure. All of this is basically reiterated at the end of Chapter XI of Book I, 'Of Wages and Profit in the Different Employments of Labour and Stock', where Smith again points to the legislature's 'attempts to regulate the differences between masters and their workmen', when 'its counsellors are always the masters' (p. 142). Wage rates and income distribution are partially a function of legally grounded and/or re-enforced positions of power operating through a process of mutual coercion in the market. Masters and workmen maximize within the market but they also, the masters with special success, maximize by influencing the institutional and thereby power structure in their favour.

Let us turn next to Smith's discussion of the relative position of the landowners, wage earners and businessmen in regard to the interests 'of the public', and the advantageous position of the businessmen in having the public interest increasingly defined in their terms – because of 'their having a better knowledge of their own interest' – and his doctrine that

> The interest of the dealers, however, in any particular branch of trade or manufacturers, is always in some respects different from, and even opposite to, that of the public. To widen the market and to narrow the

> competition, is always the interest of the dealers. To widen the market may frequently be agreeable enough to the interests of the public; but to narrow the competition must always be against it, and can serve only to enable the dealers, by raising their profits above what they naturally would be, to levy, for their own benefit, an absurd tax upon the rest of their fellow-citizens. The proposal of any new law or regulation of commerce which comes from this order, ought always to be listened to with great precaution, and ought never to be adopted till after having been long and carefully examined, not only with the most scrupulous, but with the most suspicious attention. It comes from an order of men, whose interest is never exactly the same with that of the public, who have generally an interest to deceive and even to oppress the public, and who accordingly have, upon many occasions, both deceived and oppressed it. (p. 250)

Let us not dwell on his judgement that the interests of the landlords and of the wage earners are inseparably connected with the general social interest whereas the interest of those who live by profit 'is always in some respects different from, and even opposite to, that of the public', nor let us dwell on his judgement as to the propensity of businessmen to deceive and oppress the public, for these judgements are matters on which reasonable men will differ both in the large and in detail. What is important is that here too Smith points to a system of mutual coercion, with jockeying for positions of power, positions of power from which 'to levy, for their own benefit, an absurd tax upon the rest of their fellow citizens'. Here is a system of mutual coercion whose results are explicitly articulated in terms making them roughly equivalent to those of government, namely, the power to tax by raising prices, the power to get something for nothing, or at least nothing directly. The genius of Smith's system, of course, is competition, but competition operates within and upon a structure of rights and power (which in turn operates through the competitive market). Smith recognizes that in a business society nothing is more natural than for the business class to have the ear of the statesman and public opinion generally as to what is in the interest of the public. Here the competition is for that public opinion which controls (*pro tanto*) legislation and elections, and for the state itself. I repeat: it is not of present importance whether the businessmen ought to be treated with caution and suspicion; what is important is the fact of their power play in a system of mutual coercion as they attempt to structure the market and its operation to their own advantage. There must be *some* structure of rights and position, and their goal (like that of the landowners and wage earners) is to skew it to their own advantage. The workings of mutual coercion, hence the allocation of resources and distribution of income, reflect the pattern of advantage and disadvantage embodied in the structure of rights and power.

Much the same lesson emerges from Smith's earlier and well-known statement that

> People of the same trade seldom meet together, even for merriment and diversion, but the conversation ends in a conspiracy against the public, or in some contrivance to raise prices. It is impossible indeed to prevent such meetings, by any law which either could be executed, or would be consistent with liberty and justice. But though the law cannot hinder people of the same trade from sometimes assembling together, it ought to do nothing to facilitate such assemblies; much less to render them necessary. (p. 128)

Here again mutual coercion takes the form of manipulations of alternatives open to consumers and/or workers by concentrated or collusive private power, with or without state aid. To Smith, both the mercantile and agricultural systems were systems of extraordinary restraints and extraordinary encouragements in the interest of one social class or another, in each case the state serving one set of interests as opposed to others. In the case of Physiocracy, albeit 'in representing perfect liberty as the only effectual expedient for rendering this annual reproduction the greatest possible, its doctrine seems to be in every respect as just as it is generous and liberal' (p. 643), in preferring agriculture to manufactures and trade it is essentially a substitution phenomenon *vis-à-vis* mercantilism (pp. 650–1) and a perverse one at that inasmuch as Smith found that 'agricultural systems . . . really and in the end discourage their own favourite species of industry' (p. 650). But business, too, that is, trade and manufacturing generally, not just mercantile interests, seeks extraordinary restraints and encouragements both private and public. It is another matter as to just when a restriction or encouragement is 'extraordinary' and when a matter of private rights or justice; here what counts is that business will seek positions of advantage in the market directly and indirectly through legal aid, all in a system of mutual coercion. Arrangements agreed to or liked will be spoken of as a matter of right and justice, and others as coercion in the pejorative sense, but they all involve coercion in the analytical sense used here, including power strategies and moves undertaken unilaterally or individually and not collusively or collectively.

I take us next to some of the most important and revealing discussions in the *Wealth of Nations*. In the relatively short (twelve pages) second part of the long (150 pages) first chapter of Book V, Smith discusses the expenses of justice. Now justice in the Smithian scheme of things covers a great deal; it includes his theory of the role of government as an instrument for ordering social relations and resolving conflicts, 'that of protecting, as far as possible, every member of the society from the injustice or oppression of every other member of it, or the duty of establishing an exact administration of justice' (p. 669). In the *Theory of Moral Sentiments* Smith made it clear that whereas situations of *beneficence* do not involve any obligation to attend to the interests of others, situations of *justice* have to do with those acts the omission of which or the commission of which incurs injury,[7] i.e., generalizing, the production of negative externalities as the substance of mutual coercion. So the domain of *justice* to Smith covers a great range. In this part of the *Wealth of Nations*, Smith presents his theory of the origin and role of civil government. It is a theory in which government is both a dependent and independent variable in the general system of mutual coercion, and Smith could not be clearer in his understanding and description of the forces of mutual coercion at work. Smith begins by pointing out that 'Among nations of hunters, as there is scarce any property, or at least none that exceeds the value of two or three days labour; so there is seldom any established magistrate or any regular administration of justice. Men who have no property can injure one another only in their persons or reputations' (p. 669).

After comparing the economics of injuries to person and reputation with those to property (the former is typically negative-sum and the latter often zero-sum), he continues:

> Men may live together in society with some tolerable degree of security, though there is no civil magistrate to protect them from the injustice of those passions. But avarice and ambition in the rich, in the poor the hatred of labour and the love of present ease and enjoyment, are the passions which prompt to invade property, passions much more steady in their operation, and much more universal in their influence. Wherever there is great property, there is great inequality. For one very rich man, there must be at least five hundred poor, and the affluence of the few supposes the indigence of the many. The affluence of the rich excites the indignation of the poor, who are often both driven by want, and prompted by envy, to invade his possessions. It is only under the shelter of the civil magistrate that the owner of that valuable property, which is acquired by the labour of many years, or perhaps of many successive generations, can sleep a single night in security. He is at all times surrounded by unknown enemies, whom, though he never provoked, he can never appease, and from whose injuries he can be protected only by the

> powerful arm of the civil magistrate continually held up to chastise it. The acquisition of valuable and extensive property, therefore, necessarily requires the establishment of civil government. Where there is no property, or at least none that exceeds the value of two or three days labour, civil government is not so necessary. (p. 670)

There is more and as interesting and important yet to come, but let us pause and take notice of the evident system of mutual coercion, by both rich and poor insofar as they can get away with it, indeed, a system of mutual coercion even without inequality. Moreover, given that the property which the law shall protect is precisely that property which the law recognizes and enforces, and given that wealth is, *ceteris paribus*, a function of such property, no wonder 'For one very rich man, there must be at least five hundred poor, and the affluence of the few supposes the indigence of the many': for the state is an instrument whereby those who can get it to recognize their claims as property rights, through which they become *de jure* wealthy; whereas those who are not in such a position remain disadvantaged, being unable to get their interests recognized as property rights which become a cost to others.[8] The private property that requires civil government is the interests which social powers get government to declare as private property and thereby protectable as private property. No wonder property means inequality: private property and civil government are correlated, and both emerge out of the system of mutual coercion and its companion and asymmetrical structure of social power. Here, then, is Smith:

> Civil government supposed a certain subordination. But as the necessity of civil government gradually grows up with the acquisition of valuable property, so the principal causes which naturally introduce subordination gradually grow up with the growth of that valuable property. (p. 670)

The rise of both private property and civil government depend upon *and* reinforce the pattern of subordination in society: private property, civil government, and the structure of subordination are three dependent and independent variables in a dynamic general equilibrium system; or to say the same thing in different words, mutual coercion, power structure, and civil government are three dependent and independent variables in a dynamic equilibrium system of choice and power. The allocation of resources takes place within a dynamic system of mutual coercion and power; the market operates only within that system and gives effect to it at the same time that the invisible hand channels it.

Smith next discusses 'The causes or circumstances which naturally, introduce subordination, or which naturally, and antecedent to any civil institution, give some men some superiority over the greater part of their brethren' (p. 670). These causes are superiority of personal qualifications, of age, of fortune, and of birth. No surprises there. But when he next discusses the introduction of civil government, Smith lays bare and in no uncertain terms the system of mutual coercion and power which characterizes the economic system:

> It is in the age of shepherds, in the second period of society, that the inequality of fortune first begins to take place, and introduces among men a degree of authority and subordination which could not possibly exist before. It thereby introduces some degree of that civil government which is indispensably necessary for its own preservation: and it seems to do this naturally, and even independent of the consideration of that necessity. The consideration of that necessity comes no doubt afterwards to contribute very much to maintain and secure that authority and subordination. The rich, in particular, are necessarily interested to support that order of things, which can alone secure them in the possession of their own advantage. (p. 674)

This is powerful stuff! Whether one interprets Smith to the effect that government is used to protect the rights which the rich get government to define as property rights and thereby contribute to making them rich, and thence protect their wealth, or to the effect that government is simply used by them to protect their wealth, government becomes an instrument with which the rich are able to maintain their superordination, their authority in their favoured order of things, their own advantages. Yet I am not here really concerned with the inequality, or with the fact (or assertion) that there may be social advantage in all this, including the inequality. Transcending all this is the fact and importance of the system of mutual coercion, of advantage and disadvantage, into which government only fits first as a dependent variable and later as both a dependent and independent variable. This is not a Marxist, to whom the state is the instrument of the ruling class; this is Adam Smith, to the same effect. Whatever one thinks of this, it is clear that it has to be examined and comprehended in the context of a paradigm of choice and power far more complex than that of modern microeconomics and welfare economics, in a broader model in which resource allocation is a dependent and independent variable *vis-à-vis* the dynamics of mutual coercion and inequality of power. Smith continues:

> Men of inferior wealth combine to defend those of superior wealth in the possession of their property, in order that men of superior wealth may combine to defend them in the possession of theirs. All the inferior shepherds and herdsmen feel that the security of their own herds and flocks depends upon the security of those of the great shepherd or herdsman; that the maintenance of their lesser authority depends upon that of his greater authority, and that upon their subordination to him depends his power of keeping their inferiors in subordination to them. They constitute a sort of little nobility, who feel themselves interested to defend the property and to support the authority of their own little sovereign, in order that he may be able to defend their property and to support their authority. (p. 674)

It is easy, of course, to extend this analysis to any economic system, including that of (small and large) business firms and workers and others of various degrees of affluence or property. The symbiotic relation between large and small holders of property in their jockeying for position in the larger authority system is but part of the total system of power and process of mutual coercion. Property rights, indeed the very institution of private property, has to be seen in the context of a general theory of conflict and mutual coercion.[9] In any economic system, the view that most people have of the specifics of mutual coercion (of what they consider 'coercive' in the pejorative sense or alternatively 'freedom') is a function of their relative position and other variables. But in any system there is a process of mutual coercion and it is given substance by the very processes to which Smith refers. Finally, Smith lays it on the line:

> Civil government, so far as it is constituted for the security of property, is in reality instituted for the defence of the rich against the poor, or of those who have some property against those who have none at all. (p. 674)

These statements, and particularly this last, can readily be taken out of context and have Smith appear as a revolutionary. Just as Smith did not draw the inference of exploitation from his analysis of the wage system he did not draw the inference of revolution from his doctrine of the role of civil government, just stated. The point here, again, is a very different one. Smith was not only a realist but he was a powerful and explicit realist; he was radical in the sense of getting down to fundamentals; he made no bones about what he considered to be fundamental social and economic processes, the processes out of which the modern economy and the modern state both developed and which characterize their operation. Smith analysed the simple and obvious system of natural liberty and the role of the invisible hand of competition in the market allocation of resources and in the checking of market power; but he also analysed the economy as a broader system of power, with power operating through the competitive market, and in this broader paradigm of power and mutual coercion he considered the use of government as an economic variable.

In 1971, *History of Political Economy* published George Stigler's query as to 'how could he [Smith] have failed to see the self-interest written upon the faces of politicians and constituencies?'[10] Stigler is puzzled over this because he poses as something of a principle, ignored by Smith, that 'the procuring of favourable legislation is a commercial undertaking',[11] and generally discusses how economic legislation tends to be a function of economic interest groups. Stigler's principle is exceptionally well taken; but as for Smith, on the contrary, I urge that he *did* see the operation of self-interest in and through government. He did see the state as an instrument for the achievement of economic objectives, as well as the economy as a means to legal ends; in both cases, the state being an object of capture and use by economic actors. Smith saw the state as but one variable in a dynamic general equilibrium-type system of choice, power, and mutual coercion, in which the simple allocation of resources through market forces pales in comparison. The wisdom of Smith lies not only in his brilliant perception and exposition of a model of so-called voluntary market exchange but also in his continued contemplation of a model of power and coercion in which it can be said both that an individual's set of opportunities is a function of the total structure of power and process of mutual coercion, and that the total structure of power and process of mutual coercion is a function of choices by individuals from within their opportunity sets at any point in time and over time, choices not only in spending their income but in jockeying for positions of market and political advantage. Smith's wisdom resides both in his analysis of maximizing market actors and in his analysis of the forces and factors governing the structure and composition of opportunity sets and the impact of power structure upon the operation of the market mechanism. The paradigm of market resource allocation is an incomplete substitute for the paradigm of mutual coercion; indeed the former must be understood in terms of the latter if we are to begin to comprehend the economic system as Smith understood it.

Let us return to the *Wealth of Nations* once more. Smith envisions religion as a sanctioning force of social control; but the same Smith who saw in private economic activity both the beneficent workings of self-interest and the processes of power and mutual coercion, also saw in religion both an instrument of social control and a power player; indeed,

Smith's ability to see both facets of each case accounts in no small way for his brilliance as a political economist and social analyst. Smith thus calls attention to the history of symbiotic relations between political factions and religious sects and the establishment and public endowment of whatever sect is associated with the conquering political faction, the two sharing the spoils of power play. Religion is not (perhaps only rarely) aided and endowed by the polity because of some rational estimation of the benefits to society of ecclesiastical establishment in the case of a particular sect (though they may be rationalized as such in each instance) but rather because of considerations of political expediency. I would add that intertwined with the intrigues of politics and religion are the machinations of economic interests but Smith does not go this far, so let us stay within the confines of his analysis:

> Times of violent religious controversy have generally been times of equally violent political factions. Upon such occasions, each political party has either found it, or imagined it, for its interest, to league itself with some one or other of the contending religious sects. But this could be done only by adopting, or at least by favouring, the tenets of that particular sect. The sect which had the good fortune to be leagued with the conquering party, necessarily shared in the victory of its ally, by whose favour and protection it was soon enabled in some degree to silence and subdue all its adversaries. Those adversaries had generally leagued themselves with the enemies of the conquering party, and were therefore the enemies of that party. The clergy of this particular sect having thus become complete masters of the field, and their influence and authority with the great body of the people being in its highest vigour, they were powerful enough to over-awe the chiefs and leaders of their own party, and to oblige the civil magistrate to respect their opinions and inclinations. Their first demand was generally, that he should silence and subdue all their adversaries; and their second, that he should bestow an independent provision on themselves. As they had generally contributed a good deal to the victory, it seemed not unreasonable that they should have some share in the spoil. They were weary, besides, of humouring the people, and of depending upon their caprice for a subsistence. In making this demand therefore they consulted their own ease and comfort, without troubling themselves about the effect which it might have in future times upon the influence and authority of their order. The civil magistrate, who could comply with this demand only by giving them something which he would have chosen much rather to take, or to keep to himself, was seldom very forward to grant it.

> Necessity, however, always forced him to submit at last, though frequently not till after many delays, evasions, and affected excuses. (p. 744)

The process of mutual coercion thus characterizes both the political and religious arenas as well as the narrowly economic; and in all cases the hegemony of the state is an object of capture and use by power players. What Smith says of the effect of certain clergy upon magistrates parallels what he earlier said of the effects of certain businessmen (and landowners and workers, though with less success in the case of the workers) upon the civil magistrate.

Given this system of mutual coercion in religious matters, Smith then commits himself to the same principle by which he prefers to see economic affairs regulated:

> But if politics had never called in the aid of religion, had the conquering party never adopted the tenets of one sect more than those of another, when it had gained the victory, it would probably have dealt equally and impartially with all the different sects, and have allowed every man to choose his own priest and his own religion as he thought proper. There would in this case, no doubt, have been a great multitude of religious sects. Almost every different congregation might probably have made a little sect by itself, or have entertained some peculiar tenets of its own. Each teacher would no doubt have felt himself under the necessity of making the utmost exertion, and of using every art both to preserve and to increase the number of his disciples. But as every other teacher would have felt himself under the same necessity, the success of no one teacher, or sect of teachers, could have been very great. The interested and active zeal of religious teachers can be dangerous and troublesome only where there is, either but one sect tolerated in the society, or where the whole of a large society is divided into two or three sects; the teachers of each acting by concert, and under a regular discipline and subordination. But that zeal must be altogether innocent where the society is divided into two or three hundred, or perhaps into as many thousand small sects, of which no one could be considerable enough to disturb the public tranquillity. The teachers of each sect, seeing themselves surrounded on all sides with more adversaries than friends, would be obliged to learn that candour and moderation which is so seldom to be found among the teachers of those great sects, whose tenets, being supported by the civil magistrate, are held in veneration by almost all the inhabitants of extensive kingdom and empires, and who therefore see nothing round them

> but followers, disciples, and humble admirers. The teachers of each little sect, finding themselves almost alone, would be obliged to respect those of almost every other sect, and the concessions which they would mutually find it both convenient and agreeable to make to one another, might in time probably reduce the doctrine of the greater part of them to that pure and rational religion, free from every mixture of absurdity, imposture, or fanaticism, such as wise men have in all ages of the world wished to see established; but such as positive law has perhaps never yet established, and probably never will establish in any country: because, with regard to religion, positive law always has been, and probably always will be, more or less influenced by popular superstition and enthusiasm. (pp. 744–5)

As in the case of economic affairs the invisible hand of competition would regulate the pretensions of ecclesiastics, rendering their zeal innocent, moderated and free of absurdity and imposture; optimality would here too be a function of whose preferences counted, and Smith would have a free market for ideas of mortality, a free market for the play of the principles of approbation and disapprobation out of which moral rules were experientially generated. The market would be free in the sense of having a multiplicity of sects rather than religious monopoly or duopoly; but it would still represent and comprise a process of mutual coercion as each attempted to get credence and sanction for its notions of morality, as well as converts, and the interaction would be both a consequence and a cause (a dependent and an independent variable) of the structure of position of power enjoyed by each sect relative to the others. The genius of the Smithian prescription lies not in the absence of social power and mutual coercion but of the type of social structure advocated, in a word, pluralism.

II

My objective in this chapter, however radical, is relatively limited. As already noted I have elsewhere suggested that the attainment and distribution of economic welfare is a function not only of the process of market choice contemplated in neoclassical terms erected on recognized Smithian concepts but also of a broader and more complex system of choice and power. The former involves constrained maximization through choice from within opportunity sets; the latter involves the forces and factors governing the structure and composition of opportunity sets. My limited objective here has been to suggest that there resides in the *Wealth of Nations* this second and larger paradigm of choice and power. To assert the existence of such a second and larger paradigm may be unsettling to many, especially perhaps to find it in Smith; but I suggest that this means that the discipline has been richer, and Adam Smith even deeper, than has heretofore been given official recognition. Elsewhere I have suggested that there is an inchoate and as yet unsystematized second tradition within economics that has to do with the organization and control of the economic system, essentially the distribution of power;[12] Smith's second paradigm is fully consistent with and is indeed expressive of this second tradition.

In the case of Smith, it will be noticed that, apart from the concept of pluralism, I have not committed Smith to (or specified his ideas in terms of) any particular analysis of the structure and process of power and mutual coercion or to any particular solution or position on any specific issue of policy, nor have I set forth anything like a complete theory of Smith's model of policy. Although I necessarily have relied upon Smith's particular discussion, I am not directly interested in the details thereof but rather in his recognition, both explicit and implicit, of an underlying structure of power and process of mutual coercion within which market activity is ensconced.

Part of this second Smithian paradigm is the role of government. As I pointed out in my study of the general classical theory of economic policy, one can be misled by the distinction between framework-filling actions and particular interventions of government, the problem being the impossibility of conclusively designating any particular action as 'framework-filling' or as a 'particular intervention' when each and every government action provides the framework within which individual opportunity sets form and individuals choose, and yet may appear as 'intervention' or 'framework-filling' to some, whatever the underlying motivation or source. But even if we limit our analysis to the category of framework-filling operations (which is the stronger case: 'interventions' are unquestionably interest-oriented), the framework operates to form and structure power and is therefore an object of power play. The legal framework is both a dependent and independent variable in a general equilibrium system of power, mutual coercion, and resource allocation.

The crux of the second Smithian paradigm herein suggested is the problem of whose interests will count and the processes of social choice involved in the continuing resolution of that problem. The paradigm is one of power and mutual coercion, and market competition is neither more nor less than a dependent and independent variable in that larger general equilibrium system. In the past, the narrowing of economic categories and models, and the felt demands of ideological purity, as well as of scientific convenience, have obscured this second paradigm. But it is in the *Wealth of Nations* and it is an important correlate to Smith's analysis of the market.

Notes

1. Lionel Robbins, *The Theory of Economic Policy in English Classical Political Economy* (London: Macmillan, 1953); Samuels, *The Classical Theory of Economic Policy* (Cleveland: World, 1966).
2. Samuels, 'Interrelations between Legal and Economic Processes', *Journal of Law and Economics*, vol. 14 (1971).
3. **Opportunity set**: available alternative lines of action or choices each with a relative opportunity cost.
   Coercion: impact of the behaviour and choices of others upon the structure of one's opportunity set; is mutual or reciprocal, ergo a system of mutual coercion: includes both injuries and benefits visited through action or choices of others; is non-pejorative (designation of an action, choice or impact as 'coercive' in the pejorative sense requires an additional normative premise of psychological valuation or identification).
   Power: the means or capacity with which to exercise choice, ergo to coerce; e.g., property, position.
   Working rules: the rules of law and morality etc. governing access to and use of power.
4. See generally, Joseph J. Spengler, 'The Problem of Order in Economic Affairs', *Southern Economic Journal*, vol. 15 (1948), reprinted in Joseph J. Spengler and William R. Allen (eds), *Essays in Economic Thought* (Chicago: Rand McNally, 1960); and 'Hierarchy vs. Equality: Persisting Conflict', *Kyklos*, vol. 21 (1968).
5. Samuels, 'Welfare Economics, Power, and Property', in G. Wunderlich and W. L. Gibson, Jr. (eds), *Perspectives of Property* (University Park, Pa: Institute for Research on Land and Water Resources, Pennyslvania State University, 1972).
6. Adam Smith, *The Wealth of Nations* (New York: Modern Library, 1937): all page references are to this edition.
7. Discussed in Samuels, *The Classical Theory of Economic Policy*, pp. 193 ff.
8. A. Allan Schmid, 'Nonmarket Values and Efficiency of Public Investments in Water Resources', *American Economic Review, Papers and Proceedings*, vol. 57 (1967), pp. 162 ff; R. H. Coase, 'The Problem of Social Cost', *Journal of Law and Economics*, vol. 3 (1960), p. 44.
9. Armen A. Alchian, 'Some Economics of Property Rights', *Il Politico*, vol. 30 (1965), p. 816.
10. George J. Stigler, 'Smith's Travels on the Ship of State', *History of Political Economy*, vol. 3 (1971), p. 274.
11. Ibid., p. 266.
12. Samuels, 'The Scope of Economics Historically Considered', *Land Economics*, vol. 4 (August 1972), pp. 248–68.

4 The Political Economy of Adam Smith*

THE INTERPRETATION OF ADAM SMITH

Adam Smith and John Locke are the premier philosophers of modern Western civilization. Such stature is Smith's in part because he comprehended and analysed the deepest levels of the newly developing industrial market economy.[1] I propose to interpret Smith's picture of the market economy in terms of his total system of thought and analysis. This system, with all its oppositions and tensions, comprises Smith's solution to the problem of order, or of the organization and control of the economic system. Expressed somewhat differently, I shall inquire into the significance for economic policy of the central argument presented in the *Wealth of Nations*. Smith speaks to the ages, or at least he is still being heard in our age. What does he have to say on the most fundamental level? What is really going on in our economic system, according to Adam Smith?

I first must acknowledge certain considerations involved in the retrospective interpretation of the history of thought in general and of specific classic literature in particular.[2] These considerations necessarily limit my analysis and argument.

First, each generation has the task and the opportunity of reinterpreting Smith for itself. There is no escaping this, nor would we desire to.[3]

Second, it should be clear that the understanding of Adam Smith is influenced by the problems, interests, and values which each interpreter, whether an individual or a generation, brings to his work. This is one facet of the inescapable tension between the data (or 'facts') of history and the mind of the historian. Furthermore, the history of the interpretation of Smith influences our subsequent perceptions of problems, interests, and values. In both respects, the meaning of the man arises in and through our efforts to apprehend him. It is therefore both necessary and difficult to pierce several

---

* C. Woody Thompson Address, Midwest Economics Association, April 1, 1976, originally published in *Nebraska Journal of Economics and Business*, vol. 15 (Summer 1976), pp. 3–24, reprinted in *Ethics*, vol. 87 (April 1977), pp. 189–207. Reprinted in J. C. Wood (ed.), *Adam Smith: Critical Assessments* (London: Croom Helm, 1984) vol. 1.

Comments and suggestions, upon an earlier draft, by John Henderson, Elizabeth Johnston, Herbert Kisch, Sylvia Samuels, and Warner Wick, are gratefully acknowledged.

veils, not the least being one's own ideology, in order to approach Smith more closely.

Third, the interpretation of Smith has been influenced by a selective filtration process,[4] which has permitted certain views to remain viable and others not, a process deeply channelled by ideology, power, and whatever governs professional or disciplinary concerns, including the felt needs of both orthodoxy and heterodoxy in economics, each of which has had its own dogmas and preconceptions about the past and present. No less perceptive an authority than Alex Macfie has remarked, with regard to the historical overemphasis upon the economic side of Smith's work, that 'the immense economic impact of the *Wealth of Nations* [arose] considerably out of the way it could be used to support the more dominant economic forces of his and later times'.[5] Similarly, John Maurice Clark attributed the immediate success of the *Wealth of Nations* to a shift of 'class interest'.[6] Ideological and other filtration has permitted most economists and non-economists to have only an aphoristic appreciation of Smith's view of the economic world. One wonders whether he would have thought the notoriety worthwhile if, in achieving it, his work and analysis were caricatured.

Fourth, I would recall the mixed reception that has been given to the *Wealth of Nations* as, in Frank Knight's phrase, 'a propaganda for economic freedom'.[7] Of course, the book and its reasoning have been frequently invoked and made increasingly sophisticated as an argument in favour of the market and commercial freedom. Yet many, like Knight, have perceived that Smith was too deep and subtle, and too admitting of unsafe thoughts, to permit his book to be readily effective propaganda once one looked beyond certain obvious passages. The reception and status given to the *Wealth of Nations* has depended upon many variables, including the interpreters' perceptions of Smith and of the necessary and desirable course of social and economic policy in their own times.[8]

Fifth, I would urge that the most significant aspect of Smith and the *Wealth of Nations* resides in the total matrix of interpretations and mutual critiques, not in any single one, however attractive, useful, ostensibly complete, or accurate it may be. No one interpretation can capture the complexity and fecundity of Smith's mind or the social meaning of his work.

Sixth, I should say that the history of the interpretation of Smith is as interesting and instructive, and as difficult to fathom, as the interpretation of Smith himself. Suffice it to say that the very nature and identity of vulgar Smithism is itself a matter of interpretation; that there is a tension between the confidence that one can determine 'what Smith really meant' and the needs of reinterpretation; that it is difficult to transcend the filtration process, in part because its result inevitably help select our perceptions; and that I intend here not some 'final' word, but one contribution to the continuing matrix of interpretations.[9]

Adam Smith was no ordinary economic writer; he was a premier philosopher of Western civilization. He worked out many of the distinctive principles of a civilization newly coming into being,[10] and the complexity of such a task can hardly bc overestimated. A philosophy of civilization deals with what Joseph Spengler has called the problem of order, requiring continuous readjustments between freedom (or autonomy) and control, continuity and change, and hierarchy and equality.[11] Each such philosophy encompasses not only freedom or continuity, but also the systematic handling of freedom *and* control and continuity *and* change, according to the authoritative principles of the civilization or of those who determine them. *Vis-à-vis* other civilizations and on its own terms, each civilization and its philosophy evolves a more or less distinctive resolution of the problem of order. This may be perceived and defined in terms of some view of freedom, or otherwise, but it includes within it all the elements which comprise the problem of order: freedom, control, continuity, change, hierarchy, and equality. Each civilization and its philosophy is thus a synthesis of often seemingly contradictory or antinomial elements, such as the controls necessary to permit a particular freedom to exist, and so on. Civilizations represent systems of social control, whatever the character and scope of perceived and actual freedom therein, whatever their resolution of hierarchy versus equality and of continuity versus change. At the level of a civilization, the problem of order is holistic, and one must speak of *patterns* of freedom and control, and so on. On a lower level there exist particular conflicts regarding the details of the problem of order. Adam Smith must be interpreted in terms of such a context and on the level of abstraction required by the general problem of order.

Let there be no mistake about acknowledging the obvious: Adam Smith most distinctively stood for private enterprise, private property, self-interest, voluntary exchange, the limited state, and the market. He was the philosopher of a system of spontaneous economic activity, or resource allocation through market forces, and of efficiency (as it has come to be called) comprehended in terms of self-interest or maximization of personal well-being. The market, in the Smithian view, is a mechanism for resolving basic economic problems and for producing order without elaborate central direction, the 'mystery', as Mark Blaug expressed it,[12] of order achieved through exchange entered into by private individuals manifesting 'the uniform, constant, and uninterrupted effort of every man to better his condition'.[13] All this does in fact characterize the distinctive argument presented in the *Wealth of Nations*, which heralds the market system and its conceptions of freedom, welfare, and the nature, origin, and mode of their realization.

Yet, as I suggested several years ago, there is a second model of order in the *Wealth of Nations*, a model of the economy as a system of power.[14] Smith understood the deep forces of organization and control at work in the economic system. He realized how market forces operate only within, and give effect to, the structure of power and, especially, how those with access to and (in some sense) control over government use it. Market order is achieved only within the structure of power. Both the market and power govern whose interests will count in the economy. Markets are structured by power, and market solutions are power-structure specific. Power and market relations both constitute sets of variables in a general interdependent system.

It is possible to exaggerate the analysis of conflict and power in Smith, but it is also possible to exaggerate the analysis of voluntary market exchange, and it is the latter which has developed as a consequence of the filtration system governing the development of interpretation. Smith's realism and fecundity include both market exchange narrowly considered and the power play over rights and other bases of access to and participation in the market, including the complex economic role of government. Smith includes both market and power models in his conception of how society works out resolutions to the problem of order. What is distinctive about the market economy is not the absence of fundamental power relations, but their particular form. It is necessary to examine the system on more than its own (ideological) terms and consciousness, and it is this which Smith largely did.

SMITH'S SYNOPTIC AND SYNTHETIC SYSTEM

The juxtaposition and combination of power and market models must be seen, however, as but one part of Smith's total conception of the economic system and its underlying processes. Smith, many of his contemporaries, such as David Hume, and many successors, such as Karl Marx, Carl Menger, Vilfredo Pareto, and Max Weber, each had a synoptic grasp upon or approach to the world. Smith, and the Scottish school in general, 'thought of economics only as one chapter (not the most important) in a general theory of society involving psychology and ethics, social and individual, law, politics, and social philosophy as well'.[15] Smith had not only a synoptic view of the world but also, and most suitably, a synthetic way of thinking;

results were a consequence of the integration or composition of complex and often seemingly contradictory elements.

Let me outline the important points which must be added to the juxtaposition and combination of market and power.

First, a fact that is quite well-known but whose significance is not so well appreciated, is that Smith's approach to moral philosophy encompassed four realms of thought and action: natural theology, ethics, justice (or jurisprudence), and expediency (by which he meant concern for wealth, power and prosperity). The domain of ethics was explored in the *Theory of Moral Sentiments*; expediency, or wealth and associated power, in the *Wealth of Nations*; and justice was to be the object of another discourse, to consist of 'an account of the general principles of law and government, and of the different revolutions they have undergone in the different ages and periods of society, not only in what concerns justice, but in what concerns police [policy], revenue, and arms, and whatever else is the object of the law'.[16] In lieu of this latter volume we have had one transcription of his lectures.[17] The point is that the moral, market, and legal orders are distinguishable interacting subprocesses of a larger whole and that their interaction is an important part of their operation and explanation.

Second, it was Smith's view that what transpired in the life of the individual and society was a synthesis of a number of forces. These included self-love, self-interest, self-command, sympathy, benevolence, moral rules and legal control. Individual thought and behaviour represented a balance or synthesis of motives, each of which had complex origins. Social and individual phenomena were a product of both reason and feeling and of both rationalism and authority. There is both deliberative and non-deliberative choice in society.[18]

Third, society exhibits tendencies toward both harmony and conflict, with tension between them. There are great conflicts in society, and such harmony as exists does so within the existing system and structure and is very rough and limited; moreover, it is a created and not a fully spontaneous harmony.[19]

Fourth, it is easy to lose sight of the foregoing because in both the *Theory of Moral Sentiments* and the *Wealth of Nations* Smith himself presented a synthesis of naturalistic deductive lines of reasoning and factual inductive arguments. Needless to say, tensions exist between these two procedures.[20] As for society itself, there is a synthesis of 'experience, induction from it, and the final faith'.[21]

Adam Smith's mind encompassed both the broad, dynamic, interactive, and open-ended process of resolving the problem of order and the set of its ongoing solutions. The process was at any point constrained by the status quo and, for Smith himself, by certain normative pluralistic requirements (however ambiguous they may appear in retrospect).[22] Smith's was an essentially modern, albeit undeveloped, theory of society. Inevitably, the tendency of interpreters is to see and emphasize portions of his analysis, but we must not lose sight of Smith's synoptic and synthetic whole, with its interdependence, ambiguity, and tensions. The strength of partial analysis is necessarily associated with its limits, including the neglect both of interaction between subprocesses and of the general interdependent character of the whole. What happens to or in one subprocess profoundly affects and is affected by what transpires in the others. This is a system which Gunnar Myrdal calls cumulative causation. Interpretation cannot properly reduce Smith's analysis to single-factor explanations or to narrow normative systems without doing injury to his synoptic and synthetic view of the realities of economic life. Apparent closure, *vis-à-vis* the open-endedness of his analysis, is a result of ideological filtration which, however inevitable, necessary, and even salutary, nonetheless fails to present the entire Smithian analysis. His work serves to caution us that basic problems must be defined in such a way as not to foreclose analytical consideration of important variables and forces but rather to stress certain critical antinomies ensconced within them. There are inevitable interactions, tensions, and problems which are characteristic of the working out of solutions to the problem of order.

The greatest difficulty in both positive and normative analysis is to project adequately the system of freedom under analysis while providing an important and explicit place for the system of control necessary for that system. The same is true with regard to continuity and change. It was Adam Smith's genius to have treated this as a critical part of his synthetic and synoptic analysis. As Macfie remarks, 'Some of Smith's arguments seem to conflict with others, and the charge of inconsistency has been brought against him, with undoubted justice. But while consistency is certainly a virtue and an ideal, we live in a world shot through with inconsistencies. In this regard, I like to remember the saying of Emerson: "With consistency a great soul had simply nothing to do": an exaggeration, no doubt; but in due measure true, at least for geniuses.'[23] The same point has been made by others: Reinhold Niebuhr wrote that 'life is full of contradictions and ambiguities' and that 'we live our lives in various realms of meaning which do not cohere rationally'.[24] F. Scott Fitzgerald wrote that 'the test of a first-rate intelligence is the ability to hold two opposed ideas in the mind at the same time, and still retain the ability to function'.[25] Niels Bohr distinguished between 'minor truths, whose opposites are plainly false, and great truths, whose opposites are also true'.[26] However much ideological filtration may have distorted and emasculated Smith's analysis, his was a first-rate intelligence. He did comprehend great truths whose wisdom and accuracy resided in their synthesis with opposites which were also true in distinguishable respects. Nowhere is this insight more important than in regard to his analysis of market and power and of freedom and control, but it is also true, and important, in regard to his analysis of moral rules, law, and institutions generally.

INTERDEPENDENCE AND TENSIONS

This section will sketch the interdependence and tensions contained within Smith's synoptic and synthetic analysis. Most of the discussion concerns the nature and role of the market, its relation to other institutions of social control, and the relation of self-interest to the market and to moral and legal rules, all involving the socialization of the individual. We will see that the usual formulation of his message 'completely short-circuits much of the real substance of Smith's work'.[27]

Smith viewed the market as a regulatory system, itself an institution of social control. The invisible hand is supposed to control individual conflicts and the excesses of competition and to 'safeguard the public good through healthy competition. Such is his faith'.[28] The market above all is an institutional mechanism to compel men to pursue self-interest in social rather than antisocial ways.[29] As Rosenberg has said, 'The price system, as Smith saw it, was an intensely coercive mechanism [which] tied the dynamic and powerful motive force of self-interest to the general welfare. Its free operation would, in most cases, leave the individual producer no alternative but to pursue his economic interests in a manner conducive to the national welfare.'[30] Smith's emphasis is not solely, or not so much, upon the self-regulatory character of the market as upon the regulation of self-interest by the market. The regulatory function of the market is quite neglected by the modern emphasis upon market solutions as being *a priori* optimal or upon an *a priori* free market. This often blind invocation of the market neglects the fact that Smith's simple and obvious system of natural liberty was a shrewd method of harnessing and releasing the human propensities deemed favourable to the creation of opulence and good order and suppressing the unfavourable ones.

Notice the merely tentative propriety attributed by Smith to market results. It is true that the individual's search for 'the most advantageous employment for whatever capital he can command . . . naturally, or rather necessarily leads him to prefer that employment which is most advantageous to the society'.[31] But his most elaborate statement of the general principle is considerably qualified:

> As every individual, therefore, endeavors as much as he can both to employ his capital in the support of domestic industry and so to direct that industry that its produce may be of the greatest value; every individual necessarily labours to render the annual revenue of the society as great as he can. He generally, indeed, neither intends to promote the public interest, nor knows how much he is promoting it. By preferring the support of domestic to that of foreign industry, he intends only his own security; and by directing that industry in such a manner as its produce may be of the greatest value, he intends only his own gain, and he is in this, as in many other cases, led by an invisible hand to promote an end which was no part of his intention. Nor is it always the worse for the society that it was no part of it. By pursuing his own interest he frequently promotes that of the society more effectually than when he really intends to promote it.[32]

Notice that Smith here does not say that in *all* cases self-interest is led by an invisible hand to promote the public interest; only 'in this, as in many other cases' does this occur. Again, pursuit of self-interest does not *always* promote the interest of society, only 'frequently'. The market, as a regulatory system, is seen by Smith as a more or less newly discovered institution of social control, but its operation is not *a priori* optimal. The market must be associated with the operation of other institutions of social control; there is no presumptive optimality of market solutions. The principle of the optimality of markets and market solutions, in all its forms, is a later principle with both explanatory and legitimizing roles and does not adequately reflect Smith. The market must be seen as qualified in its operation by the impact of moral and legal rules and other institutions which are themselves a matter of choice and evolution.

The market, in Smith's total scheme, operated within and gave effect to the rest of the institutional system as well as to individual choice within the system. Voluntary exchange takes places only within legal and moral rules as well as the market. The market, according to Smith, must be comprehended within the larger system involved in the continuing resolution of the problem of order, however much it may contribute thereto. The order produced by markets can only arise if the legal and moral framework is operating well; as Rosenberg has written, the 'decisive superiority' of the price system 'as a way of organizing economic life lay in the fact that, *when it was surrounded by appropriate institutions*, it tied the dynamic and powerful motive force of self-interest to the general welfare'.[33] The market does not do so alone.

It is a fundamental argument of Adam Smith that institutions, including moral and legal rules and rule making, function as social control. Morrow, Macfie, and Rosenberg have elaborately spelled this out.[34] As Macfie has argued, for example, 'the central and fruitful proposition of the *Moral Sentiments* is not the natural theism, but the inductive argument based on the sympathetic feelings of the impartial spectator, with its historical setting of societies developing through the growth of social institutions, education, custom, moral rules and the institutions of justice'.[35] For Rosenberg, 'one of the major themes of the *Wealth of Nations*, of course, is its exhaustive examination of the manner in which institutional arrangements structure the decision-making of the individual, sometimes in a manner which harmonizes private interest and social interest, and sometimes in a manner which disrupts them'.[36] 'The question is, in each case, whether institutions do, or do not, harness man's selfish interests to the general welfare.'[37] The *Wealth of Nations*, then, is Smith's 'attempt to define, in very specific terms, the details of the institutional structure which will best harmonize the individual's pursuit of his selfish interests with the broader interests of society'.[38]

Among other things, in Smith's analysis institutions govern distribution. For example, he was concerned with the social gains and costs of the division of labour. One of his points, in modern terms, is that institutions govern their distribution among classes. In other words, there is a complex set of distributional, hierarchical, and aggregate-income level trade-offs and related choices to be made through institutions.[39] As expressed by Rosenberg, 'Smith is constantly searching out the impact of specific institutional forms upon the human actor. Given his basic conception of human motivations and propensities, the specific kinds of behavior which we may expect of any individual will depend on the way the institutions surrounding him are structured, for these determine the alternatives open to him and establish the system of rewards and penalties within which he is compelled to operate.'[40]

For Smith as for Hume, predictability of human behaviour was brought about by the continuity generated by stabilized relationships embodied in institutions. 'Once the institutional framework is specified', says Rosenberg, 'human behavior becomes highly predictable'.[41]

Institutions also govern the answer to the question of whose liberty is to be achieved. (Or, liberty for what?[42]) Smith was surely influenced by Stoic natural liberty and natural harmony doctrines, but he was also aware that social action of one form or another was necessary to discriminate between liberties and between actions. Selectivity is necessary unless *all* action be deemed harmonious and *all* exercise of liberty be sanctioned as 'natural'. Belief in ultimate rationality and harmony does not avoid the problem of evaluating the status quo with regard to the actual elements of harmony and disharmony and of rationality and irrationality in accordance with the principles of approbation and disapprobation. It is precisely the role of moral and legal rules, and their respective underlying processes, to govern such evaluation. It is the business of morality and law, as well as of the market, to regulate the detailed realities of freedom and of exposure to freedom. Speaking of banking regulations and fire walls, Smith said that 'those exertions of the natural liberty of a few individuals, which might endanger the security of a few individuals, are, and ought to be, restrained by the laws of all governments; of the most free, as well as of the most despotical'.[43] Moral and legal controls constitute part of the basis of the market, so that sympathy as well as division of labour may serve as social cement; whatever harmony and freedom exists is a function of other institutions besides the market.[44]

The process involved in the foregoing may be examined by surveying Smith's conception of the socialization of the individual. Self-love is restrained by the growth of moral rules and social institutions which control it 'appropriately' through informed sympathy.[45] Smith 'concentrated on the social sanctions of morality rather than the individual one' of conscience.[46] The critical factor to Smith is not individual self-interest as such, but the moralization of the passions 'through the gradual establishment of general rules, in the course of social progress, and through the reactions of individuals to such rules and conventions, in the course of their social living'.[47] As Morrow explains, 'It is because the individual is in his very nature socialized, a product of the social environment, that he can in general be left without external interference to act in accordance with the demands of his individual nature.'[48]

The Smithian model is one of controlled freedom; freedom of behaviour and choice exists only within the socially established norms of conduct. Smith 'certainly believed that it was only on ethical grounds that controlled liberty for individuals was justified and essential. This justified freedom (within limits) is the personal foundation of his individual and moral economic theory. The strategic factor, however, is not so much the freedom of the individual, which has received too unqualified attention since 1776, as the limitations on freedom which Smith always added were necessary, if freedom to pursue self-interest were to be moralized'.[49] Hence the paradox that 'in his main argument, Smith was always fundamentally the sociologist, though in his equally basic argument for the (suitably controlled) freedom of the individual he was the eternal radical'.[50] The individual is elevated to be the prime element in the economic system, but the individual not only operates within a moral and legal framework but is also a socialized or moralized individual. We might also say that the individual is a legalized individual. Self-love and self-interest go hand in hand with social control and socialization. It is true both that vanity has a social function in motivating self-interest *and* that 'the great secret of education is to direct vanity to proper objects'.[51] In Smith we have both self-interested behaviour *and* the control of self-interest by moral and legal rules. Self-interest exists only within social control.[52] Self-interest not only is operated upon by the market but also is defined, channelled, and restrained by moral and legal rules and by the operation of benevolence, sympathy, and the principle of the impartial spectator. Socialization operates through sympathy and the impartial spectator as internalized social control.[53]

Smith charts the operation of individual conscience (the impartial spectator plus the sense of propriety) and of social conscience (the general rules of conduct) which interact and together constitute the formation and internalization of social control. Individual choice and rationality exist within collective choice and rationality, which are in turn influenced by individual choice and rationality. The operation of the principles of approbation and disapprobation applied to the actions of oneself and others both govern and are influenced by the sense of propriety and moral rules. The impartial spectator principle helps build up the moral rules and customs which serve as social cement, yet the principle depends for its content on already internalized social control. It is truly a process of cumulative causation or general interdependence and *not* one in which particular rules or particular patterns of socialized behaviour may be taken as given once and for all. Interdependence signifies endogenous change.

Several other topics warrant brief notice. Two concern the role of social conditioning in Smith's analysis. Of these, the first treats the social basis of man's general motivational system. I refer, in part, to Smith's argument that it is the deception of the 'pleasures of wealth and greatness' which 'rouses and keeps in continual motion the industry of mankind'.[54] This has, of course, profound implications for Smith's individualism.[55] He took for granted an organization of life which promoted material welfare, the propriety of which was channelled and reinforced by the dominant socio-economic philosophy of life, that is, by socialization processes. In part this performed the social role of overcoming indolence.[56] But it is important also to recognize that Smith was clearly interested in other, non-material dimensions of welfare; that he recognized the moral corruption of overemphasizing wealth and success;[57] that he distinguished between the role of the lure of wealth and the corrupting influences of wealth acquired by both oneself and others;[58] and that he felt that self-interest is not to be equated with selfishness, although he provided no conclusive principle for differentiating useful self-interest from selfishness, holding instead that such had to be worked out in society.

The second aspect of social conditioning involves Smith's view that preferences are endogenously determined within the economic system broadly considered. They are a partial function of moralizing and socializing processes which help define self-interest, including, of course, the proper objects of vanity.[59] Institutions, in Smith's analysis, help form the incentive and reward system of individuals.[60] And of course the market itself is a partial source of endogenously generated preferences; as Rosenberg says, 'The growth of commerce is instrumental in shaping character, in altering tastes, and in providing new and more powerful incentives.'[61]

Next, I would reiterate that the dualism of power *and* the market should not be forgotten. Both complement Smith's analysis of the origin, operation, and impact of moral and legal forms of social control. In this connection, three incidental points may be made. First, Smith appreciated the complexities of power. He appears, for example, to have been quite sophisticated in his understanding of how the union of Scotland and England served in the former to diffuse power (by limiting that of the local aristocracy), notwithstanding the somewhat more apparent centralization of power.[62] Second, it appears that institutionally produced inequality was more important to Smith than natural inequality.[63] Third, I note the open question of the relation(s) of the division of labour to the power structure in Smith's work.

Another point worth noting is Smith's policy consciousness, a product of his relative empiricism, secularism, and down-to-earth realism. He treats institutions not as inevitable, but as subject to redesign and change, as the product of past choice and subject to revised choices. He did not revere the institutional status quo; rather, he represents the eighteenth-century version of concern to increase deliberative decision making in modern society.[64] Nonetheless, there is in Smith a sense of both the possibility of improving man and his condition *and* the severe limits thereof.[65]

Smith, it should be apparent, blended methodological individualist and methodological collectivist levels of analysis, and he used both the individual and society as units of analysis. There is both voluntary exchange and a system, structure, and process of power. The individual is in one sense the prime element or unit in the economic system, but the individual exists and acts only within the evolving moral, legal, and institutional framework as a socialized individual. There are both individual choices and social forces. As Morrow has argued, Smith used two analytical procedures: the method of regarding society as a derivative of the individual *and* that of regarding the individual as a product of society. Apropos of his consideration of the concrete social environment 'in explaining the nature of the individual man . . . Smith is one of the very few thinkers of his time who had any realization of this complementary point of view'.[66] The filtration system has substantially worked to disregard this aspect of his thought.

The last of these points, treated only in passing, relates to Smith's complex attitude toward businessmen *vis-à-vis* (or, should I say, versus) consumers. His views may be summarized as follows: (1) a functional emphasis upon the critical role of the business class in regard to the organization and direction of production and thereby growth; (2) a normative and perhaps positive emphasis upon consumption as the 'sole end and purpose of production' and upon the consumer as the primary beneficiary;[67] (3) a view of the market as a system of control to overcome indolence but also to control the businessman through socialization; and (4) a celebration of the business system but not of the individual businessman. Indeed his views of the behaviour of businessmen were often critical; as Heilbroner notes, Smith was 'an admirer of their work but suspicious of their motives'.[68] In sum, Smith provided no defence of the market on pro-business terms; there is no more presumptive optimality of market solutions than of business decisions in Smith; all that came much later with more sophisticated formulations of the central myth of capitalism.

This brings me to the central topic of the evolution of legal and moral rules and institutions. Smith acknowledges, and indeed emphasizes, the inductive development of moral and legal rules, their changing character and content.[69] There is an evolutionary dimension to the evaluative process in society.[70] Moral and legal rules evolve through the principles of approbation and disapprobation operating through the impartial spectator principle, expressing a refined sympathy and moral sensibility, as part of the larger evolving system.[71] 'It is by our gradual evolution of moral rules and customs from innumerable cases that we develop those human institutions which are at once the safeguards and the growing points of human societies. In them the clashes of "self-love" and benevolence, of sentiment and reason, are so far reconciled – reconciled in no absolute way, but pragmatically *ambulando*.'[72] Smith's argument in the *Theory of Moral Sentiments* is that moral and legal rules must be worked out and revised over time and cannot be set down once and for all.[73] Not all unintended consequences of the market are, or are to be accepted as, beneficent. Such consequences may have adverse impact upon desired legal and moral rules or upon human welfare, and such rules may be changed to correct for adversity.[74] As I noted earlier, the historical interpretation of the *Wealth of Nations* had been part of the process through which moral and legal rules have been revised, sometimes in one direction and sometimes in another.

Smith's analysis thus provides for re-evaluation: of institutions, including the market, in regard to the incidence of the reward and incentive system;[75] of legal rules in the light of changing norms and circumstances;[76] of the congruity of received values with new economic realities, including the terms of fellow feeling, for example, in regard to the distinction of ranks and respect for wealth and greatness;[77] of the reformulation (redefinition and reassignment) of property and other rights through law; of wealth *vis-à-vis* other considerations; of the definition of injury in regard to the doing of what one likes so long as it does not injure others;[78] of the meaning of 'extraordinary' in what Smith referred to as 'extraordinary restraints' and 'extraordinary encouragements';[79] of the proper objects to which education is to direct vanity; and, *inter alia*, the substance and exercise of self-interest and egoism.[80]

It follows from this understanding of Smith that the interactions which mark his synoptic and synthetic system involve inevitable tensions. There is tension as to the content and direction of social control. There are tensions between the market, market forces, and institutions, and between market social control and legal and moral social control. There is tension between self-interest and the market as a regulatory system: individuals seek to escape from market control, there are conflicts of self-interest, and the market has an open-ended role as a conflict resolving system which, perhaps paradoxically, is capable of being channelled by those who can control it.[81] There is tension over the appropriateness of institutions, over the nature of injuries which should be avoided or prevented by rules and rights, and over when the liberty of one is endangering the liberty of another in such a way as to call for remedial action. There is tension over all the incidents of the socialization process: if the great secret of education is to direct vanity to proper objects, there is tension as to *which* (or *whose*) objects are proper and as to how vanity is to be so directed. There are inevitable tensions over the evaluation of aspects of the general motivational system, for example, over the morality and immorality of wealth and self-interest, including the structure of 'institutional arrangements [within which] to cut off all avenues (and there are many) along which wealth may be pursued without contributing to the welfare of society', that is, over 'the conditions under which [the] market mechanism would operate most effectively'.[82] There is tension over the power structure as such;[83] and, *inter alia*, over the conditions 'wherein consist[s] the happiness and perfection of a man, considered not only as an individual, but as the member of a family, of a state, and of the great society of mankind'.[84] These tensions characterize the processes of socialization, collective action, and group existence. They were recognized as such by Smith, although they have been obscured by some interpreters, who seem to have sought to sanction certain resolutions of the problem of order, and thereby of these tensions, and not others, all in the purported image of Smith. Such interpretations presumptively overstate the degree and overspecify the substance of the closure which Smith's system permits.

I urge, then, that change, re-evaluation, and tension are necessarily critical aspects of Smith's synoptic and synthetic analysis. It is only by a static partial equilibrium-like approach to the problem of order, one which abstracts from the larger analysis, that one can reach conservative and *laissez-faire* doctrines and conclusions. I say this notwithstanding Smith's role as premier philosopher of the market system and the important conservative and free market elements in his analysis and without trying to make a case for any particular set of moral and/or legal controls or of changes therein. The deepest understanding of these aspects of Smith's analysis require consideration of his larger system. Without doing so we will not understand the conflict between those who see any act of government as an impediment of the market and those who see in government activity a change in the legal and moral foundations of the market.

PRESENT SIGNIFICANCE

What, then, is the significance of Smith for contemporary analysis and policy? Smith can be and is, of course, interpreted, evaluated, and applied from any number of specific positive or normative perspectives. His analysis is broad enough to encompass quite a wide range of applications. His larger analysis – his total system, of which the central invisible hand argument in the *Wealth of Nations* is but one interacting part – permits and indeed has an important place for many diverse phenomena. There are two key points here: the scope of his system is broad, and its details, that is, the details which characterize a market economy and its moral and legal elements, are quite open and subject to revision. There is in Smith's total system what may be called a joint determination process: on the one hand is the determination of optimality through markets as individuals engage in voluntary exchange, and on the other is the ongoing socialization process which governs the reformulation of legal and moral rules, institutions, the power structure, and thereby the substantive conditions or content of optimality, always in combination with individual choice. Smith is quite obviously pro-market, but not in a way that deems market solutions optimal *per se*. He does not propose, let alone establish, the exclusive or *a priori* presumptive optimality of market solutions. Rather, he articulates the role of the market as a regulatory system which performs well or not, depending upon the role of institutions and other forces of social control. Smith did not use his economic theory to justify conclusions which were beyond its scope, given the terms of his larger analysis, although he is easily enough interpreted as having done so. To Smith, reality is not a simple question of market-optimality versus standards or norms of legal and moral social control; rather, the market gives effect to and operates upon such social control. His system is much larger than the dominant view of his work has admitted. Indeed, his larger analysis actually serves to explain the continued conflicts over proposed changes of moral and legal rules, institutions, power, values, and so on: such conflicts are central to his conception of the evolution of the total economic system. And herein lies a major contemporary significance of Smith. Interpretive overkill, perhaps in an effort to make Smith's analysis safe for the system, has tended to obfuscate the larger process he deemed to be a crucial part of the social system.

Contrary, then, to the more typical usages of Smith and especially of the *Wealth of Nations*, I would urge that he provides not a set of immediate policy solutions or presumptions but a framework within which, given that it postulates and legitimizes a market economy, there can be no unequivocal or conclusive *a priori* determination of practical policy issues. It is Smith's message that these issues need to be worked out through the principles of approbation, disapprobation, the impartial spectator, and so on. Policy requires more than market-premised economic theory, in part because there is more to the operation of the economy than such theory incorporates. The theory of the market does not itself explain the larger system of which the market is a part, nor does it conclusively assert the superiority of market solutions within the existing systemic structure. Smith's emphasis upon the market tells us much about the general character of his economic system and how it works in general, but it tells us very little about the details of the continuing resolution of the problem of order under its aegis. Smith was aware of the limited probative value of his economic reasoning and therefore of the limits of what science can and cannot do.[85] The ultimate message of his synoptic and synthetic analysis is the openness – the empty boxes – which it presents and therefore the choices which it both permits and requires. This conclusion stands in marked contrast to the more conventional view that Smith's message is to leave things alone. His inclusion of the tensions, which I have discussed, serves to indicate the vacuousness of that view. To Smith, such tensions were not going to be resolved once and for all, nor were market solutions the only ones permitted or justified. It is a result of past filtration of

Smith's analysis that such a view as I have given may be perceived as statist.

The evolution of the interpretation of Smith, and of the doctrinal defence of the ongoing system of which that interpretation has been a part, has been a process of both filtration and conversion. Through filtration much of the substance and significance of Smith's larger system has been excluded, including some fundamental social processes and many continuing tensions. Through conversion, his analysis of the market, the invisible hand, has been transformed from an analysis and justification of relatively small-scale individual activity to that of large-scale enterprise to which some economists refer as the corporate system. Both filtration and conversion are inevitable processes. They function not only to rationalize selected aspects of the changing status quo, but also, in that respect and others, as important parts of the social valuational process. The point here is that in all these respects Smith's total system and analysis have been transformed.

Much has changed since Smith's time; the modern world is vastly different in technology, institutions, political geography, historical experience, world-view, social stratification, and economic organization and control. One does find in the *Wealth of Nations* the germs of many of the conflicts of modern Western civilization, but Smith largely antedated the conflicts between capital and labour and between property and non-property rights and positions in the economy. Yet these conflicts have a place in his system. He offers no genuine, unequivocal, and conclusive solution to any of those conflicts, but the probability that they will arise is predictable from the total analysis. Nevertheless, past usages of Smith have functioned either to deny the propriety of many of those conflicts or to channel their resolution. There is no more conclusive ground for citing Smith in favour of a pro-business or property solution than there is for citing him in repudiation of the conflicts themselves. Given a market system, Smith's is a relatively open system. His analysis also recognizes, of course, that labour and capital are each jockeying for position to control the other, that government is an instrument of those who are in a position to use it, and that much asymmetry of position characterizes both conflicts.[86] Neither the conflict between labourer and capitalist nor that over property rights was considered essentially antimarket by Smith.

The fact of the matter, of course, is that the defence of the market, quite properly often in the name of Smith, has also served as a defence of existing power structures. Market theory has been used to obfuscate the problems of power, of moral and legal rules, and of the use of government, and to canonize existing power positions and their use of morality and law. One does not find in Smith the gains-from-trade and voluntarism arguments used in such a way as to rationalize the existing power structure. Rather, Smith delineates the deep processes, however laden with controversy, through which institutions, legal and moral rules, and power structures are made subject to non-market revision. One cannot speak for Smith's reaction to a world of large-scale economic units, but it seems obvious to me that he might say that moral and legal controls, indeed the very corporate institution, should be subject to revision.[87] Surely Smith would have sympathized with Henry Simons's statement that 'we may recognize, in the almost unlimited grants of powers to corporate bodies, one of the greatest sins of governments against the free-enterprise system'.[88] In Smith's view, market solutions are not necessarily optimal; one must consider the power structure and other factors before one can reach that conclusion. It is a gross and misleading oversimplification of Smith to invoke his conception of the market without further examination of these other factors.[89]

Adam Smith was a premier philosopher of the market economy, more so than our intellectual heritage has often allowed. The greatness of his analysis is that it is an *open* system in much the same sense that the market economy itself is an *open* system – notwithstanding the efforts of the already established and powerful to the contrary. If we understood Smith better, it might be an even more open system, but that is quite another story.

Notes

1. True, he has some interesting if not important things to say about practical issues and details of economic organization and policy, not all of which, by any means, we are obligated to accept. His views on interest rate regulation and the corporation are two examples. But his opinions often are of interest because he is taking a position, more or less idiosyncratic, about some practical aspect of the fundamental structure and process of the market economy and/or its political correlatives.
2. Several of these considerations are discussed in Warren J. Samuels, 'The History of Economic Thought as Intellectual History', *History of Political Economy*, vol. 6, no. 3 (Fall 1974), pp. 305–23.
3. Interpretation, of course, serves several functions, among them social control. In the *Wealth of Nations* and in the *Theory of Moral Sentiments*, Smith examined the social control mechanisms of the existing society and economy. One indicator of the historic importance of Smith's work has been that the interpretation of the *Wealth of Nations* has become a facet of the social control system of the Western economies. Yet this only illustrates the general view that the entire history of economic thought has meaning as knowledge, social control, and psychic balm, since economics may serve as both explanation and rationalization. The interpretation of the *Wealth of Nations* has become part of the quest for moral and legal rules, a quest which to Adam Smith, as we will see, is a very important part of the socioeconomic system.

4. See Warren S. Gramm, 'Natural Selection in Economic Thought: Ideology, Power, and the Keynesian Revolution', *Journal of Economic Issues*, vol. 7, no. 1 (March 1973), pp. 1–28.
5. A. L. Macfie, *The Individual in Society* (London: George Allen & Unwin, 1967), p. 13.
6. John Maurice Clark, 'Adam Smith and the Currents of History', in *Adam Smith, 1776–1926* (Chicago: University of Chicago Press, 1928), p. 73.
7. Frank H. Knight, 'Theory of Economic Policy and the History of Doctrines', *Ethics*, vol. 63 (July 1953), p. 279.
8. For example, see the disparate interpretations of the significance of the *Wealth of Nations* presented at the Political Economy Club centennial celebration; Political Economy Club, *Revised Report of the Proceedings at the Dinner of 31st May, 1876, Held in Celebration of the Hundredth Year of the Publication of the* Wealth of Nations (London: Longmans, Green, Reader & Dyer, 1876).
9. The interpretation given below is largely in the tradition of Jacob Viner, Glenn Morrow, Alex Macfie, and Nathan Rosenberg, among others, all of whom deserve prior exculpation for the uses to which I have put their ideas. The influence of Joseph Spengler also will be evident.
10. Wesley C. Mitchell, *Types of Economic Theory*, ed. Joseph Dorfman (New York: Kelley, 1967), vol. 1, p. 165.
11. Joseph J. Spengler, 'The Problem of Order in Economic Affairs', *Southern Economic Journal*, vol. 15 (July 1948), pp. 1–29, and 'Hierarchy vs. Equality: Persisting Conflict', *Kyklos*, vol. 21 (1968), pp. 217–36.
12. Mark Blaug, *Economic Theory in Retrospect*, revised edn (Homewood, Ill.: Irwin, 1968), p. 6.
13. Adam Smith, *The Wealth of Nations* (New York: Modern Library, 1937), p. 326.
14. Warren J. Samuels, 'Adam Smith and the Economy as a System of Power', *Indian Economic Journal*, vol. 20 (January–March 1973), pp. 363–81.
15. Macfie, *The Individual in Society*, p. 16; see p. 147 and *passim*.
16. Adam Smith, *The Theory of Moral Sentiments* (New York: Kelley, 1966), p. 503.
17. Adam Smith, *Lectures on Justice, Police, Revenue and Arms* (New York: Kelley, 1964).
18. Macfie, *The Individual in Society*, chs 5, 6, and *passim*; Warren J. Samuels, *The Classical Theory of Economic Policy* (Cleveland: World, 1966), ch. 2 and *passim*.
19. Lionel Robbins, *The Theory of Economic Policy in English Classical Political Economy* (London: Macmillan, 1953), pp. 25–29; Samuels, *Classical Theory*, pp. 7–9.
20. Macfie, *The Individual in Society*, pp. 108, 122, and *passim*; Glenn R. Morrow, 'Adam Smith: Moralist and Philosopher', in *Adam Smith, 1776–1926* (Chicago: University of Chicago Press, 1928), pp. 168–71.
21. Macfie, *The Individual in Society*, pp. 102–3, n. 4.
22. Samuels, *Classical Theory*, ch. 5; Robbins, *Theory of Economic Policy*, ch. 6; and A. W. Coats, *The Classical Economists and Economic Policy* (London: Methuen, 1971), pp. 5 ff.
23. Macfie, *The Individual in Society*, p. 139. On the problem of Smith's consistency, see Ralph Anspach, 'The Implications of the *Theory of Moral*

Sentiments for Adam Smith's Economic Thought', *History of Political Economy*, vol. 4, no. 1 (Spring 1972), pp. 203–5.

24. Russel B. Nye, 'The Thirties: The Framework of Belief', *Centennial Review*, vol. 19 (Spring 1975), p. 52.
25. Quoted in James Cerruti, 'Stockholm', *National Geographic*, vol. 149, no. 1 (January 1976), p. 59.
26. Richard Schlegel, Book Review, *Journal of Economic Issues*, vol. 7, no. 3 (September 1973), p. 480.
27. Nathan Rosenberg, 'Some Institutional Aspects of the *Wealth of Nations*', *Journal of Political Economy*, vol. 68 (December 1960), p. 557.
28. Macfie, *The Individual in Society*, p. 62.
29. Rosenberg, 'Institutional Aspects', p. 558.
30. Ibid., p. 560.
31. Smith, *The Wealth of Nations*, p. 421.
32. Ibid., p. 423.
33. Rosenberg, 'Institutional Aspects', p. 560.
34. Morrow, 'Adam Smith'; Macfie, *The Individual in Society*'; Rosenberg, 'Institutional Aspects' and 'Adam Smith on the Division of Labour: Two Views or One?', *Economica*, vol. 32 (May 1965), pp. 127–39.
35. Macfie, *The Individual in Society*, p. 107.
36. Rosenberg, 'Adam Smith on the Division of Labour', p. 129.
37. Rosenberg, 'Institutional Aspects', p. 560.
38. Ibid., p. 559.
39. Rosenberg, 'Adam Smith on the Division of Labour', pp. 136–8.
40. Rosenberg, 'Institutional Aspects', p. 563.
41. Ibid., p. 563.
42. Macfie, *The Individual in Society*, p. 148.
43. Smith, *The Wealth of Nations*, p. 308.
44. Rosenberg, 'Institutional Aspects', pp. 559, 560, and *passim*; Macfie, *The Individual in Society*.
45. Macfie, *The Individual in Society*, p. 81.
46. Ibid., pp. 97–8.
47. Ibid., p. 117; see p. 118.
48. Morrow, 'Adam Smith', p. 178; see pp. 166–7, 172, 177. See also Gladys Bryson, *Man and Society* (New York: Kelley, 1968); and Louis Schneider, *The Scottish Moralists on Human Nature and Society* (Chicago: University of Chicago Press, 1967).
49. Macfie, *The Individual in Society*, p. 117–18.
50. Ibid., p. 91, n. 23.
51. Ibid., pp. 72–3; Smith, *The Theory of Moral Sentiments*, p. 380.
52. Morrow, 'Adam Smith', pp. 166–7, 172, 177–8.
53. Macfie, *The Individual in Society*, pp. 70–1, 75, 128, and *passim*; Anspach, 'Implications'; and A. W. Coats, 'Adam Smith's Conception of Self-Interest in Economic and Political Affairs', *History of Political Economy*, vol. 7, no. 1 (Spring 1975), pp. 132–6.
54. Macfie, *The Individual in Society*, pp. 47, 53–4, 60–76, 122–4; Nathan Rosenberg, 'Adam Smith, Consumer Tastes, and Economic Growth', *Journal of Political Economy*, vol. 76 (May–June 1968), p. 371; and Samuels, *The Classical Theory of Economic Policy*, p. 37.

55. Smith's element of cynicism here (Macfie, *The Individual in Society*, p. 54) may be compared with Milton Friedman's criticism of what he considers intellectuals' 'contempt for what they regard as material aspects of life'. See Milton Friedman, *Capitalism and Freedom* (Chicago: University of Chicago Press, 1962), p. 8.
56. Rosenberg, 'Adam Smith on Profits – Paradox Lost and Regained', *Journal of Political Economy*, vol. 82 (November–December 1974), p. 1187, and *passim*.
57. Macfie, *The Individual in Society*, p. 78.
58. Rosenberg, 'Institutional Aspects', pp. 557 and *passim*; 'Adam Smith, Consumer Tastes, and Economic Growth'.
59. In general, see Rosenberg, 'Adam Smith, Consumer Tastes, and Economic Growth', pp. 367, 370, 372.
60. Rosenberg, 'Adam Smith on the Division of Labour', pp. 129–30.
61. Rosenberg, 'Adam Smith on Profits – Paradox Lost and Regained', p. 1185.
62. Macfie, *The Individual in Society*, p. 137.
63. Ibid., p. 120, n. 43.
64. Ibid., pp. 49 ff; Samuels, *Classical Theory*, chs 2 and 5.
65. Macfie, *The Individual in Society*, p. 117.
66. Morrow, 'Adam Smith', p. 172.
67. Smith, *The Wealth of Nations*, p. 625.
68. Robert L. Heilbroner, *The Worldly Philosophers*, 4th edn (New York: Simon & Schuster, 1972), p. 51.
69. Macfie, *The Individual in Society*, pp. 83–7 and *passim*.
70. Ibid., pp. 89–90.
71. Ibid., pp. 83, 87, 89; Morrow, 'Adam Smith'.
72. Macfie, *The Individual in Society*, p. 57.
73. Smith, *The Theory of Moral Sentiments*, pp. 499 ff.
74. Jacob Viner, 'Adam Smith and *Laissez-Faire*', in *Adam Smith, 1776–1926* (Chicago: University of Chicago Press, 1928), pp. 116–55.
75. Rosenberg, 'Institutional Aspects', p. 562.
76. Viner, 'Adam Smith and *Laissez-Faire*'; Samuels, *Classical Theory*, chs 4 and 5.
77. Macfie, *The Individual in Society*, p. 124.
78. Smith, *The Wealth of Nations*, p. 308; Viner, 'Adam Smith and *Laissez-Faire*'.
79. Smith, *The Wealth of Nations*, p. 650.
80. Macfie, *The Individual in Society*, p. 78 and *passim*; Morrow, 'Adam Smith'.
81. Samuels, 'Adam Smith and the Economy as a System of Power'.
82. Rosenberg, 'Institutional Aspects', pp. 560, 569.
83. Clark, 'Adam Smith and the Currents of History', pp. 58, 62, 73–4.
84. Smith, *The Wealth of Nations*, p. 726.
85. Macfie, *The Individual in Society*, p. 13.
86. Samuels, 'Adam Smith and the Economy as a System of Power'.
87. Macfie, *The Individual in Society*, p. 120; Clark, 'Adam Smith and the Currents of History', pp. 54, 75.
88. Henry C. Simons, *Economic Policy for a Free Society* (Chicago: University of Chicago Press, 1948), p. 52.
89. Rosenberg, 'Institutional Aspects', p. 570.

5 The Classical Theory of Economic Policy: Non-Legal Social Control*

> Man is a Religious Animall, and onely men hope that their Earthly Soveraines will deale very justly, when such soveraines believe there is a most Just God above them.
>
> Men, either for the Love of God or the feare of Hell, will forbeare doing such mischief to their Neighbor as the Law cannot reach.
>
> Men, after prayer to God, proceede more cheerfully on their businesses when they believe that such prayers shall procure them successe.
>
> Men beare paines & wrongs more patiently, when they hope that God will ballance all in the next life.
>
> Marquis of Landsdowne (ed.), *The Petty Papers* (London: Constable, 1927). Two volumes. Vol. I, pp. 116–17.

The objective of this essay is to suggest the necessity of a definition of wider scope for the concept, 'theory of economic policy', particularly in the case of the classical economists. The conventional definition of 'theory of economic policy' limits its scope to the role of law. Thus Lord Robbins defines the concept as 'the general body of principles of governmental action or inaction – the *agenda* or *non-agenda* of the state as Bentham called them – in regard to economic activity'.[1] This definition, it is contended, is incomplete for it does not adequately acknowledge the fact that the state is but one reciprocally interacting part of a larger structure of power which comprises the total system of social control.

---

* Originally published as a two-part paper in *Southern Economic Journal*, vol. 31, no. 1, pp. 1–20; no. 2, pp. 87–100.

This study was a partial result of research facilitated by a sub-grant of a NSF institutional grant to the University of Miami. Helpful suggestions and comments were kindly offered on an earlier draft by Harvey J. Botwin, Grover A. J. Hoetzel, J. Ben Stalvey, James C. Vadakin, and Charles G. Werner. I am especially indebted to Almarin Phillips for extensive editorial suggestions. Responsibility for the interpretation presented is solely the author's. Invaluable research assistance, and suggestions, was provided by Jose A. Lopez. More than the customary praise belongs to personnel of the Main Library and Law Library of the University of Miami. A summary of this paper was presented at the November 1963 meeting of the Southern Economic Association.

The market-plus-framework interpretation of the classical theory of economic policy is taken as the most meaningful analysis yet formulated.[2] This view has, however, understated the significance and content of the social control system considered as the framework. Such understatement is significant in the case of the classical economists, for the non-legal, or non-deliberative, forces of social control, operating as morals, religion, custom, and education, were deemed necessary in the policy process.[3] Such deliberate policy making as would or could take place had to operate under conditions of order and with socialized individuals, both of which were to a substantial extent the result of the working of the non-deliberative forces of social control.

In brief, insofar as the idea of a framework is itself meaningful, (1) the framework is more significant than has as yet been made clear in the literature on classical policy; (2) this significance is in part the result of the classical emphasis on the non-legal forces of social control; and (3) the failure to recognize such significance is in no small part the result of an inadequate definition of the scope of the theory of economic policy.

It should be pointed out that the relevant cosmology of the classical economists is not that of an *Harmonielehre*[4] but rather that of the *createdness* of such harmony as could be created. According to Lord Robbins, there was no harmony at all except under certain conditions, and 'the harmony which would be established was a very limited kind of harmony'.

> In general, on any dispassionate view of the literature, it is really very hard to maintain that it gives any strong support to cosmic optimism, still less to belief in a comprehensive pre-established inevitable harmony of interests. The most that can be said of the Classical Economists in this respect is that they believed that, in a world of free enterprise, certain relationships would arise which were of a mutually advantageous kind to the individuals concerned and superior to those resulting from alternative systems . . .[5]

In the view of the classicists such harmony would have to be created by developing an appropriate and effective institutional system. Both society and market were seen as artifacts,[6] and as artifacts that were evolving.[7] The classicists did not take the institutional environment for granted.[8] It is rather the institutions of social control which were to channel individual interests into amenable lines and thereby create harmony. These are the institutions 'within which action is so limited and co-ordinated as to create the good society', withdrawing 'from the sphere of the pursuit of self-interest those possibilities which do not harmonize with the public good'.[9] To the classical economists an order is harmonious largely to the extent to which the system of social control, and largely the non-legal forces thereof, perform their functions well.[10] As expressed by Ricardo,

> To keep men good you must as much as possible withdraw from them all temptations to be otherwise. The sanctions of religion, of public opinion, and of law, all proceed on this principle, and that State is most perfect in which all these sanctions concur to make it in the interest of all men to be virtuous, which is the same thing as to say, to use their best endeavour to promote the general happiness.[11]

Moreover, and this is of great importance, the classicists' case for the relative de-emphasis of the legal forces was in effect premised on the effective operation of the non-deliberative forces of social control.[12] To the drama of the forces of morals, religion, custom, and education, as the non-legal forces of social control, we now turn.

NON-DELIBERATIVE SOCIAL CONTROL

Classical economic liberalism has had as its distinctive characteristic the resounding pleas for human freedom, for the importance of human development, for individual independence of thought and action, for freedom from arbitrary control. The classical economists from Smith to Stuart Mill shared the historic theme of liberalism – meaningful human freedom as a value – and the cognate importance of an open and pluralist society. To the fervent believers in this ideal the opposite – both philosophical and political monism – was anathema. Conceived as economic organization to achieve freedom through progress and progress through freedom, theirs was a system of private participation in economic affairs, or individualism, and was basically an argument for the market economy, or free enterprise, and private property. The classical economists stood for the market system, retrospectively against mercantilism and special interests and, in effect, prospectively against state socialism or a planned economy. Individuals were to be free in pursuit of their economic objectives, and resource allocation and income distribution were to emerge as the result of the interaction of market forces in a resolution of the basic economic problems reflecting the interplay of ostensibly spontaneous individual private demanders and suppliers.

But correlative to this *desideratum* of human freedom was a recognition of the fact and necessity of the extant system of social control, extending to both the non-legal and legal forces thereof. The classicists acknowledged the dualism of freedom and control, the desire for meaningful freedom *vis-à-vis* the necessity of control, and the necessity and complexity of choice governing the pattern of freedom and control. The system of control as a whole greatly conditioned and integrated individual behaviour patterns by channelling the exercise of choice, the range of which choice in any given circumstance was more or less flexible depending upon the pattern of historical accretion of control and the exigencies of time and place. More important in a way, the pattern of social control related to and perhaps provided more or less specifically the institutional conditions of life and behaviour patterns. One's freedom was freedom only within the pattern of freedom reigning at the time and place. Freedom was, then, largely circumstantial.[13] It reflected, first, the more encompassing notion that the character of man was in part social and situational,[14] and, second, the idea that the crucial element in the situation, given the pattern of latent passions of human nature, was the system of social control, particularly the non-legal forces ranging from the moral code and ideology or cosmology to education. Freedom was thus essentially relative and historical, and with it also the pattern of rights into which the developing structure of freedom was crystallized and in terms of which it was discussed and argued.[15] But notwithstanding the circumstantial nature of freedom and the situational character of man, the role of social control was crucial in establishing *order* as a condition of life and of progress. The exercise of social control was then in some respects to *discipline* man in the interests of order and the manifestations of order (e.g., discipline in effect directed at inducing the orderly practice of economic pursuits).

Thus the classicists acknowledged that individual behaviour and decisions were channelled by the forces of morals, religion, custom and education. The economy, considered as a decision-making process in the resolution of the basic economic problems, was also seen governed by these non-deliberative forces of social control, which were important with respect to both the *structure* of that process and the *content* of the decisions as the system channelled the exercise of choice. That the non-legal forces were non-deliberative and unobtrusive did not detract from their importance.

This section will examine Morals and Religion, Custom, and Education, in that sequence, in each case examining first Smith, in some detail, and then showing the consonance of Smith's views with those of the later classicists.

Morals and Religion

It is appropriate to turn first to Smith's *Theory of Moral Sentiments*, for not only was this remarkable essay a treatise on 'natural theology' and a great work in social analysis, but it was held in high repute by the English classicists at least through Stuart Mill.[16] Its basic ideas on morals and religion as control forces, it will be seen, were largely adhered to by the later classicists. Smith was primarily concerned with the operation and perforce the immediate or observable source of the moral sentiments. Reflecting the ambivalent character of his age and possibly the influence of Hume, Smith's analysis finds the origin of the *content* of morals in experience, so as to be perhaps ultimately indistinguishable from revered custom.[17] Through the working of sympathy and the principles of approbation and disapprobation of the conduct of one's self and of others, operating through the guidance of the 'impartial spectator' ('reason, principle, conscience, the inhabitant of the breast, the man within, the great judge and arbiter of our conduct'),[18] Smith charts the incremental development of standards of conduct which evolve and emerge as general rules of conduct.

> Our continual observations upon the conduct of others, insensibly lead us to form to ourselves certain general rules concerning what is fit and proper either to be done or to be avoided.
>
> The general rule . . . is formed, by finding from experience, that all actions of a certain kind, or circumstanced in a certain manner, are approved or disapproved of.
>
> . . . The general rules which determine what actions are, and what are not, the objects of each of those sentiments, can be formed no other way than by observing what actions actually and in fact excite them.
>
> When these general rules, indeed, have been formed, when they are universally acknowledged and established, by the concurring sentiments of mankind, we frequently appeal to them as to the standards of judgment . . . [19]

These general rules not only vary, however, in respect to time and place,[20] but were seen as imprecise and ambiguous.[21] Yet this very ambiguity is derived from and tends to promote the pervasive functioning of the rules to provide both flexibility and individual spheres of autonomy within the requirements and restraints of order. The ambiguity, that is, provides the flexibility necessary to attain workable adjustments between freedom and order.

Thus it is that the needs of *order* is a central preoccupation of Smith in the *Moral Sentiments* and to the provision of which it is the task of morals and religion alike to contribute. Indeed, the *Moral Sentiments* places great weight on *order*, which is perhaps to be expected in a work on the role of morals as an instrument of social control.

> Man, it has been said, has a natural love for society and desires that the union of mankind should be preserved for its own sake, and though he himself was to derive no benefit from it. The orderly and flourishing state of society is agreeable to him, and he takes delight in contemplating it. Its disorder and confusion, on the contrary, is the object of his aversion, and he is chagrined at whatever tends to produce it. He is sensible too that his own interest is connected with the prosperity of society, and that the happiness, perhaps the preservation of his existence, depends upon its preservation. Upon every account, therefore, he has an abhorrence at whatever can tend to destroy society, and is willing to make use of every means, which can hinder so hated and so dreadful an event.[22]

Justice is important because of its contribution to order, which is ergo the higher value. 'Beneficence', wrote Smith, 'is less essential to the existence of society than justice. Justice, on the contrary, is the main pillar that upholds the whole ediface. If it is removed, the great, the immense fabric of human society . . . must in a moment crumble into atoms. Society may subsist, though not in most comfortable state, without beneficence; but the prevalence of injustice must utterly destroy it.'[23] Indeed, 'The peace and order of society, is of more important than even the relief of the miserable.'[24]

Smith demonstrates, then, that morals, manifest through the general rules of conduct, conduce to social order, serving as an instrument of control in the process. Says Smith:

> The regard to those general rules of conduct, is what is properly called a sense of duty, a principle of the greatest consequence in human life, and the only principle by which the bulk of mankind are capable of directing their actions.[25]
>
> The coarse clay of which the bulk of mankind are formed, cannot be wrought up to such perfection. There is scarce any man, however, who by discipline, education, and example, may not be so impressed with a regard to general rules, as to act upon almost every occasion with tolerable decency, and through the whole of his life to avoid any considerable degree of blame.
>
> Without this sacred regard to general rules, there is no man whose conduct can be much depended upon. . . . But upon the tolerable observance of these duties depends the very existence of human society, which would crumble into nothing if mankind were not generally impressed with a reverence for those important rules of conduct.

> Upon whatever we suppose that moral faculties are founded, . . . they were given us for the direction of our conduct in this life. They . . . were set up within us to be the supreme arbiters of all our actions, to superintend all our senses, passions, and appetites, and to judge how each of them was either to be indulged or restrained.
>
> All general rules . . . have a much greater resemblance to what are properly called laws, those general rules which the sovereign lays down to direct the conduct of his subjects. Like them they are rules to direct the free actions of men: . . .[26]

Morality serves, according to Smith, as a social cement through its role as an instrument of social control. Whatever the theological status of the general rules of conduct, Smith acknowledged the operation, non-deliberatively, of control through social interaction.

> The all-wise Author of Nature has, in this manner, taught man to respect the sentiments and judgments of his brethren; to be more or less pleased when they approve of his conduct, and to be more or less hurt when they disapprove of it. He has made man, if I may say so, the immediate judge of mankind; and has, in this respect, as in many others, created him after his own image, and appointed him his vicegerent upon earth, to superintend the behaviour of his brethren.[27]

Wrote Morrow: 'The individual's moral consciousness with its judgments of approval and disapproval is a reflection, or a derivative, of the social consciousness; it grows through experience in society, and represents the demands of his fellow-men upon the individual'.[28]

The promulgation of morals is a concern of religion, though it is clear that Smith and the other classicists considered morals as having sources other than from religious offices. Religion was, however, a participant in the development of morals, and had to do, at the minimum, with the 'impulse to reverence', the 'sense of duty' or of 'being good'.

With respect to religion, or organized religion, as such, the classicists as a group generally: (a) advocated religious liberty with toleration and without persecution, (b) were critical of totalitarian religious institutions, (c) were critical of what Bentham referred to as the 'mischief' of religion, and (d) generally were, or at least tended toward, humanism. But most important for present purposes, the classicists (e) acknowledged the role of religion as a restraint, or source of restraint, upon behaviour. In this respect the classicists often analysed organized religion as another social institution. In so doing, they somewhat ambiguously acknowledged or developed the customary character of the content of religious or other moral codes. But they clearly envisioned religion as a force at least tending to operate as an effective instrument of social control. Religion itself might not be sufficient to produce moral behaviour, nor was belief in the existence of a Supreme Being necessarily sufficient (but compare Smith and Stuart Mill, below), but even in a humanist regime (Stuart Mill acknowledged) such belief would be efficacious. Religion was seen as inculcating a compulsion or feeling of necessity to be good (Smith's 'sense of duty'), whatever the moral system, and thereby serving to enforce the extant moral system – and of course participating in defining the content of the moral system. Religion also was seen as serving to induce a feeling of consolation or resignation, which was understood as a derivative of the necessity for order but also as the basis of meaningful social improvement.

There is some question as to how far several of the classical economists would have relied upon organized religion as part of the institutionalized ethical system. The preceding paragraph is generally correct, though there is ambivalence. Thus Smith, whose religiosity is ambiguous, nonetheless evidences a greater willingness to rely upon religion than Stuart Mill – but the difference may reflect the passage of three-quarters of a century in time, manners, sentiments, and openness of speech.

Smith was lucid in his discussion of the role of religion as an instrument of control. After stressing that 'upon the tolerable observance of these duties depends the very existence of human society, which would crumble into nothing if mankind were not generally impressed with a reverence for those important rules of society', he declares that

> This reverence is still further enhanced by an opinion, which is first impressed by nature, and afterwards confirmed by reasoning and philosophy, that those important rules of morality are the commands and laws of the Deity, who will finally reward the obedient and punish the transgressors of their duty.
>
> These natural hopes, and fears, and suspicions, were propagated by sympathy, and confirmed by education; and the gods were universally represented and believed to be the rewarders of humanity and mercy, and the avengers of perfidy and injustice. And thus religion, even in its rudest form, gave a sanction to the rules of morality, long before the age of artificial reasoning and philosophy. That the terrors of religion should thus enforce the natural sense of duty, was of too much importance to the happiness of mankind, for nature to leave it dependent upon the slowness and uncertainty of philosophical researches.
>
> Since these, therefore, were plainly intended to be the governing principles of human nature, the rules which they prescribe are to be

> regarded as the commands and laws of the Deity, promulgated by those vicegerents which he has thus set up within us.
>
> When the general rules which determine the merit and demerit of actions, come thus to be regarded as the laws of an all-powerful Being . . . they necessarily acquire a new sacredness from this consideration. That our regard to the will of the Deity ought to be the supreme rule of our conduct, can be doubted of by nobody who believes his existence. The very thought of disobedience appears to involve in it the most shocking impropriety . . . The idea that, however we may escape the observation of man, or be placed above the reach of human punishment, yet we are always acting under the eye, and exposed to the punishment of God, the great avenger of injustice, is a motive capable of restraining the most headstrong passions, with those at least who, by constant reflection, have rendered it familiar to them.
>
> It is in this manner that religion enforces the natural sense of duty: and hence it is, that mankind are generally disposed to place great confidence in the probity of those who seem deeply impressed with religious sentiments. Such persons, they imagine, act under an additional tie, besides those which regulate the conduct of other men.[29]

Nonetheless, Smith is rather sophisticated about the role of religion so far as the content of morality is concerned. Though he cautions that there can be 'no solid happiness to any man who is not thoroughly convinced that all the inhabitants of the universe, the meanest as well as the greatest, are under the immediate care and protection of that great, benevolent, and all-wise Being',[30] and that religion is the source of 'magnanimous resignation',[31] he stresses an activism with respect to man and acknowledges ambiguity in the obligations enforced by religion. With respect to the former, Smith's division of responsibility has a place for both God and man:

> The administration of the great system of the universe . . . the care of the universal happiness of all rational and sensible beings, is the business of God and not of man. To man is alloted a much humbler department . . . the care of his own happiness, of that of his family, his friends, his country . . . The most sublime speculation of the contemplative philosopher can scarce compensate the neglect of the smallest active duty.[32]

On the ambiguity of obligation, Smith recognizes that 'Religion affords such strong motives to the practice of virtue, and guards us by such powerful restraints from the temptations of vice, that many have been led to suppose, that religious principles were the sole laudable motives of action.' They are not, and, what is more,

> That the sense of duty should be the sole principle of our conduct, is no where the precept of Christianity; but that it should be the ruling and the governing one, as philosophy, and as, indeed, common sense directs. It may be a question, however, in what cases our actions ought to arise chiefly or entirely from a sense of duty, or from a regard to general rules; and in what cases some other sentiment or affection ought to concur, and have a principal influence on our conduct.

It 'will depend upon the natural agreeableness or deformity of the affection itself, how far our actions ought to arise from it, or entirely proceed from a regard to the general rule', and 'it will depend partly upon the precision and exactness, or the looseness and inaccuracy of the general rules themselves, how far our conduct ought to proceed entirely from a regard to them'.[33] Religion, then, serves to promote morality but is no unequivocal answer to the problem of the content of moral rules: 'The general rules of almost all the virtues . . . are in many respects loose and inaccurate, admit of many exceptions, and require so many modifications, that it is scarce possible to regulate our conduct entirely by a regard to them.' Although the rules of justice are 'precise, accurate, and indispensable', the rules of the other virtues 'are loose, vague, and indeterminate, and present us rather with a general idea of the perfection we ought to aim at, than afford us any certain and infallible directions for acquiring it'.[34] Like the general cosmology of the time (discussed below), the general moral system, while unable to unequivocally resolve all the particulars of moral content, gains in strength as an instrument of social control what it otherwise loses in precision, for its *general* attractiveness is most important as a force of social control.

Moreover, analysing religion as merely another social institution, Smith finds that its operation is not always unobjectionable. 'False notions of religion are almost the only causes which can occasion any very gross perversion of our natural sentiments in this way; and that principle which gives the greatest authority to the rules of duty, is alone capable of distorting our ideas of them in any considerable degree.' Notwithstanding the foregoing, Smith again subsumes equity and justice to order:

> That to obey the will of the Deity, is the first rule of duty, all men are agreed. But concerning the particular commandments which that will may impose upon us, they differ widely from one another. In this, therefore, the greatest mutual forbearance and toleration is due; and though the defence of society requires that crimes should be punished, from whatever motives they proceed, yet a good man will always punish them with reluctance, when they evidently proceed from false notions of religious duty.[35]

It is no accident, then, that Smith even in the *Wealth of Nations* applauded 'the uniformity of faith, the fervour of devotion, the spirit of order, regularity, and austere morals in the great body of the people'.[36] To Smith, says Bittermann, 'Religion is a natural response to human needs for ethical sanctions'.[37] Religion coordinated with the pressures generic to any moral system, served, in the eyes of Smith, as a force of social control. It restricted and channelled behaviour, always in terms of the more or less ambiguous content of the extant moral system, and thereby governed the ostensibly 'spontaneous' activities of men as economic and non-economic actors and consequently also governed the resolution of the basic economic problems. Yet it was stressed above that such control is itself but a facet of any system of freedom and control only in terms of which both freedom and control acquire substantive meaning. As Commons would have put it, morals and religion-sanctioning morals are non-deliberative collective action in con-trol of but also in enhancement and liberation of individual action.

Certain facets of the non-deliberative forces are of such profound import as to render the term 'non-deliberative' a meaningful synonym for 'non-legal'. This underscores the importance of these forces for the classical theory of economic policy. Smith, and other classicists, acknowledged and demonstrated the significance of morals and religion, and the non-deliberative forces in general, by subscribing (albeit often reluctantly, as with Bentham and Stuart Mill) to the at least partial necessity of what has come to be known as the operation of *ignorance* (or deception) and *indirection.* That is to say, the classicists had a place for the practice and force of *ignorance* and *indirection.* The basic idea of the concept and role of *ignorance* is the functional necessity of 'social actions and arrangements intended by no one and *unknown* to some (unspecified) proportion of actors',[38] such that greater long-run benefits are to be accrued from not confronting (or not publicizing the confrontation) directly and openly the resolution of some social problem or goal. Thus *indirection* has to do with the achievement of ends through the non-deliberative institutions and forces, the benefits accruing through focusing attention and activity on 'intermediate' attractions or goals conducive to securing the 'intended' goal(s). The underlying reasoning is complex, but two points may be noted: first, that order to some extent at least may be held to require that there not be much (open) questioning of received arrangements, and, second, that the effectiveness of goal achievement may be adversely affected if the participants are directly knowledgeable of what is at stake. The operation of religion and the sanctions of religion has long been recognized as a prime example.[39]

Adam Smith, as Schneider recognizes, is a 'prime text' in these matters:

> we may take Adam Smith's famous and familiar observation that the individual 'neither intends to promote the public interest, *nor knows* [italics supplied] how much he promotes it' when he pursues his own gain, but that, nevertheless, 'by pursuing his own interest he frequently promotes that of the society more effectually than when he really intends to promote it'. This significantly represents the individual as ignorant of the circumstance that he promotes public interest, indicates that the pursuit of the individual's interest leads indirectly to public interest, and asserts that this combination of ignorance and indirection is 'more effectual' than would be an alternative combination of knowledge of one's objects and effort to attain them. The locus of wisdom, one may say, is neither in the individual nor in any combination of individuals deliberately seeking to attain some large social end such as public welfare; it is in a set of arrangements, well-worn and traditional paths of action, that older organic theories were inclined to regard as providentially given.[40]

The strength of Smith's adherence to these ideas, fundamental to the operation of the non-deliberative forces, is evidenced throughout his writing.[41] With respect to religion, in passages already quoted, Smith maintains that reverence for the general rules of morality is 'still further enhanced *by an opinion* . . . that those important rules of morality are the commands and laws of the Deity', that the prescribed rules 'are *to be regarded as* the commands and laws of the Deity', that the general rules have 'come thus *to be regarded as* the laws of an all-powerful Being', and that requires that man be '*thoroughly convinced* that all . . . are under the immediate care and protection of that great, benevolent, and all-wise Being'.[42] Throughout the *Moral Sentiments* it is clear that the process of moralization, through the internalization of the moral sentiments, is a process involving the attention on intermediate ends rather than upon ultimate confrontations; thus for example, partiality to one's own interests is check upon the 'spirit of innovation':

> It tends to preserve whatever is the established balance among the different orders and societies into which the state is divided; and while it sometimes appears to obstruct some alterations of government which may be fashionable and popular at the time, it contributes in reality to the stability and permanency of the whole system.[43]

And on the dangers of tinkering, of failing to abide by the principles of ignorance and indirection, Smith is no less explicit.[44] With respect to the role of religion as a sanction operating upon these principles, Smith is clear that the obligation 'not to hurt or disturb in any respect the happiness of our neighbour, even in those cases where no law can properly protect him' is or should be a matter of a 'sacred and religious regard'.[45] Since Smith held with Hume that the value and esteem of the 'artificial' virtues derived from their role intermediately promotive of the higher or natural virtues, including in the former 'all the virtues connected with Property',[46] it is no surprise that he refers to property as 'sacred and inviolable'.[47]

It is especially noteworthy that Smith explicitly utilizes the idea of deception itself in connection with economic activity. 'The pleasures of wealth and greatness', he tells us, ' . . . strike the imagination as something grand and beautiful and noble, of which the attainment is well worth all the toil and anxiety which we are so apt to bestow upon it. And it is well that nature imposes upon us in this manner. It is this deception which rouses and keeps in continual motion the industry of mankind.'[48] As Bonar notes, 'It is, too, "the (world's) bustle and business" that have trained "the man of real constancy and firmness", who keeps his self-control and is always mindful of his inward monitor.'[49] Moreover, these '"deceptive pleasures" find their justification or utility in the beauty of the system',[50] i.e., in order. In this and in the other respects noted, the profound significance of the non-deliberative forces is clear: Smith's doctrine is precisely 'an effort to think of the social order as a genuine organic unity, with principles of structure and functioning which maintain themselves independently of the wills of individuals'.[51]

One specific significance of this, and another facet of the operation of the non-deliberative forces, concerns the disciplining of those very 'wills of individuals'. The operation of any system of social control, by its very nature, 'disciplines' the individuals involved by governing the range and content of private choice. By disciplining is then meant the effective defining of opportunities – here economic opportunities – and consciousness, including the acceptability of one's limited range of opportunities. It has to do with, first, fitting the individual into the economy as a satisfactorily performing and satisfied economic actor, and, second, fitting the individual into the thoughtways of the time, the success of the latter being important for the success of the former. It has already been pointed out that Smith understood industry to serve as a controlling force over behaviour and traits (text at note 49, above), but Smith also saw that the individual would have to be disciplined *into* that same system of industry. Thus he contends that 'Our admiration of success is founded upon the same principle with our respect for wealth and greatness, and is equally necessary for establishing the distinction of ranks and the order of society.' Moreover, 'By this admiration of success we are taught to submit more easily to those superiors, whom the course of human affairs may assign to us; to regard with reverence, and sometimes even with a sort of respectful affection, that fortunate violence which we are no longer capable of resisting'.[52] The absolute importance of this reasoning, of the need for not only discipline in industry but also in the industrial system, cannot be discounted. The role of discipline extends to satisfy the requirements of an industrial labour market and wage system, and of the market economy itself. This is related to the need for some group in society to have an interest in and power to seek and attain greater material abundance. As de Schweinitz has indicated, 'growth during the classical period of the industrial revolution required not so much free choice for all individuals regardless of their position in society as opportunities for the capitalists at the expense of the workers and landlords. . . . The industrial labour force had been formed and was committed to the disciplinary requirements of the economic order'. Thus future economic development 'requires that a minority imbued with a growth perspective take it in hand, and regardless of individual preferences, create the institutions favorable to growth. . . . Saving must be forced out of society.'[53] Among other things, then, the moral sentiments, and their sanctions, discipline the economic actors in the process of ordering and integrating them.

Returning to the matter of primary concern, namely, the status of morals and religion as non-legal forces of social control, the classical economists other than Smith evidence much the same position. Ricardo (note 11, above) acknowledged the 'sanctions of religion' as one of the forces directing behaviour to those 'virtues' promotive of the 'general happiness'. Ricardo did not write much on morals and religion, but he liked to walk and ride with James Mill and discuss moral philosophy, as well as politics and political economy.[54] In Parliament, seconding a motion (of Joseph Hume) for free discussion of religious opinions, Ricardo acknowledged 'the moral interests of society' and the fact and need for the 'control of moral impressions'. With respect to religion, while it was not the only obligation, 'It was, in fact, one which was superadded to the general force of moral impressions – it were a libel upon human nature to say otherwise'.[55] In the discussion Ricardo was primarily interested in showing 'that the obligation of religion was not alone considered as the influential test of moral truth, and that a man might be very sceptical upon doctrinal points, and yet very positive in the control of moral impressions distinct from religious faith'. He quoted John Tillotson, former Archbishop of Canterbury, to the effect, in part, of recognizing the role of religion in inculcating the obligation to duty and as a source of restraint upon behaviour.[56] It is not surprising, therefore, to find in the essay, 'On Christianity as an Organ of Political Movement', by

Ricardo's disciple de Quincey, a clear recognition of both the moral element in economic issues and of Christianity as part of the total system of social control and social change.[57] Nor is it surprising to find McCulloch concerned over the ties of sympathy and the content of what amounts to the moral sentiments.[58]

We have recently been told that Robert Torrens 'expressed great satisfaction at . . . efforts to revive public interest in religious matters'. In a letter to the editor of the Edinburgh Review, Torrens applauded the 'symptoms of a reviving taste' for what he called 'the science of mind' and looked forward to 'the national intellect . . . [engaging] in profound enquiries and . . . metaphysical studies again prevalent among our educated classes'.[59]

But the most extensive attention, next to Smith, given to morals and religion by classical economists was rendered by Jeremy Bentham and John Stuart Mill (who reflected the views of his father). In the writings of both of these men, the necessity of a system of morals, and of some religion as a sanctioning force, was clearly acknowledged. It is unfortunate that important but essentially tangential or marginal differences between them and other writers on the subjects have obscured the great sophistication they clearly possessed. While they were critics of the established churches and not sympathetic to components of the extant moral code considered out-of-date,[60] and while both were exponents of rational or humanist religion and were, further, exponents of more extensive deliberate legal participation than many consider 'classical', it remains true that in their respective total systems the non-legal forces have an important place.[61] They appreciated that freedom was freedom only within the context of the larger pattern of freedom and control.

It is necessary to understand that Bentham's felicific calculus, the pleasure-pain principle, considered only in respect to morals or ethics, was not a complete system. Its significance lies not as a self-contained ethical system but rather as a manifestation of an underlying quest for reasoned knowledge as the basis of action, both private and public, with the calculations of pleasure and pain, as he put it, serving to force reasoned analysis of alternatives. The felicific calculus is thus a manifestation of the transition from non-deliberative to deliberative collective and private decision making.[62] The significant point for present purposes is the place nonetheless left for the non-deliberative forces. To Bentham, the *content* of pleasure and pain would be given or conditioned by, among other things, the operation of the system of morals and religion. Social interaction, and perforce internalized controls (i.e., customary morals) is the relevant force, not the autonomous individual, however relevant the latter is in other respects and for other problems.

In the third chapter of his *Introduction to the Principles of Morals and Legislation*,[63] having discussed in the preceding chapters 'the principle of utility' and 'principles adverse to that of utility', Bentham examines 'the four sanctions or sources of pain and pleasure', namely, the physical, political, moral and religious, which are the 'sources from which pleasure and pain are in use to flow'.[64] Considering the origin of the word 'sanction', Bentham relates that 'Sanctio, in Latin, was used to signify the act of binding, and, by a common grammatical transition, any thing which serves to bind a man: to wit, to observance of such or such a mode of conduct [italics deleted] and that 'among the Romans, with a view to inculcate into the people a persuasion that such or such a mode of conduct would be rendered obligatory upon a man by the force of what I call the religious sanction'.[65] 'A Sanction then', says Bentham, 'is a source of obligatory powers or *motives*: That is, of *pains* and *pleasures*; which according as they are connected with such or such modes of conduct, operate, and are indeed the only things which can operate, as *motives*.'[66] All of the four sanctions 'can be experienced in the present life', and 'from each of these sources may flow all the pleasures or pains of which, in the course of the present life, human nature is susceptible. With regard to . . . any one of those sanctions, [they] differ not ultimately in kind from those which belong to any of the other three: the only difference there is among them lies in the circumstances that accompany their production'.[67] Thus the sanctions (for present purposes, the non-legal *vis-à-vis* the legal) have a common basis in their functioning as forces of social control notwithstanding the different 'circumstances that accompany their production', i.e., their genesis. Bentham has a place for morals, then, as well as the other sanctions,[68] and it is particularly instructive in this regard that he defines *ethics* in terms generic to social control analysis:

> Ethics at large may be defined, the art of directing men's actions to the production of the greatest possible quantity of happiness, on the part of those whose interest is in view.[69]

Bentham's utilitarianism, placed in proper perspective, must have an appropriate place for morals as an instrument of social control. Davidson quite correctly holds that 'Bentham insists that, in a civilized community, conduct is moulded for us in large measure by convention and society, and that social rules are generated and laws enacted embodying results of actions as they have been crystallized by centuries of experience, so that individual deliberate calculation is rather the exception than the rule.'[70] Clearly this statement applies equally to Smith as to Bentham. And further note Leslie Stephen with respect to Bentham's utilitarianism: '"The dictates of utility", as he (Bentham) observes, are simply the "dictates of the most extensive and enlightened (that is, *well advised*) benevolence".'[71]

Bentham's moral sanction, though his language is ambiguous,[72] appears to be essentially that of Smith's moral sentiments, i.e., through social interaction, or experience. While his specific definition of the religious sanction is ambiguous with respect to the theology involved,[73] the role of religion as a sanction, i.e., as an instrument of social control, is clear. ' . . . what place is left for *religion*?', asked Bentham and his answer was that religion could serve for social control purposes in a manner beyond the power of the state:

> But whether or no a man has done the act which renders him an object meet for punishment or reward, the eyes of those, whosoever they be, to whom the management of these engines is entrusted cannot always see, nor, where it is punishment that is to be administered, can their hands be always sure to reach him. To supply these deficiencies in point of power, it is thought necessary, or at least *useful* (without which the *truth* of the doctrine would be nothing to the purpose), to inculcate into the minds of the people the belief of the existence of a power applicable to the same purposes, and not liable to the same deficiencies: the power of a supreme invisible being, to whom a disposition of contributing to the same ends to which the several institutions already mentioned are calculated to contribute, must for this purpose be ascribed. It is of course expected that this power will, at one time or other, be employed in the promoting of those ends: and to keep up and strengthen this expectation among men, is spoken of as being the employment of a kind of allegorical personage, feigned, as before, for convenience of discourse, and styled *religion*. To diminish, then, or misapply the influence of religion, is *pro tanto* to diminish or misapply what power the state has of combating with effect any of the before-enumerated kinds of offences; that is, all kinds of offences whatsoever. Acts that appear to have this tendency may be styled *offences against religion*.[74]

Indeed, Bentham considered 'the ministers of religion . . . as charged with the maintenance of one of the sanctions of morality (the religious sanction) . . . They are a body of inspectors and teachers of morals, who form, so to speak, the advanced guard of the law; who possess no power over crime, but who combat with the vices out of which crimes spring; and who render the exercise of authority more rare, by maintaining good conduct and subordination'.[75]

In an important chapter of the *Morals and Legislation* (chapter 6, 'Of Circumstances Influencing Sensibility'), which strongly shows his position affirming the circumstantial or social character of the content of the moral sentiments,[76] Bentham directly discusses the effect of varying religious beliefs upon the resolution of the basic economic problems:

> The ways in which a religion may lessen a man's means, or augment his wants, are various. Sometimes it will prevent him from making a profit of his money: sometimes from setting his hand to labour. Sometimes it will oblige him to buy dearer food instead of cheaper: sometimes to purchase useless labour: sometimes to pay men for not labouring: sometimes to purchase trinkets, on which imagination alone has set a value: sometimes to purchase exemptions from punishment, or titles of felicity in the world to come.[77]

Moreover, Stark has disclosed an instance in which Bentham was even prescriptive in regard to the content of religious preaching to be utilized for purposes of economic policy.[78]

Like Smith, then, Bentham acknowledged the usefulness[79] and operation of religion as an instrument of social control. Coupled with this rather reluctant place given to the religious sanction, was, however, an opposition to totalitarian religion,[80] an acknowledgement of the 'mischief' of religion,[81] and criticism based on the fallacy of appeal to authority,[82] as well as criticism of governmental interference with religion.[83] Morals and religion had their place, but, as with classicism as a whole, that place was in an essentially pluralist society.[84]

John Stuart Mill provides the most extensive analysis of the functioning of religion in society of all of the classicists, many facets and ramifications of which are beyond the scope of this essay. Mill's various writings demonstrate a profound appreciation of the subtleties of balancing freedom and control, and his liberalist antagonism to concentrated power, as in the form of organized religion, does not detract therefrom: his individualism and liberalism did not obscure from him the necessities of social control. This, it is suggested, is true, whatever one thinks of his personal (and inherited) liberal humanism as a partial solution to the problems of social control. One may disagree with his solution, but he *knew* the problem. Critical analysis of his writings (as, for example, *The Spirit of the Age*) clearly evidences that the younger Mill's idealism was coupled with a realism far more sophisticated than possessed by realists of lesser stature.

Mill's essay, 'On Liberty', is perhaps the most moving and eloquent plea ever composed promotive of meaningful human and individual freedom. Yet his presentation of the grand theme of liberty is not naive. He carefully indicates that the liberty that he is endeavouring to promote is not only liberty *versus* the state but liberty *within* the state. Thus Mill declares:

> Protection, therefore, against the tyranny of the magistrate is not enough: there needs protection also against the tyranny of the prevailing opinion and feeling; against the tendency of society to impose, by other means than civil penalties, its own idea and practices as rules of conduct on those who dissent from them; to fetter the development, and, if possible prevent the formation, of any individuality not in harmony with its ways, and compels all characters to fashion themselves upon the model of its own. There is a limit to the legitimate interference of collective opinion with individual independence; and to find that limit, and maintain it against encroachment, is as indispensable to a good condition of human affairs, as protection against political despotism.
>
> But though this proposition is not likely to be contested in general terms, the practical question, where to place the limit – how to make the fitting adjustment between individual independence and social control – is a subject on which nearly everything remains to be done. All that makes existence valuable to anyone, depends on the enforcement of restraints upon the actions of other people. Some rules of conduct, therefore, must be imposed, by law in the first place, and by opinion on many things which are not fit subjects for the operation of law. What these rules should be is the principal question in human affairs.[85]

Stuart Mill was an avowed critic of non-rational supernatural religion; but he was also cognizant of the necessity of moral controls. While he discounts the role of religion in connection therewith[86] and is critical of the dehumanizing and tyrannical tendencies of orthodox religion, his humanist religion (advocated as a more humane and progressive mode of control) is a sanctioning instrument nonetheless. Throughout his writings on the subject, Mill is in favour of extensive liberty for the cultivated minds or 'best informed',[87] within some social control of course, but is opposed to debilitating and oppressive controls over the rest of mankind precluding their individual development. His position on this is correlated with his defense of power-diffused pluralistic capitalism or 'competition' against the Socialists' 'declamations against competition'.[88]

On the necessity and operation of morals as an instrument of social control, Mill writes in the 'Utility of Religion':

> Undoubtedly mankind would be in a deplorable state if no principles or precepts of justice, veracity, beneficence, were taught publicly or privately, and if these virtues were not encouraged, and the opposite vices

> repressed, by the praise and blame, the favourable and unfavourable sentiments, of mankind. . . . the influence in human affairs which belongs to any generally accepted system of rules for the guidance and government of human life.[89]
>
> Over the immense majority of human beings, the general concurrence of mankind, in any matter of opinion, is all powerful. Whatever is thus certified to them, they believe with a fulness of assurance which they do not accord even to the evidence of their senses when the general opinion of mankind stands in opposition to it. When, therefore, any rule of life and duty, whether grounded or not on religion, has conspicuously received the general assent, it obtains a hold on the belief of every individual, stronger than it would have even if he had arrived at it by the inherent force of his own understanding.[90]
>
> It is reasonable to think that any system of social duty which mankind might adopt, even though divorced from religion, would have the same advantage of being inculcated from childhood, and would have it hereafter much more perfectly than any doctrine has it at present, society being far more disposed than formerly to take pains for the moral tuition of those numerous classes whose education it has hitherto left very much to chance. Now it is especially characteristic of the impressions of early education, that they possess what it is so much more difficult for later convictions to obtain – command over the feelings. . . . [and] which operate[s] through men's involuntary beliefs, feelings and desires.[91]

The inculcation of morals, as a constraint upon behaviour, is thus clearly acknowledged.

With respect to religion as one source of such inculcation, Mill would prefer a non-supernatural religion, but the sanctioning also clearly needs to be performed, and there are other roles as well. Despite the fact that there is much historical truth supporting 'these nobler spirits [who] generally assert the necessity of religion, as a teacher, if not as an enforcer, of social morality . . . that religion alone can teach us what morality is; . . . That, only when a morality is understood to come from the Gods, do men in general adopt it, rally round it, and lend their human sanctions for its enforcement',[92] Mill contends that moral truths are 'strong enough in their own evidence',[93] and that:

> The essence of religion is the strong and earnest direction of the emotions and desires towards an ideal object, recognized as of the highest excellence, and as rightfully paramount over all selfish objects of desire.

> This condition is fulfilled by the Religion of Humanity in as eminent a degree, and in as high a sense, as by the supernatural religions even in their best manifestations, and far more so than in any of their others.[94]

It is significant, then, that the 'direction' has to be done, whatever the character of the religion serving the role. Mill would have the 'moral influences' 'cultivate the unselfish feelings',[95] and 'The deeply rooted conception which every individual even now has of himself as a social being, (which) tends to make him feel it one of his natural wants that there should be harmony between his feelings and aims and those of his fellow creatures. . . . This conviction is the ultimate sanction of the greatest happiness morality.'[96] Indeed, Mill's defence of utilitarianism acknowledges the necessity of a moral system and the operation of utilitarianism as a moral system.[97]

It would be misleading, however, not to note that Mill was not as absolute about the role of supernaturalism as he sometimes seems: the realist does win out over the idealist, so far as the theory of social control is concerned. Wrote Mill: 'So long as human life is insufficient to satisfy human aspirations, so long there will be a craving for higher things, which finds its most obvious satisfaction in religion. So long as earthly life is full of sufferings, so long there will be need of consolations, which the hope of heaven affords to the selfish, the love of God to the tender and grateful.'[98] Writing of Mill's Religion of Humanity, Stephen maintains, 'That religion, "with or without supernatural sanctions", will be the religion of the future; but it will be strengthened by the feeling that we are "helping God" and supplying "co-operation" which "he, not being omnipotent, really needs".'[99] The ideas of John Stuart Mill were basically consonant with the other classicists concerning the role of *order* in human affairs (to the sophistication of his ideas on this *The Spirit of the Age* is ample testimony) and the role of morals and religion as a social cement and controlling and socializing instrument. And his personal and intellectual antipathy to deception did not preclude a place for it in his theory of social control.

The classical economists clearly acknowledged the operation of morals and religion as instruments of social control. In the same manner the later classicists exhibited a position equivalent to that of Smith as to the operation of ignorance and indirection, as well as discipline. Thus Ricardo, who adhered to the necessity of the 'sanctions of religion', also contended that it was 'essential . . . to the cause of good government, that the rights of property should be held sacred'.[100] And the same Ricardo who shared Dr Tillotson's concern over the passive and non-deliberate but necessary operation of the restraints of religion, also most certainly sympathized (in principle at least) with his friend Trower, against the background of London riots opposing a proposed Corn Law, who, (wrote Trower), 'if I were to consider this question with the eye of a *moralist*, rather than that of a *statesman*, I should strenuously recommend that employment of the public industry which leads to the peaceful pursuits of agriculture, in which

> With silent course that *no loud storms* annoy
> Glides the smooth current of domestic joy.'[101]

Nor was Ricardo alone among the post-Smithian classicists who so held: Malthus thus wrote that,

> it is so absolutely necessary for the general interests of society to consider private property as sacred,[102]

and Bentham, that,

> a state can never become rich but by an inviolable respect for property.[103]

One of the most interesting aspects of the classical approach to non-legal control relates to their partial substitution of ideas-in-general (cosmology or ideology) for what Smith included in the moral sentiments. The role as non-deliberative constraint remains the same and reflects the operation of the principles of ignorance and indirection through the pervasive influence of an Hayekian collective wisdom. In this the classicists certainly concurred with de Tocqueville, who wrote that:

> men will never cease to entertain some opinions on trust and without discussion. . . .
>
> But obviously without such common belief no society can prosper; say, rather, no society can exist; for without ideas held in common there is no common action, and without common action there may still be men, but there is no social body. In order that society should exist, and, *a fortiori*, that a society should prosper, it is necessary that the minds of all the citizens should be rallied and held together by certain predominant ideas; and this cannot be the case unless each of them sometimes draws his opinions from the common source and consents to accept certain matters of belief already formed.
>
> . . . he is reduced to take on trust a host of facts and opinions which he has not had either the time or the power to verify for himself, but which men of greater ability have found out, or which the crowd adopts. . . .
>
> A principle of authority must then always occur, under all circumstances, in some part or other of the moral and intellectual world. Its

place is variable, but a place it necessarily has. The independence of individual minds may be greater or it may be less; it cannot be unbounded. Thus the question is, not to know whether any intellectual authority exists in an age of democracy, but simply where it resides and by what standard it is to be measured.[104]

The classicists' reliance upon the non-deliberative forces indicates their general adherence to these ideas; as Hume put it, 'Though men be much governed by interest, yet even interest itself, and all human affairs, are entirely governed by *opinion*.'[105] S. G. Checkland thus wrote, 'As Malthus himself knew, it is often more important and more productive of lasting effects to condition minds than to instil in them particular ideas.'[106] But the most extensive analysis of this subject by a classical economist is to be found in Stuart Mill's *The Spirit of the Age*, wherein he substantively concurs with de Tocqueville. The importance of the essay for present purposes and for understanding Mill warrants quotation at length. The 'spirit of an age', says Mill

is deeply important: for, whatever we may think or affect to think of the present age, we cannot get out of it; we must suffer with its sufferings, and enjoy with its enjoyments; we must share in its lot, and, to be either useful or at ease, we must even partake of its character.

. . . the multitude (by which I mean the majority of all ranks) have the ideas of their own age, and no others. . . .

The proofs of these truths may be brought down to the level of even the uninformed multitude, with the most complete success. But, when all is done, there still remains something which they must always and inevitably take upon trust: and this is, that the arguments really *are* as conclusive as they appear; that there exist no considerations relevant to the subject which have been kept back from them; that every objection which can suggest itself has been duly examined by competent judges, and found immaterial.

In these circumstances the people, although they may at times be unhappy and consequently discontented, habitually acquiesce in the laws and institutions which they live under, and seek for relief through those institutions and not in defiance of them. Individual ambition struggles to ascend by no other paths than those which the law [and, we should add, institutions, particularly of the non-deliberative sort] recognizes and allows.

In endeavouring to give an intelligible notion of what I have termed the *natural* state of society, in respect of moral influence – namely, that

> state in which the opinions and feelings of the people are, with their voluntary acquiescence, formed *for* them, by the most cultivated minds which the intelligence and morality of the times call into existence.
>
> . . . howsoever defective the morality which (the early church) taught, they had at least a mission for curbing the unruly passions of mankind, and teaching them to set a value upon a distant, paramount to immediate temptations, and to prize gratifications consisting of mental feelings above bodily sensation.[107]

Mill's analysis of the *natural* and *transitional* states of society remains a most brilliant analysis in the theory of social change, in effect a theory of the conditions of *order* (*vis-à-vis* change) and of the role of the non-deliberative forces in connection therewith, relying upon the principles of ignorance and indirection through the operation of 'the spirit of the age'. And, as was seen above in connection with 'On Liberty', Mill is demonstrating that the conditions of *order* also specify the character and conditions of the *freedom* that exists coordinately. As with de Tocqueville, to whom 'salutary restraint' necessarily complemented a free society,[108] Stuart Mill argued that continuity and order required that the multitude adhere to the cosmology of the time as an indirect instrument of social control,[109] but that within its constraints free minds could pursue with a meaningful measure of independence. While 'It is, therefore, one of the necessary conditions of humanity, that the majority must either have wrong opinions, or no fixed opinions, or must place the degree of reliance warranted by reason, in the authority of those who have made moral and social philosophy their peculiar study', still, 'It is right that every man should attempt to understand his interest and his duty. It is right that he should follow his reason as far as his reason will carry him, and cultivate the faculty as highly as possible.'[110]

On the operation of discipline the views of the classicists were also essentially the same as those of Smith, as suggested, for example, by the letter of Trower to Ricardo, quoted above. Ricardo himself would have impressed 'on the poor the value of independence, by teaching them that they must look not to systematic or casual charity, but to their own exertions for support, that prudence and forethought are neither unnecessary nor unprofitable virtues'.[111] McCulloch also favoured inculcating 'the spirit of emulation, industry, and invention', and argued that discipline was necessary to induce acquiescence in the industrial order and to assure progress within the constraints of scarcity and the given industrial order. Wrote McCulloch, appreciative of the need to make the manufacturing population 'in general orderly, and disposed to respect and support the right of property and the established institutions of the country',

> Something, perhaps, may be done to strengthen the existing institutions of the country, by improving the education of the poor, and showing them how closely their interests are identified with those of their employers, and with the preservation of tranquillity and good order.
>
> By raising the intelligence of the poor, and enabling them the better to appreciate the worthlessness of the nostrums on which they are so often called to depend, and to estimate the more remote, as well as the immediate consequences of their actions, it could hardly fail to contribute materially to their advantage.

And he quotes Bentham:

> To enjoy immediately – to enjoy without labour, is the natural inclination of every man. This inclination must be restrained; for its obvious tendency is to arm all those who have nothing against those who have something. The law which restrains this inclination, and which secures to the humblest individual the quiet enjoyment of the fruits of his industry, is the most splendid achievement of legislative wisdom – the noblest triumph of which humanity has to boast.[112]

Indeed, so far as the classicists were concerned, the poor law controversy turned on the interference thereby with the disciplining forces of the market through poverty and industrial competition.[113] Bentham's criticism precisely turned on the matter of the disciplining forces of the market:

> The law which offers to poverty an assistance independent of industry, is, so to speak, a law against industry itself; or at least, against frugality. The motive to labour and economy is the pressure of present, and the fear of future, want: the law which takes away this pressure, and this fear, must be an encouragement to idleness and dissipation. This is the reproach which is reasonably brought against the greater number of establishments created for the poor.[114]

Bentham considered idleness and prodigality to be 'offenses against the national wealth', and would have relied upon the discipline of market forces, or as he called it, 'the gentle motive of reward', to promote material well-being.[115] So also with Stuart Mill, who wrote in his 'Chapters on Socialism', that

> In the case of most men the only inducement which has been found sufficiently constant and unflagging to overcome the everpresent influence of indolence and love of ease, and induce men to apply themselves unrelaxingly to work for the most part in itself dull and unexciting, is the prospect of bettering their own economic condition and that of

> their family; and the closer the connection of every increase of exertion with a corresponding increase of its fruits, the more powerful is this motive. To suppose the contrary would be to imply that with men as they now are, duty and honour are more powerful principles of action than personal interest, not solely as to special acts and forbearances respecting which those sentiments have been exceptionally cultivated, but in the regulation of their whole lives; which no one, I suppose, will affirm.[116]

Indeed, 'Education, habit, and the cultivation of the sentiments, will make a common man dig or weave for his country, as readily as fight for his country.'[117] The operation of discipline, which de Schweinitz has stressed as perhaps a *sine qua non* of economic development, was thus recognized by the classical economists as a group, and constituted one facet of the operation of the non-deliberative forces functioning as part of the system of social control conditioning the grand pattern of freedom and control.

Custom

The classicists differentiated between morals and custom. They generally referred to 'morals' in the context of discussions of social control, wherein individuals were seen as bound together, integrated and channelled; and 'custom' in contexts having to do with the import and impact of the non-deliberative forces (e.g., Smith's general rules) on particular usages affecting market forces of demand and supply. Custom would govern the structure of economic organization and condition the substance of the resolution of the basic economic problems through structuring the economic decision-making process and through influencing or conditioning the content of behaviour. In particular, customs operated on tastes, expectations, and capacities to participate as an economic factor. In their formal analysis such factors were ruled out by utilizing the logic of *ceteris paribus*. In his well-known chapter, 'Of Competition and Custom', Stuart Mill indicated the importance of this consideration when he wrote, 'that only through the principle of competition has political economy any pretension to the character of a science'.[118] The methodology of the Ricardian economic analysis has been erroneously criticized as if Ricardo *et al.* were not aware of broader considerations and other determining causes than were included in the model.

In *The Theory of Moral Sentiments* Smith devoted a short but lucid discussion to the influence of custom and fashion (which is 'a particular species'[119] of custom). In the first of two chapters comprising Part V, Smith shows the influence of custom and fashion upon the sense of what he calls 'beauty and deformity' and ergo upon what present-day economists would call *taste*. It is thus of the greatest significance for the present essay that Smith considers the operation of custom as extending to the field of consumption, or demand: his examples include dress, furniture and decoration. It is clear from these pages that Smith's analysis therein may be reduced to considering custom as a governing influence upon relative demand schedules. (The scarcity of diamonds exists, after all, because of its *customary* status whatever their value-in-use.)[120]

In the second chapter of Part V of *Moral Sentiments*, Smith discusses the influence of custom and fashion upon the moral sentiments as they relate to conduct. Smith's analysis here is not entirely clear (largely due to the ambiguity of his differentiation between morals and custom), but there is no question that custom governs the usages that are so much the stuff of life. Wrote Smith:

> But though the influence of custom and fashion upon moral sentiments, is not altogether so great, it is however perfectly similar to what it is every where else. When custom and fashion coincide with the natural principles of right and wrong, they heighten the delicacy of our sentiments, and increase our abhorence for every thing which approaches to evil.
>
> All these effects of custom and fashion, however, upon the moral sentiments of mankind, are inconsiderable, in comparison of those which they give occasion to in some other cases; and it is not concerning the general style of character and behaviour, that those principles produce the greatest perversion of judgment, but concerning the propriety or impropriety of particular usages.
>
> It is not therefore in the general style of conduct or behaviour that custom authorises the widest departure from what is the natural propriety of action. With regard to particular usages, its influence is often much more destructive of good morals, and it is capable of establishing, as lawful and blameless, particular actions, which shock the very plainest principles of right and wrong.[121]

Indeed, what people 'have been familiarized with . . . from their infancy, custom has rendered . . . habitual to them, and they are very apt to regard it as, what is called, the way of the world'.[122] (In another context, Smith argues that, 'It is absurd to preserve in people a regard for their old customs, when the causes of them are removed.')[123] Looked at another way, it is not surprising for Smith to have discussed 'the Influence of Commerce on Manners',[124] or, given the relativity of custom acknowledged in the *Moral Sentiments*, for him to write:

> The difference between the most dissimilar characters, between a philosopher and a common street porter, for example, seems to arise not so much from nature, as from habit, custom, and education.[125]

In Ricardo's *The Principles of Political Economy and Taxation*, the chapter on rent is a model of brilliant theorizing, as is the work as a whole, with scarce reference to institutional and other data. But despite the theoretical character of the *Principles*, its author is not really justifiably open to the charge that *he* neglected institutional data. His chosen task in the *Principles* was simply different from that of, say, Richard Jones in his well-known complementary work. Elsewhere Ricardo gives ample evidence in his written works to support the claim that he was a master realist whatever the structure and compass of his theory.

Thus Ricardo, in a letter to Trower, acknowledges that the pricing of the rent of land and the distribution of the proceeds is, in part to be attributed to the particular institutions of time and place.[126] But perhaps the general principle applicable to Ricardo that is relevant here was in the form of a question by Wesley Mitchell: 'And whenever there is occasion to go back of prices, are not wants standardized and made dependable for business purposes by "habits and custom"?'[127] That there is such a role for custom and habit in the Ricardian (and classical) theory of economic policy is further supported by the recognition that the level of wages in the Ricardian system depended on several factors one of which clearly was custom and habit. Indeed, Ricardo states in his *Principles* that

> It is not to be understood that the natural price of labour . . . is absolutely fixed and constant. It varies at different times in the same country, and very materially differs in different countries. It essentially depends on the habits and customs of the people.[128]

Irma Adelman concludes that 'Ricardo's natural wage rate is therefore a function of the socio-cultural environment and of the marginal productivity of land. In fact, the variations of customs and agricultural productivity with time are responsible for the time-dependent behaviour of the natural wage rate'. Discussing further the 'influence of the socio-cultural environment' in the Ricardian system, she writes: 'By affecting the economy's subjective minimal standards of living, changes in outlook and in institutions can modify the rates of growth of the labor force, of investment, and therefore of output, and the nature of the stationary state of the economy.'[129]

Moreover, Ricardo's awareness of the role of custom as a factor in the economic decision-making process is well illustrated by the following excerpt from another letter to Trower: 'Great evils however result from the idea which the Poor Laws inculcate that the poor have a *right* to relief.'[130] And in a letter to McCulloch, Ricardo demonstrated the realism with which he interpreted or applied his own basic theory:

> You think otherwise because you are of opinion that capital will be constantly drawn away from this country whilst the corn laws are in force. I acknowledge the tendency of capital to flow from us, but I think you very much overrate it. I have always said that the desire to stay in our own country is a great obstacle to be overcome.[131]

There can be no question but that custom and habit (or, differential institutions) had a place and an important place in the Ricardian theory of economic policy: custom and habit dictated much of the substance of resource allocation and income distribution, i.e., governed the operation of market forces, and comprised part of the structure of the economic decision-making process.

The foregoing interpretation is further supported by reference to Malthus and McCulloch. Both acknowledge the circumstantial character of the determination and distribution of rent,[132] and both consider that wages depend in part upon custom and habit. McCulloch, after quoting Smith to the same effect, contends that the 'natural or necessary rate of wages' depends 'essentially on the physical circumstances under which every people is placed, and on custom and habit'.[133] It is also relevant to note that it is largely through the reconstruction of custom (i.e., the preventive checks) that the possible adverse consequences of the Malthusian law of population are to be overcome. It can be said that the classicists would all have concurred in the statement that beneficial changes in customs, together with improvement of the 'moral and intellectual condition of mankind',[134] would have operated to improve the economic and social conditions of both higher and lower orders of humanity.

Passing to Bentham, it is clear that just as the operation of the greatest happiness principle was conditioned on the moral and religious sanctions, so also was the content of the solutions to the problems of man achieved by using the felicific calculus also dependent upon custom and its role in providing continuity. Bentham was aware of the mantle of custom and the fixity of authority bestowed by habit, just as he recognized that the accumulation of property required the appropriate customs (and laws) to produce security.[135] Moreover, his emphasis on gradual change (characteristic of all the classicists, including Stuart Mill) related in part to his cognizance of the importance of custom.[136] As a matter of general principle, Bentham and the other classicists emphasized that the structure of the decision-making process that was the market economy required reliance upon custom, as Mitchell stated in the case of Ricardo. Writing of the principle of utility, Lord Robbins has contended that

> It was perfectly consistent with this principle to attach, as indeed there was attached, the greatest value to stable institutions and general rules of conduct. The greatest happiness was not the greatest happiness at the moment, but the greatest happiness over time; and, on the basis of this principle, the most powerful arguments could be deployed in favour of security of expectation and consistency in behavior, which in turn afforded strong grounds for more or less settled codes of law and morals. On the utilitarian outlook, social arrangements were not provisional in the sense that they were liable to day-to-day change and upset; they were provisional only in the sense that they were all liable to the ultimate test of their ability to promote human happiness.[137]

Perhaps the most intense sentiment on the role of custom was held by John Stuart Mill. First, Mill is at one with the other classicists in holding that custom is important in determining the structure of property rights, and thereby the structure of private participation in the economy.[138] Second, Mill contended that, unlike the production of wealth, the distribution of wealth is a matter of institutions. In his chapter on property, Mill wrote:

> The distribution of wealth, therefore, depends on the laws and customs of society. The rules by which it is determined are what the opinions and feelings of the ruling portion of the community make them, and are very different in different ages and countries; and might be still more different, if mankind so chose.[139]

This position is reflected in his consideration of rent, which he held to be regulated by custom.[140] Third, and most general, for his analysis extends in effect to both income distribution and resource allocation, Mill contends that custom is coordinate with competition (by which he meant the operation of market forces) in governing the resolution of the basic economic problems. In his chapter 'Of Competition and Custom', Mill accepts the practice by political economists of assuming competition as the field of their concern: 'The political economist justly deems this his proper business: and as an abstract or hypothetical science, political economy cannot be required to do, and indeed cannot do, anything more.' 'But', he goes on to say, 'it would be a great misconception of the actual course of human affairs, to suppose that competition exercises in fact this unlimited sway'. This is because there are cases 'in which the result is not determined by competition, but by custom or usage'. In these cases, competition 'rather acts, when it acts at all, as an occasional disturbing influence; the habitual regulator is custom, modified from time to time by notions existing in the minds of purchasers and sellers of some kind of equity or justice'. Thus, 'Where competition, though free to exist, does not exist, or where it exists, but has its natural consequences overruled by any other agency, the conclusions will fail more or less of being applicable',[141] unless the operation of custom etc. is brought into account. The matter of methodology is, as indicated above, not presently important. What is decisive is the recognition, for purposes of the classical theory of economic policy, that custom is one of the forces comprising the decision-making structure of the market economy and governing the play of market forces.

Education

To the classical economists, the provision of education was one one of the crucial functions of society whether instruction be handled privately or institutionally. As a matter of fact, the classicists' understanding of the importance of education was responsible for their unanimous holding that the provision of instruction be a preeminent function of the state. Seen against the context of the preceding pages, the provision of education, which is so inextricably bound up with the role of knowledge in society, reflects the profoundly complex problems of freedom and control, and continuity and change. Thus the classicists acknowledged that education was a social control force operating through the inculcation of individuals in the prevailing moral code, training individuals for a place in the status quo, and impressing upon individuals the existent cosmology within the constraints of which private thought takes place. Yet this understanding of the role of education as an instrument of social control was coupled with the fervent desire for pluralism shown, for example, in Stuart Mill's 'On Liberty', and with a vision that education could provide *the* means whereby future if not present generations of the common man could improve their intellectual, social, political and material status.[142] Not many of the other classicists shared Stuart Mill's hopes for cooperativism, but they all shared the view that progress for the common man required his education, and perhaps all were aware that education, by redistributing opportunity, was a means of social transformation. Here, however, the concern is mainly with one facet of this complex area, the role of education as a non-deliberative force of social control.

In the *Moral Sentiments*, the promulgation and dissemination of the general rules of morality is essentially an educative process such that the foregoing discussion of Smith's notions of the social control function of morals is, in effect, appropriate here. Both the logic and the importance of Smith's ideas thereon are well underscored by the following terse but seminal line from the *Moral Sentiments*: 'The great secret of education is to direct vanity to proper objects.'[143] Perhaps no other single sentence from any work by a classicist so well illustrates and specifies the role of the non-legal forces of social control in the market system: freedom to choose is freedom only within the pattern and range of choice allowed or inculcated by the society within which the choosing individual lives.

In both the *Lectures* and *The Wealth of Nations* Smith called for the utilization of education as a remedy for some of the disadvantages of an industrial civilization.[144] It is in the concluding paragraph of the relevant section of *The Wealth of Nations* that Smith expresses most clearly the social control role of education in a society that is 'free' only in the context of the constraints of that control:

> The same thing may be said of the gross ignorance and stupidity which, in a civilized society, seem so frequently to benumb the understandings of all the inferior ranks of people. A man without the proper use of the intellectual faculties of a man, is, if possible more contemptible than even a coward, and seems to be mutilated and deformed in a still more essential part of the character of human nature. Though the state was to derive no advantage from the instruction of the inferior ranks of people, it would still deserve its attention that they should not be altogether uninstructed. The state, however, derives no inconsiderable advantage from their instruction. The more they are instructed, the less liable they are to the delusions of enthusiasm and superstition, which, among ignorant nations, frequently occasion the most dreadful disorders. An instructed and intelligent people besides, are always more decent and orderly than an ignorant and stupid one. They feel themselves, each individually more respectable, and more likely to obtain the respect of their lawful superiors, and they are therefore more disposed to respect those superiors. They are more disposed to examine, and more capable of seeing through, the interested complaints faction and sedition, and they are, upon that account, less apt to be misled into any wanton or unnecessary opposition to the measures of government. In free countries, where the safety of government depends very much upon the favourable judgment which the people may form of its conduct, it must surely be of the highest importance that they should not be disposed to judge rashly or capriciously concerning it.[145]

It is a manifestation of this view of the social control role of education that Ricardo wrote to McCulloch,

> I have long been convinced that our security for good government must rest on the institutions themselves, and the influence under which those who govern us act, and not on the more or less virtue in the character of our governors. The conduct of two different sets of men educated nearly in the same manner, acting under the same checks, and with the same objects in view, as far as their own personal interest is concerned, cannot be materially different.[146]

Malthus also saw education as necessary to raise the 'standard of wretchedness' and to 'chasten' individuals by inculcating individuals in the ways of the time; indeed, Bonar would have Malthus hold that 'education will not do its perfect work if it has not included the particular doctrines which it has fallen to me more than any man to bring home to the public mind'.[147] The Reverend Malthus must have been quite sophisticated in these matters.

McCulloch, who sincerely desired the improvement in the conditions of the working classes that they themselves variously sought, was afraid of the disorders accompanying this quest by the workers, and, in his *Principles*, indicated the danger to order from education itself reducing the sentiments of resignation and generating discontent, radicalism, and in particular Chartism. Education, he says, is valuable,

> but it is by no means clear that it is at all calculated to reconcile the labouring classes to their lot. A stupid or an ignorant individual most commonly regards the privations incident to his situation as the effect of circumstances beyond human control, and submits to them as to the dispensations of Providence, without reflection or murmur; but he who is instructed, who is acquainted with the constitution of society, and with the privileges and advantages enjoyed by other classes, will not be so apathetic, nor, probably, so resigned to his fate. We are not, we confess, of the number of those who can contemplate the condition and prospects of the labourers in our great manufacturing towns without serious apprehensions . . . workmen have less chance than formerly of advancing themselves. . . . But, under these circumstances, can anything be more natural, than that instructed workmen, who are thus condemned as it were to perpetual helotism, to continued poverty and hard labour, should become discontented?

It is a few lines after this that McCulloch writes,

> Something, perhaps, may be done to strengthen the existing institutions of the country, by improving the education of the poor, and showing them how closely their interests are identified with those of their employers, and with the preservation of tranquillity and good order. But,

after all, we incline to think that but little stress can be safely laid on education. A man must have a lively and grateful sense of the advantages he derives from established institutions before any species of training will make him anxious for their preservation.

These passages are from his chapter dealing with the different employments of capital and labour; in a chapter on the education of the poor in the same work, McCulloch relates how he would counter the foregoing tendency, and it is not by having the poor remain uninstructed:

> it is most for the interest of the poor, as well as of the other classes, that they should be well informed. To render education productive of all the utility that may be derived from it, the poor should, in addition to the elementary instruction now alluded to, be made acquainted with the duties enjoined by religion and morality, and with the circumstances which occasion that gradation of ranks and inequality of fortunes that usually exist; and they should be impressed, from their earliest years, with a conviction of the important truth, that they are, in a great measure, the arbiters of their own fortune; that what others can do for them is but little compared with what they may do for themselves; and that the most tolerant and liberal Government, and the best institutions, cannot shield them from poverty and degradation, without the exercise of a reasonable degree of forethought, frugality, and good conduct, on their part.

(This view is clearly consonant with that interpretation of the Malthusian doctrine on population which has it not a statement of inevitable adversity and thereby pessimism but which sees in it a statement of the conditions (or some of them) necessary for the improvement of the life of the masses.) But, says McCulloch,

> It would be unreasonable, indeed, to expect that it should produce any very immediate effect on their habits; and we are not of the number of those who expect that any system of education will ever ensure tranquillity in periods of distress, or that it will obviate the vicissitudes and disorders inherent in the manufacturing system. But . . . the harvest of sound instruction . . . [by] raising the intelligence of the poor, and enabling them the better to appreciate the worthlessness of the nostrums on which they are so often called to depend, and to estimate the more remote, as well as the immediate consequences of their actions, . . . could hardly fail to contribute materially to their advantage.[148]

The danger to order is thus not averted, but education, argues McCulloch, can contribute to both order and progress in a compatible manner; what is instructive here is the role of education as social control instrumental in securing both order and progress.

Jeremy Bentham was also cognizant of the possible ill effects of education,[149] but he also supported governmental education as control promotive of morality but within the constraints of a free society.[150] His understanding of the role of education as the inculcator of the cosmology of the time and place has been well put by Mitchell: 'Since whatever is amiss in the opinions or conduct of mankind is due to "intellectual weakness, indigenous or adoptive", education must be the one great agency of reform. And since the understanding is made up of associations among ideas, the forming and strengthening of proper associations must be the one great aim of education.'[151] James Mill, of course, was instrumental in the development of associationism.

John Stuart Mill, his idealism notwithstanding, is basically at one with his predecessor and contemporary classicists on the role of education as an instrument of social control. In his posthumously published 'Chapters on Socialism', Mill applauded the gradual improvement in the intellectual character of man through education to transcend the necessities of market inducements to effort;[152] and in his *Autobiography* he seconds his father's views on the matter:

> In psychology, his fundamental doctrine was the formation of all human character by circumstances, through the universal Principle of Association, and the consequent unlimited possibility of improving the moral and intellectual condition of mankind by education. Of all his doctrines none was more important than this, or needs more to be insisted on: unfortunately there is none which is more contradictory to the prevailing tendencies of speculation, both in his time and since.[153]

But, as has been seen above in other respects, Mill coupled his optimism with realism, and his quest for meaningful freedom with an understanding of the operation of the social control system. Thus, in the 'Utility of Religion', the main theme of which has already been stated, Mill asks,

> consider next how tremendous is the power of education; how unspeakable is the effect of bringing people up from infancy in a belief, and in habits founded on it.
>
> . . . what vast efficacy belongs naturally to any doctrine received with tolerable unanimity as true, and impressed on the mind from the earliest childhood as duty.[154]

> The power of education is almost boundless: there is not one natural inclination which it is not strong enough to coerce, and, if needful, to destroy by disuse.[155]

CONCLUSION

This essay has had a relatively limited objective, and, underscoring Schneider, 'it would be a gross misinterpretation of the paper to take it as a paean in praise of ignorance';[156] rather, with Robbins, the aim has been 'to describe and to analyse rather than to judge'.[157]

Classical economics was an attempt to provide a meaningful understanding of the market economy, perhaps of economic life in general, that would comprise a body of knowledge capable of serving as the basis of policy. In this the concern of the classicists was with the role of the deliberative action or inaction of the state and that it be appropriate given the classical body of knowledge of the economy. Clearly, then, the classicists were preoccupied with the governmental or legal facet of the theory of economic policy. But it has been the limited objective of this essay to demonstrate the classical acknowledgement of the non-legal forces of social control, and the important role attributed thereto, and therefore the necessity and meaningfulness of including such non-legal forces as an additional facet of the classical theory of economic policy.

This requires the extension or broadening of the definitional scope of 'theory of economic policy' in the case of the classicists at least, to include the non-legal forces. The classicists were aware, or their analysis may be reduced to the proposition, that the economy *in toto* is a decision-making process in which both private, legal and non-legal participating forces interact and together resolve the basic economic problems within the constraints of the dual problems of 'freedom and order' and 'continuity and change'. By 'theory of economic policy' must be meant, then, the principles of the respective roles of all the participants in the economic decision-making process.

The economy of the classical economists was a market system with primarily individual participation. Critics of classicism have long objected (among other things) to a supposed tendency to anarchism, or failure to appreciate the claims and problems of order. If the classicists had merely premised some natural beneficent harmony of interests or of results, the criticism would have merit. But *Harmonielehre* has no central place in the classical theory of economic policy. Rather the foregoing paragraphs indicate that whatever the role of government in the economy attributed to the classicists, and even aside from 'competition', there would not be chaos; and, further, that competition (by which the classicists meant the market system) itself depends for its orderly process and the content of its decisions upon the functioning of the non-legal forces. Insofar as the market-plus-framework interpretation is meaningful, the non-legal component of the framework is clearly of coordinate importance with any other facet; for example, the market considered independently of the role of government, or government *per se*. Professor Knight's criticism[158] of institutionalists for ostensibly having ignored the historically developed and largely non-deliberative institutions (however appropriate a criticism of the institutionalist) should be translated into praise for the classicists for their appreciation of such institutions. This is required notwithstanding the Ricardian methodology.

It has been seen that the non-deliberative forces were, in the consensus of the classicists, in part at least, responsible for the maintenance of order, for the achievement of social control constraining individual behaviour. Moreover, the non-legal forces and their promulgating and sanctioning complements, with which they are often indistinguishable, are in many respects responsible for the specific content of the market resolution of the basic economic problems. To the extent that government is passive and the forces of demand and supply operate, relatively wide scope, however unobtrusive, is given to the non-legal forces, no less in the modern than in the medieval age, though the genesis of the non-legal forces is at present more diffused. The non-legal forces may also be said to comprise and shape not only the content of resource allocation but also the structure of the decision-making process operating to resolve the basic economic problems and thereby both directly and indirectly influence the resolution of those problems.

The theory of economic policy defined as suggested above has to do with the structuring of the economic decision-making process as a whole and thereby with the way in which society organizes for and controls economic development. It is not surprising, then, nor inappropriate to note, that economists increasingly concerned over problems of economic development have returned to the classical view of the economic problem, which after all was how to increase the material well-being of nations.[159] Students of economic development theory and policy have learned anew the lessons of Weber and Tawney that were known to the classicists: that economic development requires recourse to the non-deliberative forces of social control and social change.[160] Finally, it is a tribute to the genius of the institutionalists, primarily of the Commons–Witte variety, that they were preoccupied with the problems of institution building that are at the heart of promoting economic development; what Usher says of the classicists is equally applicable to the instutitionalists whatever one thinks of the content of their respective contributions, for both groups 'made substantial contributions to state policy designed to develop or modify private institutions essential to economic activity'.[161]

Notes

1. Lionel Robbins, *The Theory of Economics Policy in English Classical Political Economy*, hereafter cited as *Theory of Economic Policy* (London: Macmillan, 1953), p. 2.
2. *Theory of Economic Policy*, e.g., pp. 190–1. See also B. A. Corry, *Money, Saving and Investment in English Economics, 1800–1850* (New York: St Martin's Press, 1962), p. 71. For a critique of the market-plus-framework approach, see S. G. Checkland, 'The Prescriptions of the Classical Economists', *Economica*, n.s., vol. 20 (1953), pp. 68–72.
3. It is no accident that two outstanding contemporary advocates of the classical tradition of economic liberalism, Frank H. Knight and F. A. Hayek, both stress the unobtrusive workings of the non-deliberative forces. *In re* Wilhelm Roepke, see notes 10 and 12, below. Hayek, however, concludes that the non-legal forces are important only in the case of Adam Smith, and that 'the classical economists of the nineteenth century, or at least the Benthamites or philosophical radicals among them', had much less and perhaps progressively less of a place for them, coming increasingly to emphasize deliberateness and conscious design. It will be seen below that there is a much greater degree of consonance among the classicists in these matters than Hayek envisions. Friedrich A. Hayek, *Individualism and Economic Order* (Chicago Ill.: The University of Chicago Press, 1948), p. 4; see pp. 11, 26, 28–29. Compare Overton H. Taylor, *The Classical Liberalism, Marxism and the Twentieth Century* (Cambridge, Mass.: Harvard University Press, 1960), p. 26.
4. The notion of harmony was, like that of the labour theory of value, 'among the shibboleths of the time, a convenient weapon against mercantilist thinking'. M. Blaug, *Economic Theory in Retrospect* (Homewood, Ill.: Richard Irwin, 1962), p. 52. But the 'idea that individuals, each following his own interest, created laws as impersonal, or at least as anonymous, as those of the natural sciences was arresting. And the belief that these must be socially beneficial quickened the spirit of optimism that was a feature of the revolution in industry'. T. S. Ashton, *The Industrial Revolution, 1760–1830* (London: Oxford University Press, 1948), p. 139. The crucial question for policy analysis is of course 'harmony of interests' by what criteria, on what terms, and in the context of what system of social control (or decision making process). Moreover, the ideas of an invisible hand or of a pre-existent and pre-eminent order or of harmony itself, were epistemologically either mere assertion or hypothesis. The history of subsequent economic thought may be

viewed as efforts aiming at the specification of the conditions of mutuality or harmony of interests.

5. *Theory of Economic Policy*, pp. 25, 26, 28–29.
6. Ibid., pp. 55, 57. Compare Checkland, 'Prescriptions of the Classical Economists', p. 71.
7. The sophistication of the classicists concerning social control was at least equalled by their sophistication concerning the dynamics of social change. An analysis of the classical theory of social change is beyond the scope of this essay.
8. Compare, for example, the views of Edwin Cannan and Karl de Schweinitz, Jr. Wrote Cannan: 'Throughout history society has been fashioning and modifying its institutions so as to make it the interest of its members to do the right thing . . . the very fact which Smith ignored, namely, that such harmony as is found between the pursuit of self-interest and the general good is dependent on the existence of suitable human institutions. . . . (Smith) failed to see that self-interest had been put in the shafts and harnessed by law and order, products of collective wisdom' ('Adam Smith as an Economist', *Economica*, vol. 6 (1926), pp. 132–3, 134). But compare de Schweinitz: 'Unlike neo-classical economics, classical economics never was far removed from the social and political institutions which formed the framework of economic activity . . . the classical economists could not take the institutional framework of the economy for granted, simply because it too was being transformed. Especially could they not take for granted the maintenance of social order, so severe were the strains imposed on the community by the industrial revolution. The classical economists, therefore, were very much aware of the coercive relationships of economic and social organization and not inclined to apply freedom to the former indiscriminately. Adam Smith, for example, was not so far convinced of the harmony of interests in society that he lost sight of the coercive role of the state' ('Free Enterprise in a Growth World', *Southern Economic Journal*, vol. 29 (1962), p. 105). See also notes 10 and 12, below .
9. *Theory of Economic Policy*, pp. 41–2, 56.
10. Writing of *The Theory of Moral Sentiments*, Glenn R. Morrow concludes that, 'It is because the individual is in his very nature socialized, a product of the social environment, that he can in general be left without external interference to act in accordance with the demands of his individual nature' (*Adam Smith, 1776–1926* (Chicago, Ill.: University of Chicago Press, 1928), p. 178). And Wilhelm Roepke: 'The market is only one section of society. It is a very important section, it is true, but still one whose existence is justifiable and possible only because it is part of a larger whole which concerns not economics but philosophy, history, and theology. . . . Adam Smith, whose fame rests not only on his *Wealth of Nations* but also on his *Theory of Moral Sentiments*, would have known better' (*A Humane Economy: The Social Framework of the Free Market* (Chicago, Ill.: Regnery Co., 1960), p. 92). For similar interpretations of the *Theory of Moral Sentiments* and of Smith in general, see Henry J. Bittermann, 'Adam Smith's Empiricism and the Law of Nature', *Journal of Political Economy*, vol. 48 (1940), pp. 487–520, 703–34; Albert Salamon, 'Adam Smith as Sociologist', *Social Research*, vol. 12 (1945), pp. 22–42; J. Bonar, '"The Theory of Moral Sentiments", by Adam

Smith, 1759'. *Journal of Philosophical Studies* (now *Philosophy*), vol. 1 (1926), pp. 333–53; A. L. Macfie, 'Adam Smith's *Moral Sentiments* as Foundation for his *Wealth of Nations*', *Oxford Economic Papers*, n.s. vol. 11 (1959), pp. 209–228; Nathan Rosenberg, 'Some Institutional Aspects of the *Wealth of Nations*', *Journal of Political Economy*, vol. 68 (1960), pp. 557–70; and K. W. Kapp, *The Social Costs of Private Enterprise* (Cambridge, Mass.: Harvard University Press, 1950), pp. 28–9. See also Jacob Viner, 'Bentham and J. S. Mill: The Utilitarian Background', *American Economic Review*, vol. 39 (1949), pp. 365, 367; William D. Grampp. 'On the Politics of the Classicial Economists', *Quarterly Journal of Economics*, vol. 62 (1948), pp. 730–1, 741–2; Overton H. Taylor, *Economics and Liberalism* (Cambridge, Mass.: Harvard University Press, 1955), chs 2 and 3, and *The Classical Liberalism, Marxism and the Twentieth Century*, pp. 26, 27, 96, 97; and William L. Davidson, *Political Thought in England* (New York: Holt, n.d.), p. 17.

11. J. R. McCulloch (ed.), *The Works of David Ricardo* (London: John Murray, 1881), p. 554. See also W. Stark, *Jeremy Bentham's Economic Writings* (New York: Burt Franklin, 1954), vol. 3, p. 311; and James Mill, 'An Essay on Government', in Edwin A. Burtt (ed), *The English Philosophers from Bacon to Mill* (New York: Modern Library, 1939), p. 858.

12. Thus Roepke quotes Burke: 'Society cannot exist unless a controlling power upon will and appetite be placed somewhere, and the less of it there is within, the more there must be without.' (Roepke, *A Humane Economy*, p. xiii.) In the *Moral Sentiments* Smith wrote: 'What institution of government could tend so much to promote the happiness of mankind as the general prevalence of wisdom and virtue? All government is but an imperfect remedy for the deficiency of these' (Adam Smith, *Essays Philosphical and Literary* (London: Ward, Lock, & Co., 1880), p. 165). (Hereafter cited as *Essays*.) A number of writers compare Smith's 'natural' identicity of interests with Bentham's 'artificial' identicity of interests (J. Bartlet Brebner, 'Laissez Faire and State Intervention in Nineteenth-Century Britain', *Journal of Economic History*, vol. 8, Supplement (1948), pp. 61–3; Elie Halevy, *The Growth of Philosophic Radicalism* (Boston, Mass.: Beacon Press, 1955), pp. 88–120; Wesley C. Mitchell, *The Backward Art of Spending Money* (New York: Kelley, 1950), pp. 195–6. See also *Theory of Economic Policy*, pp. 188–92; Viner, 'The Utilitarian Background', pp. 368–70; and Overton H. Taylor, *A History of Economic Thought* (New York: McGraw-Hill, 1960), pp. 131, 133). All of the classical economists contemplated the use of both the deliberative and non-deliberative forces of social control, but with relatively greater emphasis on the latter. The idea of 'natural', defined as inevitable is simply wrong or question-begging (see John Stuart Mill, 'Utilitarianism', in Burtt, *The English Philosophers*, pp. 919–20; Leslie Stephen, *The English Utilitarians* (New York: Peter Smith, 1950), vol. III, pp. 436–7; William Ashley, 'A Retrospect of Free-Trade Doctrine', *Economic Journal*, vol. 34 (1925), pp. 502, 513; and Taylor, *Economics and Liberalism*, chs 2, 3); conceived as independent of legal controls, logically allows for the role of the non-deliberative forces but fails to specify their existence – a frequent and misleading practice. With respect to Bentham, it will be seen below that he had no unimportant place for religion, morals, custom and education (see,

e.g., G. W. Keeton and G. Schwarzenberger (eds), *Jeremy Bentham and the Law: A Symposium* (London: Stevens, 1948), essay by A. J. Ayer, at p. 253, and see text at note 75, below); and with respect to Smith, Rosenberg has contended that 'Smith's search [was] for an institutional scheme which will establish and enforce an identity of interests between the public and private spheres', and that 'Far from assuming a "spontaneous" identity of interests (in the mere absence of government restrictions) . . . Smith was obsessed with the urge to go beyond the ordinary market-structure definition of competition and to evaluate the effectiveness of different institutional forms in *enforcing* this identity' (Rosenberg, 'Institutional Aspects', pp. 567, 559; see Taylor, *Economics and Liberalism*, pp. 92–5). See also Irma Adelman, *Theories of Economic Growth and Development* (Stanford, Calif.: Stanford University Press, 1961), p. 28; and V. B. Singh, 'Adam Smith's Theory of Economic Development', *Science and Society*, vol. 23 (1959), pp. 108–9, 113. (Also see below.) If there is any meaning to the differentiation between Smith and Bentham, it is not that of an automatic *vis-à-vis* artificial harmony, for both adhered to the *createdness* and ergo 'artificiality' of harmony, but on the basis of Bentham's great*er* reliance upon law: but note Smith's emphasis upon the dependence of private property on law. (See de Schweinitz, 'Free Enterprise', pp. 105–6; and William D. Grampp, 'Adam Smith and the Economic Man', *Journal of Political Economy*, vol. 56 (1948), pp. 326–7.)

13. Thus Mortimer J. Adler considers Smith, Bentham and Stuart Mill as adhering to what Adler calls the 'circumstantial self-realization' concept of freedom, the circumstances in part depending upon the pattern of legal and non-legal controls (*The Idea of Freedom* (Garden City, N. Y.: Doubleday, 1958), e.g., pp. 592–3, 226–7, 234–5). See also Rosenberg, 'Institutional Aspects', p. 567; Grampp, 'Adam Smith and the Economic Man', pp. 326, 332, 335, 336; and de Schweinitz, 'Free Enterprise'.
14. The material comprising the substance of this paper is evidence of the classical recognition or premise of the social and situational character of man. In addition to the articles by Salomon, Rosenberg, Macfie, Bonar, Morrow, etc., cited above, note 10, see also H. M. Robertson, 'The Adam Smith Tradition' (London: Oxford University Press, 1950), p. 12; Davidson, *Political Thought in England*, pp. 65–7; Joseph J. Spengler, 'Adam Smith's Theory of Economic Growth', Part I, *Southern Economic Journal*, vol. 25 (1959), notes 1, 10, 14, 67; Burtt, *The English Philosophers*, pp. 919, 920; *Autobiography of John Stuart Mill* (New York: Columbia University Press, 1924), p. 75; and Adam Smith, *An Inquiry into the Nature and Causes of the Wealth of Nations*, hereafter cited as *The Wealth of Nations* (New York: Modern Library, 1937), p. 726.
15. See, e.g., Adam Smith, *Lectures on Justice, Police, Revenue and Arms*, hereafter cited as *Lectures* (New York: Kelley & Millman, 1956), pp. 35ff. and 107ff.; Jeremy Bentham, *The Limits of Jurisprudence Defined*, C. W. Everett (ed.) (New York: Columbia University Press, 1945); Harold A. Larrabee (ed.), *Bentham's 'Handbook of Political Fallacies'* (Baltimore, Md.: Johns Hopkins Press, 1952); C. K. Ogden, *Bentham's Theory of Fictions* (London: Kegan Paul, 1932), pp. 118–21; John Stuart Mill, 'Chapters on Socialism', *Fortnightly Review*, vol. 31 (1879), pp. 526–30; Philip Wheel-

wright (ed.), *Selected Writings of Jeremy Bentham, James Mill and John Stuart Mill* (Garden City, N.Y.: Doubleday, Doran & Co., 1935), pp. 211ff.

16. Mill's *Three Essays on Religion*, 3rd edn (London: Longmans, Green & Co., 1885), particularly the essay, 'Utility of Religion', his *The Spirit of the Age*, with Introductory Essay by F. A. Hayek (Chicago: University of Chicago Press, 1942), and 'Utilitarianism' (Burtt, *The English Philosophers*, pp. 895ff.), were in a sense sequels to the *Moral Sentiments*, for Mill shared Smith's humanism, his ambivalent recognition of the role of religion as an instrument of social control, and his sophistication regarding social change. The same may be said of his *Autobiography*.
17. In *The Wealth of Nations*, Smith wrote: 'In every age and country of the world men must have attended to the characters, designs, and actions of one another, and many reputable rules and maxims for the conduct of human life must have been laid down and approved by common consent' (p. 724). Smith differentiated between the moral sentiments and custom, as is being done in this study, though he says: 'But though the influence of custom and fashion upon moral sentiments, is not altogether so great, it is however perfectly similar to what it is everywhere else' (*Essays*, p. 177; see also pp. 185–7).
18. *Essays*, p. 120.
19. Ibid., pp. 139–40.
20. The different situations of different ages and countries are apt, in the same manner, to give different characters to the generality of those who live in them, and their sentiments concerning the particular degree of each quality, that is either blameable or praise-worthy, vary according to that degree which is usual in their own country, and in their own times. . . . And as this varies, according as their different circumstances render different qualties more or less habitual to them, their sentiments concerning the exact propriety of character and behaviour vary accordingly.' (Ibid., p. 181.)
21. Thus Smith states that 'situations may occur, in which it is doubtful, whether the highest propriety of conduct consists in observing or in receding from what, in ordinary cases, are the rules of our duty', (Ibid., p. 303; see also pp. 150–8, 203, 290–1; and see Bittermann, 'Adam Smith's Empiricism', p. 513.)
22. *Essays*, pp. 80–1.
23. Ibid., p. 79.
24. Ibid., p. 200. Thus 'Our respect for the great, accordingly, is most apt to offend by its excess; our fellow-feeling for the miserable, by its defect', with a resulting corruption of our moral sentiments. But, 'The distinction of ranks, the peace and order of society, are in a great measure, founded upon the respect which we naturally conceive for the former. . . . Nature has wisely judged that the distinction of ranks, the peace and order of society, would rest more securely upon the plain and palpable difference of birth and fortune, than upon the invisible and often uncertain difference of wisdom and virtue' (p. 200; see pp. 224–5).
25. 'Many men behave very decently, and through the whole of their lives avoid any considerable degree of blame, who yet, perhaps, never felt the sentiment upon the propriety of which we found our approbation of their conduct, but acted merely from a regard to what they saw were the established rules of

behaviour . . . if the regard to the general rules of conduct has been very strongly impressed upon them.' (Ibid., pp. 142–3.)
26. Ibid., pp. 143–6.
27. Ibid., p. 114.
28. *Adam Smith, 1776–1926*, p. 177. 'This theory, therefore, looks upon the individual not as an absolute and irreducible entity existing prior to social experience, but as a product of his social environment' (p. 177). 'The concrete social environment must also be taken into consideration in explaining the nature of the individual man, and Adam Smith is one of the very few thinkers of his time who had any realization of this complementary point of view. . . . 'This concrete social point of view is best expressed, not in the *Wealth of Nations*, but in the *Theory of Moral Sentiments*' (p. 172). 'In short, unregulated self-interest is no more advocated in the *Wealth of Nations* than it is in the *Moral Sentiments*, whereas in the latter work the moral value of the inferior virtues, when properly regulated, is fully recognized' (p. 167). Both the *Moral Sentiments* and the *Wealth of Nations* were part of a larger sociology and cosmology, with the former comprising essentially the analysis of the non-deliberative forces of social control within which the autonomous (or almost autonomous, save for the further control through law and competition) individual 'spontaneously' acted.
29. *Essays*, pp. 144, 145, 149–50.
30. Ibid., p. 208.
31. Ibid., p. 209; see pp. 210, 243–5.
32. Ibid., p. 210.
33. Ibid., pp. 150–1, 153.
34. Ibid., pp. 153–4, 155.
35. Ibid., p. 156.
36. *The Wealth of Nations*, p. 765. Having quoted Petty at the head of this essay, it is appropriate to note that one of his twelve criteria for promoting 'the most convenient, commodious, and comfortable livings' is 'For peace and uniformity in religion'. He criticized the proliferation of parishes and thereby of sermons, such that 'it were a miracle, if a million of sermons composed by so many men, and of so many minds and methods, should produce uniformity upon the discomposed understanding of about 8,000,000 of hearers'. He would rather have 'an uniformity of common prayer, (and) in preaching also' (Sir William Petty, *Essays on Mankind and Political Arithmetic* (London: Cassell, 1888), pp. 42, 43, 46).
37. Bittermann, 'Adam Smith's Empiricism', p. 716. 'Smith's argument, then, is that the sanctions for morals are to be found directly in human nature. . . . Religion provided an external sanction, at least in men's thought, but religion itself was in accord with basic passions of human nature' (*Loc. cit.*). On the psychological role of religion, to Smith, see pp. 716–17.
38. Louis Schneider, 'The Role of the Category of Ignorance in Sociological Theory: An Exploratory Statement', *American Sociological Review*, vol. 27 (1962), p. 493.
39. 'Durkheim's analysis has repeatedly raised the question of how effectively religion would function, or how nearly it would still have the consequences he claims for it, if the "veil" were penetrated by the ordinary participants in religious exercises. By penetration of the veil is meant the acquisition by the

participants in the exercises of the knowledge that feelings of awe and of the presence of the transcendent are simply occasioned by the attributes and constraints of society and that actions initially addressed in good faith to subjectively significant religious objects merely lead to outcomes like group solidarity. . . . But more than this: Durkheim's view was that the solidarity, cohesiveness, integration of the individual with the group, and the like, that religion brought about, were brought about indirectly. *Indirection* is the first in a set of terms bearing on ignorance that will be specified here. Social solidarity is not achieved in the religious context through a deliberative fixing of solidarity as an end to be achieved. It is achieved, in Durkheim's theory, through actions subjectively addressed to other ends, and "ends" such as solidarity are achieved in ignorance *and* indirectly' (Ibid., pp. 495–6). Schneider subsequently proceeds to an analysis of Hayek as a theorist who 'is partial to the general notion that historically evolved institutions, as they stand at any particular time, are likely to incorporate considerable "wisdom" based on past experience and reflection. This wisdom is not necessarily present to the minds of those who act in the terms of the institutions; it is indeed more likely to be unknown to them, but that does not preclude its having "beneficient" effects. From Edmund Burke to Friedrich Hayek, law, polity, language, religion, the market and other phenomena have been lauded . . . for their supposed incorporation of a wisdom that was never direct and deliberate but, rather, indirect and inadvertent. The organic, spontaneously developed institutions are opposed to deliberate, rationally constructed social arrangements . . . (and the) claim for the superiority of the organically evolved is associated with an insistence that the organically evolved institutions attain their efficacy precisely *because* they involve indirection and ignorance' (pp. 497–8).

40. Ibid., p. 498; cf. p. 500. See also Salamon, 'Adam Smith as Sociologist', p. 36; Macfie, 'Adam Smith's *Moral Sentiments*', pp. 210–11, 224–5; Morrow, *Adam Smith, 1776–1926*, pp. 171–2; and Ashley, 'Retrospect of Free-Trade Doctrine', pp. 508–9.
41. Including his interest in the formation of language: see *Essays*, pp. 305–25. Bentham also, for example, had an interest in language. John Bowring (ed.), *The Works of Jeremy Bentham* (New York: Russel & Russell, 1962), vol. 8, pp. 295–338. In both Smith's essay, 'Considerations Concerning the Formation of Language', and Bentham's 'Essay on Language', particularly the latter, one can perceive strains of language serving as a non-deliberative force shaping the cosmology of the users. See also Ogden, *Bentham's Theory of Fictions*, pp. ixff. and 7ff.
42. *Essays*, pp. 144, 145, 149, and 208. (Italics added.)
43. Ibid., p. 205; see also pp. 136, 163–4, 196–7. Note also, for example, the interesting reasoning of Stuart Mill, who 'earnestly hoped that Owenite, St Simonian, and all other anti-property doctrines might spread widely among the poorer classes; not that I thought those doctrines true, or desired that they should be acted on, but in order that the higher classes might be made to see that they had more to fear from the poor when uneducated, than when educated' (*Autobiography*, p. 121; quoted also in Hayek's introductory essay to *The Spirit of the Age*, pp. xxxi–xxxii).
44. 'The man of system . . . seems to imagine that he can arrange the different

members of a great society with as much ease as the hand arranges the different pieces upon a chess-board. He does not consider that the pieces upon the chess-board have no other principle of motion besides that which the hand impresses upon them; but that, in the great chess-board of human society, every single piece has a principle of motion of its own, altogether different from that which the legislature might choose to impress upon it. If those two principles coincide and act in the same direction, the game of human society will go on easily and harmoniously, and is very likely to be happy and successful. If they are opposite or different, the game will go on miserably, and the society must be at all times in the highest degree of disorder' (*Essays*, p. 207).

45. Ibid., p. 193.
46. Bonar, 'The Theory of Moral Sentiments', p. 347.
47. Smith, *The Wealth of Nations*, pp. 121–2. See also C. R. Fay, 'Adam Smith and the Dynamic State', *Economic Journal*, vol. 40 (1930), pp. 32–3: 'Liberty goes with justice, and both rest on the bosom of natural right, as in the frequent phrase, "evident violation of natural liberty and justice".'
48. *Essays*, p. 162. See also Bittermann, 'Adam Smith's Empiricism', p. 721; Singh, 'Theory of Economic Development', p. 128; and George J. Stigler, *Five Lectures on Economic Problems* (London: Longmans, Green & Co., 1949), p. 4.
49. Bonar, 'The Theory of Moral Sentiments', p. 342. See Smith, *Essays*, p. 48, and *Lectures*, pp. 253–5; and Cannan, 'Adam Smith as an Economist', p. 130.
50. Macfie, 'Adam Smith's *Moral Sentiments*', p. 211; See Smith, *Essays*, pp. 163–4.
51. Morrow, *Adam Smith, 1776–1926*, pp. 171–2. See Taylor, *Economics and Liberalism*, pp. 89–91.
52. *Essays*, pp. 224–5; see p. 74.
53. de Schweinitz, 'Free Enterprise', pp. 106, 107, 108, 109. 'The price system, as Smith saw it, was an intensely coercive mechanism' (Rosenberg, 'Institutional Aspects', p. 560). See also Francis A. Walker, 'Recent Progress of Political Economy in the United States', American Economic Association, *Publications*, First Series, vol. 4 (1889), p. 39; and Edwin Cannan, *A Review of Economic Theory* (London: King, 1929), p. 433.
54. Piero Sraffa (ed.), *The Works and Correspondence of David Ricardo* (Cambridge: Cambridge University Press, 1952), vol. 9, p. 377.
55. Ibid., vol. 5, pp. 325–6, 327, 328.
56. Ibid., p. 328. The quote from Tillotson reads as follows: 'As for most of those restraints which Christianity lays upon us, they are so much both for our private and public advantage, that, setting aside all considerations of religion, and of the rewards and punishments of another life, they are really good for us; and if God had not laid them upon us, we ought in reason, in order to our temporal benefit and advantage to have laid them upon ourselves. If there were no religion, I know men would not have such strong and forcible obligations to these duties; but yet, I say, though there were no religion, it were good for men, in order to temporal ends, to their health and quiet, and reputation, and safety, and, in a word, to the private and public prosperity of mankind, that men should be temperate, and chaste, and just, and peaceable,

and charitable, and kind, and obliging to one another, rather than the contrary. So that religion does not create those restraints arbitrarily, but requires those things of us, which our reason, and a regard to our advantage, which the necessity and conveniency of the things themselves, without any consideration of religion, would in most cases urge us to' (p. 327). On Tillotson, see Louis G. Locke, *Tillotson* (Copenhagen: Rosenkilde and Bagger, 1954; *Anglistica*, vol. IV), e.g., p. 88.

57. Thomas de Quincey, *Theological Essays* (Boston, Mass.: Ticknor, Reed, & Fields; 1854), vol. 1.
58. J. R. McCulloch, *The Principles of Political Economy* (Edinburgh: Tait, 1843), pp. 187, 265; see 432.
59. S. A. Meenai, 'Robert Torrens – 1780–1864', *Economica*, n.s., vol. 23 (1956), p. 55.
60. See, e.g., Bowring, *The Works of Jeremy Bentham*, vol. 1, p. 192.
61. See note 12, above.
62. Thus, wrote Alfred Marshall some years later, 'It is deliberateness, and not selfishness, that is the characteristic of the modern age' (*Principles of Economics*, 8th edition (New York: Macmillan Company, 1920), p. 6).
63. Jeremy Bentham, *An Introduction to the Principles of Morals and Legislation*, hereafter cited as *Morals and Legislation* (London: Oxford University Press, 1907); also in Bowring, *The Works of Jeremy Bentham*, vol. 1. The juxtaposition of morals *and* legislation is very suggestive, particularly since Bentham is considered to be the father of the science of legislation.
64. *Morals and Legislation*, p. 24.
65. Ibid., pp. 24–5.
66. Ibid., p. 25.
67. Ibid., p. 26.
68. Thus Bentham has a clear place for 'moralist' and moral leaders; on this see Viner, 'The Utilitarian Background', pp. 364, 365, 367; Stephen, *The English Utilitarians*, vol. 1, p. 312; and Elmer Louis Kayser, *The Grand Social Enterprise* (New York: Columbia University Press, 1932), who concludes his chapter on 'Public Opinion and the Moral Sanction', in respect to Bentham, 'In good government, that "harmony established between legislation and enlightened opinion", the work of the legislator would become lighter and lighter and many of his functions would be assumed by the moralist' (p. 64). The following, from Bentham's 'Constitutional Code', is instructive: 'Thus, on taking, on the one hand, a view of the deleterious influence of the temptation presented by arrangements which, in the first instance, may have presented themselves in no other character than that of arrangements of civil or distributive law, operating on no other than the passive faculty, care should be taken, on the other hand, not to suffer to pass unheeded, the moral forces by which, in the character of tutelary sanctions, the force of temptation may be, and, in the ordinary state of things, is, effectually resisted' (Bowring, *The Works of Jeremy Bentham*, vol. 9, pp. 20–1).
69. *Morals and Legislation*, p. 310.
70. Davidson, *Political Thought in England*, p. 67; see *inter alia*, p. 60.
71. Stephen, *The English Utilitarians*, vol. 1, p. 257.
72. *Morals and Legislation*, p. 25.
73. Ibid., *loc. cit.*

74. Ibid., pp. 219–20. In his 'View of a Complete Code of Laws', Bentham puts it essentially the same way:

> The distribution of rewards and punishments is often opposed or misdirected, or rendered useless, because the state has neither eyes which can see everything, nor hands which can attend to everything. Religion is calculated to supply this deficiency of human power, by inculcating upon the minds of men the belief that there is a power engaged in supporting the same ends, which is not subject to the same imperfections. It represents the Supreme Invisible Being as disposed to maintain the laws of society, and to reward and punish according to infallible rules, those actions which man has not the means of rewarding and punishing. Everything which serves to preserve and strengthen in the minds of men this fear of the Supreme Judge, may be comprehended under the general name of Religion; and for the purpose of clearness of discourse, we may often speak of religion as if it were a distinct being, an allegorical personage, to whom certain functions are attributed. Hence, to diminish or pervert the influence of Religion, is to diminish or pervert, in the same proportion, the services which the state might derive from it, for the repression of crime or the encouragement of virtue. Everything which tends to weaken or mislead the operations of this power, is an offence against Religion.
> (Bowring, *The Works of Jeremy Bentham*, vol. 3, p. 170.)

75. Bowring, *The Works of Jeremy Bentham*, vol. 1, p. 316.
76. Like Smith, Bentham acknowledges the ambiguity of content: 'The dictates of religion are, under the infinite diversity of religions, so extremely variable, that it is difficult to know what general account to give of them, or in what rank to place the motive they belong to' (*Morals and Legislation*, p. 124). See the text at the following note. See 'Of the Influence of Time and Place in Matters of Legislation', in Bowring, *The Works of Jeremy Bentham*, vol. 1, pp. 171ff.
77. *Morals and Legislation*, p. 64.
78. 'That a homily to be read in churches be composed by the authority and under the direction of the persons by whom forms of prayer for particular occasions are composed, recommending to the labouring classes the acquisition of Annuity Notes by showing the advantages that may be derived from this species of property as well in a moral as in an economical point of view by industrious persons to themselves and their families, by laying up a provision against sickness, accidents and old age, to the encouragement of sobriety and frugality, and the proportionable discouragement of drunkenness and every other species of dissipation and extravagance' (Stark, *Jeremy Bentham's Economic Writings*, vol. 3, p. 480).
79. Bentham did not completely bridge the gulf between private interests and the general interest, but neither did he deny the existence of such a gulf, and he did propose two ways, education and government, by which the gulf could be somewhat narrowed – with religion, though grudgingly, accepted as a useful part of education in so far as it educates for virtue' (Viner, 'The Utilitarian Background', p. 371).

80. See, e.g., Bowring, *The Works of Jeremy Bentham*, vol. 8, pp. 546ff.; vol. 9, p. 35; vol. 10, p. 70.
81. See, e.g., Bowring, *The Works of Jeremy Bentham*, vol. 1, pp. 75–6, 412, 566; vol. 5, pp. 457–8; vol. 6, p. 117 (note); vol. 8, p. 547; and vol. 10, p. 70. For Petty's enumeration of the 'disadvantages to the world' of 'Worshipping, honoring, & glorifying God', see *The Petty Papers*, vol. 1, pp. 117–18.
82. See, e.g., Bowring, *The Works of Jeremy Bentham*, vol. 2, p. 393; and Larrabee, *Bentham's 'Handbook'*, pp. 17–82.
83. See, e.g., Bowring, *The Works of Jeremy Bentham*, vol. 1, p. 147.
84. The position of Bentham, however, is made ambiguous by consideration of his anti-religious works, even allowing for their polemic character. In these writings, Bentham was severely critical of organized religion, its theological creed and sacerdotal class. It is instructive, nonetheless, that Bentham does temper his often outspoken criticism with a recognition of religion as a promulgating and sanctioning instrument of social control. (Jeremy Bentham, *Church-of-Englandism and Its Catechism Examined* (London: Wilson, 1818); Philip Beauchamp, *Analysis of the Influence of Natural Religion on the Temporal Happiness of Mankind* (London: Carlile, 1822); and Gamaliel Smith, *Not Paul, But Jesus* (London: Hunt, 1823).)
85. Burtt, *The English Philosophers*, p. 952. 'The rules which obtain . . . appear . . . self-evident and self-justifying. This all but universal illusion is one of the examples of the magical influence of custom, which is not only, as the proverb says, a second nature, but is continually mistaken for the first. The effect of custom, in preventing any misgiving respecting the rules of conduct which mankind impose on one another, is all the more complete because the subject is one on which it is not generally considered necessary that reasons should be given, either by one person to others or by each to himself' (p. 952). On the latter point, see *The Spirit of the Age*, and below.
86. The theme of his essay on the 'Utility of Religion' concerns the ostensible effect of supernatural religion which he attributes not to the supernatural character of religion but rather to the opportunity for organized religion to educate and inculcate morality. (*Three Essays on Religion*, pp. 72, 74, 78–9, 83, 87, 100.) See note 154, *infra*.
87. *The Spirit of the Age*, pp. 17, 25, 29, 30–2, 75, 86.
88. John Stuart Mill, *Principles of Political Economy* (New York: Kelley, 1961), p. 792.
89. *Three Essays on Religion*, pp. 77–8.
90. Ibid., pp. 78–9.
91. Ibid., pp. 81, 84.
92. Ibid., p. 96.
93. Ibid., p. 97.
94. Ibid., p. 109.
95. Ibid., p. 111. 'What is called morality in these times is a regulated sensuality; in the same manner exactly as the love of gain is regulated by the establishment of a law of property' (Hugh S. R. Elliot (ed.), *The Letters of John Stuart Mill* (London: Longmans, Green & Co., 1910), vol. 2, p. 376 (Diary entry for 4 March 1854)).
96. Burtt, *The English Philosophers*, p. 922.

97. Ibid., pp. 918–19.
98. *Three Essays on Religion*, p. 104.
99. Stephen, *The English Utilitarians*, vol. 3, p. 449. See *Three Essays on Religion*, pp. 256–7. For further discussion by Mill on the role of religion as an instrument of social control, see the concluding section of *The Spirit of the Age*, e.g., pp. 61ff, 76–7, 79, 83.
100. Such that, 'I would agree to deprive those of the elective franchise against whom it could justly be alleged that they considered it their interest to invade them' (McCulloch, *The Works of David Ricardo*, pp. 554–5). For an example of Ricardo's use of the sacredness of private property as an argument against a legislative proposal, see Sraffa, *Works and Correspondence of Ricardo*, vol. 5, p. 69.
101. Sraffa, *Works and Correspondence of Ricardo*, vol. 6, p. 184. Wrote Ricardo to Malthus on the same rioting: 'I am too much a friend to good order to wish to succeed through such means, besides that I am persuaded that they hurt rather than promote the object which they and I have in view' (Ibid., p. 180). See, however, Sraffa, vol. 5, pp. 28–9, and vol. 8, p. 80. Note also Sraffa, vol. 8, p. 102.
102. T. R. Malthus, *The Principles of Political Economy* (The London School of Economics and Political Science, Series of Reprints of Scarce Works on Political Economy, no. 3, 1936), p. 410.
103. 'The more the principle of property is respected, the more is it strengthened in the minds of the people. Small attacks upon this principle prepare for greater' (Bowring, *The Works of Jeremy Bentham*, vol. 1, pp. 310, 321). In other instances, where Bentham was an advocate of a more conscious deliberative approach, he was critical of what amounts to the operation of indirection and ignorance; see *Morals and Legislation*, p. 125, 220; Bowring, *The Works of Jeremy Bentham*, vol. 3, pp. 310, 484; and Ogden, *Bentham's Theory of Fictions*, pp. xvii, 121.
104. 'In the United States the majority undertakes to supply a multitude of ready-made opinions for the use of individuals, who are thus relieved from the necessity of forming opinions of their own. Everybody there adopts great numbers of theories, on philosophy, morals, and politics, without inquiry, upon public trust; and if we examine it very closely, it will be perceived that religion itself holds sway there much less a doctrine of revelation than as a commonly received opinion' (Alexis de Tocquevile, *Democracy in America* (New York: Vintage Books, Two Volumes, 1954), vol. 2, pp. 9, 10, 11–12).
105. Quoted by Brebner, 'Laissez-Faire and State Intervention', p. 60. See James Bonar, *Philosophy and Political Economy* (New York: Macmillan, 1893), pp. 128, 318.
106. S. G. Checkland, 'The Propagation of Ricardian Economics in England', *Economica*, n.s. vol. 16 (1949), p. 51.
107. *The Spirit of the Age*, pp. 4, 16, 28, 36, 75–6, 79. On the subject of religion, or, rather, the practice of religion, de Tocqueville was more orthodox than Stuart Mill, but it is crucial that both men acknowledged the role of ignorance and indirection. (Stuart Mill's first review of *Democracy in America* deeply gratified de Tocqueville. See de Tocqueville, *Democracy in America*, vol. 2, pp. 412–13.) Perhaps the difference lies in de Tocqueville's greater affection or adherence to the idea of religious orthodoxy (e.g., de Tocqueville,

Democracy in America, vol. 2, pp. 21–3). Wrote Mill: 'I think that few men of my father's intellect and public spirit, holding with such intensity of moral conviction as he did, unpopular opinions on religion, or on any other of the great subjects of thought, would now either practise or inculcate the withholding of them from the world, unless in the cases, becoming fewer every day, in which frankness on these subjects would either risk the loss of means of subsistence, or would amount to exclusion from some sphere of usefulness peculiarly suitable to the capacities of thc individual. . . . Such an avowal would put an end, at once and for ever, to the vulgar prejudice, that is called, very improperly, unbelief, is connected with any bad qualities either of mind or heart.' Then Mill acknowledges the practice of deception, or ignorance, and indirection: 'The world would be astonished if it knew how great a proportion of its brightest ornaments – of those most distinguished even in popular estimation for wisdom and virtue – are complete sceptics in religion; many of them refraining from avowal, less from personal consideration, than from a conscientious, though now in my opinion a most mistaken apprehension, lest by speaking out what would tend to weaken existing beliefs, and by consequence (as they suppose) existing restraints, they should do harm instead of good' (Mill, *Autobiography*, pp. 31, 32). Mill was clearly torn between a sense of the necessity of indirection etc. with respect to social control and a feeling of intellectual disapprobation toward deception (see also Stephen, *The English Utilitarians*, vol. 2, pp. 109–19).

108. de Tocqueville, *Democracy in America*, vol. 2, pp. 22–3.
109. But Mill's sympathies were clearly not with what General Francis A. Walker later called 'the aristocratic economics of the early part of the century'. Wrote Walker: 'I don't think that I exaggerate when I say that, among those who deemed themselves the guardians of the true faith, it was considered far better that a man should know nothing about economic literature, and have no interest whatever in the subject, than that, with any amount of learning and any degree of honest purpose, he should have adopted views varying from the standard that was set up' (Walker, 'Progress of Political Economy', pp. 33, 26). See also Ronald L. Meek, 'The Decline of Ricardian Economics in England', *Economica*, n.s., vol. 17 (1950), for excerpts from the writings of Longfield, Scrope, Read and Cooper, of whom Meek concludes, 'Their fundamental approach, in other words, was determined by a belief that what was socially dangerous could not possibly be true' (p. 61).
110. 'But reason itself will teach most men that they must, in the last resort, fall back upon the authority of still more cultivated minds, as the ultimate sanction of the convictions of their reason itself' (*The Spirit of the Age*, p. 31.) In 'Utilitarianism' Mill wrote: 'Any condition, therefore, which is essential to a state of society, becomes more and more an inseparable part of every person's conception of the state of things which he is born into, and which is the destiny of a human being' (Burtt, *The English Philosophers*, p. 920).
111. David Ricardo, *The Principles of Political Economy and Taxation* (Everyman's edition) (New York: Dutton, 1911), p. 62.
112. McCulloch, *Principles of Political Economy*, pp. 265, 181, 182, 432, 88–9.
113. See James Bonar, *Malthus and His Work* (New York: Harper, 1885), pp. 176ff.
114. Bowring, *The Works of Jeremy Bentham*, vol. 1, p. 314.

115. Ibid., vol. 3, p. 170, and vol. 1, p. 312.
116. *Fortnightly Review*, p. 516.
117. Mill, *Autobiography*, p. 163. In *The Spirit of the Age*, Mill notes the difficulty of securing discipline in an age of transition: 'Who can hope to sway the minds of the public by the old maxims of law, or commerce, or foreign policy, or ecclesiastical policy? . . . Nay, what landlord could call forth his tenants, or what manufacturer his men?' (pp. 7, 8).
118. Mill, *Principles of Political Economy*, p. 242. See also Viner, 'The Utilitarian Background', pp. 379–80. See note 127, below.
119. *Essays*, p. 172.
120. *The Wealth of Nations*, p. 28; *Lectures*, p. 253.
121. *Essays*, pp. 177, 185–6.
122. Ibid., p. 177.
123. *Lectures*, p. 235.
124. Ibid., pp. 253ff.
125. *The Wealth of Nations*, p. 15. See also p. 734: 'But the understandings of the greater part of men are necessarily formed by their ordinary employments.' See Stigler, *Five Lectures*, p. 4.
126. Sraffa, *Works and Correspondence of Ricardo*, vol. 7, p. 297; and see vol. 9, p. 314. See also Mitchell, *The Backward Art of Spending Money*, p. 215.
127. Mitchell, *The Background Art of Spending Money*, p. 220. David Hume had stressed that the principle of continuity underlying scientific analysis rested upon custom and habit. See O. H. Taylor, *Economics and Liberalism*, pp. 47–8.
128. Ricardo, *Political Economy*, pp. 54–5. In the note commencing at p. 54, Ricardo quotes Torrens' *Essay on the External Corn Trade* to the same effect.
129. Adelman, *Theories of Economic Growth*, pp. 49, 59; cf. p. 141. See also Blaug, *Economic Theory in Retrospect*, p. 68, and *Ricardian Economics* (New Haven: Yale University Press, 1958) p. 22; and Cecil Clare North, 'The Sociological Implications of Ricardo's Economics', *American Journal of Sociology*, vol. 20 (1915), p. 812. On the social relativity of custom, law, and religion, see Sraffa, vol. 7, pp. 227–8.
130. Sraffa, *Works and Correspondence of Ricardo*, vol. 7, p. 248.
131. Ibid., vol. 8, p. 357.
132. See McCulloch, *Principles of Political Economy*, pp. 263–6, and *A Treatise on the Succession to Property Vacant by Death* (London: Longman, Brown, Green, & Longmans, 1848); and Malthus, *Principles of Political Economy*, pp. 372ff.
133. McCulloch, *Principles of Political Economy*, pp. 390–1. See also Malthus, *Principles of Political Economy*, pp. 223ff.
134. John Stuart Mill, *Autobiography*, p. 75.
135. See, e.g., Stark, *Jeremy Bentham's Economic Writings*, vol. 3, pp. 411, 482; and Bowring, *The Works of Jeremy Bentham*, vol. 6, p. 7.
136. See, e.g., Bowring, *The Works of Jeremy Bentham*, vol. 1, p. 181 (really the entire work 'Of the Influence of Time and Place in Matters of Legislation').
137. Robbins, *Theory of Economic Policy*, pp. 178–9. Stephen's interpretation of Bentham is too narrow when he criticizes Bentham for allegedly failing to consider custom as the basis of law. (Stephen, *The English Utilitarians*, vol. 1, p. 304.)

138. Mill, 'Chapters on Socialism', *Fortnightly Review*, pp. 527, 530; and 'The Claims of Labor', in *Dissertations and Discussions* (New York: Holt, 1882), vol. 2, pp. 260ff. All of the classicists recognized custom as one of the foundations or sources of the particular rules of the institution of private property. On Hume, for example, see Robbins, *Theory of Economic Policy*, p. 54, and Bernard Wand, 'Hume's Non-utilitarianism', *Ethics*, vol. 72 (1962), p. 193 (cf. p. 196).
139. *Principles of Political Economy*, p. 200. In his 'Preliminary Remarks', Mill wrote that the laws of distribution 'are partly of human institution: since the manner in which wealth is distributed in any given society, depends on the statutes or usages therein obtaining' (p. 21) but in the chapter on property he writes that the distribution of wealth 'is a matter of human institution solely. The things once there, mankind, individually or collectively, can do with them as they like' (p. 200).
140. See Alexander Bain, *John Stuart Mill: A Criticism* (London: Longmans, Green, & Co., 1882), pp. 200–1. See also, e.g., *Dissertations and Discussions*, vol. 5, pp. 225ff., particularly, but not only, pp. 279ff.
141. *Principles of Political Economy*, pp. 242, 242–3, 246–7, 247. Among other interesting passages, note the following: 'In many trades the terms on which business is done are a matter of positive arrangement among the trade, who use the means they always possess of making the situation of any member of the body, who departs from its fixed customs, inconvenient and disagreeable' (p. 247). This is undoubtedly one of the earliest references to what has come to be called standardized contracts, or contracts of adhesion. See also Bain, *John Stuart Mill*, pp. 200–1, and Richard T. Ely, 'The Past and the Present of Political Economy', *Johns Hopkins University Studies in Historical and Political Science*, vol. 2 (1884), p. 39.
142. With respect to the vision of improvement through education, Frank H. Knight has written: 'Education provides no formula by which a society can lift itself culturally by its bootstraps, and the faith in education now appears as one of the most pathetic items in the entire creed of liberalism.' 'Organized education, democratically controlled, is, on its face, as regards fundamental ideals, an agency for promoting continuity, or even for accentuating accepted values, not a means by which "society" can lift itself by its own bootstraps into a different spiritual world.' *Freedom and Reform* (New York: Harper, 1947), pp. 32, 40.
143. *Essays*, p. 230.
144. *Lectures*, p. 259; *Wealth of Nations*, pp. 734–8.
145. *Wealth of Nations*, pp. 739–40. Thus wrote Grampp: 'As long as freedom was in danger of being abused, authority had necessarily to be great. As the danger lessened, authority would be diminished, and the maintenance of government by law would rest in ever growing measure on the self-responsibility of individuals. For such a condition to come about, it was essential to increase the political intelligence of the masses – to make it possible for them to acquire an interest in peace.' 'This condition, the economists believed, depended on the material welfare of the people.' ('On the politics of the Classical Economists', p. 747.)

    It is the very next paragraph, commencing the section 'Of the Expence of the Institutions for the Instruction of People of all Ages', that Smith begins,

'The institutions for the instruction of people of all ages are chiefly those for religious instruction' (p. 740). In the *Lectures*, Smith is reported to have said, 'We may observe an utility in this constitution of our nature that children have so long a dependence upon their parents, to bring down their passions to theirs, and thus be trained up at length to become useful members of society. Every child gets this piece of education, even under the most worthless parent' (p. 74; see p. 160.)

146. Sraffa, *Works and Correspondence of Ricardo*, vol. 8, p. 317; see *Principles of Political Economy and Taxation*, pp. 61–2.
147. Bonar, *Malthus and His Work*, pp. 194–5, 199.
148. McCulloch, *Principles of Political Economy*, pp. 181–2, 431–2. McCulloch then quotes from Sumner's 'Records of the Creation', including the following: 'As fast as the standard of intelligence is raised, the poor become more and more able to cooperate in any plan proposed for their advantage, more likely to listen to any reasonable suggestion, more able to understand, and therefore more willing to pursue it. Hence it follows, that when gross ignorance is once removed, and right principles are introduced, a great advantage has been already gained against squalid poverty' (p. 432). On the role of government promotive of morals see also p. 294; also see Bowring, *The Works of Jeremy Bentham*, vol. 1, p. 568, and vol. 4, p. 493; John Stuart Mill, *The Spirit of the Age*, p. xx, and *Principles of Political Economy*, pp. 887–8; *per contra*, see e.g., Bowring, *The Works of Jeremy Bentham*, vol. 1, p. 147, and (Nassau Senior), Book Review, *Edinburgh Review*, vol. 88 (1848), p. 331.
149. Bowring, *The Works of Jeremy Bentham*, vol. 1, p. 318.
150. Ibid., vol. 1, pp. 568–9; Bentham, *Morals and Legislation*, pp. 311–12.
151. Mitchell, *The Backward Art of Spending Money*, p. 194.
152. *Fortnightly Review*, p. 516.
153. *Autobiography*, pp. 75–6.
154. *Three Essays on Religion*, pp. 80, 78. 'A little reflection will, I think, lead us to the conclusion that it is this which is the great moral power in human affairs, and that religion only seems so powerful because this mighty power has been under its command' (p. 78).
155. Ibid., p. 82. See also the passage from p. 81, quoted above, text at note 93. Thus wrote Stephen: 'Now Mill, believing even to excess in the power of education, included in education the whole discipline of life due to the relations of the individual to his social environment; and it is his essential principle that this force should be directed to enforcing a sense of "responsibility" in the widest acceptation of the word' (Stephen, *The English Utilitarians*, vol. 3, p. 273.)
156. Schneider, 'Category of Ignorance', p. 494.
157. Robbins, *Theory of Economic Policy*, p. 6.
158. Frank H. Knight, *On the History of Method of Economics* (Chicago: University of Chicago Press, 1956), p. 18.
159. Hla Myint, 'The Classical View of the Economic Problem', *Economica*, n.s. vol. 13 (1946), pp. 119–30; reprinted in Joseph J. Spengler and William R. Allen (eds), *Essays in Economic Thought* (Chicago: Rand McNally, 1960), pp. 442–53.

160. See, e.g., Clark Kerr *et al.*, *Industrialism and Industrial Man* (Cambridge: Harvard University Press, 1960), and Everett E. Hagen, *On the Theory of Social Change* (Homewood, Ill.: Dorsey Press, 1962).
161. A. P. Usher, in *Explorations in Economics: Notes and Essays Contributed in Honor of F. W. Taussig* (New York: McGraw-Hill, 1936), p. 407.

6 Introduction to Thomas Robert Malthus, 'An Essay on the Principle of Population', 1798*

(with John P. Henderson)**

THE ARGUMENT OF THE ESSAY

The argument in Thomas Robert Malthus's *Essay on Population*, the first edition of which was published anonymously in 1798, is one of the most dramatic in the history of human thought. It is no wonder that it is a classic not solely of economic thought but of all human writings whatsoever.

Although ultimately quite complex, the argument is fundamentally simple and straightforward: the inescapable tendency is for population to increase more rapidly than the food supply, thereby causing severe problems for individuals and for society. Malthus elaborated this argument in several ways.

First, Malthus argued that the power of population is greater than the power of production of subsistence; or, as he expressed it, population tends to grow geometrically (1, 2, 4, 8, 16, 32, etc.) whereas food tends to increase arithmetically (1, 2, 3, 4, 5, 6, etc.).

Second, Malthus argued that population necessarily will be kept down to the level of subsistence, and that there are several operative processes by which this is done. These means are principally the positive check of misery and the preventive check of vice. By misery Malthus meant premature death due to malnutrition, starvation and illness; by vice he meant war, infanticide, geriatricide, and promiscuity before and outside marriage. Misery, he thought, was an absolutely inevitable consequence; vice, due to the operation of virtue, was not, but was nonetheless prevalent.

---

* '*Zu Malthus' Essay über die Entwicklung der Bevolkerung*' was first published in German in Engels, Hax, Hayek and Recktenwald (eds), *Klassiker der Nationalokonomie* (Dusseldorf/ Darnstadt: Verlag Wirtschaft und Finanzen GmbH, 1986) pp. 11–28.

** John P. Henderson is Professor of Economics, Emeritus, Michigan State University.

Third, Malthus summarized his argument in a series of propositions. First, the increase of population is necessarily limited by the means of subsistence; population cannot increase without an increase in the means of subsistence (although population will increase in proportion to the removal of the checks – misery and vice – upon it, thereby, however, increasing the likelihood of their presence in the future, as increasing pressure is thereby placed on the food supply); a permanent increase in population is possible only with an increase in the means of subsistence, for which he held out little hope. Second, population invariably increases when the means of subsistence increases, as more people live longer as the mortality rate declines. Third, the superior power of population, the perpetual tendency for population to increase faster than and beyond the means of subsistence, cannot be checked without producing misery or vice; that is, the actual population tends to be adjusted to the means of subsistence by the forces of misery and vice.

Fourth, there emerges a large-scale demographic model comprising at least the following variables: the geometrical growth potential of population, the arithmetic growth potential of the food supply, the positive check of misery, and the preventive check of vice, to which is added (and emphasized in the second edition) the preventive check of moral restraint.

Fifth, the major implication of Malthus's argument is that the combination of the two different growth potentials of population and food supply with the checks of misery and vice constitutes, as he put it, an insurmountable barrier to the perfectibility of man and society. Utopian schemes for the regeneration of man and society, such as were then being advanced by William Godwin and the Marquis de Condorcet, were, unfortunately, inevitably to be doomed by the pressure of population growth upon food supply and the resultant checks of misery and vice.

Sixth, a derivative, less dramatic but no less pressing, implication is that efforts to help the poor, such as that proposed by William Pitt the Younger (which he subsequently withdrew upon becoming convinced of the merit of Malthus's argument), would result in a larger number of people being miserable and resorting to vice.

Seventh, although not fully developed in the first edition of the *Essay*, Malthus's argument actually involved three sets of consequences. There was, first, the obvious tendency for population pressure to lower average real incomes to the minimum of subsistence, a condition enforced by the means of misery and vice. There were also, however, second, adverse effects on the overall quality of life, and third, the increasing need to rely upon formal social control, to wit: government and police, to cope with the interrelated problems consequent to greater population, greater population density (especially in the towns and cities), greater complexity of human interaction, and poverty and the human reactions thereto. In no respect was the human condition, or its prospects for improvement, sanguine.

THOMAS ROBERT MALTHUS, THE PERSON

Such were the ideas of the 32-year-old Fellow of Jesus College, Cambridge, and curate at the small parish of Albury, in southern Surrey. The economist's father, Daniel Malthus, was a man of independent wealth, though not in the class of the highest landed gentry. An eccentric individual, Daniel travelled a good deal, not only in his native land but on the Continent as well. He cultivated the famous minds, though not a great intellect himself, and thus befriended David Hume and Jean-Jacques Rousseau. Hume the inductivist philosopher and Rousseau the humanist and social critic both greatly influenced Daniel Malthus as he became an advocate of their ideas and beliefs. His own eccentricity was intensified by their contrasting views, especially Rousseau's, on the question of education.

Thomas Robert Malthus was born on 13 February 1766, the second son in an age of primogeniture, and the victim of a cleft palate and hare-lip. It was probably because of his son's affliction, and Rousseau's view on education, that Daniel Malthus took on the major task of Robert's early education, aided in turn by tutors. In addition to the usual grammar and the Latin and Greek classics, young Malthus was also exposed to mathematics and the ideas of the Scottish and French radicals as espoused by his father. In the winter of 1784, at the age of 18, Malthus became a pensioner of Jesus College, one of the less prestigious colleges at Cambridge University, but nonetheless a centre of good learning. Malthus was active in his college, not only academically but in sports and debate, achieving the distinction of Ninth Wrangler, that unique Cambridge tradition of awarding University honours in mathematics.

Judging from his letters to his father and the memoirs of his contemporaries at Cambridge, Malthus was very much aware of current literature and commentary, read Edmund Burke, Edward Gibbon and the rush of pamphlets pertaining to events in France. It was this breadth of understanding and wide interest which lead Malthus to the heights of achievement with the writing of the *Essay on Population*.

As with all Oxbridge graduates at the time, Malthus was required to take Holy Orders in the Church of England. As the event of his graduation neared, there was considerable question as to whether he could be ordained, because of the defect in his speech. Preaching would be a problem, not to mention the social prejudice against an afflicted member of the clergy. The problem of his ordination was resolved when Malthus convinced the head of his College that his only wish was to live a quiet life in the country. Through family connections he was offered the position of curate in Albury. In 1788, aged 22, Malthus graduated from Jesus College and took Holy Orders.

For the next decade, Malthus pursued two careers, one as a Fellow of Jesus College, for which he received £100 annually, and the curateship at Albury. He spent most of his time in the country, except for frequent trips to Cambridge to attend lectures and seminars. It appears that his personal library was modest, and this may account for the fact that the first *Essay* was essentially that of an *a priori* argument of only about 50,000 words. There is little evidence of research on earlier writers on population, except for Godwin and Condorcet, something which led Marx to believe, mistakenly, that Malthus plagiarized the work of Robert Wallace. This was also the reason that Marx gave for the *Essay* being published anonymously.

THE DEVELOPMENT OF THE DOCTRINE

Malthus's concern with population was not original but it was consequential. Other writers, not the least of whom were Adam Smith and the very authors whose allegedly grandiose ideas he was challenging, had recognized the problem of population pressure. But Malthus's *Essay*, a polemic which was also a constructive critique of sorts, was evidently timed just right: it became one of the single most influential writings on human affairs. In the history of economic thought, to be a Classical Economist was to be someone not only who was concerned with population pressure and its significance for both economic performance and the human prospect, but whose initial and fundamental attack on any analytical or policy problem consisted in no small part in the search for the implications thereof for population growth. But this was not all. Population pressure became an important explanatory variable explaining or helping to explain all manner of domestic phenomena as well as war and imperialism. It became the great conservative argument for the status quo. Malthus's analysis was suggestive to *both* Charles Darwin and Alfred Russell Wallace in their independent development of the idea of natural selection as the critical component in the theory of evolution. As Anthony Flew, in his Introduction to the Pelican edition of the *Essay* (1970), has pointed out, Malthus's 'main achievement is to have brought questions of national population and individual family size within the sphere of morality and prudence, of policy and decision'.

Flew continues: 'Of course, to say this is not to say that individuals and organizations do not still pretend that this is not so.'

One eventual facet of the development of the idea of population as a moral question has undoubtedly been the study of sex as a psychological and socioeconomic problem, something with which Malthus, equally undoubtedly, would not have been comfortable. Another facet, correlative to that of population *per se*, has been the recognition of poverty as an analytical and social, if not also a political, problem. Finally, Malthus's argument became one of the major analytical and policy checks on human idealism in an age in which mankind's consciousness of the policy nature of human institutions was enhanced and assorted schemes for social reconstruction and progress were rampant.

The *Essay*, with its author now both acknowledged and celebrated, went through several editions during his lifetime. Indeed, the first edition was somewhat superseded but by no means fully eclipsed by the revision of his argument presented in the second and subsequent editions. Discarding the *a priori* approach of the first edition, Malthus turned to induction, in an attempt to lend historical support to his very simple proposition of population pressure. The octavo volume of the first *Essay* became the two-volume quarto work of the second edition. By the fifth edition, the *Essay* ran to 250,000 words. Samuel Coleridge, one of Malthus's greatest critics, exclaimed 'we now have a quarto of verbiage and senseless repetition' in an attempt to prove that there must be poverty.

Besides the methodological change in the second edition, to the checks of misery and vice, Malthus now added a second preventive check, comprising 'moral restraint' or sexual abstinence before and during marriage without any accompanying increase in vice. His own marriage at the age of 38, and the three children his wife bore him, bear some evidence of his new convictions.

Malthus's total demographic model was now evidently complete and the harsh conclusions of the first *Essay* were now deliberately softened, as he noted in the Preface to the second edition published in 1803. There are, however, two extraordinary twists to Malthus's having emphasized the preventive check in moral restraint in the second and subsequent editions.

In both respects one has to recognize that the gravamen of the argument in the first edition was directed against the prospect advanced by Godwin, in response to the critique of his ideas given by Robert Wallace, of the perfectibility of man and the development of intellectual pleasures in place of the gratification of sexual passion. In 1798 Malthus had admitted that it would be better for population to be checked by foresight than by want and sickness and the other modes of misery and vice. While he recognizes the possibility of delaying or avoiding marriage, he argues that this is likely to lead to an increase in vice. More importantly, he says that intellectual improvement is possible but he finds no observable progress towards either the extinction or the substantial weakening of what he calls 'the passion between the sexes', adding that it is certainly improbable for the lower classes to obtain any high degree of intellectual improvement, because they are insufficiently free from both want and labour. Both Godwin and Condorcet, Malthus argues repeatedly, exaggerate the prospects for the development of rational intellect. Models of perfection may actually, he warns, impede improvement. Man, he stresses, is not susceptible of perpetual improvement, nor is society, especially the lower classes; the argument against both the perfectibility of man and 'any great and decided amelioration of the conditions of the lower classes of mankind' is said to appear to be 'conclusive'.

The first point to be emphasized is that already in the final two chapters of the first edition, having earlier identified but minimized the relevance of moral restraint, Malthus stresses the formation (read 'improvement') of the human mind, including the 'production of moral excellence'. Malthus is here concerned with the objections of the pious to the implications of his previous discussion with regard to the nature, role and intentions of God. Malthus says that the population-pressure based problems of man are evidence of neither divine impotence, lack of divine goodness or goodwill towards man, nor a state of human trial. These problems are rather the evidence of a creative process for man, a process which is a divine product and one acting through general laws. Its principal feature is the awakening of matter into mind, the improvement of the mind. The first great awakeners of mind seem, he says, to be the wants of the body. More important, evil seems necessary to create the exertion by man to create mind and moral excellence, through the cultivation of intellectual wants; and there is no more evil in the world than is absolutely necessary as an ingredient in this mighty process. Indeed, the very role of the population principle is to improve and exalt the human mind and thus fulfil the will of mankind's Creator; the evils of population increase themselves facilitate the growth of mind. God could produce food for man without requiring the latter's exhausting labour and avoiding the consequences of overpopulation, but the exertion and travail by man is 'necessary to create mind' and to 'rouse man into action, and form his mind to reason'. Seemingly, more than the foundation for an emphasis on the prospects of moral restraint is thus laid; the very idea has already become a basic conception in the first edition. Nonetheless, for whatever concatenation of reasons the promise of moral restraint therein was eclipsed.

The greater irony, of course, is that Malthus, stressing the creative formation of mind, and specifically the development of intellectual wants, in the first edition, and the overall preventive role of moral restraint in the second and subsequent editions, not only deflated the reasoning used against Godwin but adopted his own version of the perfectibility of man.

These two twists, as it were, only point to the vagaries of literary development. What is nonetheless of enormous consequence is that Malthus made the question of population a, if not for a time the, critical issue facing mankind. Or perhaps we should say that the question of population was made a critical issue by the sum of all those who, each in their own fashion, addressed the issue: Godwin, Wallace, Malthus, *et al.* Still, the focus has, not inappropriately, long been on Malthus's *Essay* for its dramatic formulation of the problem as such.

CRITIQUE

Malthus's analysis, in the form of either the basic argument of the tendency for population to outrun the means of subsistence or the full demographic model inclusive also of preventive and positive checks, is a powerful and indeed compelling matter. But it can and indeed must be subjected to careful criticism, of which several elements are very important.

First, although the concept is not central to the explicit discussion in the *Essay*, the notion of a minimum of subsistence is logically critical to the argument. It is when the minimum of subsistence is reached that the more offensive results of the positive checks come to fruition; and it is the tendency of population pressure to reduce average real incomes to the minimum of subsistence that is crucial. But the precise content of the minimum of subsistence, especially whether it is an absolute physical or a malleable social phenomenon, is not specified, which leads to at least some ambiguity in the fundamental argument itself. It should be understood that this was a crucial problem for all the classical political economists, for unless one can determine the minimum it is not possible to determine the surplus available for growth.

Second, Malthus's sole focus with regard to the means of subsistence is on foodstuffs. Indeed, manufactured goods are seen by him as a detraction from the ability of society to produce foodstuffs, an indication of his general disregard of improvements in productivity. But, while food is obviously important, there is more to the means of subsistence than food. We shall return to this point below.

In passing, it ought to be noted that what may be considered the second great theme of the *Essay* is an argument in favour of the promotion of agriculture. Malthus deprecates the tendency for society to develop along commercial and industrial lines, to the disadvantage of agriculture, a theme he stressed over and over again in his other writings. This relates to still another point discussed below, but it does suggest a further ambiguity in Malthus's principal theme: the growth of agriculture, given the continued operation of the tendency of population to increase faster than the production of goods, would only permit more persons to live at the means of subsistence. Perhaps the answer is that such is precisely the predicament of human society revealed by the population doctrine: all efforts to improve mankind's lot are destined to be self-defeating. Still, it is conceivable that one might argue that morally it is better for fewer than more to suffer. In any case, Malthus leaves unposed and unanswered two key questions: what is the optimal population, and by what criterion(ia) is it optimal?

Third, Malthus, at least in retrospect, clearly does not give enough weight to increases in productive power leading to increases in the means of subsistence, even if only food. The comparison of arithmetic to geometrical ratios of foodstuff and population growth, respectively, has been in fact considerably deficient. While the law of diminishing returns is an important part of population doctrine for Malthus, the law was to be overcome, at least in the developed countries, by technological progress.

In broad summary, the empirical situation is roughly as follows. In the almost two centuries since the publication of the first edition of the *Essay*, there have been two historical experiences. In the developed countries, there have been enormous increases in both longevity and population (and these due to lowering of death rates and not to increasing birth rates); substantial reductions in the length of the working week; enormous increases in both production and productivity in both food and manufacturing industries; food has become a decreasing proportion of the wherewithal of life; and, while it is difficult to make meaningful or at least exact physical and welfare comparisons over two centuries, astounding increases in *per capita* real income. In the developed countries, Malthus's projection has not been realized or even approached.

In the non-developed countries, however, Malthus's argument and prediction, to the misfortune of countless hundreds of millions of persons, has been realized. The capacity to sustain life, not to say to improve real living conditions, often has not increased faster than population; multiplied numbers today live pretty much at the same minimum of physical subsistence level as did generations of their ancestors and have little if any prospect of escaping from that predicament.

The empirical test, then, of Malthus's doctrine both refutes and confirms his argument. The empirical situation is diverse. Malthus's doctrine is logically and psychodynamically compelling but is empirically inconclusive, except as a tendency, and it was as a tendency that he always couched his argument. It is a statement of neither an absolute truth nor an inexorable resultant condition, but of a serious and difficult problem to be overcome, indeed, of a problem which may not always and everywhere be overcome. Flew underscores the point made by Archbishop Richard Whately in 1832 distinguishing 'between two senses of the word "tendency": that in which a tendency to produce something is a cause which, operating unimpeded, would produce it; and that in which to speak of a tendency to produce something is to say that that result may reasonably be expected in fact to occur'.

Thus it is not surprising that modern growth and development analysis suggests that the Malthusian model of arithmetic versus geometric ratios and preventive *vis-à-vis* positive checks is simplistic, and that the interaction of economic growth with population growth is much more complex. Both historical experience and theoretical understanding now suggest that Malthus's doctrine on population can be interpreted either as a prognosis of a dismal future or as a statement of the conditions and limits of progress. For all the evident power of Malthus's model, the limits of reasoning within a limited model are equally manifest.

Moving on to a quite different point, it may be remarked in passing that Malthus's theological arguments in the last two chapters of the first *Essay* are not conclusively persuasive, however much they open the door to moral restraint and irony in relation to Godwin and Condorcet. There are three points, at least the first and third of which seem manifestly important. First, why did not God make man fully formed? Why was the creative process, through which man has so much to suffer, necessary? Could not God have generated the final result, fully formed man, whose matter has been formed into mind? Whatever one might prefer to think, Malthus provides no answer to this question. Second, what is the place in the physical and social universe of fully formed man? Again, there are answers to this, more or less compelling, but Malthus neither raises nor resolves the matter. Third, if full revelation by God of the plans for man would inhibit or repress the formation of the human mind and its appreciation of virtue, which requires the presence of moral evil, as Malthus argues, why is this reasoning not applicable to Malthus's own publication of his argument? If the answer is that the formation of mind is still necessary even after Malthus wrote, the response is that this is true even if God reveals the situation. Perhaps the conclusive response to all these questions is that whatever the personal piety of Malthus, the doctrine of population is most proximately a secular, human, empirical matter, to which the discursive system of theology may be applied but is not necessarily applied nor is it necessarily conclusively dispositive.

Finally, we need to consider the question of power manifest in the institutional and class structure of society, because ideas thereon are presented throughout the *Essay*. Malthus's ideas, not surprisingly, are rather complex with regard to power. Inequality is a result of population increase; population pressure would force Godwin's society to adopt the institutions of private property and marriage and therefore inequality of conditions; some must draw a blank, as he puts it, in the great lottery of life. But inequality is also a check to, or limit upon, population increase; Godwin's proposed egalitarian institutional changes, for example, would lead to population growth. While he says that the present degree of inequality is neither necessary nor useful, Malthus affirms both the necessity of class division and that the positive check is chiefly confined to the lower orders of society.

These points raise certain questions. Is Malthus more concerned with the population problem or with Godwin's and Condorcet's respective systems of equality? If the tendency is for population to increase more rapidly than the means of subsistence, if, that is, institutions are irrelevant (perhaps governing only the number and not the fact of individuals living at the minimum of subsistence or subject to the working of the preventive and positive checks), then why does he give so much attention to the maintenance of certain institutions and the rejection of others? Why the emphasis on an agricultural economy, which may only permit more to live subject to misery and vice?

Perhaps the answer is that the power structure is recognized by Malthus to be functional to the *distribution* of misery. The misery, he says 'falls chiefly, as it always must do, upon that part whose condition is lowest in the scale of society. . . . Where there is any inequality of conditions . . . the distress arising from a scarcity of provisions, must fall hardest upon the least fortunate members of the society'. That is tautological, for otherwise the lowest would not be the lowest and the least fortunate would not be the least fortunate. But it is nonetheless instructive, for it suggests that there are two interwoven elements to the *Essay*. One concerns the tendency for population to increase more rapidly than the means of subsistence, with respect to which the same problems would exist, says Malthus, even if the rich and the poor somehow were to change places. 'The rich might become poor, and some of the poor rich, but a part of the society must necessarily feel a difficulty of living, and this difficulty will naturally fall on the least fortunate members.' The second concerns the participation by Malthus in the process through which the distribution of misery is effectuated. And here, while Malthus showed evident sympathies with the mass of the suffering poor, he reflected the position of the land-owning class and agricultural system with which he always identified.

This places in perspective the later uses made by others in support of the hierarchical power structure as it then existed and to oppose reform. Malthus's doctrine, his law of population as it has been called, though it is at best a statement of tendency (in one of Whately's senses and not the other), became part of the selective conservative defence of the status quo. To the population argument was added a particular strategy intended ultimately to reproduce the hierarchical power structure as it governed and represented the distribution of misery.

All of this, however, was upset by a multiplicity of developments, not the least of which was the spread of effective contraceptive techniques and a decline in fertility rates in the developed countries. While the technology of contraception was in its earliest stages during Malthus's time, it was nonetheless practised, apparently with some effectiveness. On this matter Malthus is silent. But it completes, in a sense, the 'Malthusian' demographic model, however much it may be considered, along with abortion, as but another means of vice. The genius of Malthus is indicated by his continued relevance, in all areas of the world, though his population doctrine is not by itself conclusive with respect to policy.

With the publication of Malthus's second edition in 1803, his popularity increased and he moved into the centre of English society. In 1804 he married, a change which required his relinquishing his Cambridge Fellowship, and the next year he was appointed Professor of Modern History and Political Economy at the newly organized East India College at Haileybury. In the later years of the Napoleonic Wars he became interested in the broader issues of political economy, and less concerned with demographics, though it was as the author of the *Essay on Population* that he was known, and it continued as a cornerstone of British classical political economy.

7 Introduction to Thomas Robert Malthus, *Principles of Political Economy*, 1820*

(with John P. Henderson)**

Thomas Robert Malthus's *Essay on Population* (1798) contributed one of the central propositions by which British classical political economy came to be defined. His *Principles of Political Economy*, however, is one of the truly great iconoclastic, dissenting treatises in the history of political economy. Malthus here dissented from the received doctrine of David Ricardo's theory of value and deductive methodology. He dissented from the 'law of the market' associated with James Mill and J. B. Say and embraced by Ricardo and his followers. He further dissented from, or at least was strongly revisionist of, Ricardian and indeed his own prior rent theory, as well as many lesser Ricardian themes. He also dissented from the very negative Whiggish, middle-class perception of the landed, *rentier* and aristocracy.

Malthus was unquestionably a British classical economist, indeed he was one of the school's leading figures. But he may also be interpreted as a forerunner of neoclassicism in his theory of value, of John Maynard Keynes in his understanding of how the income-determination mechanism works, and of institutionalism in his attention to induction, systemic dynamics, cumulative causation, and the operative consequences of institutions for economic performance. Malthus was neither neoclassicist, nor Keynesian, nor institutionalist, but the inclusion of such elements of economic analysis in his *Principles* made his version of classical political economy remarkably different from that of Ricardo. Malthus's *Principles* contained a running critique of the second edition of Ricardo's *Principles of Political Economy and Taxation* (1819), and it elicited from Ricardo a detailed annotated commentary on Malthus (though not published for over a century). As Keynes has noted, the mystery of what British economics might

* 'Malthus als Theoretiker', in *Uber Malthus' 'Principles of Political Economy'*, was first pubished in German in Engels, Hax, Hayek and Recktenwald (eds), *Klassiker der Nationalokonomie* (Dusseldorf: Verlag Wirtschaft und Finanzen GmbH, 1989) pp. 35–9.

** John P. Henderson is Professor of Economics, Emeritus, Michigan State University.

have become, had its development followed Malthus rather than Ricardo and the later marginalist reorientation, is impenetrable, as is also the question whether Malthus was a dedicated apologist championing the conservative landed interest or simply (but for us, instructively) gave effect to an assumption of the traditional institutional order of his time and place. For all Malthus's evident greatness, his place in the history of economic thought, therefore, is subject to varying interpretation and evaluation.

By 1820, when he published his *Principles*, Malthus was one of Britain's most outstanding and recognized economists. He had been in the centre of every important dispute for over thirty years, and probably was at the height of his distinguished career. He had moved from being an anonymous author, of the first edition of the *Essay on Population*, to having published four subsequent editions (1803–17) and the volume was now twice the length of the original. At the time of the famous bullion controversy (1810–11), Malthus had reviewed the pamphlets of the main contributors in the leading journal of the day, the *Edinburgh Review*. He presented both sides of the issues, as he believed that Britain's monetary difficulties were caused by both the war-related trade imbalance and the excessive issue of paper currency by the Bank of England, which had been relieved of the responsibility of redeeming bank notes in gold bullion. Unlike the bullionists, who traced all of the problem to the trade imbalance, or Ricardo and Robert Mushet, who placed the blame solely on the Bank, Malthus saw both sides as did the official *Bullion Report* from the House of Commons.

As the long Napoleonic Wars drew to an end in 1815, Malthus opposed Ricardo's free trade doctrines which called for a repeal of the Corn Laws, because of the adverse effects on the agricultural sector, and the dislocations which would follow. In 1815, the Malthus–Ricardo controversy over the effect of repealing the Corn Laws was carried on with pamphlets, most of which were published in February of that year. There was no repeal of the Corn Laws, and Ricardo published his *Principles of Political Economy* in part in order to continue the debate, the first edition in 1817, the second in 1819. Malthus took opposition by publishing this volume.

Malthus's *Principles* begins with a methodological introduction followed by a specification of certain fundamental concepts. The remainder of the book is devoted to the theory of value (Malthusian microeconomics), the theory of distribution (rent, wage and profit theory), and, after a pause to consider the relation between wealth and value, Malthusian macroeconomics, under the heading of 'the immediate causes of the progress of wealth'. This latter is almost precisely one-third of the main text of the book (which is followed by a detailed 70-page summary). Within each subsection his typical procedure is to first state his theoretical position, or opposition, and then give examples illustrating, perhaps intended to demonstrate or to prove, the argument. The book as a whole is readily sensed to be as much a sequel to Adam Smith's *Inquiry into the Nature and Causes of the Wealth of Nations* (1776), which it both lauded and criticized, as a response to Ricardo's *Principles.*

METHODOLOGICAL AND DEFINITIONAL CONSIDERATIONS

Malthus's distinctive methodological position, which has particular consequences for his substantive analysis, seems to be predicated upon his vision of the economic system and the relationships of which it is comprised. The economy, in his view, is a complex, interactive system. He is critical of precipitant attempts to simplify and generalize, especially of unwillingness to acknowledge the operation of more causes than one in the production of observed effects, the same approach he had taken with his review of the bullion issue. Contrariwise, Malthus sees both multiple causation and mutual interdependence among variables, or what Gunnar Myrdal later was to call cumulative causation; relationships are dual, reciprocal and interactive. Thus, for example, he stresses that demand is as necessary for an increase of capital as an increase of capital is for an increase in demand. He opposes the drawing of deductive inferences on the basis of assumptions of single causes, perhaps especially for the showing of what Ricardo called 'strong cases'. He would like, ideally, to consider all the causes which concur in the production of particular phenomena, and not just the major cause. His interpretation of the Newtonian emphasis, that one should not admit more causes of any phenomenon than are necessary to account for it, is to stress the implication that all those causes which are necessary must be admitted, even if their significance is slight. One needs all the causes, not just the major ones. Recognizing that his approach would engender a danger of the opposite kind to that which arises from a tendency to (over)simplification, he calls for practice to follow a just mean between the two extremes as a way of arriving at the truth. The need to make the number of explanatory variables manageable is thus not totally elevated over realism and relevance.

It is because of this view of the economy and how it must be studied that Malthus emphasized and himself became an advocate of an empirical, inductive and experiential, rather than an *a priori* and deductive, approach to political economy. He believed both that a comprehensive attention to facts is necessary and that theories should be brought to the test of experience; only thereby would economic analysis fit the open-ended complexity of its material; only thereby would conclusions be adequately seen to be both relative and relevant to circumstances (for example, diverse soil fertility, population pressure, institutions, labour supply, and so on). The major weakness of such an approach is that it is a poor guide to policy recommendations, except the policy is doing nothing.

Malthus's methodological perspective has ramifications beyond those of empiricism to such factors as the importance of 'proportions', the sense in which variables are to be understood as operative, and the problem of certainty in analysis. With regard to the matter of proportions, Malthus did not believe that variables were to be considered in isolation, certainly not in a world in which the relationships between variables were characterized by mutual, interactive interdependence. Malthus repeatedly stressed that all the great results in political economy respecting wealth (which, as we shall see, is its central focus) depend upon proportions. The point is emphatically articulated in regard to the relation between production and distribution and the division of landed property. In the former case it involves the centrality not of saving alone but of a *balance* between consumption and investment. With regard to saving in relation to investment, for example, it is necessary that the level of saving be economically meaningful, not on its own, but in relation to the level of investment. Since the latter has limits, so does saving require limits.

Malthus also insists that, in this complex interactive system, variables are to be considered as limiting rather than narrowly regulating factors. Thus, he would prefer to say that the rate of profit is limited by the powers of the last land taken into cultivation and that this is essentially different from saying that the latter 'regulates' (in some ultimate or uniquely determinative sense) the former, again stressing the duality, or multiplicity, of causation.

Malthus stresses, too, the inexorability of uncertainty in economic analysis. At both the beginning and the end of his *Principles*, he states that the science of political economy resembles more the sciences of morals and politics than the science of mathematics. This may seem odd coming from a writer who, in his 1814 pamphlet, *Observations on the Effects of the Corn Laws*, had written that 'Many of the questions both in morals and politics seem to be of the nature of the problems *de maximis et minimus* in fluxions; in which there is always a point where a certain effect is the greatest, while on either side of this point it gradually diminishes.' But defending 'the main doctrine' that 'the progress of wealth depends upon proportions' against the objection 'that it necessarily opens the way to differences of opinion regarding these propositions, and thus throws a kind of uncertainty over the science of political economy which was not supposed to belong to it', he urges that 'If, however, the doctrine should be found, upon sufficient examination, to be true; if it adequately accounts for things as they are, and explains consistently why frequent mistakes have been made respecting the future, it will be allowed that such objectors are answered. We cannot make a science more certain by our wishes or opinions; but we may obviously make it much more uncertain in application, by believing it to be what it is not.' Malthus thus seemed fundamentally to appreciate that there is a difference between the theoretical–hypothetical and the 'actual state of things' and that, in a world in which phenomena were the result of proportions between variables, the predictive power of political economy was severely limited; that is, that there is a difference between a prediction within the context of a particular model and a prediction of actual future phenomena; and, perhaps also, that seeking absolute or unique solutions to analytic and policy problems was a question-begging practice.

One deficiency of Malthus in these respects is noteworthy. While establishing and emphasizing that certain pairs of phenomena are 'connected', he does not always comprehend that the connections are multiple and accordingly can be interpreted (for example, with regard to causation and normative status) in more than one way. Thus, while his analysis of the connectedness of wealth and value is relatively unobjectionable, that of rent and production interprets cause and consequence in the context of taking the landlord–tenant property system as given.

Finally, it ought to be noted that while Malthus's understanding of the scope of political economy was broad, it was not unlimitedly expansive. In his long seventh chapter on the causes which are most effective in calling forth the powers of production in different countries, he says that moral and political causes are, in this respect, of primary importance; but it is here intended by him chiefly to consider those which are more directly within the province of political economy. Accordingly, he concentrates on certain technical economic considerations although he does rather frequently introduce moral (by which he refers to factors of habit and motivation) and political variables and indeed does so quite effectively.

FUNDAMENTAL CONCEPTIONS

Malthus's *Principles* is very much in the tradition of Smith: the object of political economy is to study the causes of the progress of wealth, and wealth is defined as the *material* objects which are necessary, useful or agreeable to mankind. Malthus thus follow Smith in distinguishing between productive and unproductive labour. Saying that the question of productive labour is dependent upon the definition of wealth, he confined the definition of productive labour to that labour which is productive of wealth, in the form of material objects, so directly as to be estimated in the value of the objects produced.

The distinction is striking because Malthus, as we shall see, traces exchange value (price) to the forces of demand and supply and not to any single ultimate governor of value, such as embodied labour or capital. While ultimately perhaps of only semantic significance, this terminology, for the unwary, can potentially be seriously misleading: in the final chapter he makes a case for 'unproductive consumption' in which, in modern terms, he calls for spending on services (in contrast to material objects) in order to maintain the flow of spending leading to the generation of revenue, or gross domestic product, a view which seems to, but does not, authorize waste. His critic, Ricardo, claimed that 'unproductive consumption' was as useful as a fire.

Malthus recognizes that all paid labour might be called productive of value but he objects that such a position would make the payment for labour, instead of the quantities of material product, the criterion of productiveness. In his view, if we once desert matter, every human exertion to avoid pain and obtain pleasure is productive labour; the very same kind of labour will be productive, or not, according as it is paid for, or not. Again, this surely is odd coming from someone who has an open-ended demand and supply theory of price. But he sticks by his definition of wealth, arguing that while unproductive labourers are of great importance in the production of wealth indirectly, as demanders, and even though some unproductive labour is much more useful and important than productive labour, their labour is incapable of being the subject of the gross calculations which relate to national wealth, and they cannot with propriety be said to create the wealth which pays them.

One reason why Malthus prefers the material-object definition of wealth is its ostensible estimational accuracy. Here Malthus argues that capability of definite valuation is necessary to enable us to estimate the amount of wealth obtained by any kind of labour, or what Smith called vendible commodities. The labour realized upon material products is the only labour, he says, which is at once susceptible to both accumulation and definite valuation. Apropos of this, three points may be made: first, labour is not directly and specifically counted by the analyst, and nowhere does Malthus really try to do so; second, nor is wealth measurable solely by labour, as Malthus insists that varying capital/labour ratios require a major alteration in Ricardo's labour theory of value (a view to which Ricardo already adhered in his second edition of 1819); and third, Malthus here anticipates Alfred Marshall's effort to limit economic analysis to what is measurable. In Malthus's case the problem of measurability was compounded by his additional requirement that the product be susceptible of accumulation, that is, a material object. A ramification of the last point is the questionable belief that income is ultimately constituted solely of material objects, thus the view that producers of services do not create the (material) wealth which pays them and by which they live, a proposition which placed him squarely in the classical tradition. Notwithstanding Marshall's focus on what is measurable, he did not adopt the classical distinction between productive–unproductive labour (between commodities and services).

THEORY OF VALUE

Malthus's theory of value in the *Principles* is exceedingly complex and subtle; although couched in terms of the labour theory of value it rejects the Ricardian embodied labour theory for the labour command theory, holds cost of production subordinate to demand and supply, and centres on the prices necessary to be paid to induce the supply of products. His discussion is concerned, first, with the nature (source) of value and, second, with the measurement of value, although the two are difficult to keep separate.

Malthus is concerned with the reason for value in exchange; value in use, defined awkwardly as the intrinsic (sic) utility of an object, he discards as metaphorical, but nonetheless considers it essential to exchange. Value in exchange presupposes exchange and exchange requires both the power and the will to exchange, and is thus in part a function of utility, or value in use. Exchange is a matter of reciprocal demand, and reciprocal demand depends upon the relative estimations in which each commodity is held, and is founded upon the relative desire to possess as well as the difficulty or facility of procuring possession. Malthus makes a point of arguing that if nature distributed commodities in the pattern now achieved through exchange prior to consumption, then exchangeable values could not be known. Exchange value requires exchange for its determination, and exchange is dependent upon individual use values.

Notice, then, that of Malthus exchange value abets the production of both commodities and exchangeable value, because of the use value, or utility, which underlies reciprocal demand. To Malthus, *inter alia*, the adaptation of production to consumer wants is necessary to fully secure the exercise of the power of production. There is thus a fundamental microeconomic foundation to his macroeconomic emphasis on effective demand: great stimulus to production is produced by a wide extent of the market and by high prices reflective of high value in use. Moreover, it is fundamental to his view that the effect of an advantageous exchange is to increase the value of both products; this is because it enables or gives effect to reciprocal demand, or mutual value in use. Each receiver places a higher use value on the commodity than the reciprocal receiver. Demand and supply allocates resources (he uses the terminology of distribution in a physical sense) and both encompass and give effect to a multiplicity of interacting forces, including value in use. Effective demand is important on both the microeconomic and the macroeconomic level.

Malthus rejects the system in which price is a function of cost of production, in favour of one in which cost of production is subordinate to demand and supply. Cost of production has a powerful effect on price, however, but the true way, in his view, of viewing costs of production in their effects on prices is as the necessary conditions of the supply of the objects desired. These conditions constitute what Smith called the 'natural price', which Malthus prefers to term the 'necessary price', encompassing the supply prices or costs imposed by labour (as modified by wage turnover), capital (as weighted by the capital/labour ratio and modified by durability of capital), taxes and land rent. Thus, in the determination of value, cost of production is subordinated to demand and supply; labour command is elevated over both cost of production and embodied labour; and exchange value in general is said to reflect the costs necessary to bring the product to market; labour alone does not determine relative exchange value – all three of Smith's component parts of price must be admitted.

Nor does the quantity of labour employed on a commodity constitute a correct *measure* of its exchangeable value. Malthus says that while labour is the principal ingredient in the component parts of price, all the other parts must be reckoned with. *Ceteris paribus*, the quantity of labour which a commodity will command will be in proportion to the quantity it has cost, but the labour which a commodity requires is only one of the circumstances which influence exchange value, although the most important one. Moreover, while labour approaches the nearest of any one object to a measure of real value in exchange, still, since labour itself (like all other exchanged things) is subject to variations in demand and supply, it cannot be considered as a standard. Nor can any one commodity justly be a standard measure of real value in exchange. He suggests, but does not actually put to use, a mean between corn and day-labour as a measure, recognizing that this neglects varying division of labour and varying capital/labour ratios. The prices of corn and of day-labour he sees as varying reciprocally but he is not bothered by any further difficulties in affirming such a measure of real value in exchange. *Vis-à-vis* Ricardo's cost of production approach to measurement, Malthus says that we must choose between an imperfect measure (labour command as measured by a mean between corn and day-labour) and one which is fundamentally erroneous as a measure of cost.

We come finally to the relationship between wealth and value, the subject of a short, eight-page sixth chapter. As may be anticipated, Malthus argues that exchangeable value is necessary to the production of wealth (wealth and value are thus 'connected') but that any discussion of the relation between value and wealth requires an enlarged notion of value, and not merely the quantity of labour employed in production. Exchangeable value must focus on price as both governed by, and governing, demand and supply.

A country possessing the greatest abundance of commodities without labour might be rich, writes Malthus, but the commodities would be without exchangeable value. But in the real state in which man is placed on earth, wealth and exchangeable value are connected most intimately by the necessity of the latter to the production of the former. It is the value of commodities, he argues, that, in the actual state of things, may be said to be the sole cause of the existence of wealth in any quantity. The market prices of commodities are the immediate causes of all the great movements of society in the production of wealth, and these market prices express (in terms of money) their exchangeable values. It will be remembered that demand and supply govern all prices, those of productive and unproductive activities, commodities and services, but the category of wealth applies only to commodities. The idea that demand and supply govern *pro tanto* the production of all things, whether denominated productive or unproductive, material goods or services, is central to Malthus's value and macroeconomics theories but irrelevant to his conception of wealth. Even services which have value in use are excluded from the latter, however much they may figure in the determination of exchangeable value and gross domestic product. Both the classical concern with wealth creation and the neoclassical concern with value in exchange, are to be found in Malthus, for he is one of the few economists who tried to deal with both macro (wealth creation) and micro (value in exchange) problems.

DISTRIBUTION THEORY

The central proposition of Malthus's theory of distribution is that functional distribution is a matter of demand and supply between and among the owners of land, labourers, and the owners of capital. For Malthus, although there are key influencing or limiting variables, there are no single ultimate governing principles determining, respectively, rents, wages, and profits. Although congruent with the general theory of how markets work, this approach has never been central in distribution theory, having been eclipsed by the dominant quest for regulating principles. Malthus's approach reflects his belief that the economy is a complex interactive system, with functional income distribution a result of a multiplicity of mutually interacting technical economic factors, as well as institutions and relative market power.

This approach is amply manifest in his treatment of the factors governing the level of rents. Increasing rents are principally due to (1) accumulation of capital which lowers the rate of profit, (2) increase in population which both lowers the wage rate and raises the demand for, and therefore the price of, food, and (3) improvement of agricultural technology which lowers the cost of production in agriculture. Decreasing rents are due to the opposite conditions.

In Malthus's view, high prices for agricultural commodities and high rents are generally 'connected' with wealth; they are the necessary consequence and sign of prosperity. Low prices and low rent are indications of poverty and decline.

The return of rent by the landlord to the tenant, he argues, would neither cheapen agricultural commodities nor cause an increase in their quantity. This view is consistent with the central thrust of the theory of rent prior to this book, that agricultural prices are high not because the rent of land is high but the rent of land is high because agricultural prices are high, the latter ultimately because of population pressure on an inelastic supply of land. Malthus retains this position here, acknowledging that rent is a consequence of the price of agricultural commodities. But he has two other, related themes in which he is here much more interested, the first of which at least is derivative of his general demand and supply model.

Malthus argues, first, that even though at one level of abstraction, rent is price-determined, still land rent is not 'regulated' by product price and, more importantly, land rent in most instances enters into price as a condition of supply. Malthus thus adopts the microeconomic allocative argument that the payment of rent is necessary for production as a condition of supply of the product produced on land, and that therefore in that sense or respect rent is a necessary part of the price of agricultural produce. This obviously is congruent with his adoption of Smith's notion of natural price or what Malthus called necessary price, and in opposition to his previously held view that marginal land yields no rent.

Second, Malthus builds on his argument that high agricultural prices and high rents are 'connected' with prosperity. He argues that in countries which are self-sufficient in agricultural commodities and countries which import them, the interest of no other class is so nearly 'connected' with the interests of the state as that of the landlord. In Malthus's view, the landlords' rent represents surplus produce of great benefit to society, although it is regrettably not generally seen as such. The surplus is a bountiful gift of Providence, providing much relief from labour. Curiously, however, Malthus also argues that there could not be a more disastrous present to man than an unlimited power of producing food in a limited space. It is all a matter of proportions, here in relation to population growth and its problems other than food supply. Malthus's defence of the landlords' receipt of rent is fairly wide-ranging. He argues that high rents enable a leisure class and thus the creation of culture. He downplays the importance of increased price occasioned by increased difficulty of production (brought into play through population increase under conditions of decreasing returns) as the cause of increases in rent, arguing that improvements in agriculture (due of course to landlords) have been the main cause of increased rents. He goes so far as to emphasize that it is the rich, more fertile, lands which yield the rents, not the poor ones. And he argues that everything which enriches a country increases rents, and everything which impoverishes it, diminishes them; thus the interests of the landlord and of the state are closely connected if not united. Even granting the allocative role of rent, the apologia is clear, as Malthus bends over backwards to defend the interest of the landlords.

With regard to wages, it is again Malthus's central argument that all prices, including wage rates, are determined by demand and supply. Cost of production, for example, affects wages only as a necessary condition of supply; the prices of the necessaries of life affect wages only as they affect the supply of labour by affecting the cost of producing labour. Other variables include the level of a country's resources and the demand for labour and their respective rates of increase; the increase in fixed capital (which he says is not likely to decrease the demand for labour, though he does discuss the adjustment process pertaining to the substitution of fixed for circulating capital); and, of course, the level of population, which, as Malthus discusses at some length, is due to the habits of the labouring classes. All in all, it is a matter of both the union of all the variables and their respective proportions, not any one regulating principle, which is essential to the formulation of the science of political economy. More so than the *Essay on Population*, the *Principles* suggests that population increase interacts in quite complex and open-ended ways with other variables in the generation of economic growth.

Malthus affirms a desire for the maximum possible increase in the demand for and wealth of labour. He recognizes, as did not too many of his contemporaries, that an inferior mode of living is a cause as well as a consequence of poverty. But high wage rates, he urges, can lead to increasing population or to improved modes of subsistence. Which of these alternatives materialize depends in large part on the ability or inability of the lower classes to reason with regard to the future consequences of their present gratification as well as on their civil and political liberty; and their elevation of character and education, as well as their civil and political liberty, is dependent upon their ability and opportunity to plan for the future. This is, indeed, a complex political and economic model but nothing less is to be expected of the author of the *Essay on Population* than his continued insistence that the prudent habits of the poor can alone give them command over a fair proportion of the necessaries and conveniences of life.

Finally, Malthus's discussion of profits encompasses a large number of limiting factors: the relative abundance of capital compared to labour, improvements in agriculture (which affect both agricultural productivity and the demand for capital), increased personal exertion among the working classes, the interest rate on government securities, and so on, all operating, as it were, in a general equilibrium distribution system within the context of a general demand and supply analysis. The principle stressed by Ricardo, that profits are regulated by the wage rate and the wage rate by the cost of production on the last land taken into cultivation, is deemed always operative but operative only within the laws of demand and supply. Also, while there is a tendency for the rate of profit to equalize in all sectors, the tendency is counteracted and overcome by the action of new causes. Congruent with his general methodological position, a position perhaps compelled by his general interactive system, he argues that the effect on profits of any particular increase in capital accumulation cannot be predicted beforehand, as it must always depend upon all the relevant variables, that is, upon the principles of demand and supply.

MACROECONOMICS: GROWTH OF WEALTH AND EFFECTIVE DEMAND

Earlier writers, such as François Quesnay, had developed careful and relatively sophisticated analyses of the interrelated problems of the level of economic activity and economic instability. But Malthus's seventh chapter, long and somewhat rambling and repetitious as it is, is a dramatic analysis all the more striking because it so closely (though by means completely) prefigures John Maynard Keynes's *General Theory of Employment, Interest and Money* (1936) with its emphasis on effective demand. (It should be said that Malthus had quite weak analytical tools with which to analyze the varying causes and consequences of price level changes, changes in liquidity preference, and the relationships between real and money wage rates, not that Keynes had the last word on those subjects.)

The structure of the chapter only hints at the central argument. In separate sections Malthus examines four 'stimuli' to the continued increase of wealth: population growth, capital accumulation (equated with saving), soil fertility, and labour-saving inventions. After a suggestively titled section on 'the necessity of a union of the powers of production with the means of distribution, in order to ensure a continued increase of wealth', he takes up three 'means of increasing the exchangeable value of the whole produce': the division of landed property, internal and external commerce, and unproductive consumption (or the employment of unproductive labour). The chapter concludes with an application of his argument to the post-1815 'distresses of the labouring classes'.

The core of the argument is that apropos of warranting either the translation of saving into capital or the use of capital, accumulation itself does not necessarily ensure sufficient desire for more goods. While saving is a necessary condition for the production of wealth, there must be an effective demand for the output of capital. Increases in saving can result from decreases in consumption which can constitute reductions in effective demand.

Effective demand is as necessary, he says, for the increase of capital as an increase of capital is for the increase in demand. There is mutual interdependence between the two. The problem is that demand has generally produced capital, though capital has sometimes failed to produce demand. The crux of the matter is what Keynes called the marginal efficiency of capital, or the expected rate of profit. The motive to accumulate and to employ capital can be checked, Malthus argued, by want of effective demand: the motive which leads to the extension of both domestic and foreign commerce is profits, an increase of profits or the prevention of their fall. For Malthus, habitual demand for necessaries and, especially, for conveniences, as well as for luxuries, is crucially important for economic growth, an importance that places the landlord class in a peculiarly significant role. The landlord class is the one most capable of possessing the necessary habitual demand for luxuries.

Malthus's argument is essentially that there must must be a balance between consumption and saving and therefore between consumption and investment; there must be the correct proportion between consumption and investment, or between consumption and production. (Malthus sometimes seems to assume that all saving goes into investment, and at other times not;

some problems diagnosed by him arise because saving leads directly to capital formation and others because saving is not transformed into investment, a problem later stressed by Marx.) Capital can be greatly deficient compared with territory and population, but also redundant compared with the effective demand for commodities and for the capital which is used to produce them. Saving may add to capital formation more rapidly than the growth of desire for the goods produced by capital and therefore the demand for the capital itself. Increases in saving and thereby investment can be accompanied by decreases in consumption which limit the market for output. Investment at the expense of consumption can limit the market for the product of investment. The want of demand rather than the want of capital may retard the progress of wealth. The analysis is both oversaving and underconsumption, but the crux of the argument is the necessity for balance proportions in the growth of consumption, saving, and investment, in which consumption and saving–investment are doubly linked: investment leads to income and thereby consumption growth, and consumption, through the marginal efficiency of capital, is the warrant for investment utilization. For saving to lead to investment, or for the employment of capital already accumulated, there must be adequate consumption; otherwise capital is redundant with regard to limited effective demand. Saving must be limited to the amount which, when translated into investment, can be advantageously employed in satisfying the actual, effective demand for products. Capital deficient in relation to population implies a high rate of profit and can be corrected by increased saving; capital deficient in relation to effective demand implies a low rate of profit and will only be aggravated by increased saving.

Malthus thus rejects the denial by Say's law of the possibility of a general glut. He avers, ironically in view of more recent invocations of the law, that the law contradicts the great principles regulating demand and supply: saving may supply investment greater than is warranted by effective demand. Say's law assumes insatiable wants, that all income is spent, and that there is no trade-off of goods for leisure, thus taking for granted the very points in dispute. Say's law, by considering commodities only in relation to each other, neglects the possibility of deficient expected profits consequent to deficient effective demand. Further, by assuming that accumulation will itself ensure effective demand, Say's law neglects the possibility that the passion for accumulation of capital can increase the supply of goods beyond consumer demand. Saving pushed beyond a certain point can destroy profits and employment. There is for Malthus no adjustment mechanism (as is affirmed by Say's law) which guarantees stable full employment growth.

Thus the four stimuli to the increase of wealth – population, saving and capital accumulation, soil fertility and inventions – represent possible but not inexorable growth of production; each requires a suitable market for output, an effective demand ultimately yielding an adequate marginal efficiency of capital. There must therefore be, argues Malthus, a union of the powers of production and consumption. Whenever there is a diminished demand for products, the capitalist will soon lose both the will and the power to employ labour. There must be a proper proportion between production and consumption, centring on the balances between consumption and saving and therefore consumption and investment.

As a limiting factor the division of landed property is also a matter, says Malthus, of proportions. Wide diffusion of ownership will enhance effective demand but there is a trade-off with the requirements of the division of labour (scale economies in production). Moreover, even if wide ownership unlimitedly promoted effective demand and thereby production, still this would not be conclusive support for such a social policy: Malthus's acceptance of the landed aristocracy and the correlative system of liberties and privileges finds an outlet in his argument that the British constitution could not be maintained without an aristocracy and that an effective aristocracy, and therefore good government, could not be maintained without the right of primogeniture. The trade-off is between effective aristocracy and effective demand and Malthus opts for the former, nonetheless emphasizing that analytically, whatever laws of succession may prevail, the principle applies that the institutionalized division of landlord–tenant landed property is a means which governs the exchangeable value of the whole produce. In other words, output is legal-structure specific, just as it is to the level of domestic and foreign commerce.

Malthus's argument concerning the utility of unproductive consumers, or of unproductive labour, is, given his definitions of productive and unproductive, far less radical and controversial than appears at first glance. Once it is recognized that gross domestic product includes both the nominally productive and unproductive, the basic macroeconomic argument is not really compromised. The argument that the tendency to consume is powerfully counteracted by the love of indolence and the desire to save in order to better our condition, with its implications for imbalance between consumption and capital accumulation, is far more important than the semantics of productiveness with its emphasis on material output. His narrow definition of wealth does not restrict the effective substance of Malthus's macroeconomics of income determination.

The fundamental ambiguity of Malthus's analysis lies elsewhere. For all his attention to instability involving imbalanced or disproportionate growth of consumption and saving–investment, and for all his recognition of the distresses of the labouring classes following the end of the Napoleonic Wars, he concludes that the whole question of saving may safely be left to the uninfluenced operation of individual interests and feelings. If there is imbalance between consumption and saving, then there is so much more pressure on the habits of the working class. Therein, arguably much more than his affection for the landed aristocracy, lies Malthus's economic conservatism; though perhaps the one is simply the obverse of the other.

8 Edgeworth's *Mathematical Psychics*: A Centennial Notice*

Francis Ysidro Edgeworth (1845–1926) published his *Mathematical Psychics* in 1881.[1] While not an architectonic classic, such as Alfred Marshall's *Principles*,[2] it was a major work in the history of economics. It was, in retrospect, a book remarkable for its time in its emphasis on mathematical formalism, its depth of technical sophistication and formulation, and its studied application of utilitarian analysis to matters of economic and political policy, as well as its particular substantive contributions to the discipline. A book now apparently largely unread, it is striking for what it did, for what it tried but did not accomplish, and for what it contained that was neglected by subsequent writers until redeveloped much later. More important, it prefigured both the form which economic analysis was subsequently to take and the problems of applying economic analysis to problems of policy. It is a book worthy of centennial notice, indeed, perhaps capable of providing further insight.

We may note, first, that Edgeworth equivocated in the terminology which he used to describe his use of mathematics to explicate the role of utility and maximization in exchange. The phrase 'mathematical psychics' is used in the title and the text (p. 138) but Edgeworth also employed 'psychical mathematics' (p. 126), 'economical mathematics' (p. 127), 'mathematical economics' (pp. 127, 138), 'mathematical theory of exchange' (p. 119), and 'a general theory of contract' (p. 146). All these are found in the appendices (comprising almost one-half the book) in which he attempted to apply and to justify the application of his approach to problems of analysis and policy.

The book essentially was a brief for the use of what Edgeworth called 'mathematical reasoning without numerical data' or 'unnumerical mathematics'. Although Edgeworth, always characteristically modest, was apparently anxious over the degree of his mastery of mathematics, he

* Originally published in *Eastern Economic Journal*, vol. 7 (July–October 1981), pp. 193–8. The author is indebted to Norman Obst for discussions at an early stage of the preparation of this article and to two anonymous referees.

presented the case for the axiomatic method using formal mathematical symbolism. His mathematical formulation of economic problems was remarkable *vis-à-vis* the great bulk of the economic literature of his day and for some time thereafter. Edgeworth was aware, of course, of the relatively inconspicuous mathematical tradition which had been slowly developing in economics in the work of Augustin Cournot and Leon Walras, among others, and, in England, William Stanley Jevons and Alfred Marshall. Nonetheless, for 1881, Edgeworth published a high degree of sophisticated formalism and abstract mathematical rigour. The growth of mathematicization was to be considerable in the years ahead but remained largely secondary until after Paul Samuelson's *Foundations* helped to rechannel economic theory two-thirds of a century later.

Samuelson's maximization economics rather precisely echoed Edgeworth's vision. Edgeworth argued for mathematical reasoning as constituting science. He included in his argument the idea of verification by mathematical reasoning (p. 3). But he justified the use of mathematics, particularly, of course, the calculus, on the grounds that the economics of exchange could be analyzed as a series of maximization problems in the hypothetico-deductive mould. Indeed, he envisioned the problems of social science as problems of individual and collective maximization, and two sections of the substantive Part II of the *Psychics* treated precisely those problems. Economics as social mechanics was recognized and extolled, the conception of man as a pleasure machine both facilitating and justifying the employment of mechanical terminology and mathematical reasoning (pp. 12, 15).

It is not clear whether Edgeworth considered his economics to be a corpus of descriptive truth or a set of analytical tools or, for that matter, whether he seriously considered the question when writing the *Psychics*. Constrained maximization seems to have been, in his *Psychics*, both a technique and a substantive paradigm. In any event, from the perspective of the present, Edgeworth's mode of economic analysis, in contrast with the Walrasian or neo-Walrasian, is clear: an emphasis on inter-agent behaviour rather than prereconciled choice; individual exchange rather than marketwide outcomes; recontracting rather than market adjustments as the exchange process; attention to disequilibrium difficulties; atomistic units in a completely unorganized market; and an emphasis on contract(ing) rather than equilibrium.

The *Psychics* is recognized for its presentation of the contract curve, perhaps less for its author's understanding that it also is a conflict curve (p. 29). It also is recognized for Edgeworth's defence of a conceivable measure of cardinal utility (pp. 7ff., 59–60, 98–102 and *passim*). But also to be found within the pages of the *Psychics* are a willingness to settle for ordinal utility (pp. 8–9); the idea of interdependent utility functions (pp. 12, 53, 102–3); a theory of public choice or of utilitarian politics (pp. 128ff.); a theory of combinations or of collective action (pp. 44–5, 134ff.); and, actually, a centrepiece of Edgeworth's substantive analysis, a theory of imperfect competition.

As interesting as the other topics may be, Edgeworth's handling of the question of imperfect competition (so called by him) is perhaps more instructive. For Edgeworth, the affirmative focus of his analysis of individual maximization was the 'field of competition': 'A *perfect* field of competition professes in addition certain properties peculiarly favourable to mathematical calculation; namely, a certain indefinite *multiplicity* and *dividedness*, analogous to that *infinity* and *infinitesimality* which facilitate so large a portion of Mathematical Physics (consider the theory of Atoms, and all applications of the Differential Calculus)' (p. 18). But competition enabled not only the use of mathematical symbolism. It also engendered determinate solutions. 'That contract in a state of perfect competition is determined by demand and supply is generally accepted, but is hardly to be fully understood without mathematics' (p. 30). Moreover, 'The advantage of this particular method is that it is applicable to the particular cases of imperfect competition; where the conceptions of *demand and supply at a price* are no longer appropriate' (p. 31). Applicable it was, but imperfect competition yielded indeterminate solutions for both economic actors and economic analysts.

In 1939, John Hicks[3] lamented that

> It has to be recognized that a general abandonment of the assumption of perfect competition, a universal adoption of the assumption of monopoly, must have very destructive consequences for economic theory. . . .
>
> It is, I believe, only possible to save anything from this wreck – and it must be remembered that the threatened wreckage is that of the greater part of economic theory – if we can assume that the markets confronting most of the firms with which we shall be dealing do not differ very greatly from perfectly competitive markets. . . . At least, this getaway seems worth trying.

Much the same response was made by Edgeworth to his recognition of the problem posed by non-competitive conditions:

> . . . it does not seem very rash to infer . . . a considerable extent of indeterminateness.

> Of this inference what would be the consequence. To impair, it may be conjectured, the reverence paid to *competition*; in whose results – as if worked out by a play of physical forces, impersonal, impartial – economists have complacently acquiesced. . . . But if it should appear that the field of competition is deficient . . . if competition is found wanting, not only the regularity of law, but even the impartiality of chance . . . economics would be indeed a 'dismal science', and the reverence for competition would be no more. (p. 50).

In the real-world economy, the 'characteristic evil of indeterminate contract' brought about by noncompetitive conditions was '*deadlock*, undecidable opposition of interests' between buyers and sellers (p. 29). Such situations permitted strategic bargaining and gains from combination. There also would result 'a general demand for a *principle of arbitration*' (p. 51), which would lead to the resolution of economic and political conflicts in accordance with some principle of justice or equity, especially distributive equity. This was of great theoretical and practical concern to Edgeworth and he argued that '*Justice* requires to be informed by some more definite principle . . . a superior luminary – utilitarianism' (p. 52): '*competition requires to be supplemented by arbitration, and the basis of arbitration between self-interested contractors is the greatest possible sum-total utility*' (p. 56). Edgeworth thus was led, reluctantly, by consideration of the importance of economic power to the necessity for deliberative conflict resolution and a strategy for economic policy.

The greatest happiness principle was, to Edgeworth, the first principle of economics and ethics (p. v) and more of the *Psychics* was devoted to the practical application of it than to the economics of individual exchange in competitive markets. Both Keynes[4] and Schumpeter[5] distinguished Edgeworth's philosophical utilitarianism from his theoretical, positive economics but Edgeworth firmly believed that the two were inseparable and he directed considerable attention to the subtleties of utilitarian reasoning and the contemporary psychological literature.

It is possible and perhaps often necessary to debate the degree of Edgeworth's appreciation of the complexities and conditions of individual and collective utility maximization, especially the degree to which the greatest happiness principle is capable of providing unambiguous and unequivocal answers to problems of policy in the absence of severely limiting and prefiguring, channelling assumptions (see below). In Edgeworth's favour is his recognition that realization of the greatest possible quantity of happiness is 'under conditions' (p. 12) and that the conclusions, or rules, provided by his mathematical psychics were only general instructions, not detailed regulations; a very general, abstract and rough pattern requiring checking by experience and modification in practice (pp. 71, 126). It would be unfair to attribute to Edgeworth the sins of extreme rationalism, determinateness, and exclusiveness of policy implications perpetrated by later generations of economic analysts.

Two important characteristics of Edgeworth's work in collective maximization warrant attention. First, Edgeworth's utilitarianism constituted an *administrative*, not a methodological individualist approach to collective utility maximization.[6] Using Vilfredo Pareto's terminology, Edgeworth dealt with utility *for* a society, not *of* a society. Thus, his definition of the problem of the collective utilitarian calculus is to 'find the distribution of means and of labor and the quality and number of population, so that there may be the greatest possible happiness' (p. 56, paraphrased). We shall see in a moment that Edgeworth's utilitarianism was distinctly conservative (or hierarchic) but it was a problem-oriented, activist utilitarianism, one taking the central decision maker's or planners' point of view and not the optimality of markets *per se*. His was a utilitarianism for the statesman, a style of policy analysis which typified the late nineteenth-century departure from the eighteenth-century natural order approach to social phenomena.[7]

The second characteristic of Edgeworth's analysis of collective maximization was his insistence on individuals' differential capacity for happiness (p. 57; and also for work, pp. 59, 66), as well as the diminishing marginal utility of means (p. 61). Accordingly, we find in the *Psychics* a conservative theory of economic policy. He would allocate the means of education to the highest in order of evolution, as the group most capable of improvement (pp. 68, 79). He would limit population differentially for each section of population in order to maximize the happiness of the next generation (pp. 69, 71). He would sacrifice the interests of the least favoured class in the utilitarian community to the happiness of the higher classes (compare John Rawls!) (but the limit is somewhere above the starvation point, determined by reference to disincentive effects, the relation of diminishing marginal utility to privation, population control, and political instability (p. 75 and *passim*)). Finally, *inter alia*, the happiness of the present generation may have to be sacrificed to that of the future (pp. 74–5). Overall, he felt 'that in order to the greatest possible sum total of happiness, the more capable of pleasure shall take more means, more happiness' (p. 10), thus 'negativing the assumption that *Equality* is necessarily implied in Utilitarianism. For, if sentients differ in *Capacity for happiness* . . . there is no presumption that equality of circumstances is the most felicific arrangement; especially when account is taken of the interests of posterity' (p. vii).

Edgeworth insists that the importance of each class is not necessarily in proportion to its numbers (p. 89n) and that true utilitarianism is not that each person counts for one but that each increment of marginal utility counts for one (p. 122). Unequal capacity means unequal distribution of means (pp. 124–5).

Edgeworth does insist that the final result may be aristocratic or egalitarian but that equality, although part of, is not the whole of distributive justice, weight having to be given to differences in the capacity for pleasure, considerations which enter his discussions of income, work, and the treatment of women (pp. 77ff.). A critical question, of course, is the relation of existing institutions to the 'natural' distribution of such capacity. Edgeworth's answer with respect to women is clear: 'Altogether, account being taken of existing, whether true or false, opinions about the nature of woman, there appears a nice consilience between the deductions from the utilitarian principle and the disabilities and privileges which hedge round modern womanhood' (p. 79; Edgeworth never married).

There are other defences of inequality, of course, but Edgeworth's admits several ironies. First, insofar as differential capacity for happiness is institutionally determined (unequal distribution of means produces unequal capacity), Edgeworth's utilitarian calculus operates to reproduce social structure and its artificial differential capacity for happiness. Second, Arthur Cecil Pigou's later assumption is rich and poor likely had similar temperaments (that is, had roughly equal capacity to derive utility), involved a quite different variant of utilitarianism. After all, Bentham's greatest happiness principle had long posed the further problem whether the object to be maximized was the number or percentage of happy people or the happiness of those most intensively happy;[8] and the Benthamite left and right took quite different positions on this, the fundamental distributive issue. Third, the indifference curve used by Edgeworth to further his utilitarian analysis was later used to exorcise utilitarianism from economic analysis.[9]

Edgeworth's combination of constrained maximization, unorganized markets, and mathematics went through several reformulations until it is now lauded as a promising alternative to neo-Walrasian model building[10] – if it is not already, through Samuelson, the principal and most distinguishing characteristic of economics although this writer, for one, believes that there is more than this to economics.

But there are several problems which have been, it is tempting to say, perennial in economics. Edgeworth's *Mathematical Psychics* is significant, in part, because these problems arose in modern form for the first time with its publication. Let me state the problems from the point of view of the 'critic'. First, neither Edgeworth nor many modern economists seem to have adequately recognized the limits of formalism with regard to description, explanation, and policy. Formal rationalism, while productive of deep, pointed theoretical insights, is unable uniquely to solve questions of policy. Second, Edgeworth's marriage of utilitarianism with a conservative, hierarchic view of social order seems to illustrate the ease with which utilitarianism can be combined with antecedent normative premises with regard to whose interests ought to or can count. Conversely, Edgeworth's felt necessity to resort to some version of the greatest happiness principle in order to reach determinate solutions to conflict problems suggests that determinate solutions are achieved only by introducing, explicitly or implicitly, channelling and prefiguring assumptions as to whose interests are to or can count. Third, Edgeworth's resort to the greatest happiness principle as an approach to collective utility maximization is (as I already have noted) an inadequate treatment of the methodologically collectivist (not normatively collectivist) forces at work with respect to social organization and structure.

It may be said that no economist really has believed differently. Certainly, Edgeworth (and Pareto, for that matter) would have agreed, but he carried his utilitarianism so far, abetted by his conservative assumption of differential capacity for happiness, that the limits were easily obscured if not forgotten. Paradoxically, Edgeworth's utilitarianism implies (1) that atomistic individualism is inevitably informed by considerations (whatever they are) of social structure and (2) that economic analysis necessarily contains and should make explicit its normative premises (whatever they are).

To Edgeworth's credit, he made his normative premise explicit. That he considered differential capacity for happiness a *fact*, not a valuational premise, does not weaken that point very much. (In a different connection, Randall Bartlett[11] has shown that implicitly treating differentially or unequally situated persons equally may give unobserved effect to the actual inequality, whereas making the inequality of circumstance explicit enables quite different conclusions to be reached.) Rather, it suggests the difficulties which the discipline subsequently has had in identifying the normative premises, and their grounds, in its analysis.[12] Edgeworth subtitled his *Mathematical Psychics* 'An Essay on the Application of Mathematics to the Moral Sciences'. He surely went too far in declaring that the limits of mathematics can 'only . . . be decided by the authority and in the presence of Mathematics herself' (p. 3) and that '"Mécanique Sociale" may one day take her place along with "Mécanique Celeste", throned each upon the double-sided height of one maximum principle, the supreme pinnacle of moral as of physical science' (p. 12). He did recognize, however, that the realization of the maximum sum-total of happiness was subject to constraints, including structural considerations (pp. 9, 11–12). To his credit, notwithstanding his conversatism, he recognized the applicability of technique 'to the political struggle for power, as well as to the commercial struggle for wealth' (p. 16). As to whether mathematical psychics has anything to teach with regard to the political (read 'power') aspects of problems, Edgeworth said, 'Nothing as to practical politics; but as to the first principles of political theory perhaps something' (p. 127; see also p. 133), and that 'about a subject so illusory, where the vanity and the very virtues of our nature, oligarchical pride, democratical passion, perturb the measurements of utility; not slight the advantage of approaching the inquiry in the calm spirit of mathematical truth' (p. 134). Edgeworth surely overestimated that advantage, as he overestimated the non-normative character of the uses of mathematics in social science, but he was not totally captivated or blinded by his principle of the differential capacity for happiness.

Notes

1. F. Y. Edgeworth, *Mathematical Psychics*, 'An Essay on the Application of Mathematics to the Moral Sciences' (London: Kegan Paul, 1881). Subsequently reprinted for Economist's Book Club by Augustus M. Kelley. All page references are to this work.
2. The *Mathematical Psychics* was published when Edgeworth was 36; the *Principles*, when Marshall was 48. Both men lived into their early eighties.
3. John R. Hicks, *Value and Capital* (Oxford: Oxford University Press, 1939), pp. 83–5.
4. John Maynard Keynes, *Essays and Sketches in Biography* (New York: Meridian Books, 1956), p. 107.
5. Joseph A. Schumpeter, *History of Economic Analysis* (New York: Oxford University Press, 1954), pp. 408–9, 780, 831, 1056.
6. See S. Todd Lowry, 'Recent Literature on Ancient Greek Economic Thought', *Journal of Economic Literature*, vol. 17 (March 1979), pp. 65–86; and Keith Tribe, *Land, Labour and Economic Discourse* (London: Routledge & Kegan Paul, 1978), especially chs 3 and 5.
7. Ellen Frankel Paul, *Moral Revolution and Economic Science* (Westport: Greenwood Press, 1979).
8. Overton H. Taylor, *A History of Economic Thought* (New York: McGraw-Hill, 1960), p. 134: 'leaving unanswered the question *which* is really to be maximized, the number or percentage of (more or less) happy people, or the intensity of the happiness of those most largely benefited'.
9. Henry W. Spiegel, *The Growth of Economic Thought* (Durham: Duke University Press, 1971), p. 526.
10. E. Roy Weintraub, *Microfoundations* (New York: Cambridge University Press, 1979).

11. Randall Bartlett, *Economic Foundations of Political Power* (New York: Free Press, 1973). See Warren J. Samuels, Book Review, *Journal of Economic Issues*, vol. 10 (March 1976), pp. 181–5.
12. See Warren J. Samuels, 'Ideology in Economics', in Sidney Weintraub (ed.), *Modern Economic Thought* (Philadelphia: University of Pennyslvania Press, 1977), pp. 467–84; and 'Normative Premises in Regulatory Theory', *Journal of Post Keynesian Economics*, vol. 1 (Fall 1978), pp. 100–14.

9 Ashley's and Taussig's Lectures on the History of Economic Thought at Harvard, 1896–7*

If each generation of economists has the task of interpreting the history of the discipline for itself, then the history of the history of economic thought is itself an important and viable field of inquiry. It should instruct us, among other things, on how the minds and paradigms of economists have developed, in part, through informing us as to how earlier generations received still earlier economic concepts and theories.

This chapter reports on student notes from two year-long courses in the history of economic thought given at Harvard in 1896–7 by leading figures in the profession. Economics 15 was taught by William James Ashley and began with the Greeks, concentrated upon the mercantilists, and concluded with Smith and Malthus. Economics 2 was taught by Frank William Taussig and covered Ricardo through Böhm-Bawerk and Marshall, concentrating upon the latter.[1] The notes were taken by A. Piatt Andrew, then a doctoral student (and Taussig's assistant in Economics 1)[2] and subsequently a member of the Harvard economics faculty.[3] The two courses were quite different, in part because of their respective subject-matter but in part, too, because of the interests of the professors. But there were similarities, not the least of which is the apparent relative absence of narrow doctrinal interpretation. Moreover, although there is much fairly standard interpretation found in the notes, there also are some interesting variations and departures.

This chapter also reports on a set of undated and untitled notes from other lectures by Taussig primarily comprising an overview of the entire history of economic thought. Some pages are marked 'Pol. Econ.' and the name 'Political Economy' will be used here. The lectures most likely had been given in Economics 1.

The three main sections of this chapter will report on the notes from Ashley's Economics 15, Taussig's Economics 2, and Taussig's lectures on Political Economy, in that order.[4]

* Originally published in *History of Political Economy*, vol. 9 (Fall 1977), pp. 384–411.

I ECONOMICS 15: THE HISTORY AND LITERATURE OF ECONOMICS TO THE MIDDLE OF THE NINETEENTH CENTURY

Andrew's notes from Ashley's course run to 102 pages for the first half-year and 97 for the second. The main divisions of the course were these: Greek thought (49 pages), Patristic and Scholastic thought (11 pages), Mercantilism (92 pages), Adam Smith (19 pages), and Thomas Robert Malthus (5 pages). Other individuals, including those covered under Mercantilism, were Plato, Aristotle, Pierre Dubois, Nicholas Oresme, Thomas Mun, Josiah Child, Sir William Temple (1628–99), John Locke, Sir William Petty, Dudley North, Nicholas Barbon, Charles Davenant, and David Hume, with the greatest number of pages devoted to Plato, Aristotle, Locke, and Hume (20, 21, 30 and 11 pages, respectively). Conspicuous by their absence, except for occasional references,[5] are the Physiocrats, perhaps explained by a required thesis on '"Physiocracy" (with a discussion of Turgot's relation thereto)'. However, a second thesis on '"Mercantilism" (illustrated from Mun, or any other important mercantilist writer)' was also required notwithstanding the extensive lectures thereon, including seven pages on Mun (15.a.1).

The reading list provided for John Kells Ingram's *History of Political Economy* and Frank W. Taussig's *Wages and Capital* as texts, supplemented with material from Plato's *Republic*, Aristotle's *Politics*, Ashley's own *Economic History*, Mun's *England's Treasure by Foreign Trade*, Locke's *Some Considerations of the Consequences of the Lowering of Interest and Raising the Value of Money*, Hume's *Essays*, A. R. J. Turgot's *Reflections on the Formation and the Distribution of Riches*, Smith's *Wealth of Nations*, Malthus' *Essay on the Principle of Population* (1st and 2nd editions). David Ricardo's *Principles of Political Economy and Taxation*, and John Stuart Mill's *Essays on Some Unsettled Questions of Political Economy* (15.a.1). The notes for the first half-year include the mid-term exam.[6] Ten of the first twelve pages of notes include summaries of chapters from Sir Henry Maine's *Ancient Law* and Ashley's *Economic History* and summary notes on Greek thought, Patristic and Scholastic writers, and Mercantilism.

Ashley's treatment of Plato and Aristotle covered the traditional subjects of the basis of the state and the role of property; the nature of human nature; the division of labour; the place of exchange, wealth, and money; and the sociopolitical foundations of economic order, including their concern over class conflict and related discord and disunity. His analysis of the Stoic and Epicurean schools concentrated upon their different views of natural law.

Discussion of the Church Fathers centred on the topics of slavery, property, and the relation of the individual to the state. Ashley stressed the Augustinian dichotomy as 'in a sense a vital blow at the old conception of the state; the state thereafter became secular, a thing of this world – of this age (saeculo), [sic] as opposed to that which is eternal – the church' (15.a.76). He urged that 'the modern individualism could never have come to be except for the intermediary stage when the spiritual interests had been separated from the interests of the state' (15.a.77). His discussion of the Schoolmen and Canonists stressed the maintenance-of-social-structure interpretation of the just price.

As will be further discussed below, Ashley's course developed the theme that the history of economic thought reflected economic and political circumstances. Mercantilism thus was interpreted as a complex set of intellectual and policy responses: the discovery of new sources of the precious metals naturally resulted in the attachment of excessive importance to the new means of exchange, and mercantilism as the economic aspect of sixteenth-century absolutism, including the Roman-law revival of governmental absolutism (15.a.86–7).[7]

Accordingly, Ashley sympathetically presented the array and interplay of mercantilist concerns and thinking: money as wealth versus money as a means to wealth (the importance of the circulation of money); interrelations of the quantity of money, the volume of transactions, and the price level; perceived shortages of the precious metals; promotion of employment; coalescence of favourable-balance-of-trade and protectionist ideas in the sixteenth century, arguing that tariff policy only slowly came to a prominent place in Mercantilist minds (15.b.7); control of the interest rate; concern over population; industrial regulation; and, *inter alia*, coinage and debasement. Ashley envisioned three stages: prohibition of export of the precious metals, the balance of bargain system, and balance of trade orientation. He also surveyed historians' varying ideas on the nature of mercantilism. Most interesting is his repeated argument that mercantilism – particularly (as in Child's view) when internal restrictions came to be juxtaposed to protectionism *per se* – played a role in breaking down the old system of industrial regulation and prepared the way for freer trade. The notes read, in part:

> It may be worth considering how far mercantilism, by breaking down industrial regulations for the benefit of foreign trade, prepared the way for the free trade attack on restrictions all around, and in foreign trade in particular. Hildebrand recognized the control of industry as the essence of mercantilism, but taking a larger view, is not the mercantilist temper simply the earliest stage in the modern movement to which Smith and

> the free trade school belong? While they differed as to the results to be expected from particular measures, there was an underlying unity of feeling as to the ultimate principles by which things were to be tested. (15.b.16)

And again, weeks later: 'So, says Ashley in a sense, the Mercantilists led the way for the naturalist school of liberty. They wanted to break down the internal regulation of industry' (15.b.53).

Ashley discussed Locke's ideas on interest, value of money, government and property, labour theory of value, and tax shifting, maintaining that his quantity theory was envisioned 'only as an instance of the wider law of supply and demand – so we have here a theory of money and a theory of price intertwined' (16.b.25). Ashley also drew attention to Locke's holding that interest and rent were a function of private property institutions (15.b.27). Dudley North was held by Ashley to have contributed to the 'movement which led to A. Smith' (15.b.56), stressing the ideas that interest was similar to rent, that trade implies its profitability, that a nation always has the money supply it needs, and that the whole world is as to trade as one nation (15.b.58). As for Barbon, Ashley juxtaposed his own generally deprecatory view to what he criticized as Stephen Bauer's exaggerated opinion. Barbon, the notes have Ashley saying, was 'discovered and monopolized by Stephen Bauer' (15.b.60).

Hume's essays were given close attention, Ashley concentrating upon the relations of wealth and power, the irrelevancy and relevancy of the quantity of money, the distinction between money and capital, and taxation. On the latter topic, Ashley suggested that the theory that all taxes fall on land was 'a pretty familiar idea at the time' (15.b.73).

Ashley's treatment of Smith was limited in the notes to the eleven chapters of Book I of the *Wealth of Nations*, and concentrated upon the relations of Smith's value theory to Locke's and Cantillon's. He called attention to the germ of the idea of surplus value in Smith 'which has played so great a part in Socialism, the idea which regarded the product as entirely due to the labour applied in production, and regarded the payment to the landlord and capitalist as an unfair deduction. 'But', Ashley went on to say, 'Adam Smith had in mind not the idea that the same result was to be shared between capitalist and laborer but it was the increased result of facilitated labor' (15.b.82–3). Ashley returned to the subject later. After restating the Smithian idea that 'with the introduction of capital and rent the laborer has to allow a "*share*" to the landlord and employer'. Ashley argued that 'it seems to be suggested that it is the same product which the laborer has foregone a *share* of. Of course Smith did not mean this, but it has been so understood by Socialists who demand for laborers "the total produce of labor"' (15.b.87). Interestingly, at the same point, after asserting Ricardo's excessive attention, *vis-à-vis* Smith, to natural price, Ashley is noted as saying that 'recently the Austrians have so exalted *market* price as almost to overlook the *natural* price of commodities' (15.b.86).

The discussion of Malthus centred on population *vis-à-vis* diminishing returns. The Economics 15 notes conclude with this evaluation of Malthusian ideas:

> The mischief of the Malthusian teaching in *England* is that it has caused the forces of reproduction to be isolated, to be regarded as a great blind overmastering force dominating the whole economic situation, whereas it is only one power out of many, and its effect will vary with surrounding conditions.
>
> The most important consideration is whether or not the supply of employment in the future is calculable. If you have an organization of society in which men can make some reasonable forecast of the future, and are mentally able to make such a forecast, the forces of prudential restraint are active.
>
> So that in the end we come to a position intermediate between that of Malthus and that of Godwin – namely that '*institutions*' do really play an important part. (15.b.96–7)

Ashley characterized the development of economic thought as 'concerning the material basis of human life' (15.a.21). He held that the first sustained economic thought was in ancient Greece; that 'economics as a "*science*" – as a systematic study – only emerged with the later mercantilists' and 'in the narrower sense of the word "science" – meaning a study of the causes and sequences of things – economics only came into existence with the Physiocrats' (15.a.13). But 'until our own time economics has not been distinguished from other fields. It was a part of general political, general ethical speculation' (15.a.14). Ashley's conception of the scope of economics included the philosophic foundations of order. Inasmuch as thought reflected circumstances, it tended to rationalize the status quo order; and it reflected class conflict (haves and have-nots) and other antagonisms as well as the dimensions of contemporary idealism-versus-realism conflicts over continuity versus change (see, for example, 15.a.10, 21, 34).

According to the notes, Ashley described the course in these terms: 'We are only going to study writers who have been of historic importance – who have represented the ideas of the time or country or have influenced later thinkers. We are not to follow ideas with a purely "antiquarian" interest' (15.a.13). The antipathy to antiquarianism was repeated at least one other time, as part of a critique of Wilhelm Roscher's *Geschichte der Nationalökonomik in Deutschland*: 'It sometimes falls into the common danger of all historical writers – antiquarianism' (15.a.18). This is found in six pages of notes critiquing the existing history of economic thought literature. Included in the comments recorded are these: John Ramsay McCulloch as treating all with the 'narrowest dogmatism' (15.a.16); Smith as failing to trace through the relations between mercantilism and Physiocracy 'and the events of their times' (15.a.15). Roscher's, Karl Knies's and Bruno Hildebrand's stress on the relativity of economic thought; and that Roscher's work, notwithstanding the tendency to antiquarianism, was 'the first thoroughly objective and impartial work in spirit and method' (15.a.17).

Ashley also expounded upon 'the value of a study of the history of economic thought':

1. In Political Economy the subject-matter is subject to change. The economic activities of men are affected by internal and external changes and differences. Hence, economic generalizations must be relative – or hypothetical, i.e., true only under certain conditions. And so the economic teaching of the past can not be condemned *merely* because it differs from the present.
2. Economic ideas of one period are connected with the ideas of preceding periods both by genetic relations of sequence and by *conscious reaction*. As Hegel says – 'error is a moment in the development of truth'.
3. Even what were in their own times errors were in so far the outcome of contemporary conditions, that they contribute to the understanding of the past.
4. The thoughts of men have often powerfully affected whole communities, e.g., Mercantilism was of great importance in bringing about the change from feudalism to the state in which we live – by developing international trade. (15.a.13)

The most distinctive theme running through the notes is that ideas reflect circumstances. The basic notion is found in a discussion of Aristotle on slavery: 'The ancient world rested on slavery, the mediaeval world on serfdom, and the modern world on *legal* freedom of contract in the laborers. Hence the problem of the means of obtaining the material basis of life has presented itself in these forms . . . the successive stages of the world's history' (15.a.48). Thus in discussing the Schoolmen and Canonists, the notes have Ashley saying that 'the questions of serfdom and slavery did not emerge as questions – they seemed to belong to the nature of things' (15.a.78). The ideas of Plato were said to reflect circumstances, namely, unchecked democracy and the loss of power after the Persian wars; Stoic and Epicurean individualism was 'principally due to contemporary political conditions' (15.a.63); then the difference in societies between the time of the Patristic writers and the Schoolmen, especially the new phenomena of trade, account for the new fields of speculation, namely, currency, coinage and debasement, and the law and morality of contracts (15.a.70, 78, 80) such that in the eleventh century, with the growth of towns, the formation of merchant bodies, and the establishment of markets, 'the economic questions were presented in a new light' (15.a.5); and, as indicated above, mercantilism was seen as a reaction to the profound impact of the great influx of precious metals and the rise of political absolutism. Throughout both terms there is continued close attention to the circumstantial bases of mercantilist issues, arguments, and policies and, so also seen above, to their circumstantial consequences.

Circumstances also include political conditions and ambitions, and Ashley dealt at some length with the motivations behind Locke's legal–economic ideas. Locke was in part reacting to Thomas Hobbes' idea that the rights of property depend upon the will of the sovereign, a view which 'cut the ground from beneath the idea of property as a revolutionary argument'. 'Locke had this in mind when he set about to find a different origin for property – in order to prove the unjustifiableness of the arbitrary interference of the king.' Out of this came the labour appropriation theory of property, however qualified – for example, by the requirement that there be enough and as good left in common (15.b.42, 43). After discussing the details of Locke's reasoning, the notes have Ashley saying, 'Of course, this is all abstract in-the-air reasoning' (15.b.46). He goes on to Locke's view that money and consent lead to inequality in the case of societies not subject to government; in the case of government, the inequality is regulated by the laws. In Ashley's interpretation:

> The first way out of the difficulty was for Locke to say that in political societies laws settle rights of property originally settled by labor, and so inequality of property comes into existence. It is a matter at first of labor. Then as societies grow up, law takes the place. But this associates property rights with political society, this comes dangerously near Hobbes' idea that property rights were created by the sovereign. This won't satisfy Locke. He wants to prove that the rights of property are prior to the formation of political society, that they belong to the state of nature.

> And for that reason he introduces the appeal to the use of money, which he regards as having existed in a state of nature. Money existed in that state by tacit consent, and since unequal conditions flow from the use of money, unequal possession may be said to have been sanctioned by the tacit consent of society. (15.b.46)

According to Ashley, this serves 'the political end of Locke's argument'.

> Men put themselves under government to preserve their property. In the state of nature there was a want of definiteness, of a tribunal to decide in case of disputes – of an executive power to insist on justice. To secure these guarantees of the existing natural rights of property, governments were established. Hobbes had maintained that rights of property had only come into existence with the institution of political society. With Locke they had existed before, and so Locke uses this ground as a base for his plea that James II had violated rights existing before political organization began. (15.b.47)

Yet, these ulterior political motivations notwithstanding, Locke is the first great theorist: 'Roscher calls Locke the first systematizer of Political Economy.' What he means, Ashley says, is that

> Locke was the first great *theorizer*. You feel this in passing from Temple and Child to Locke. With them the practical interest was dominant; and their observations were those of shrewd men giving direct impressions without stopping to examine the mental process which led to those impressions. Locke was interested in the argument for its own sake. He has that intellectual curiosity which makes for a theory of the subject. He follows a *deductive* train of argument. If men pursue self-interest, the consequences will be so and so – precisely the sort of argument that you find in Adam Smith. You feel in reading Locke the presence of a system in the background. He had the materials for a system – the foundations – but his interests being chiefly in philosophy, he never followed out his economic theories. (15.b.50)

Finally, Ashley directed attention to the sources of ideas manifest in the *Wealth of Nations*, primarily in a half-dozen pages entitled 'The literary history of the underlying conceptions of A. Smith' (15.b.75). The main influence was the conception of man's relation to political society found in Stoic and Epicurean philosophies. Eighteenth-century deification of nature was said to be primarily a revival and extension of Stoic teaching, with continuity through the Middle Ages, the channels being the study of Roman law and the Christian theologians, especially Thomas Aquinas, and later

Hugo Grotius, Pierre Gassendi, Hobbes, Samuel von Pufendorf, and Locke. Ashley found a great impact of Locke on Smith, both in general and in regard to details; and doubted that Hume was a necessary intermediary between Locke and Smith (15.b.48, 50). Locke's views were interpreted by Ashley as representing a modified Stoicism, a blend of ideas from both contract and natural rights philosophies. Rights from the 'tolerable' state of nature were retained by individuals after entering the compact which exists to safeguard them. By giving the liberal movement the weapon of appealing to indefeasible natural rights, Locke was the father of eighteenth- and nineteenth-century individualism.[8] A further and complementary aspect of Smith's thought, according to Ashley, was a large element of eighteenth-century optimistic theism (15.b.79). The Physiocratic influence was to affect 'Smith's treatment of particular topics, and his arrangement of the whole', especially the conception 'of a produce divided among the several classes of society, classes which were at the same time social classes and economic categories, laborers, landowners, capitalists, etc.' (15.b.80)

II ECONOMICS 2: ECONOMIC THEORY FROM THE MIDDLE OF THE NINETEENTH CENTURY TO THE PRESENT TIME

Andrew's notes from Taussig's course cover 71 pages for the first half-year and 85 for the second. The course was conducted partly by discussion, and Andrew apparently was careful to distinguish what were notes from Taussig's lectures and remarks and what were his own additions thereto by appending his initials to the latter. The main divisions of the course were these: David Ricardo (24 pages); John Elliott Cairnes (15 pages); Francis A. Walker and Taussig on distribution (19 pages); Alfred Marshall (48 pages); Eugen von Böhm-Bawerk (15 pages); and a fraction of a page to 2 pages each on Johann Heinrich von Thünen, Jean-Baptiste Say, J. C. L. de Sismondi, Malthus, Thomas Chalmers, Richard Jones, the Manchester School, James Mill, John Stuart Mill, McCulloch, Nassau William Senior, Frederic Bastiat, Henry C. Carey, F. B. W. von Hermann, Karl Heinrich Rau, the Historical Schools, and the Austrian School in general. The course aimed at teaching both the history of economic thought and contemporary theory, a primary technique being the comparison of key contemporary writers *vis-à-vis* each other and earlier writers, for example. Cairnes in juxtaposition to Stuart Mill. The notes also include the mid-year and final exams.[9]

The reading list for the first half-year included chapters from Ricardo's *Principles of Political Economy and Taxation* and his *Essay on the*

Influence of a Low Price of Corn on the Profits of Stock; Stuart Mill's *Principles of Political Economy*; Cairnes' *Some Leading Principles of Political Economy Newly Expounded*; Taussig's *Wages and Capital* and *The Wages Question*; Walker's *Political Economy* and *The Wages Question*; and Marshall's *Principles of Economics* (from both the 1st and 3rd editions). The list for the second half-year comprised additional chapters from Marshall and many chapters from Böhm-Bawerk's *Positive Theory of Capital*.

The general order of consideration is worth mentioning. Taussig first covered Ricardo, Cairnes, Mill, Walker, and himself (in all cases primarily on value, wages, and profits) and then Marshall, the other earlier English writers, and the non-English writers, including Böhm-Bawerk, and concluded with five pages on distribution.

The course gave elaborate consideration to the topics of value, price, cost of production, wages, and profits in the works of Ricardo, Mill, Cairnes, Walker, and Taussig, including Cairnes and Taussig on the wages fund and Walker's 'rent' theory of profits *vis-à-vis* the ideas of Sidgwick and Macvane. The extensive discussion of Marshall begins with this statement:

> The distinguishing mark of Marshall's book is that *value* and *distribution* are treated as one. From what we have seen in Cairnes these two subjects plainly dovetail more than one would suppose from Mill and Ricardo. Marshall for the first time, however, treats value and distribution intentionally in one inquiry. (2.a.58)

Taussig concentrated attention upon the Marshallian topics of consumers' rent (as consumers' surplus was called in the first three editions of his *Principles*); rent, population, and diminishing returns; costs; the maximum satisfaction doctrine; the principle of substitution, which the notes have Taussig say 'seems to me to be practically a restatement of Cairnes' position, that the employer will so divide his capital between fixed and wages fund, and between different sorts of laborers that the greatest possible return will be gained' (2.b.21); labour market conditions; quasi-rent; and interest. The several references to Macvane include his distinction between waiting (the time between the outlay of labour and the possession of the finished product) and abstinence – a considerable interval of waiting coupled with unequal possessions leading to a vicarious waiting for the labourers by the possessors of much wealth (paraphrased from 2.a.70). Finally, Taussig's treatment of Böhm-Bawerk, particularly on capital as a factor of production, the subjective theory of value, and the interest rate, showed a thorough understanding of the Austrian's doctrines.

The notes include extensive consideration of the wide array of variables seen as governing or relevant to price under the rubric of the Classical labour theory of value or cost-of-production theory. They evidence the considerable heterogeneity of nineteenth-century orthodox economic thought on these matters. Included were such factors as constant versus increasing cost; non-competing groups (see below); wages in relation to cost of production; cost of production as proportional *vis-à-vis* equal to the quantity of labour; the varying durability of fixed capital; cost versus the reward of cost; standard of living *vis-à-vis* population law *vis-à-vis* demand and supply; wages in relation to prices; money versus real wages; the effects of changes in the quantity of capital, population, and technology (including increasing returns therein); goods subject to continuous production versus goods absolutely limited in supply; relative wage rates versus the level of wages; and so on.

There are notes critical of Ricardo's assumptions; commodities whose value is determined by scarcity alone 'are probably more numerous than Ricardo supposed – including such articles as are produced by non-competing groups of laborers',[10] and the assumption that competition operates without restraint 'is decidedly open to question' (2.a.6). The same group of notes also treats Ricardo in the light of Marx:

> Ricardo also reiterates that when he speaks of the values of commodities as *governed by* the relative quantities of labor bestowed on them, he does not imply that their *cost* is exactly *equal* to those quantities of labor, for profits are an added element in the cost of many commodities. The costs of commodities are (with the exceptions mentioned) *proportional to* the quantities of labor but not necessarily *equal* to them, according to Ricardo.
>
> Karl Marx and some of the Socialists have based their doctrine that value consists of 'labor jelly' upon Ricardo, and have asserted it to be the logical implication of his doctrine that the only claim upon value was that of the laborer.
>
> The passages we have just summarized [from chapter one of Ricardo] give the answer to this claim.
>
> Ricardo distinctly recognized profits. He emphasizes the importance of labor for the purposes of measuring the exchangeability of articles, because profits were proportional to labor expended, and so needed not to be considered. Value he said was 'governed by', 'dependent upon', 'measured by' or 'proportional to' quantities of labor. He did not say that value *was* or *consisted in* quantity of labor. (2.a.7–8)

The problem of proof recurs throughout the notes and will be considered later but there is one case, in connection with Taussig's criticism of Ricardo's neglect of scarcity value, that is appropriate at this point. After mentioning Adolf Held and T. E. Cliffe Leslie to the same effect, the notes have Taussig saying,

> And the fact seems to be that Ricardo does not elaborate any proof of the assertion that value is determined by quantity of labor. He seems to assume that in general there is free competition; and that as only an insignificant number of commodities have a scarcity value, they need not be taken into account. While he does mention the fact that differences of skill are held in unequal estimation, he does not apparently appreciate the way by which those different valuations have come to be – i.e., how differences in wages have come to be – and neither does he understand their significance. Ricardo does not seem to realize that the limited number of skilled laborers tends to limit the production of commodities and to give them a scarcity value – which is not measured by the quantities of labor bestowed on them. If he did understand this, he did not think it important enough to deserve careful notice. (2.a.9–10)

But the most interesting discussions of labour, productivity, and value are those wherein Taussig gives his own view. At no fewer than three points in this course Taussig argued that 'labor alone produces'. In a discussion of Marshall's Book VI, Chapter VI, Section 3, the notes read:

> Marshall passes then abruptly to Socialists.
>
> In order to reply to the claim of Marx *et al.* that wealth is produced by labor alone, Marshall says that it is the product of labor and waiting.
>
> Taussig says that nothing is produced except by labor, but labour may be applied in different ways – either immediately or through a series of steps. In order to [have] effective application of labor, some delay is necessary, and someone must wait. If wealth is so unequally distributed that the one who works can not do the waiting, but some one else it vicariously – then the vicarious waiter must be paid for it. Labor alone produces.[11]

The topic comes up again at the beginning of Taussig's discussion of Böhm-Bawerk:

> Capital *per se* produces nothing; it is simply a mode of employing labor. This pointed out clearly by Böhm-Bawerk (as also by Macvane – and in fact Ricardo). The factors of production, he says, are nature and labor. Taussig says that the only real factor is labor. Böhm-Bawerk says (Book II, Chapter II) that the factors are labor and the *limited* natural agents. Taussig says that these latter are of slight importance. (2.b.53)

And on the very last page of notes dealing with Böhm-Bawerk, Taussig returns to the subject, criticizing him for denying that capital is an independent factor of production but so treating land. The notes go on to say: 'Taussig does not believe it, says human labor is the only real force in production.' Interestingly, Andrew put a blue-pencil question mark after this (the notes are in ink) and also wrote in regular pencil, 'If the same amount of labor spent on two fields yields a different product, then why not speak of the surplus of the greater yield as a contribution of land?' (2.b.79).

Apropos of Marshall's concept of consumers' rent, Taussig was very dubious:

> It plainly aims to go beyond the usual conceptions with which Political Economy deals. It enters the field of Hedonics. Political Economy is concerned with utility only as an element of wealth and exchange. Marshall here considers utility as the satisfaction-yielding power of commodities from a wider standpoint – one might say from the point of view of welfare or happiness rather than wealth. He tries to measure the satisfaction yielding power of commodities. But it is questionable whether he really adds anything to economic thinking by the endeavour. . . . There are many qualifications, however, to the possibility of measuring consumers' rent, and it is doubtful whether Marshall's Consumers' Rent is of any real value. (2.a.58)

Nevertheless, in his discussion of Böhm-Bawerk, the notes have Taussig saying, 'It is worthy of remark that while the conception of consumers' rent does not seem to be inconsistent with Böhm-Bawerk's reasoning, and in fact seems almost implicit in it, he never describes or names the matter.'[12]

With regard to rent, Taussig (in his discussion of Marshall) is recorded as saying that the formation of economic rent must be distinguished from the division of rent based upon institutional and market arrangements; that it is delusion to think economic rent can be automatically pared off, because there is no clear-cut line between interest, rent, and profit; and that the single tax would probably discourage 'the inventive ingenious application of capital to the land' (2.b.9, 10). Similarly, in his discussion of Richard Jones, Taussig sympathetically presented the view that Ricardo's theory of rent was circumstantially related to time and place and not an immutable natural law. 'Jones pointed out that over most of the world and throughout most of history rents had been determined by custom rather than by economic laws' (2.b.40, 41). Thus in a discussion of Böhm-Bawerk's views on rent in a socialist state, Taussig is summarized thus:

> The phenomena of diminishing returns and of varying fertility of soils would appear in a socialistic state, as much as anywhere else, but rent might not emerge as a separate element. The state might lump together the whole agricultural product of a country and sell all portions at the same price – or it might take the surplus produce of the better lands and apply it to the State's own use. (2.b.78)

Also of interest is Taussig's characterization of the new Marshallian paradigm: instead of the older view of oscillations of market about normal price, he substitutes analysis of the reestablishment of equilibrium, for example, through changes in demand eliciting changes in supply, with short-run normal price being greater than long-run normal price and with the existence of quasi-rents (2.b.7).

One of the preoccupations of Taussig running throughout the notes is the importance of non-competing groups for the determination of both wage rates and values. In commenting upon Mill's analysis of cost of production, Taussig indicated that there were two views with regard to mobility and therefore competition in labour markets. According to one view, mobility and competition are widespread, and therefore goods exchange in proportion to the quantity of labour they represent, including labour spent in preparing materials, in building the machinery, and in acquiring skill or familiarity with the business, with 'allowance also for the different degrees of attractiveness of one sort or another in various businesses. All such allowances being made, however, they are of the opinion that wages are largely determined by the "net advantages" of different occupations, and that the values of commodities are principally based on "quantities of labor"' (2.a.3). Also acknowledged are the higher values commanded by the commodities produced by those with exceptional skills or exclusive capacities. The second view is that

> the community is arranged in a vast series of different planes of labor, which are practically if not necessarily more or less fixed – that there are obstacles which as a matter of fact prevent men from turning from one mode of life to another – such obstacles are those of inborn aptitudes and inaptitudes, the need of long or expensive training and so on. Therefore it is said that different degrees of attractiveness do not determine the wages of labor – and that the values of commodities are not determined by the quantities of labor – because there is not free competition. I rather incline to this view. (2.a.4)[13]

Two pages later the notes say that Ricardo does not carefully study the causes of differences in wages 'but apparently recognizes the existence of certain noncompeting groups, which are held in different estimation, because of differences in intensity of labor, and in natural skill' (2.a.6). But four pages later one reads:

> Ricardo seems to have *assumed* free competition, and then thought it was self evident, that under such conditions when labor could move freely into any channels where extra rewards were offered, and all articles could be indefinitely multiplied according to demand – that it was self evident I say – that commodities would exchange according to the quantities of labor.
>
> And granting his premises – his conclusions would be true.
>
> Ricardo's failure to grasp the importance of monopolies of skill and capacity, and the consequent obstacles they present to freedom of movement and free competition, is I think the basal defect in his theory of value. (2.a.10)

Subsequently, in a discussion of Cairnes on normal value, Taussig reports sympathetically on his qualification that labour is subject to limitations upon its circulation (because of the 'limitations . . . set by the qualifications necessary for the various branches of trade, and the amount of preparation necessary for their acquisition') and that 'upon this account there is not effective competition among laborers. They are arrayed in classes or layers with hard barriers between'. Accordingly, the cost-of-production principle applies to the prices of goods produced by workers belonging to the same group or level, but not to the exchange of goods produced by workers belonging to different groups (2.a.34–5). Indeed, Taussig returns to the point thrice, urging that 'Cairnes' contribution to the theory of normal value lies in his application of the theory of Reciprocal Demand (usually associated only with the phenomena of international trade) to all cases of exchange between occupations where there is not complete freedom of competition' (2.a.36; cf. 2.a.38 and 2.b.68).

Taussig returns to the topic in his later discussion of Böhm-Bawerk's and Marshall's different conceptions of cost. Among other things, the notes read,

> Taussig says that the importance of the marginal utility theory depends upon the question as to whether we do have noncompeting groups or not. Marginal utility helps to interpret what determines rates of exchange between noncompeting groups, [but] this point has never been touched upon by the Austrians. (2.b.67)

If all labour is equally rewarded, marginal utility will determine the occupational distribution; the permanent regulator of value here is cost (sacrifice, or exertion plus waiting). The notes continue:

> The great defect of Marshall's book is that he does not tell us where he stands on this question. In his first edition he spoke of permanent differences of standard of living – or permanent noncompeting groups. In his later editions he tends to minimize this and to reason as if rewards tend in the long run to be proportional to sacrifice. (2.b.67–8)

Next Taussig is held to say that

> Cairnes more than anyone else has emphasized the conception of noncompeting groups and it was his great contribution to the subject (though it is only an elaboration of Mill).

And finally:

> Yet Böhm-Bawerk and the continental economists have overlooked Cairnes' writings, regarding him as only one of the epigoni. So they have never applied marginal utility to noncompeting groups, a field where it might well be discussed. (2.b.68)

Taussig made a number of comments in passing that are of some present interest. (a) Apropos of Say: 'In his consideration of value, Say had much more to say about demand and supply than about normal value and its causes. In this respect he was behind even A. Smith. Say never really understood Ricardo' (2.b.38). (b) The main difference between Malthus and Ricardo was said to reside in their mode of expressing doctrines rather than in the doctrines themselves (2.b.39). (c) Senior's work is 'today as valuable as anything that has been written in international trade' (2.b.44). (d) Proudhon was 'a confused writer, half anarchist, half socialist' (2.b.45). (e) The 'Austrian School represents a return to the deductive method – with the idea that it can still be used to advantage. Menger, Böhm-Bawerk, though conservative with regard to economic method, they are all in accord with Socialists of the chair with regard to practical policies' (2.b.53). (f) Referring to Adolf Held, Taussig seemed to concur with the idea 'that you could not understand Ricardo until you understood his intention, which was an attack on the land-owning class. He was the apostle of the capitalist class, and he wanted to have the corn laws abolished. He hoped to stir the hatred of the laborers against the landowners rather than the capitalist' (2.a.24).

A recurring criticism levelled by one writer (including Taussig) against another is that of circular reasoning – for examples, Taussig against Mill for saying both that high wages make high prices and high prices make high wages (2.a.5), and Cairnes against Mill for saying both that value is function of wages and profit and that wages and profit are determined by value (2.a.32); and also with regard to Walker's distribution theory (2.a.48), marginal productivity theory (2.b.17, 27–8), and Marshall's principle of substitution in his general theory of distribution (2.b.37). Elsewhere, the absence of a unique wage rate is acknowledged (Mill, under the influence of Thornton; 2.a.56–7) and the possibility of multiple equilibria in the long run (Marshall; 2.b.12). The absence of any impact of Léon Walras and Vilfredo Pareto is not startling; much time was yet to pass before the meaning and significance of general equilibrium were even to begin to permeate the discipline.

The question of proof, and the problems thereof, was something which Taussig frequently raised for his students. Ricardo, it was seen above, was held to only assert that value is determined by quantity of labour; no proof is elaborated by him (2.a.9). Marshall's 'mode of proof' is said to consist of this: 'He just assumes a stationary state (not as defined by Mill, the eventual state when capital has reached the point that its accumulation is barely worthwhile), by which to him means a state of things in which there is no quasi-rent – the normal state, with only *true* rent, wages, interest' (2.b.12) – and deductively reasons out the consequences of some introduced change. Thus, with respect to the rent character of extraordinary labour incomes in relation to supply price, Taussig argues, 'how can you dispute Marshall's proposition that these extraordinary incomes enter into the normal supply price, and so are not of the nature of rent?'. Taussig felt 'that in any one case you could not prove that the extraordinary rewards were no more than enough to call out the desired supply'. Yet he himself felt that 'the extraordinary incomes of a few enormously successful individuals were of the nature of rent, and did not enter into the normal supply price' (2.a.36). Whether certain incomes were of the nature of supply price or a rent was important deductively but practically the matter was impossible of proof. Neither deductive chains of reasoning nor definitional manipulation could come to grips with the matter.

Taussig also touched several times on the ideological use of economic theory. It first arises in a discussion of the 'possible practical bearing of Cairnes' ideas', where the notes have Taussig saying that 'hitherto it had been held that commodities exchanged according to sacrifice – an optimistic idea of value, but since Cairnes' time, economists have been less inclined to claim that their doctrines proved the justice of existing conditions' (2.a.38). Taussig raises the matter next in regard to McCulloch. After calling him 'a very opinionated if not conceited man', the notes read:

'Glorified laissez-faire – the ideas which Smith had inherited from 18th century philosophy. McCulloch glorified the existing conditions of modern industry – and advocated noninterference of government with industry. Freedom would give such a stimulus to production and the national dividend would be so enlarged that all social problems would be done away with.' But Taussig apparently next said that 'the enormous expansion of industry after the abolition of the corn laws, probably due to many other causes, prepared the way for an easy shattering of economic faith' (2.b.42). Nor was that all: 'Another tendency was the capitalistic view of McCulloch.' Seeing profits as the barometer of the successful industry, and approaching 'a belief in the harmonies of Political Economy', 'McCulloch rather believed that whatever was in industry was right. So, with McCulloch and his school, economic teachings were mixed up with preaching of non-intervention' (2.b.42, 43). A more favourable view was given of Senior, who 'stands as the representative of the man of a different kind – the trend which tried to limit Political Economy to a deductive science like mathematics. He said that it had nothing to do with giving advice; its object was to analyze the phenomena of trade, wages, etc. The only method was that of deduction from certain premises' (2.b.43–4). He acknowledged that various German critics felt that Senior's type of economics was too abstract and unrealistic, and that 'this naturally caused a reaction' (2.b.44). The point that 'they hold a general belief in laissez faire – have a strong faith in effects of international free trade, – believe that existing state of things is on the whole just' was also made in regard to the Manchester School (2.b.41). And Cairnes is favourably cited for having pointed out the fallacy of Bastiat that rent presumes private property in land, and the latter is taken as given to prove it is justified: Bastiat 'said that if A had land and loaned it to B, he did B a service and deserved a reward – which obviously contains a fallacy as a justification of property in land' (2.b.45–6).

Finally, of interest are notes which are clearly Andrew's but which undoubtedly reflect Taussig's views, at least in part. Andrew, in a series of notes carrying his initials, discussed Böhm-Bawerk's theory of value. He argued that marginal utility is conditioned by supply and that supply is largely a function of cost of production. 'Böhm-Bawerk fails to look deep enough' and 'marginal utility does not go deep enough. It is determined by supply and supply is determined by cost of labor' (2.b.62). Moreover, throughout several pages of notes, 'supply and demand' is equated with marginal utility, and Andrew finds no 'very great difference between Böhm-Bawerk's subjective value, and the old exchange value of the classic writers. Both are determined for the moment by supply and demand (marginal utility)' (2.b.62). This view of Andrew's was facilitated by a literal and close reading of Böhm-Bawerk's Chapter 10 and the 'Austrian case': in the event of an inelastic supply of the factors of production, product values are a function of demand and supply (marginal utility); in the case of an elastic factor supply, product values are a function of cost of production (2.b.62). Thus a few pages later, the notes say that Böhm-Bawerk admits that the marginal-pairs theory is only a more refined statement of the law of demand and supply; that the marginal utility of the seller is acknowledged by Böhm-Bawerk as insignificant under conditions of organized production; that the principle of marginal pairs therefore really does 'not concern the business world as we know it'; and that, in regard to the theory of market value, Böhm-Bawerk is close in result to Mill (2.b.66).

III 'POLITICAL ECONOMY'

These notes are unidentified as to date and course origin but on page six they are marked as 'Prof. Taussig's lectures'. The pages prior thereto contain abstracts and other notes from and/or on Stuart Mill, Henry George, Walker, Silas Marcus Macvane, Marshall, and Henry Sidgwick on wages, profits, and related topics. Altogether there are 50 pages of notes, including the cover, which has a brief outline of the course. As with the other two sets of notes, a few pages have writing on both sides.

Prior to the main historical lectures are brief comments on certain history of economic thought texts. Jerome Adolphe Blanqui's *History of Political Economy* is said to be 'Rather old fashioned. Not worth much.' Luigi Cossa's *Guide to the Study of Political Economy* is 'Very useful as a list of writers; not so much as an analysis.' Ingram's *History of Political Economy* is 'Very useful – but somewhat radical; more philosophical treatment.' Julius Kautz's *Die geschichtliche Entwickelung der National-Oekonomik und ihrer Literatur* is 'inexecrable German – very learned, just – but long winded'. And Roscher's *Geschichte der Nationalökonomik in Deutschland* is 'prodigiously learned – but unfortunate in taking Germany as centre' (PE. 6).

Taussig's lectures covered Greece and the Middle Ages (2 pages), post-Middle Ages to the Physiocrats (7 pages), the Physiocrats, Cantillon, and Smith (11 pages), William Godwin and Malthus through John Stuart Mill (9 pages), Bastiat and Carey (2 pages), German political economy (3 pages), Marshall (11 pages), and Böhm-Bawerk (7 pages).

The notes record Taussig as saying that the treatment of economic topics in Greece was sporadic and had no perceptible influence upon the modern development of political economy. The theme of circumstantial conditions is presented. The medieval attitude towards interest is said to have been conditioned by borrowing not for production but for necessities; and the analysis of the just price is related to the fact of custom cum guild cum government regulation of trade and price (PE.7). Political economy arose in the fifteenth and sixteenth centuries in the study of the new conditions of that period; there had been little previous economic analysis because of the predominance of slavery (PE.6). The first conscious economic thinking awaited the subjects of money and prices elicited by the new phenomena, including coinage debasement and the inflow of specie from the New World (PE.8). As for mercantilism, it was not a consolidated, uniform system. Its merits and defects both have been exaggerated. It had no single dominating doctrine; and all its doctrines were closely connected with economic and industrial conditions and problems of those days (PE.9–10). The steady growth of manufactures was a new thing and was added to the inherited ideas of official regulation and governmental control (PE.11). Similarly, the Physiocratic notion of the single tax is said to have been influenced by the circumstances:

> Single tax. All economists are influenced by the circumstances of their day. The tax system in France at that time was heavy. All taxation must come out of net product; they said it might come out all at once as well as not. They made it about one-third.
>
> All privileges in taxes were to be abolished. Heretofore the clergy and nobility were exempt. (PE.15)

Cause and effect analysis is said to have come only after Smith (PE.7).

With regard to Smith, the notes record Taussig as saying that he emphasized production, not distribution; and that Smith's 'natural' is Cairnes' 'normal' (PE.19). Ricardo is interpreted as having a measurement, not an embodiment, labour theory of value; and one that is qualified through assuming 'all through the book . . . that all capital is simply resolvable into labor' (PE.20). John Stuart Mill is said to represent 'on the one hand, the last representative of the old classic economy – and, on the other, stood for the beginning of the transition' (PE.27). Apropos of Mill's distinction between production and distribution in regard to the role of natural laws, the notes state, 'Taussig thinks this is rather an imaginary difference' (PE.27). Bastiat is interpreted as having taken 'up pen for private property' and 'a systematic refutation of Socialism and its doctrines' in response to the revolutions of 1848 (PE.28). The few lines dealing with the general Austrian School include these: 'Uses strictly deductive and quasi-metaphysical reasoning' and 'The feeling of national Austrian pride may have something to do with the independence of their economics' (PE.33).

(In the notes from Economics 2, Taussig mentions Marshall's national pride *vis-à-vis* Böhm-Bawerk; 2.b.33).

Here, too, Cairnes is lauded for his ideas on non-competing groups: 'Cairnes' great contribution – noncompeting groups, a permanent cause of differences of wages – contrary to Ricardian theory that commodities exchanged according to quantity of labor in them. Commodities need not so exchange' (PE.36). The problem of proof is posed with regard to distinguishing the absence of competition from differences in training between occupations, in the explanation of differences in wage rates (PE.36). Taussig is said to think that the principle of substitution 'will explain very little in regard to differences of wages' (PE.39); the standard of comfort, and therefore custom and social forces, is important with regard to wage rates, so that 'here the unity of Distribution and Exchange disappears' (PE.40).

In these notes also are found the themes that waiting does not produce, that roundabout production is more productive and involves waiting, but waiting itself is no factor or production. 'Labor alone *produces*' (PE.40). But if labour is the only source of value and waiting is no factor of production, nevertheless interest may be founded and justified on utilitarian grounds, although not as an ethical necessity: 'Interest flows as the inevitable accompaniment of effective modes of production, not as an ethical necessity' (PE.41). In addition, emphasizing instead demand and supply forces, Taussig is critical of the view that 'individual earnings are in proportion to their contribution to society', which he finds implicit in Marshall's law of substitution. 'But as Marshall shows, those who contribute the really great elements of progress often get small reward' (PE.41). And the thought is repeated twice: 'It cannot be said that each man gets according to his productivity' (PE.41), and 'Taussig himself does not believe there is any adjustment of reward to services performed. If one so argues, he is probably reasoning in a circle' (PE.43).

Taussig also apparently had this to say: 'Marshall's treatment of questions is much more complex than Mill, Ricardo and Walker. The general impression which one gets is of a great confusion and diversity of tendencies and elements. The general outlines of economics he does not emphasize – the old problems of general wages etc. disappear'. Apropos of wages: 'Jevons says there is a great hodge podge of conditions and the problem is for everyone to get what he can. Marshall gives a somewhat similar impression' (PE.42). And finally: 'Marshall's whole teaching is to justify present conditions' (PE.43).

The discussion of Böhm-Bawerk's *Positive Theory of Capital* is, here too, clear and straightforward. Taussig compares Karl Rodbertus' distinction between social capital and private capital (essential and historic capital) with Böhm-Bawerk's approach to capital (PE.44–5). Böhm-Bawerk is also interpreted in these terms: 'He approaches questions of capitalistic production from the side of production. The Socialists approach from the other side – distribution. His whole book deals with the mechanism of production' (PE.46).

CONCLUSION

The notes for Economics 15 and 2 reveal two solid courses in the history of economic thought; and in Taussig's case insight is supplemented by the notes entitled 'Political Economy'. The courses dealt with the mainstream of orthodox economic thought, and both professors discussed deep problems and issues in a frank, candid and straightforward, non-ideological way, although their personal sympathies do tend to show through. Yet one could appreciate how a socialist would see, especially in Taussig's lectures, an attempt to defend the system from attack; and one could envision Frank Knight reacting to the same notes to the effect that Taussig's theories and arguments were not a very powerful propaganda for economic freedom.[14]

The continuity (or discontinuity) of past thought and argument with regard to current issues often shows through. Also evident are the different twists and angular interpretations that have come down to the present. All schools of thought and theories are more complex and heterogeneous in reality than they seem in retrospect. General summaries – what usually come down to subsequent generations – are often sterile and devoid of any vestige of kaleidoscopic complexity and incipient heterodoxy.

No attempt is made here to assess the accuracy or propriety of the interpretations recorded in Andrew's notes. Clearly various doctrines and bodies of ideas had different meanings attributed to them than are now assigned to them. The lectures evidence a view that the history of economic thought is not a movement from error to truth, but rather a sympathetic interpretive account of the development of ideas accompanying the development of the economy, an account which also manifests the heterogeneity of the subject-matter and the diversity of human imagination.

Socialist thought was not seen to exist within the confines of the discipline, but the history of economic thought presented was no ideological whitewash. But it should be noted that the economics department at Harvard did list courses in 'Socialism and Communism – History and Literature' (Economics 14) and 'The Labor Question in Europe and the United States – The Social and Economic Condition of Workingmen' (Economics 9), taught by Edward Cummings and John Cummings. The former course is said to lead 'to a discussion of the foundations of existing institutions'. Indeed, the problem of distribution between workers and capitalists – as both an analytical and ideological matter – was perhaps more central to late nineteenth-century orthodox thought than is generally now recognized. So also with the conflict of conservative versus reformer over the power and class structures – and the political origins of certain economic thought and of the assumptions of other, often later, economic thought. Both sets of notes testify to this. Problems of power and order were discussed quite directly, especially in the case of Taussig, through the concept of non-competing groups. Taussig thereby raised serious questions as to the operation of the economy and the realism and relevance of economic theory: for example, what is the relevance of the pure theory of the market in the face, not of 'market imperfections', but of inequality and hierarchical elements? Contrary to the appreciation of most contemporary economists, the problem of power, both broadly and narrowly contemplated, was a very widely discussed matter in the decades around the turn of the century.[15] But that is a broader question than can be taken up here, although the notes reported on herein make a contribution thereto. Moreover, although the economic system as it existed was taken as a given, its evolutionary character also seems to have been taken for granted, although not with the force that was then brewing in the mind of Thorstein Veblen.

What is important is not only what people should believe (say, because of its accuracy or propriety) but what they in fact do believe. Economic theories, perhaps particularly those of entire schools of thought, are sufficiently complex that they permit of heterogeneous specification. There is something of a spectrum of alternative possible interpretations of theories and certain forces work as sieves in sifting out certain interpretations and permitting others. This is an important part of the development and reception of ideas and theories.

These notes suggest vast opportunities for using turn-of-the-century economic thought (if not also somewhat more recent thought) as a base with which to research the spectrum and the operation and results of the filtration or selection mechanisms by which certain interpretations survive and others pass into oblivion – except for forgotten books and articles and student notes that are occasionally discovered. As I have suggested in a different context, the history of economic thought is considerably more complex and comprises a greater variety of permutations and interpretations than is currently appreciated.[16] The notes reported on here are a small but positive contribution to broader and deeper understanding not only of the history of the discipline but to the appreciation of the realities of modern research and thought.

Notes

1. Joseph Schumpeter, it may be recalled, referred to Taussig as 'the American Marshall' (Schumpeter, *Ten Great Economists* (New York: Oxford University Press, 1951), p. 220.
2. This and other descriptive material given below is taken from the catalogue of the Departments of History and Government and Economics, Faculty of Arts and Science, Harvard University, 1896–7.
3. See Warren J. Samuels, 'The Teaching of Business Cycles in 1905–1906: Insight into the Development of Macroeconomic Theory', *History of Political Economy*, vol. 4 (1972), pp. 140–62; and with Andrew Gray, '"One Great Tragedy": A Vignette', ibid., vol. 6 (1974), pp. 114–18, and 'The Teaching of Monetary Economics in the Early 1900s: Insight into the Development of Monetary Theory', ibid., vol. 8 (1976), pp. 324–40.
4. The following notational system is used: the course member; followed by the letter 'a' or 'b', depending upon whether the notes come from the first or second half-year sequence; and the page(s). Thus '15.b.45' refers to Ashley's Economics 15, second half-year notes, page 45. The Political Economy notes are cited 'PE' plus the page number(s). The notes are unedited except for minor grammatical corrections and inserted punctuation. The notes are in the possession of Andrew Gray, Washington, D.C.
5. Ashley at one point says that the *Tableau économique* has been excessively lauded (15.b.110); elsewhere he compares Hume's and the Physiocrats' assumptions bearing on taxation (15.b.73–74), refers to Quesnay's principles of economic liberty (15.b.78), suggests that Quesnay's naturalism has been influenced by natural science (15.b.79), and compares Smith and the Physiocrats on rent (15.b.92).
6. With the instructions 'not more than eight questions must be attempted', the exam is as follows: '1. Explain the influence of the Greek conception of the State upon the economic speculation of Greek philosophers. 2. 'The sacredness of property is a notion far more fixed in modern than in ancient time.' Comment upon this remark. 3. Explain and illustrate the influence of the example of Sparta on Greek social thought. 4. In what sense is it true that Plato anticipated Adam Smith's teaching concerning division of labour? 5. In what sense is it true that Aristotle anticipated the modern distinction between Value in Use and Value in Exchange? 6. Set forth briefly Aristotle's doctrine as to Chrematistic. 7. Discuss the question as to whether Christianity destroyed slavery. 8. What sanction, if any, has Socialism or Communism in the teaching of the Christian Fathers? 9. Trace the early history of the doctrine of "interest", in the original sense of the word. 10. Distinguish between the various senses attached to the term Mercantilism. Which do you think most convenient? 11. What ideas prominent in modern Protectionist argument are absent from Mercantilism as represented by Mun?'

   The x's alongside the other numbers suggest that Andrew omitted numbers 5, 8 and 11 (15.a.1).
7. 'It has been customary for English economists to speak of the Mercantile system with contempt. Mill speaks of it as a "palpable absurdity". He compares it to "a crude fancy of childhood". [Mill, however, makes an important concession when he grants that money had an especial importance for coun-

tries which had occasion for sudden and large foreign payments, a concession, which Smith would not have made, of whose historical significance, Mill himself had no true realization.]

'On the other hand, writers of the historical school assert that any really dominant belief had a "relative validity", and tend to justify Mercantilism simply because it existed. And it is indeed conceivable that a particular policy promoted the interests of a particular people – while the reasons which they avowed for the policy were mistaken, and based upon misapprehensions. It is sometimes said that one may agree with a man's conclusions without admitting its arguments. Thus fiction may have favored progress' (15.a.89).

Later Ashley acknowledges the post-sixteenth-century influx of precious metals into Europe as a result of favourable balances and that this did stimulate industry and commerce. 'Whether this will justify Mun's language or not, Ashley will not say. He admits that there may be a remnant of what A. Smith called the "popular notion" that money is the main source of wealth' (15.b.6).

8. See 15.b.77, 78. On the subject of naturalism, Ashley said that it was 'a concept entangled with many meanings, and therefore easily conjured with, and made use of for the most diverse purposes' (15.a.56). Thus to the Stoic mind a golden age was identified with the rule of natural law, now a lost code (15.a.66–7). With Grotius, it had something of a 'fresh start', but was 'thoroughly Stoic', including 'belief in a "law of nature" prior to, or outside the civil laws – certain principles which men ought to recognize whether they can be enforced or not'. These ideas, which Grotius thought 'obtained currency throughout the civilized world', included as principles: 'abstinence from that which belongs to another': 'restitution of what we have taken from another or may gain thereby'; obligation of performing one's promises'; 'reparation for injury done by one's fault'; and 'retribution by punishment' (15.b.76, 77). Then there was Locke's blend of contract and natural rights theory discussed in the text. Finally, the notes have Ashley saying that 'the doctrine of natural liberty presented to us today had been enormously affected by a conception unknown before the present day, the state of mind produced by the "natural" sciences – the idea of "natural" as meaning unaffected by man's influence, e.g., the struggle for existence' (15.b.78–9).

9. The mid-year exam: '1. "According to Ricardo, the exchange value of commodities contains neither return to capital nor rent, but simply labor." Why? or why not? 2. Sketch concisely the development of the general theory of value at the hands of Ricardo, Mill, Cairnes. 3. "Skill, as skill, produces no effect on value; in other words, commodities do not under any circumstances exchange for each other in proportion to the degree of skill bestowed on them. Skill, though in itself inoperative on value, nevertheless affects it indirectly in two distinct ways; first, where competition is effective among producers, through the cost which must be undergone in acquiring the skill; . . . and secondly, in the absence of competition, through the principle of monopoly." – Cairnes. Explain and illustrate. 4. "If there really was a national fund the whole of which must necessarily be applied to the payment of wages, that fund could be no other than an aggregate of smaller similar funds possessed by the several individuals who compose the employing part of the nation. Does, then, any individual employer posses any such fund? Is there

any specific portion of any individual's capital which the owner must necessarily expend upon labour? . . . May he not spend more or less on his family and himself, according to his fancy, – in the one case having more, in the other less, left for the conduct of his business? And of what is left, does he or can he determine beforehand how much shall be laid out on buildings, how much on materials, how much on labour? . . . Be it observed, fixity or definiteness is the very essence of the supposed wages-fund. No one denies that some amount or other must within any given period be disbursed in the form of wages. The only question is, whether that amount be determinate or indeterminate." – Thornton, *On Labour*. State carefully, and consider critically, the answers Cairnes made to these questions. 5. Would you accede to the statement that "President Walker's theory is, in reality, not a theory of manager's earnings at all but a theory of differences in manager's earnings"? 6. "For an understanding of the machinery by which distribution is accomplished, the classification of sources of income should thus be different from that to be adopted for an explanation of the fundamental causes." – Taussig. Wherein different? 7. Explain what is meant by Consumer's Rent; and consider how its significance is affected by inequalities in wealth. 8. "As a rule, the poorer soils rise in value relatively to the richer, as the pressure of population increases." – Marshall. Why?'

The final exam: '1. Do you believe that a permanent gain for the theory of wages has been made by Walker's discussion of that subject? If so, wherein? if not, why not? 2. Does Marshall's analysis of the different grades of labor, and of the barriers between them, differ in essentials from Cairnes's? from Mill's? 3. Explain what "quasi-rent" is, wherein it differs from true rent, wherein resembles true rent; and state whether the conception seems to you a helpful one, deserving to be permanently embodied in economic theory. 4. What do you conceive the difference to be between what Walker calls "current product", Marshall "the national dividend", and the instructor in the course "real income"? 5. On what grounds does Marshall maintain that "the extra income earned by natural abilities may be regarded as a rent, when we are considering the sources of the income of individuals, but not with reference to the normal earnings of a trade"? What is your own opinion? 6. "The attribute of normal value implies systematic and continuous production." – Cairnes. Would Böhm-Bawerk accede to this proposition? Why, or why not? Give your own opinion. 7. Explain what Böhm-Bawerk means by (subjective) "value"; and consider his analysis of the relation between value and cost. 8. Enumerate the grounds on which Böhm-Bawerk maintains that "present goods have greater value than future goods of like kind and quantity"; consider to which of these grounds he gives most attention; and give your opinion as to the justice of this emphasis' (2.a.1; 2.b.1).

10. 'Adam Smith had discussed with some detail the differences of wages in different employments. Book I, Chapter X. Ricardo does not carefully study the causes of these differences in rewards – but apparently recognizes the existence of certain noncompeting groups, which are held in different estimation, because of differences in intensity of labor, and in natural skill' (2.a.6).

11. 2.b.33–4. The notes continue: 'Marshall probably would not object to this view, though occasionally he seems to. In his introductory chapters on Distribution he spoke of the marginal net product of labor, as determining the

employer to employ this or that grade of laborers. Marshall there also speaks of the marginal net product of capital. He does not mean probably that capital is an independent factor in production, but when an individual capitalist deliberates as to whether he shall employ capital or not, whether he shall buy a machine or employ a laborer, will be determined by which yields the greatest marginal return. While this is true for the individual, Marshall would probably admit that there is no net marginal return from capital as a whole. He never gives a clear cut definition of what determines the return from capital as a whole' (2.b.34). The discussion continues in terms of the effective desire for accumulation *vis-à-vis* the extension of opportunities for investment and the steady accumulation of capital as governing the rate of interest. The notes indicate that Marshall's weakness on the demand side (the effective desire for accumulation furnishing a supply schedule for capital) must be overcome by supplementing it by Böhm-Bawerk's analysis of the 'technical superiority of present goods' (2.b.34–5) – by which presumably Ashley and/or Taussig meant roundabout production.

12. The notes then give the following 'Reasons': '1. He approaches the matter from a different point of view; he seems more *directly* concerned with ascertaining the cause of the *exchange value* of commodities, and perhaps regards consumers' rent as something quite aside from that point, as it is. 2. His aim is more specific than Marshall. Marshall is writing a treatise on Political Economy in general, – in all its wider aspects; Böhm-Bawerk is simply endeavoring to find a theory of value, which he is so use in elucidating a theory of capital. "Consumers' rent" may be significant with regard to certain subjects, e.g., taxation; it would have little reference to Böhm-Bawerk's aim' (2.b.58). The notes also say that 'Böhm-Bawerk and Marshall may not really differ, but present different psychological bases of value' (2.b.56) – the former denying and the latter affirming the possibility of summing the marginal values of successive units of consumer goods.

13. The notes continue: 'In each particular plane of labor – and indeed between the different planes, allowance being made for the difference in wages – the commodities produced in those planes may be said to exchange according to the quantities of labor involved in them – and inasmuch as variations in the quantities of labor necessary for producing a commodity are more liable to occur, than changes in the wages of a particular occupation (changes in wages usually being *general*) – changes in value are generally due to modification in the *quantity* of labor necessary to produce a given commodity. It may be noted in this connection that both Mill and Ricardo, in discussing the question of value, seem to have in mind not so much the causes of *differences* in value as the causes of *variations* in value – that is to say they study not so much the conditions of values at any one time – but the conditions determining values at different times' (2.a.4).

14. Frank H. Knight, 'Theory of Economic Policy and the History of Doctrine', *Ethics*, vol. 63 (1953), p. 279. (Knight is here evaluating the English Classical economists.)

15. See, for example, Joseph Dorfman, *The Economic Mind in American Civilization*, vol. 3 (1865–1918) (New York: Viking Press, 1949).

16. Warren J. Samuels, 'The History of Economic Thought as Intellectual History', *History of Political Economy*, vol. 6 (1974), pp. 305–23.

10 The Teaching of Business Cycles in 1905–6: Insight into the Development of Macroeconomic Theory*

Traditional business cycle theories and the business cycles course were important facets of the development of what is now seen as macroeconomics, and knowledge of their development affords insight into the development of macroeconomic theory. Fortunately there is now available a set of excellent lecture notes and student reports from a course, 'Commercial Crises and Cycles of Trade', given at Harvard two-thirds of a century ago. The notes cast light on the early identity and character of the study of what is now within the domain of macroeconomic (and monetary) theory, as well as the quality of teaching in that field, during a period when macroeconomic questions hitherto have appeared to have been largely dormant. They reflect a surprisingly 'modern' business cycles course in both coverage and execution, as well as basic conceptualization, and also evidence the considerable intellectual ferment – largely forgotten and thus neglected by both macro theorists and historians of economic thought – that accompanied the acknowledged doctrine of Say's law.

The notes were taken during his senior year at Harvard by a student in the course, Robert Lee Hale, subsequently a long-time specialist in public utilities and legal economics at the Law School of Columbia University.[1] I came upon them during an examination of Hale's private papers undertaken to determine Hale's theory of the economy as a system of power and its legal bases.[2]

In this chapter I shall discuss first the course and the professor; then, the notes in general; and finally the treatment of business cycles in the course. We shall see that the study of business cycles – or the early vision of what is now macroeconomics – why by 1905 already developed, organized, and taught; that while not as sophisticated as the field developed in the 1920s, it was two decades earlier already impressive in its depth of descriptive and

* Originally published in *History of Political Economy*, vol. 4 (Spring 1972), pp. 140–62.

analytical content; and that while Say's law was allowed as orthodox doctrine, it was already challenged both directly by so-called heretics and indirectly by analyses and chains of reasoning of orthodox economists pursuing different lines of analysis, and that, in fact, Say's law coexisted with a growing body of analysis investigating the nature and causes of cycles and their recurrence and periodicity. As indicated below, this discussion of the phenomena associated with one course is no substitute for a more thorough inquiry into the state of macroeconomics and the status of Say's law at the turn of the century. But Andrew's lectures and the related materials are significant for their interpretive suggestiveness, however representative or not of early twentieth-century macroeconomic thought they may turn out to be.

I

The materials at hand are from 'Commercial Crises and Cycles of Trade', given as Economics 12b by Assistant Professor A. Piatt Andrew in the Fall term of 1905. Offered to graduate and undergraduate students, it was one of a changing bundle of courses in economic and financial history and analysis given in the middle years of the first decade of this century by such men as Frank W. Taussig, O. W. M. Sprague, Edwin F. Gay, George Charles Selden, and, among others, Andrew. According to Hale's class notes, the lectures commenced on Monday, 2 October 1905, and concluded on Wednesday, 24 January 1906, before a class meeting twice a week except for the first week, when the class also met on Friday.

By the fall of 1905, A. Piatt Andrew (1873–1936) had already established himself as a leading investigator of monetary questions and business conditions, having published a series of articles on money, currency, and reserves in the *Quarterly Journal of Economics*.[3] He subsequently became special assistant to the National Monetary Commission, helping to organize the now well-known institutional and financial studies by economists published under the aegis of the Commission. He also served as assistant secretary of the Treasury under Taft. While working for the Commission, Andrew published in 1910 his *Statistics for the United States, 1867–1909*,[4] a landmark compilation and construction of economic statistics which, among other sources, was used (and refined) by Wesley C. Mitchell in his monumental *Business Cycles* of 1913.[5] Andrew subsequently published widely, including additional articles in the *Quarterly Journal of Economics* interpreting business cycles and monetary issues and problems.[6]

II

The lecture notes proper run to 177 pages. They are in longhand, well-preserved, and legible. Taken primarily by Hale, a few days' notes were copied from another student. In addition to the lecture notes, there are four groups of summary notes appended to the main body of notes. These consist, in the order found, of five pages entitled 'Crises Theories', summarizing the discussion in the final lectures of business cycle theories; twelve pages entitled 'Crisis Barometers', summarizing the indicator-type statistics used in the course, together with some mention of theories or discussions relating to the significance of particular factors; three pages simply entitled 'Selden', summarizing, it turns out, a 1902 article by Andrew's colleague George Charles Selden,[7] which was on a reserve list; and twenty pages entitled 'Crises. History', summarizing the lectures on the history of instability phenomena from the Dutch tulip mania of 1634–8 to the situation in the United States and (to a much lesser degree) England and Germany in 1905. There follow two single pages, one dealing with Hobson versus Mill (found, interestingly, upside down), and the other comprising a library reserve list in connection with the second report prepared by students in the class (see below).

Of the 31 lectures recorded in Hale's notes all but three deal primarily with the history of business conditions, the statistical data used to demarcate the progress and change in conditions and the relations between particular events, and the conflict of interpretations of those relations and of particular panic, crisis, and cycle phenomena. The final three lectures deal with business cycle theory. As a history of business conditions, the lectures are a good example of what was later to become a more or less conventional style of rendition of events. Andrew, if the notes are accurate (and there is no reason to doubt them), gave a careful, systematic, and factual description of business and economic developments, paying primary attention to what we may call the proximate causes and manifestations of upswings, downswings, and turning points. After several lectures on the sixteenth and seventeenth century, John Law, the Bank of England, and the South Sea Company, as well as a session devoted to the organization of the course and bibliographical materials (the meeting of 6 October), Andrew began his study of the English crises between 1763 and 1815–16 with a discussion of Jevons' work on periodicity. He then shifted to the American crisis of 1818–19, the English crisis of 1825 and the situation in both countries in the 1830s. The succeeding lectures covered the major subsequent events and periods of interest to a business cycle or crisis analyst. The first 38 pages of class notes carry the discussion to the American Civil War; and the next

123 pages are devoted to the description and interpretation of the period between 1860 and 1905, with the main attention given, as would be expected, to the depression-laden decades of the 1870s, 1880s, and 1890s. Some lectures dealt primarily or exclusively with empirical data relating to some period; others sketched verbal pictures of business conditions and developments; and interspersed were discussions of particular interpretive contributions, such as the works of William Stanley Jevons, Heinrich Herkner and Alfred Russel Wallace on agriculture, Emile de Laveleye on foreign trade, and Clement Juglar on loan movements and the cycle. As already suggested, the great bulk of the discussion is of American experience, with more or less brief (in terms of the notes, at least) reference to parallel or divergent movements in Europe, especially England and Germany. Andrew paid particular attention to banking and currency data, to political factors, to price movements as pointers to underlying 'real' factors, to developments in particular industries, to foreign trade conditions – in short to the obtrusive aspects of panics, crises, and cycles as they came to be seen and known.

One important facet of the course was the extensive use of statistics. It was clearly no accident that Andrew later produced his *Statistics for the United States, 1867–1909*, for Hale's notes include no fewer than 30 tables or compilations of statistical data given by Andrew in the course of his lectures. Andrew, together with Irving Fisher and Mitchell, among others, was a leader in the empirical and quantitative approach to business cycle study and analysis. It is the lines of analysis typified by the statistical tables which Hale summarized under the title of 'Crisis Barometers'. These include bank clearings, stock exchange transactions, business failures, foreign trade, prices, wages, strikes, price and output data of particular commodities (Andrew apparently preferred iron and steel as an indicator), gross railroad earnings, agricultural production, and so on, including bank loans and reserves. The tables are collections of such data.

The prevalence if not predominance of statistical description in Andrew's lectures is but one of two striking and important general characteristics of his course. The second resides in the existence of and his extensive use of the wide literature on crises and cycles that had already been developed and which his course brought together. The existence of much of this literature has been largely forgotten. The notes present a veritable panorama of authors and works. In his organizational lecture, Andrew listed works by such men as Max Wirth, Clement Juglar, Charles Arthur Conant, H. M. Hyndman, Theodore E. Burton, Mikhail Tugan-Baranowsky, Arthur Raffalovich, Hector Denis, Eugen von Bergmann, Edward David Jones, Heinrich Herkner, William Stanley Jevons, and Pierre Vialles. The reserve list mentioned earlier, to be used in connection with the preparation of the second student report, comprised works by John A. Hobson, A. F. Mummery, John M. Robertson, Uriel H. Crocker, Karl Rodbertus, Edward David Jones, John Stuart Mill, George Charles Selden, Thomas Nixon Carver, and Frances A. Walker. Throughout the lectures reference was made to the works and/or ideas of the following writers, in addition to the names already mentioned: Richard Ehrenberg, Henry Dunning Macleod, Robert Giffen, Thomas Tooke, William Langton, Alfred William Flux, John Pease Norton, Henry L. Moore, John R. Commons, Wilhelm Roscher, Gustav von Schmoller, Arthur Twining Hadley, William Petty, Hyde Clark, William Herschel, W. W. Hunter, James Laurence Laughlin, James Edwin Thorold Rogers, Michel Chevalier, James Maitland Lauderdale, H. F. von Storch, Henry Chalmers, Eugen Dühring, Johann Georg Busch, Edwin L. Godkin, John Mills, as well as Smith, Say, Ricardo, James Mill, Malthus, and such now remote figures as Sonenbeck and Briaune. Many of these references were made in connection with Andrew's survey of business cycle theory, which will be summarized later. There are also references to governmental investigations and collections of works. Careful study of the notes and reports suggests that the two articles by Carver and Selden had a great influence on Andrew and were prominent in the intellectual structuring of the course (see below).

As already indicated, Andrew's course provided for two reports[8] by each student, one due mid-term and the other near the end of the term (the due dates seem to have been postponed to accommodate students). Hale's first report, dated 30 October 1905, is entitled 'Gross and Net Railroad Earnings, N. Y. Bank Clearings, and Price of Pig Iron – Month by Month, 1892–4 (Inclusive)'. The subject was apparently worked out through arrangement between student and professor in conference. The essay is preceded by a two-page chart plotting time series for the data indicated in the title. The first thirteen pages examine the nature and sources of the statistical data (primarily from Statistical Abstract and Commercial and Financial Chronicle), and the remaining nine pages consider 'the causes for the changes shown on the chart'.[9] Hale examined both market factors and special (i.e., exogenous) factors and their interrelation. He attempted no generalizations.

The second report, dated 3 January 1906, is entitled 'The Recurrence of Crises', and was specifically assigned to all students by Andrew. The notes relating to the assignment read as follows:

> In Dec., report on theory – reasons for recurrence of crises. Consider arguments for and against general overproduction – whether or not it's possible and in what sense. Then how far this would go to explain recurrences. List of references given.[10]

The first seven pages of Hale's 23-page longhand report present a summary of characteristic events during a typical cycle. The major lines of analysis included speculation leading to overproduction, inter-industry diffusion, and liquidity preference.[11] This is followed by two pages summarizing Hobson's theory of overproduction generated by underconsumption; this by two pages summarizing John Stuart Mill's continuation of the tradition of Say, denying the possibility of general overproduction; then by a critique of Mill, stressing the possibility of engaging in production in order to increase wealth (rather than to acquire other goods, as Say held) and the consequent possibility of general overproduction; and this, by a critique of Hobson's remedy (increasing consumption power), that production in the aggregate still need not be adjusted to consumption and the possibility of difficulties ensuing from unforeseen changes. Hale then pointed to the dichotomy in Mill resulting from the latter's adherence in one chapter to Say's law and his recognition in another chapter that cycles result from the attempt to overcome the falling rate of profit.[12] This is followed by the stipulation that better information in the hands of businessmen and better banking policy would avoid many of the 'accidental happenings bringing on crises'.[13] Hale next summarized Carver's article presenting the basic germ (in terms of value theory)[14] of what has come to be called the accelerator theory, which he then criticized as neglecting cost of production in regard to normal value. Hale concluded his paper with an affirmation of a contracyclical policy of increasing the standard of living of workers so as to at least tend to stabilize demand, which he differentiated from Hobson's view in part in that his own was 'merely a hypothetical remedy, not a cause of recurrence'.[15] Andrew gave Hale a B+ on the paper (the first paper does not indicate a grade) and commented as follows: 'Good thesis – a little too much attention was given to Hobson and too little to criticising other more important theories and developing your own.'[16]

III

As might be expected there are numerous particular points or discussions of interest in the lecture notes. Noting just a few, Andrew discussed Jevons' investigation of periodicity in eighteenth-century fluctuations without distortion because of the latter's attempt to relate cycles to sunspots.[17] Andrew, according to the notes, held that 'In general in [the] eighteenth century, we find crises more or less severe every ten or a dozen years'.[18] There is a reference to an 1818 Pennsylvania Senate investigation of business collapse and distress[19] somewhat paralleling a reference to the House of Commons investigation of the collapse of 1857.[20] Andrew discussed the conflict between currency-and-banking schools in terms of its relevance to the problem of crises and cycles, i.e., business conditions.[21] Andrew presented a Schumpeterian creative-destruction-type interpretation of economic changes bringing 'great injury to some, and undeserved benefits to others'.[22] There is a reference to 1884 US Treasury intervention to alleviate money-market stringency,[23] somewhat paralleling a reference to countercyclical Bank of England loan policy in 1825–6.[24] Finally, there is a reference to Hyde Clark's perception, in the late 1840s, of a 54-year cycle.[25]

More important is Andrew's approach to his subject, 'commercial crises and cycles of trade'. First of all, Hale perceived his professor's mind and pedagogy to run toward history, barometers, and theory; indeed, the class notes reflect a clearly articulated and well-organized set of lectures along these lines. The mould for the business cycles course had already been given form. Second, it is clear that Andrew perceived the general transformation of fluctuations from crises to cycles. Third, it is also clear that Andrew perceived that instability had to be accepted as a fact of life, and further, had to be explained. With respect to both of these latter points one can do no better than quote Mitchell, who, writing for 1913 publication, could have been describing the intellectual environment in Andrew's 1905–6 course:

> Wide divergences of opinion continue to exist among competent writers upon crises; but in recent years substantial agreement has been reached upon two points of fundamental importance.
>
> Crises are no longer treated as sudden catastrophes which interrupt the 'normal' course of business, as episodes which can be understood without investigation of the intervening years. On the contrary, the crisis is regarded as but the most dramatic and briefest of the three phases of a business cycle – prosperity, crisis, and depression. Modern discussions endeavor to show why a crisis is followed by a depression, and depression by prosperity, quite as much as to show why prosperity is followed by a crisis. In a world, the theory of crises has grown into the theory of business cycles.
>
> This wider grasp of the problem has discredited the view that crises are due to abnormal conditions which tempt industry and trade to forsake their beaten paths and temporarily befog the judgment of business men and investors, or to misguided legislation, unsound business practices, imperfect banking organization, and the like. As business cycles have continued to run their round decade after decade in all nations of highly developed business organization, the idea that each crisis may be

> accounted for by some special cause has become less tenable. On the contrary, the explanations in favor today ascribe the recurrence of crises after periods of prosperity to some inherent characteristic of economic organization or activity. The complex processes which make up business life are analyzed to discover why they inevitably work out a change from good times to bad and from bad times to good. The influence of special conditions is admitted, of course, but rather as a factor which complicates the process than as the leading cause of crises.[26]

Andrew – or Hale's record of Andrew's lectures – was not as explicit as this; but it is clear that Andrew's mind was very much in this direction, though he possibly would have resisted any implicit demotion of money and banking factors. What the lectures notes suggest, and very strongly, is that by 1905 leading thinkers in this field were well along the way to accepting the inherent and inevitable character of their subject, to treating it, as it were, as a serious subject – though popular and even much professional opinion lagged behind for several decades. There is thus in Andrew's lectures, as seen through Hale's notes, an interesting mosaic composed of the juxtaposition of the older crisis style of reasoning; an increasing cycle orientation; an historical record of boom-bust, and questions of periodicity and recurrence; and the problem of the possibility of general overproduction. There is also a complex juxtaposition of monetary, real and psychological factors.

Andrew structured his lectures on business cycle theories upon an initial distinction between two 'groups of opinion', the one maintaining that cycles are generated by such a variety of causes as to preclude generalization, and the other holding that cycles are due to 'permanent causes'.[27] In the first group were such men as Carroll D. Wright (US Department of Labor), Wirth, Laveleye, Roscher, Wallace, Busch, and Schmoller, all of whom Andrew pictured as holding that there was a plethora of immediate causes of cycles, that all the causes led to disturbance of the balance between production and consumption, and that such immediate causes were sufficient to account for crises. According to the notes, Andrew's evaluation of this point of view was that while it accounts for disturbances in trade it does not 'suggest any periodicity'.[28] The problem, as Andrew saw it, was one of periodicity and recurrence.

The second group of writers, according to Andrew, 'attributes crises to periodicity of physical or mental conditions or [the] circumstances of our capitalistic organization'.[29] Andrew then proceeded to survey the ideas of

Briaune, Petty, Hyde Clark, Herschel, Hunter, and Jevons on physical factors; John Mills and Godkin on mental conditions, i.e., 'optimism and pessimism; confidence and distrust';[30] Laughlin on the credit system (his distinction between normal and abnormal credit); Godkin and Rogers on the impact of generational succession in business control; Chevalier and Selden on credit as a magnifier rather than a fundamental cause of cyclical movements; and Walker and Carver on the propagation and cumulation of shocks.

Midway in his discussion of business cycle theories, Andrew took up the view of those who: 'have connected crises with [the] capitalistic system of production', that is, those who have said that 'there might be a general glut of all commodities – and [that] such [is] inevitable under [the] regime of private property'.[31] Here he discussed first the collective views of Lauderdale, Storch, Malthus, Sismondi, Chalmers, Hobson, Mummery, Dühring, Crocker, and Hadley. His emphasis, in addition to tying the possibility of general market gluts to private property, was upon increased investment 'resulting in production in excess of profit-paying demand'.[32] This he labelled as 'the theory of overproduction; or underconsumption'.[33]

Andrew then considered the 'opposition to this – most of [the] more distinguished English and French economists dismissed [the] notion of overproduction as heretical'.[34] His summary of the position of Say, James Mill, and John Stuart Mill was mainly in terms of the impossibility of a general glut because the provision of certain goods represents the demand for other goods (which he distinguished from the possibility of 'overproduction of particular goods due to maladjustment').[35] To this view he juxtaposed the ideas of Hobson and other 'modern believers in overproduction' who 'admit every increase in commodities increases [the] power to purchase, but [who] insist that those who have the power may not choose to use it – [or] to use it in such a way as not to be consumed at once',[36] an argument which Andrew held was 'not touched by Ricardo etc'.[37] He then presented John Stuart Mill's argument that 'men won't continue to produce unless they want to consume', but went on to say, according to the notes, 'But this argument [is] not so effective, for many persons long after [their] demands [are] satisfied continue to produce for the love of control, or habit, or providing for [a] distant future.'[38] He then moved to Mill's chapter on the tendency of profits to a minimum, 'where he admits there is a tendency for profits to decline which leads to crises',[39] and comments, 'Thus Mill seems to have reached in this chapter virtually to [the] views of Malthus etc. on over-production – [he] admits there's over-production of capital.'[40]

The last one and a third pages of the class notes cover Andrew's evaluation of the controversy. We shall quote him in the notes' entirety:

> Discussion [is] largely one of terminology. In one sense over-production [is] obviously impossible – that people could have more than they could consume. Also impossible in [the] sense that more could be produced than exchanged if properly distributed. But it does seem possible that more could be produced than could be sold with a profit.
>
> Quite another question whether over-production is a cause of crises. What happens after a crisis gives plausible ground for thinking it does cause crises. After [a] crisis [there is] an apparent excess of product – but this [is] not [the] cause but [the] result of [the] crisis – due to [a] desire to change goods into money. This occurs in every period of depression.[41]

He goes on to say a few words about socialist thought on crises and business cycles:

> This has struck the socialists as a paradox of [the] modern capitalist system – [the] coincidence of want and destitution on one hand and excess of supply on the other, as in 1893. Result is their theory that [the] only remedy is government ownership of industry. They accept [the] theory of [the] tendency of profits to [a] minimum, and when they're low, they see men thrown out of work. If production [is] carried on by [the] state it wouldn't cease periodically on account of [a] decline of profits. The socialistic schemes differ in detail.[42]

This discussion concludes the lecture notes.

Hale's summary of these notes in 'Crisis Theories' is simply that – a theory-by-theory summary of Andrew's lectures. His summary of the long passages from pp. 176–7 quoted above is as follows:

> *Over-production seems possible in [the] sense that more can be produced than sold at a profit.*
>
> Does over-production *cause* crises? Apparent excess of product after crisis is not cause, but *effect* – people trying to change *goods* for *money*.[43]

A word should be said about the two articles by Carver and Selden, inasmuch as they appear to have figured prominently in the course. Carver's article[44] is an exposition, in terms of the theory of value, of the principle of acceleration. As Haney has written, Carver here was 'the first to state it fully and in relation to the cycle theory'.[45] According to Carver, 'A satisfactory explanation of industrial depression must . . . be sought in the laws of value which govern investment in . . . [producers' goods] rather than in the examination of the conditions of the money market, or conditions of organized credit.'[46] He maintained that there is 'a general law to the effect that a slight fluctuation in the value of a product tends to produce a violent fluctuation in the value of the establishment producing it. Stated in still more general terms, the value of producers' goods tends to fluctuate more violently than the value of consumer's goods'.[47] Expanding:

> A slight rise in the price of consumers' goods will so increase the value of the producers' goods which enter into their production as to lead to larger investment in producers' goods. . . . There seems, therefore, to be a fundamental reason for the periodicity of industrial depression, which can only be removed by such a complete knowledge and understanding of the situation as would enable the business world to foresee the tendencies and take measures to overcome them.[48]
>
> A consumer's market depends upon the willingness of the public to consume, while an investor's market depends upon their willingness to invest. As was shown above, there are reasons, other than psychological, why an investor's market must be more unstable than a consumer's market.[49]

This line of reasoning, it seems clear, fits in well with Andrew's feeling that 'it does seem possible that more could be produced than could be sold with a profit'.[50] On the other hand, this line of reasoning does not presume the perfect adjustment, and full-employment equilibrium, which Say's law has been held – especially more recently – to involve.

Selden's article[51] also fits in well with Andrew's feeling about production beyond the limits of profitability and a narrow interpretation of Say's law. As Andrew summarized it in his lectures, Selden's article maintained that 'crises result from [the] effort to anticipate'.[52] In the article itself the key lines are as follows:

> The credit system is responsible for both the extent of the advance in prices and the violence of the decline, and is the sole cause of the panic which results from the hoarding of cash. As without credit there would be no fear of bank failures; but it is not the cause of that seesaw movement between goods and money which is termed the trade cycle. The effort to anticipate higher prices would still exist if credit were unknown.[53]
>
> In conclusion, the primary cause of the trade cycle is the effort of buyers and sellers to anticipate a rise in prices. This produces a fictitious enlargement of demand beyond real consumptive requirements, and finally results in the accumulation of considerable stocks of goods. . . . Price fluctuations are increased in extent and severity by the credit system.[54]

Selden's article is interesting in other respects as well. Apposite to the quotation above from Mitchell on the new attitude toward instability, published in 1913, are the opening lines of Selden's article, published in 1902:

> A large portion of the business community are accustomed to look upon the commercial crisis as much as an epidemic of smallpox was regarded before the days of Jenner – as a mysterious 'act of God' which cannot be foreseen or understood, and can only be endured with what fortitude the sufferers are able to command.[55]

It was Selden's view, however, that cycles *can* be foreseen and understood, and in the article his aim was 'to trace out a little more fully than has heretofore been done the principle which operates to produce trade cycles'.[56] The great bulk of the article is concerned, first, with elaboration of the five groups of the population 'arranged according to the degree to which business transactions are affected by the effort to speculate';[57] second, with a differentiation between stock exchange cycles, industry cycles and the trade cycle; third, with a characterization of the trade cycle into the phases of panic, depression, recovery, prosperity – in the course of which, discussing depression, he remarked, 'The people are spending less because they are receiving less, and are receiving less because they are spending less',[58] surely an interesting anticipation of later ideas; fourth, with all the while developing the notion of investment speculation in anticipation of price increase; fifth, with noting in passing (what is now called) an increase in liquidity preference at certain stages among 'the shrewdest class of business men':

> It is a maxim among such that there is a time when it pays better to allow money to lie idle than to invest it in any other form of property. . . . To put it another way, far-sighted men buy money, because that goes up when everything else goes down. As yet they are content to leave it in the banks, where interest is paid on it, while at the same time it appreciates through declining prices.[59]

This too fits in well with the problem of producing more than could be sold with a profit. Selden also discusses the situation in this manner:

> Each individual is merely seeking to protect himself from apprehended dangers. To withdraw cash at such a period is clearly unpatriotic, but for any one individual to refuse to do so on that ground might result in loss to himself without averting disaster from others.[60]

This formulation also points to a disequilibrium mechanism, along with generated overproduction as a result of production beyond profitable limits and liquidity preference. Indeed, two paragraphs further Selden states bluntly, 'It is a periodical breakdown of the social machinery, and one for which our economic and political engineers have so far been unable to suggest any adequate remedy.'[61]

Hale's three-page summary of the Selden article concentrated upon Selden's differentiation of types of cycles and characterization of the phrases of each cycle. The argument of the article is summarized in a paraphrase of Selden:

> *Credit system* responsible for extent of advance in prices and violence of decline – panic. But not cause of trade cycle, which is due to effort to anticipate higher prices.[62]

On the basis of the foregoing it seems reasonable to conclude that Say's law was acknowledged as "doctrine" but that it coexisted with additional lines of reasoning attempting to explain fluctuations and cycles; that Say's law itself was seen as enjoining overproduction as a *cause* of cycles; that overproduction could be the result of instability whose genesis still had to be explained; that Say's law did not signify for the writers involved the impossibility of either unemployment or of cycles nor for that matter the impossibility of internally generated cycles *per se*. Say's law, in other words, while of doctrinal status, applied to only a small range of considerations and was neither an absolution of the need for nor a substitute for a business cycle theory. Economic thought was not derailed by what was seen as Say's holding of the impossibility of general overproduction as a cause of cycles. These economists were seeking explanations of cycles, not using the doctrine to deny the possibility of generated overproduction and unemployment. Instead, they sought answers in terms of dysfunctional anticipations and the accelerator principle. During this same period, the assumptions of Say's law were made clearer, first through their invocation as arguments – money as a medium of exchange, flexible prices, interest-rate equilibration of saving and investment, etc. But that is another story, and one not much aided by the present materials.

We come finally to Andrew's 'philosophy' of business cycles, his mental posture in looking over the future. This philosophy or posture the notes show him articulating as he completed his analysis of 1904–5, the final period covered by him. That posture is one of down-to-earth realism and seriousness. 'Everyone', the notes have Andrew saying, 'must believe that sooner or later the extraordinary prosperity of [the] last eight years must come to an end and [the] country [USA] go through another ordeal of purging. Many undertakings have doubtless been launched [which are] controlled by reckless, unscrupulous or incompetent men. At any rate this has been the case before.'[63] He pointed out that periods of relapse 'are various in length. . . . But in each [earlier] case a factor [was] present [which is] absent today – complication of disorders in our money system'.[64] 'Those circumstances', he went on, are 'absent now, and in case of another reaction [it is] conceivable that as far as this [is] concerned [it is] not likely to be so prolonged. But in every democratic country hard times almost always [are] prolonged by some radical movement's trying to remedy it. It might take a socialistic form. On the other hand [there are] peculiarities in our currency situation [which are] especially favorable.'[65] He then surveyed the US gold supply and concluded that while inflation of the per capita circulation had been a 'cause for [a] great rise [in] prices', it had been so 'without danger of reaction which would be [the case] if paper [had been] inflated'.[66] The next crisis, he thought, would have a rapid recovery because of the strong gold position. There were also 'other factors for encouragement'. The concentration of capital, he argued, 'has made it easier [to] adjust production to consumption and prevent overproduction due to rival firms continuing production'.[67] Another factor was the 'extraordinary prosperity' of the West and the South.[68]

Andrew then moved on to England, which had, he said, 'no *great* crises etc. since 1870, but all figures show she went through [the] same periods of depression and inflation as [the] US'.[69] He generalized that transitions in England 'have been made lately without acute periods of distress and sudden collapse. Some people', he pointed out, 'say [that the] absence of crises in England [is] an unmitigated evil. They say it now takes her years to accomplish what before took [a] short time; formerly failures [were] crowded into [a] few weeks' time, now she has lingering illness, [and is] slowly purged – by this a sharp panic [is] considered as a strong cathartic. No businessman would accede to such proposition', he insisted, 'for [a] crisis besides purging is likely to bring to liquidation firms fundamentally solvent. All business [is] founded on credit, which [a] panic destroys. And as [a] matter of fact in this country we've had the panics, and also the long period [of] depression. Absence of crises', he insisted, is 'in itself a matter of congratulations, not regret – yet some of the reasons why England has escaped crises may be subjects of regret. Why has she had no great crises since 1866?'[70] To this question he answered, first, 'Her banking system [is] better adapted to meet them than ours. It's centralized, hence more control over business and more conservative';[71] second, the 'English government on the whole interferes less with business and is more respectful of property rights. No reckless experimenting with currency. Scarcely ever any apprehension as to meddlesome legislation about trade. Since 1866,[72] no apprehension regarding currency';[73] third, he saw 'England by nature more phlegmatic and conservative than we are, probably less imaginative and not too apt to lose balance. We're more apt to be carried on by [the] spirit of optimism, and to be cast down by the turn of the tide'.[74] Finally, 'most important of all – England [is] an old country which has long since reached [her] maximum speed of development. . . . This [is] the most important reason for England's lack of crises in recent years – in other industrial countries like Germany they've been as severe as in [the] US'.[75]

IV

These lecture notes, reports, and the course of which they were an emanation are both revealing and suggestive of some aspects of the early history of macroeconomic theory in this century. Most clearly they reveal that business cycles were already treated as a serious subject. The subject was taught in an organized way and underwent relatively penetrating and sophisticated treatment, both deductive and inductive. It utilized an extensive literature and developed a reasonably complex and sophisticated variety of lines of reasoning. Much if not all of this has been obscured by the enormous impact of the Keynesian revolution, by the growth of national income accounting, and by the largely ahistorical (if not antihistorical) posture of economic theory and economists generally. These materials suggest that, with respect to the subject of business cycles and macroeconomic theory, economists in the opening decade of this century were not as naive or absurd as some would have them appear and, alas, some of them sometimes appear to have been. Business cycle analysis in that period was already rich and variegated and had its own internal forces for the generation of new ideas, including the lacunae of theoretical analysis, reinforced by the facts and trends of the marketplace and world of affairs.

The materials also raise large questions of interpretation. What was the actual *interpretation* of Say's law in the three or four decades before Keynes's attack in the 1930s, and, whatever the interpretation, what was the law's *status* in that period, especially in relation to the growing body of business cycle theory, both orthodox and heterodox? Say's law was acknowledged as doctrine, but just what did it signify and what did it preclude? It was surely not as all-important as many have made it out to have been. Their view coexisted with a growing body of thoughts which did not consider Say's law either sufficient or conclusive as macroeconomics. Among the orthodox economists whose thought vibrated throughout Andrew's course, himself included, Say's law was treated in neither a cavalier nor an adversary manner; in no small part, it seems to have been left neatly on the shelf, applied negatively to one line of reasoning (overproduction as a cause of cycles), as something inadequate to the problem at hand – in effect, as part of a developing collection of lines of reasoning and approaches, all attempting to grapple with an understanding of a serious problem, a problem whose nature was approached and seen from different facets. These economists were seeking explanations for crises and cycles, for periodicity and recurrence, to use Andrew's phraseology; in short, to account for under-full-employment equilibrium.[76]

The problem of the interpretation and status of Say's law in the earliest decade of this century suggests the further problem of the process by which the meaning of a doctrine is changed, the process in which certain meanings are filtered out and others added and by which the doctrine is continually undergoing reinterpretation, if not in basic statement, then in the nuances read into and the uses made of it. What are the forces governing the change of meaning and/or application of a doctrine and its place in the development of theory? Finally, there is the problem of what is the 'correct' implication, interpretation or use of a doctrine, postulate, or theorem. Here the fact seems to be that a doctrine is what its users make of it; and that in the process of use its meaning is continually redefined.[77]

But important as these questions and issues are, the materials reported upon in this chapter, and this chapter, provide no conclusive answers. The materials point rather to needed inquiry. What they do reveal, however, is the serious and relatively sophisticated study of business cycles, hence macroeconomics, during the early heyday of neoclassical economics in this country.[78]

Notes

1. A member of a distinguished English and American family, Hale (1884–1969) received the B.A. (1906), A.M. (1907) and LL.B. (1909) from Harvard and the Ph.D. (1918) from Columbia. His non-law degrees were all in economics. He served as an assistant to Taussig, with whom he developed a friendship which was to last for decades. Hale taught in the Columbia Economics Department both before and after receiving the doctorate. He began teaching in the Law School in 1919, eventually being granted a joint appointment and finally, in 1928, transferring completely to the Law School, from which he retired as professor emeritus in 1949, continuing to teach into the mid-1950s. Biographical information is based upon Joseph Dorfman, *The Economic Mind in American Civilization* (New York: Viking Press 1959), vol. 4, pp. 160–3, and vol. 5, p. 588; J. Goebel, Jr (ed.), *A History of the Law School* (New York: Columbia University Press, 1955), pp. 324–5, 361; *Law Alumni Bulletin*, vol. 11 (Winter 1969), p. 39. Hale's research and teaching

were concentrated in public utility law and in a unique course, Legal Factors in Economic Society. He produced a stream of important articles in public utility law which had manifest eventual impact on the courts, in part through his friendship with Justices Stone, Brandeis, Cardozo, Frankfurter, Hand, and Frank, among others. He also wrote extensively on the economy as a system of mutual coercion based upon relative power and on the legal bases thereof. See, for example, Hale, 'Coercion and Distribution in a Supposedly Noncoercive Society', *Political Science Quarterly*, vol. 38 (1923), and *Freedom Through Law* (New York: Columbia University Press, 1952).

2. Samuels, 'The Economy as a System of Power and Its Legal Bases: The Legal Economics of Robert Lee Hale', *University of Miami Law Review*, vol. 27 (Spring–Summer 1973), pp. 261–371.
3. See citations listed in American Economic Association, *Index of Economic Journals* (Homewood, Ill., 1961), vol. 1, p. 161.
4. National Monetary Commission, Senate Document No. 570, 61st Cong. 2nd sess., 1910.
5. Wesley Clair Mitchell, *Business Cycles* (Berkeley, Calif., University of California Press, 1913). See also Milton Friedman, in *Wesley Clair Mitchell: The Economic Scientist*, ed. Arthur F. Burns (New York: National Bureau of Economic Research, 1952), p. 244, and the use still made of Andrew's material in Milton Friedman and Anna Jacobson Schwartz, *Monetary Statistics of the United States* (New York, Columbia University Press, 1970).
6. *Index of Economic Journals*, vol. 1, p. 161 and vol. 2 (1961), p. 262; Library of Congress, *Select List of References on the Monetary Question* (Washington, 1913); Andrew, 'Criticisms of the Note-Issue Provisions of the Owen-Glass Bill', *Proceedings of the Academy of Political and Social Science*, vol. 4 (Oct. 1913), pp. 177–83.
7. George Charles Selden, 'Trade Cycles and the Effort to Anticipate', *Quarterly Journal of Economics*, vol. 16 (1902), pp. 293–310.
8. Lecture Notes, pp. 7–8, 90.
9. First Report, p. 13.
10. Lecture Notes, p. 90.
11. For Selden's views concerning liquidity preference, see below, text at n. 59.
12. See John Stuart Mill, *Principles of Political Economy*, ed. W. J. Ashley (reprint, New York: Kelley, 1961), bk 3, ch. 14, and bk 4, ch. 4.
13. Second Report, p. 20.
14. See below, text at n. 46.
15. Second Report, p. 23.
16. Ibid., cover.
17. Lecture Notes, p. 8.
18. Ibid., p. 11.
19. Ibid., p. 16.
20. Ibid., pp. 37–8.
21. Ibid., pp. 26–7.
22. Ibid., p. 103.
23. Ibid., p. 113.
24. Ibid., p. 17.
25. Ibid., p. 165. See Joseph A. Schumpeter, *History of Economic Analysis* (New York: Oxford University Press, 1954), p. 743.

26. Mitchell, *Business Cycles*, pp. 5–6.
27. Lecture Notes, p. 163.
28. Ibid., p. 165.
29. Ibid.
30. Ibid., p. 166.
31. Ibid., p. 170.
32. Ibid., p. 172.
33. Ibid.
34. Ibid., p. 173.
35. Ibid., p. 174.
36. Ibid., p. 175.
37. Ibid.
38. Ibid.
39. Ibid.
40. Ibid., p. 176.
41. Ibid., pp. 176–7.
42. Ibid., p. 177.
43. 'Crisis Theories', pp. 4–5; emphasis in original.
44. Thomas Nixon Carver, 'A Suggestion for a Theory of Industrial Depressions', *Quarterly Journal of Economics*, vol. 17 (1903), pp. 497–500. The article is summarized in the Lecture Notes on pp. 55–6.
45. Lewis H. Haney, *History of Economic Thought*, 4th edn (New York: Macmillan, 1949), p. 677.
46. Carver, 'A Suggestion for a Theory', p. 497.
47. Ibid., p. 498.
48. Ibid., p. 499.
49. Ibid., p. 500.
50. Lecture Notes, pp. 176–7.
51. Reference given above, n. 9.
52. Lecture Notes, p. 170.
53. Selden, 'Trade Cycles', p. 309.
54. Ibid., p. 310.
55. Ibid., p. 293.
56. Ibid.
57. Ibid., p. 294.
58. Ibid., p. 301.
59. Ibid., p. 306.
60. Ibid., p. 308.
61. Ibid., pp. 308–9.
62. Selden, 'Trade Cycles', p. 3; emphasis in original.
63. Lecture Notes, pp. 153–4.
64. Ibid., p. 154.
65. Ibid.
66. Ibid., p. 155.
67. Ibid., pp. 155–6.
68. Ibid., p. 156.
69. Ibid.; emphasis in original.
70. Ibid., pp. 157–8.
71. Ibid., p. 158.

72. The text appears to read 1816, but other evidence suggests Andrew said or intended 1866.
73. Lecture Notes, p. 159.
74. Ibid., p. 159.
75. Ibid., pp. 159–60. Andrew also gave as another factor the idea he attributed to Tugan-Baranowsky that England produces producer goods more than consumer goods and 'such trade is less speculative than finished commodities' (p. 158). (This idea conflicts, of course, with Carver's accelerator concept.) Andrew's comment in this regard paralleled his comment on the first point. Concerning England's more centralized banking system, he said that her banking system was centralized before 1866 and 'this didn't prevent her having crises *before* 1866', and moreover, 'in NY recently banks have become more and more centralized, and have helped us avoid collapse in recent years' (p. 158; emphasis in original). On Tugan-Baranowsky's point he said, 'But here too no striking difference [exists] in this regard between England and [the] US, for *we* are for [the] most part providing producers' goods' (p. 158; emphasis in original). Hale's summary of these points closely follows the lecture notes; see 'Crises. History', pp. 19–20.
76. One of the referees of this paper has sensed a 'schizophrenia which must have been prevalent among economists who taught courses in "business cycles" while believing in Say's Law', and has suggested the relevance of the following statement from Samuelson concerning the situation three decades after Andrew's course: 'To know your own country you must have travelled abroad. To understand modern economics it is good to have lived long enough to have escaped competent instruction in its mysteries. When Archibald and Lipsey try to draw for Patinkin a picture of what a "classical" monetary theorist believed in, they are pretty much in the position of a man who, looking for a jackass, must say to himself, "If I were a jackass, where would I go?"

    'Mine is the great advantage of having once been a jackass. From 2 January 1932 until an indeterminate date in 1937, I was a classical monetary theorist. I do not have to look for the tracks of the jackass embalmed in old journals and monographs. I merely have to lie down on the couch and recall in tranquillity, upon that inward eye which is the bliss of solitude, what it was that I believed between the ages of 17 and 22. This puts me in the same advantageous position that Pio Nono enjoyed at the time when the infallibility of the Pope was being enunciated. He could say, incontrovertibility, "Before I was Pope, I believed he was infallible. Now that I am Pope, I can feel it".

    'Essentially, we believed that in the longest run and in ideal models the amount of money did not matter. Money could be "neutral" and in many conditions the hypothesis that it was could provide a good first or last approximation to the facts. To be sure, Hume, Fisher, and Hawtrey had taught us that under dynamic conditions, an increase in money might lead to "money illusion" and might cause substantive changes – e.g., a shift to debtor-entrepreneurs and away from creditor-rentiers, a forced-saving shift to investment and away from consumption, a lessening of unemployment, a rise in wholesale prices relative to sticky retail prices and wage rates, et cetera.

'But all this was at a second level of approximation, representing relatively transient aberrations. Moreover, this tended to be taught in applied courses on business cycles, money and finance, and economic history rather than in courses on pure theory. In a real sense there was a dichotomy in our minds; we were schizophrenics. From 9 to 9:50 a.m. we presented a simple quantity theory of neutral money. There were then barely ten minutes to clear our palates for the 10 to 10:50 discussion of how an engineered increase in *M* would help the economy. In mid-America in the mid-1930s, we neoclassical economists tended to be mild inflationists, jackasses crying in the wilderness and resting our case essentially on sticky prices and costs, and on expectations.

'Returning to the 9 o'clock hour, we thought that real outputs and inputs and price ratios depended essentially in the longest run on real factors, such as tastes, technology, and endowments. The stock of money we called *M* (or, to take account of chequable bank deposits, we worked in effect with a velocity-weighted average of *M* and *M′*; however, a banking system with fixed reserve and other ratios would yield *M′* proportional to *M*, so *M* alone would usually suffice). An increase in *M* – usually we called it a doubling on the ground that after God created unity he created the second integer – would cause a proportional increase in all prices (tea, salt, female labour, land rent, share or bond prices) and values (expenditure on tea or land, share dividends, interest income, taxes)' (Paul A. Samuelson, 'What Classical and Neoclassical Monetary Theory Really Was', *Canadian Journal of Economics*, vol. 1 (1968), pp. 1–2. A second referee 'was not disturbed by the question of "schizophrenia" in economists at the turn-of-the-century on the question of Say's Law and business cycles. Clearly, Say's Law was a recognized principle – and the business cycle was a recognized phenomenon (witness the existence of Andrew's course at Harvard)'. The suggestion in the text is that perhaps Say's law then meant something different, and had a different status, than it did in the 1930s and thereafter. It is beyond the narrow interpretive limits of this paper to attempt to resolve this question.

77. On similar and related points see Bernice Shoul, 'Karl Marx and Say's Law', *Quarterly Journal of Economics*, vol. 71 (1957), reprinted in J. J. Spengler and W. R. Allen (eds), *Essays in Economic Thought* (Chicago: Rand McNally, 1960), ch. 18; W. H. Hutt, *Keynesianism: Retrospect and Prospect* (Chicago: Rand McNally 1963); and *inter alia*, Robert V. Eagly (ed.), *Events, Ideology and Economic Theory* (Detroit: Wayne State University Press, 1968).

78. Grateful appreciation is acknowledged to Mrs Robert Lee Hale and Mr Robert Lee Hale, Jr, for making available most liberally the private papers of the late Robert Lee Hale. The lecture notes and reports described in this paper are in the possession of Mrs Hale (Folders 67 and 107) and are eventually to be deposited in the Law Library of Columbia University. A copy of the notes is in my possession. I am also indebted to Professor Arthur H. Cole of Harvard University for providing, among other things, important information concerning the course described herein; to Maury Weinrobe for comments on an earlier draft of the paper; and to two referees who made invaluable suggestions for improvement.

11 The Teaching of Monetary Economics in the Early 1900s: Insight into the Development of Monetary Theory*

(with Andrew Gray)**

I

A[bram] Piatt Andrew (1873–1936) was one of the leading monetary economists of the first two decades of the twentieth century. Beyond his professorial duties in the 1900s at Harvard, Andrew was special assistant to the National Monetary Commission, Assistant Secretary of the Treasury, Director of the Mint, and after World War I a member of the House of Representatives for fifteen years. In an earlier article, Warren Samuels (1972) reported on a student's notes from Andrew's 1905–6 course in Commercial Crises and Cycles of Trade, Economics 12b, which is of interest because of Andrew's heavy reliance upon statistical material, the highly developed study of cycles and the attendant literature reflected in the course, and his treatment of Say's Law. In a subsequent note, Samuels and Gray (1974) reported on the 1909 catastrophe in which a box of research materials and course notes, representing almost all of the materials he had prepared during his nine faculty years at Harvard, was tossed in error by a servant into Gloucester harbour only to be recovered in time by Andrew. We can now report on these salvaged materials, discovered at Andrew's home, together with a few items which survived by not being thrown into the sea.[1]

The materials in hand are primarily lecture notes used by Andrew in teaching Economics 8a, Money: A General Survey of Currency Legislation,

* Originally published in *History of Political Economy*, vol. 8 (Fall 1976), pp. 324–40. The authors appreciate the comments by John P. Henderson, Lawrence Officer, and two referees on an earlier draft.

** Andrew Gray is a private consultant and writer in Washington, DC.

Experience, and Theory in Recent Times. The notes appear to have been primarily those used during the Fall 1902 term but some were used earlier and some later. There are some notations for revision.[2]

In this chapter we shall discuss first the materials relating to monetary theory and practice. We shall get a feel for the changing compass and content of monetary economics shortly after the turn of the century as interpreted by a young economist at the leading department of economics in the country. Andrew demonstrated a wide range of knowledge, a deft capacity for integrating historical and theoretical materials, and a sophisticated and innovative mind. We shall then turn to Andrew's contribution to the National Monetary Commission and the establishment of the Federal Reserve System, as prefigured in these notes.

II

A political and economic conservative by many standards, manifest, during his Republican membership in Congress (Tugwell, p. 53; Garland, p. 383), Andrew was nonetheless policy-oriented and reformist, willing to rely upon the federal government in monetary reform, so long as the changes were consonant with his interpretation of the business system.

As a monetary theorist he held a complex combination of largely orthodox ideas. These included the quantity theory, stable prices, sound money, the gold standard, that the price level and price of gold tended to move together, and that cycles were considerably influenced by monetary conditions and policies (Fusfeld, pp. 31, 263). He opposed trusts (albeit without drastic remedies) and tariffs and supported central banking (Fusfeld, p. 24); indeed, in regard to the latter, he was the principal architect of the Aldrich Plan which would have given greater banker control over the central banking system than was effectuated by the Federal Reserve Act (Garland, p. 383; Gray, pp. 67–74).

Andrew's surviving lecture notes for Economics 8a for 1902–3 and other years comprise several hundred sheets and are not complete. The notes were originally organized in sequence by lecture, with pagination only for each lecture. Some lectures are complete; others are totally or partially missing. There are also supplementary sheets, unnumbered, which were probably inserted into the various lecture sequences.

Andrew's outline of the course for 1902–3 divided the materials into seven sections. To quote from his outline sheet, the first four lectures were introductory and dealt with the 'nature, functions, kinds of money, legal relations of money, etc.'. Then followed five lectures on 'The Precious

Metals', covering 'history of their production, consumption, flow to the east, the ratio, their value, with study of index numbers'. 'English Monetary History' (nine lectures) included six lectures on the 'history of English coinage, debasements, recoinages, and reasons for adoption of gold standard' and three lectures on 'restrictive period, bullion report and related controversies about paper money'. 'French Monetary History' (six lectures) covered four lectures on the 'history of coinage, debasements, the great nineteenth century experiment with bimetallism, the Latin Union, etc.', and two lectures on paper money in France, including John Law, the *assignats*, and the late-nineteenth-century period of suspension. Andrew next devoted six lectures to the 'Recent Monetary History of Other Countries', listing Germany, Holland and the Dutch Indies, the Scandinavian Union, Austria, Russia, Japan, British India, and the Philippines, most of which notes are missing. Next followed five lectures on 'American Monetary History', specifying 'colonial coins and bills, revolutionary money, history of US coinage, history of legal tenders', although, as with most of the lectures on other countries, especially England and France, Andrew's lectures were more of a broad-gauged financial than a narrow monetary history. The concluding four lectures were on 'Monetary Theory' and were listed as follows: '(1) Recent criticism of the quantity theory; (2) The labor and commodity standards; the ideal standard; (3) The Bimetallic arguments, general and special; and (4) The International Monetary Conferences and their failures; general survey of movement to gold and its explanation.'

The notes indicate the use of considerable statistical data – for example, gold and silver production and coinage ratios – although perhaps not as much as in his cycles course. Although his Fall 1903 course (one year later) in Economics 8a apparently gave greater emphasis to the quantity theory and 'the students were given a long reading list on the quantity theory, and were to write a thesis evaluating it' (Fusfeld, p. 30), the Fall 1902 course did use the quantity theory as an interpretive vehicle and apparently gave the students a choice of thesis topics. On a sheet entitled 'Thesis Subjects', Andrew listed nine possibilities: a history of English legislation and proclamations regarding the retention of the precious metals – the prohibition of their export, concessions made to the East India Co. etc. – as one aspect of mercantilism; a critical study of the recoinage of William III, wherein it succeeded and wherein it failed; a study of the consequences of the Restriction Act, with tables and charts illustrating the quantity of notes issued, their proportion to cash holdings, their depreciation both in terms of gold and of commodities – with the probable reasons therefor; a study of recent currency legislation in India dealing with coinage suspension and resumption, the Report of the Indian Currency Commission of 1898, subsequent progress towards a gold standard, the issue of gold certificates, the payment of officials in gold, etc.; the differences between money and measures of length, time, weight, etc.; the exchange of silver for gold in the Far East during the 16th and 17th centuries; the early history of prices (before 1800); the extent to which exchequer bills were used to serve as currency; and the relations between the agio on an abased currency and its depreciation – all as given on the sheet. At the end of this list was an additional list of charts that the students were to prepare, including one on gold and silver production in the United States since 1840, with a line for gold in California; one showing the relative imports of gold and silver into India, the rupee exchange values and the price of silver; and one showing net exports of gold and silver in France during the century. The course, which seems to have been becoming increasingly theoretical and less historical–descriptive, was already highly empirical and quantitative.

The course relied upon an already considerable literature. Included in assigned reading and/or otherwise used were books and articles (primarily in the *Quarterly Journal of Economics* and *Economic Journal* but also in some financial publications) by F. A. Walker, T. B. Macaulay, H. D. Macleod, J. L. Laughlin, F. W. Taussig, W. Roscher, K. Knies, W. S. Jevons, W. G. Summer, M. Chevalier, J. R. McCulloch, and many others, some of whom are noted below.

Sheets marked Lecture 1 surveyed the literature and bibliographical sources and also the development of monetary thought. Starting with the ancients (Plato and Aristotle as well as Aristophanes, to whom Andrew attributed the 'earliest recognition of so-called "Gresham's Law"'), Andrew covered the medieval period (including T. Aquinas, N. Oresme, and N. Copernicus), the 16th century (Bishop Latimer, J. Bodin), the 17th century (mercantilists and their opponents: A. Serra, T. Mun, G. de Malynes, J. Locke, C. Davenant, W. Temple, W. Petty, D. North), the 18th century (J. Law, I. Newton, J. Harris, J. Steuart, D. Hume), and the 19th century divided into four periods: the bank restriction controversy (D. Ricardo, N. W. Senior, T. Tooke and W. Newmarch, R. Torrens, J. W. Bosanquet), the Bank Charter Act controversy, discussion of the effects of gold discoveries (J. E. Cairnes, W. S. Jevons, M. Chevalier), and the Bimetallism debate (including W. S. Jevons, W. Lexis, W. Bagehot, R. Giffen, P. E. Levasseur, H. D. Macleod, H. White, and others). Andrew next examined barter, gold and credit systems; the functions of money; and evaluated their performance. By the functions of money he primarily meant measure of value and medium of exchange, to which he added standard of deferred payments, means of transporting value, means of storing value, means of lending capital, and means of payment for one-sided transactions (by which he meant payment of fines, taxes, insurance, indemnities, and the making of gifts). However, after enumerating these latter possible functions he wrote, 'It is at least questionable whether these are distinct functions, or whether they might not all be subsumed under the first two which we mentioned.' He next examined the commodities serving as money and analysed their development. At this point there is attached a very small, unidentified newspaper clipping which reads as follows: 'Major Ciccodicola considers the Abyssinian market a remunerative field for European enterprise. Silver dollars have been coined by Menelek, but the standard currency still includes salt bars and lengths of American calico. There is a market in the country for silks, firearms, and . . .'.

Andrew next discussed currency by weight and coinage systems and the various methods (standards) of using the two primary metals. He considered Herbert Spencer's proposal for the private manufacture of money and examined the experience of some companies privately minting coins. Andrew concluded in favour of government coinage, primarily on efficiency grounds: 'When private coins are allowed to circulate, the public is often to be put to great inconvenience. The coins require testing and weighing at each exchange, very much as did the uncoined metal in early times, and there is the further disadvantage that the monetary standard is apt to deteriorate. As a good and convenient money is a matter of vital importance for the general public, it would seem reasonable', Andrew wrote, 'that its provision should be under the control and regulation of the government'. (For Andrew's further views on the private use of the money power, see Samuels and Gray 1974.)

Andrew then reviewed the history of mining, production, coinage, the use of money in international trade, and the gold–silver ratio (the latter in quite some detail over many centuries). He next discussed the history of prices. In this and other matters he relied upon, and in part summarized, the works of W. Fleetwood, A. Smith, A. Young, T. Tooke and W. Newmarch, W. Jacob, T. E. Cliffe Leslie, L. L. Price, P. E. Levasseur, T. Rogers, M. Chevalier, and others. Part of his attention was directed to the role of gold and silver in political, economic, and military history.

His lectures on monetary history were very broad, effectively constituting a general financial history. He covered banking organization, structure, and control; coinage and currency policies; and the genesis of and policy related to financial panics. In all these subjects he introduced aspects of business cycle history as straightforward descriptions. He included information on money-market conditions, the stock market, and business conditions generally; also international monetary and trade movements, tariff history, payments problems, and related political history. The works of

C. F. Dunbar, M. Tugan-Baranowsky, R. Giffen, W. J. Ashley, among others, figured prominently. Later he covered American monetary legislation, the history of the Bank of England, and the problem of reserves.

Andrew's notes indicate his concern with the impact of gold and silver discoveries; the increased demand for gold as a function of growth; the gold versus silver controversies; mono- versus bimetallism; monetary disturbances, debasements and other manipulations; mint versus market ratios; coinage practices; inconvertible paper versus the gold standard; the impact of French coinage policies on England and the United States; the interrelations between custom, import of gold and silver, and price stability in India; and English monetary and financial history, including considerable attention to the Bullion Report and its role in stimulating analysis – almost all central strands of monetary history which consequently became part of the standard study of the field. The course thus dealt with problems of monetary theory and analysis which were closely related to the extant system of monetary organization and its associated problems of policy.

In a folder entitled 'History of Monometallic Theory' are notes and lecture notes covering the quantity theory, mono- versus bimetallism, and related questions of theory, such as the relation of the value of coined metal to bullion of the same metal, the relation of cost of production to the value of metal, the relation of interest rates and price levels, the relation of prices to increased productivity, and index numbers. Throughout is a concern with the impact of monetary matters upon enterprise and real production as well as, although to a lesser degree, distributional consequences. With regard to the quantity theory, there are many notes summarizing the contributions of particular theorists (including N. Barbon, J. Child, J. Bodin, T. Mun, J. Harris, J. Locke, J. Vanderlint, J. Paulus, W. Petty, I. Newton, R. Cantillon, J. Steuart, A. Smith, D. Hume, and apparently concluding with D. Ricardo). Andrew emphasized the use of the quantity theory to 'upset' mercantilist notions of the favourable balance of trade. He surveyed attitudes, theories and arguments (the relative advantages and disadvantages) concerning price stability *vis-à-vis* rising and falling prices.

Andrew's interest in business cycles is reflected in another folder entitled 'Crises and the Currency' which was also found with the lecture notes from Economics 8a and which likely were included as part of his lectures on American monetary history. He considered proposals to reform the currency, note, and banking organization and procedures, in order to make the supply of money more responsive to the needs of trade and to minimize its adverse contribution to cyclical conditions. He included some comparison with other countries and noted a great variety of ascribed causes of crises and, accordingly, of proposed remedies.

The course was therefore heavily policy-oriented. It also included considerable discussion of problems of theory, most of which, with the exception of the quantity theory, which was also given independent attention, were dealt with as part of his interpretation of monetary history and problems of policy. Rivalling the quantity theory in use was Gresham's Law, which Andrew employed in analysing the consequences of coinage ratios and paper *vis-à-vis* metal money throughout the history of monetary policy. Andrew was relatively traditional in his monetary teaching, but did show a critical and reforming attitude towards monetary organization. He did not applaud in class notes the virtues of any one monetary or banking principle or standard, but was ready to assess each of them in the light of experience and to adjust relevant institutions and practices accordingly. The monetary system he saw as governmental in character and therefore subject to reform through government; but he coupled this view with much concern over the misuse of the monetary system by government.

There are many interesting specific materials in the notes. One is marked Lecture 24 and deals with paper money and the French Revolution. After a survey of conditions under Louis XV and Louis XVI, Andrew presented a carefully detailed exposition of events from October 1789 to 1792, during which time the successive authorities issued series after series of *assignats*. Andrew, as is to be expected, did not fail to relate the flow of paper money to the increasing price level, but some of his remarks are interesting in other respects as well. The *assignats* were issued by the Treasury (at first bearing an interest rate of 5 per cent) in connection with the sale of confiscated ecclesiastial property, beginning late in 1789. As Andrew explained the strategy, 'They were to be paid out by the Treasury to its creditors. It was expected that many of them would be paid back into the Treasury at once in purchase of land, and that the rest would be redeemed by the specie which was brought in by the sale of the land. That is to say, these government notes were guaranteed by a general (pledge/mortgage) on the revenues derived from the sale of ecclesiastical property.' Particularly interesting is Andrew's appreciation that government had, as he expressed it,

> *two reasons* for wanting to sell this property immediately; *first* there was the *fiscal motive*, . . . the need of revenue to meet expenses and to pay off the debt. But second there was a *political motive*. They were anxious to get this land distributed as rapidly and as widely as possible among the middle classes, in order to commit them to the Revolution, and to the government which they would then be bound to support, because they owed to it the title to their property.

Andrew had a clear appreciation of the interrelations between the economics and politics of property rights, of both the politics of the devolution of property rights and the insinuation of private economic interests into government policy.

In another lecture – possibly from the principles course and not Economics 8a, however – Andrew explicated the functions of money by relating them to the inconveniences of barter; the functions were measure of value and medium of exchange. At the apparent conclusion of the lecture, Andrew's notes read:

> It is very important that we should get a clear idea of just what money is and what it does, it plays so conspicuous a part in our life. [Yet] it is very common for men to get a wrong idea of its place in the economic regime, and an exaggerated idea of its importance.
>
> Money you will see is really nothing more than a device for facilitating the exchange of goods. It offers a most convenient method of exchanging things for each other.
>
> We must not let the fact of its intervention and trade obscure the real character of transactions.
>
> Fundamentally and in the last resort things are not purchased with money, and laborers are not paid in money.

This position did not keep Andrew from the view that improper monetary policies and conditions could contribute to cycles and crises, as schizophrenic as the result may appear.

In notes marked Lecture 32 – on the first page of which Andrew wrote a reminder: 'a little short' – he went out of his way to challenge a view ascribed to Laughlin, insisting that changes in the coinage ratio were '*not* debasement'. The very next paragraph, however, after noting that the new ratio (in his example) was not the market ratio, remarked that, '*Gresham's Law* was once more brought into play'.

On a single sheet is a quotation taken by Andrew from an unspecified 'Austrian currency pamphlet':

> Even if the monetary system of the civilized world is not regulated as it should be, still it remains a necessity for Austria to conform to that system, whatever it may be. Money is like speech: it is a means of intercourse. He who would have dealings with others must speak their language, however irrational he may find it. Language is rational by the very fact that it is intelligible to others, and more rational in proportion as it is intelligible to more people or to all. There can no more be an independent money system than independent speech: indeed, the more

> universal character of money, as compared with language, appears in this, that while a national language has its justification and significance in the intercourse of the world, there is no place for a national monetary system in the world's intercourse. If Europe errs in adopting gold, we must still, for good or evil, join Europe in her error, and we shall thus receive less injury than if we insist on being 'rational' all by ourselves.

Other than indicating that this is a quotation (possibly from F. von Wieser), Andrew made no further written comment.

One group of notes, whose first page is unfortunately missing, presents a sympathetic and perceptive account of popular monetary heterodoxy and its roots and consequences. After earlier remarking that 'the party which happens to be in power during periods of hard times, always suffers first', he wrote:

> There has always been a disposition in [the USA] – it existed even in colonial times – to regard an inflation of the currency as a remedy for economic evils of any sort, whether due to crop failures, speculation, or over expanded credit or what not. It has become almost a custom to look to the government for relief when industry stagnates, and whenever the lean years have come around there have always been those who attributed the distress to insufficient currency and who tried to better matters by enlarging its supply. In fact upon several occasions unsettlement of business has been prolonged and aggravated by the general uncertainty as to the future of the monetary standard. This was emphatically the case in the 70s as it was again in the 90s, in both of which decades the depression was more than ordinarily severe and more than ordinarily prolonged.
>
> All through the 70s there was agitation about the currency. We had had only a paper currency for more than a decade, – now the amount was decreased, and now it was increased again, and there was no assurance that the notes would recover their face value in coin. . . . There were all over the country discontented persons who were suffering from the depression, or from the fall in prices which was inevitable after the war, who believed they would be better off if the country never resumed specie payments. There were professional reformers who agreed with them, – men like Wendell Phillips who wrote in 1875, 'We mean to have more democracy and less autocracy in the money market: more money in everybody's reach and less for the . . . few'.
>
> There were good men like Peter Cooper in New York who persistently argued the desirability of a 'strictly national currency', one not

> convertible into coin 'and which cannot be taken from the hands of the people by the evershifting balances of commodities between nations'.
>
> There were professional politicians too who skillfully played upon the prejudices and discontent of the masses.
>
> Mr Benjamin F. Butler who was a candidate of the Greenback party for governor of this state in 1875 and 1879, and who was candidate of the Anti-monopoly, National, Greenback, Labor, and People's parties for President in 1884, continually spoke of gold and silver as the 'money alike of the barbarian and the despot' – as 'the machinery and relic of old despotisms'. What we needed was 'an American currency' 'of some cheap and convenient material' – and an 'American system of finance'.

Andrew went on to say: 'I do not mean to imply that there was no justification whatever for the Greenback movement. I don't believe that there has ever been a movement which has appealed to great bodies of men which has not had at its basis some element of truth. . . . – that there is an element of reason mixed in with all of the errors – and that is why they make their appeal.' He continued: 'Now there can be no doubt that the fall in prices which occurred after the war wrought great injury to many and great gain to others.' It was not surprising, therefore, he argued, that there should be such controversy. But, he went on, 'It is not strange that many failed to appreciate that this continual agitation with regard to the standard of value was working tremendous injury to business, when they were confronted with such an uncomfortable falling market.' After further detailing the understandable grounds for the complaints in what is really a very sympathetic account, Andrew returned to his argument:

> I don't mean to argue in defense of the Greenbackers, except to show why the agitation with regard to the currency continued for so long a time, for until this agitation subsided, until men could once more be certain of the standard in which their loans might be repaid, they would not lend, they would not invest, business could not recuperate.

This argument brought Andrew very close to specification of liquidity preference, elements of which did enter his teaching in other connections (Tugwell, pp. 155–6 and elsewhere; and see below). Nevertheless, Andrew did comprehend the close connections between the problem of order – with its elements of freedom versus control, continuity versus change, and hierarchy versus equality – the monetary system, and business enterprise. In another lecture, numbered 34, discussing the price level and economic conditions during the years of the Civil War, consequent to the issue of the paper currency, Andrew remarked, 'You can imagine how fortunes were gained and fortunes lost during those years', and 'Little wonder that men appealed to the Supreme Court to protect themselves from such losses. This is one of the subjects upon which the Supreme Court has displayed very unfortunate vacillation when it has at different periods given diametrically opposed decisions.'

The subject of greatest interest must be Andrew's presentation of the quantity theory and related subjects. Here Andrew's close familiarity with the complexities of empirical realities led him to stress the major historic thrust of the quantity theory (coupled with Gresham's Law), but his was a highly sophisticated approach to quantity theory. He used quantity theory reasoning typically, it appears, in considering the complexities of the gold-silver-greenback 'standard' with which he and the country [USA] were then familiar. Thus, in a discussion elaborating upon the statement that 'there are several qualifications, however, which must be attached to the assertion of a definite quantitative relation between the growth of deposits and the basis of reserves' – a critical matter in application of the quantity theory at the time – his first point was that 'the proportion of deposits withdrawn in cash varies from country to country and has not always been the same even in the same country'. In elaborating the point, Andrew stressed that 'the slow growth of modern banking methods has resulted unquestionably in a continually increasing extension of monetary substitutes without any corresponding increase in their monetary foundations', and also pointed out that 'there are changes in the relation between deposits and reserves due to fluctuations in commercial confidence'. It is possible to read too much into these statements about his perceptivity as to the variations and vagaries of liquidity preference (with consequences for *M* and *V*); but consider Andrew's second point:

> There are periods of business prostration when even though there is an increase of money in the country the monetary substitutes will not increase and prices will not rise.

Beyond liquidity preference, Andrew's work evidently foreshadowed the precise working-out of the factors influencing financial multipliers in the 1920s and 1930s, including liquid asset demands closely connected to deposits.

Later in the same notes, Andrew wrote: 'In the course of the twenty-five years from 1873 to 1897, for instance, the quantity of money no doubt increased very considerably in almost every country and yet almost everywhere prices were falling. Some writers immediately jumped to the conclusion that the quantity theory was no longer valid as an explanation of prices.' This conclusion he rejected: the conclusion 'is not justified for the simple reason that [it] takes a very one-sided view of the quantity theory'. It 'only takes into account one of the two factors which Hume had found a century and a half ago to rest at the basis of monetary theory. According to the old theory prices depend upon the quantity of money – but upon that quantity taken in connection with the quantity of goods to be exchanged'. Thus contemporary critics of the quantity theory 'took no account of the vast increase in wealth and production and consequently of exchanges'. There was, then, no mechanical relationship between *M* and *P*; Say's Law did not render *V* and *T* irrelevant in Andrew's analysis.

Similarly in other notes Andrew indicated his comprehension of the complex structure of monetary velocity:

> We are so accustomed to hearing the expression '*the* rate' and '*the* rapidity' of circulation that we are liable to forget how very complicated is the matter referred to by them. Yet one can easily see that not only is money subject to great inequalities in the frequency of its employment as between different countries, but that it varies very widely in this regard in different parts of the same country as well. The rate is not the same in the *cities* as in the *towns*, nor alike in the *towns* and in the *villages*, and it differs still more widely in the *purely rural districts*. Then it varies too between the *different classes and occupations*, and even between the *particular individuals* of any given society. *Money will remain idle for instance as much as six or seven weeks on the average in the purse of a bondholder who receives his interest in cash trimestically* . . .

Finally, in another lecture, Andrew wrote:

> We saw that the premium on gold depended only in part upon the quantity of notes outstanding. The movements in the price of gold depended upon many other factors, upon whether or not gold was needed to settle unfavorable foreign balances – upon whether or no men were holding fast to their gold because of their apprehensiveness as to the outcome of the war [the Civil War].

No wonder that Andrew could readily consider variations in liquidity preference; his conception of the quantity theory was sufficiently complex to permit intrusion of a complex and changing reality. It was this same comprehensive empiricism that enabled him to juxtapose to Say's Law the realities of business-cycle history, namely, the 'periods of business prostration' referred to above. Say's Law was not used by Andrew to finesse either velocity or transactions in the quantity theory equation; nor did it preclude consideration of the causes of actual overproduction of cycles (Samuels, 1972, pp. 160–3).

III

The notes are of interest in yet another major respect. The period of Andrew's tenure on the Harvard faculty was for him, the profession, and the country a time of tortuous and groping reformulation of the nature of money and attendant reform of the banking system. The bond-secured note-issue function of banks appeared in those years to be the prime problem; everyone knew that the bond-secured currency was inelastic, or worse, perversely elastic, and nearly all schemes for banking reform concentrated upon making the note issue more flexible. Andrew, like so many other monetary economists of his time, was at first preoccupied with the traditional, as it were, problems of the monetary standard, the banking standard, the National Banking System's solution to the note-issue problem, the coinage ratio, price stability, bank solvency, radical legislation, the relation of cost of production to the value of the money metals, the inability of an inelastic currency system to adjust supply to changes in demand, and so on. But during this time, the question of what 'money' is took on new meaning as the relation of both cheques and deposits, on the one hand, and paper currency, on the other, to gold came to be better understood. This newer comprehension was hindered by many factors even beyond the aforementioned preoccupations: the aura of gold as *money* and the discredited past of paper currency experiments, ergo of notions of 'sound money', and the concern with price stability and the hold of the quantity theory, which reinforced the 'sound money' conceptions and thereby reinforced the gold and antipaper images and sentiments. Many if not all clung to the idea of money as something independent and tangible and were at first unable to perceive or admit its transformation to something decidedly intangible and artifactual, with its sources in the bookkeeper's pen. But in time bank obligations came to be seen as money, albeit with considerable delay and hesitation if not reluctance on the part of such eminent authorities as Irving Fisher, Charles Conant, J. Lawrence Laughlin, and Andrew himself. The well-known Fisherian formulation of the quantity theory was a long time in coming and it did not come easily. By the same token, Andrew did not discover the Cambridge formulation of the quantity theory or the motives for holding money.

Similarly the nature and role of fractional reserve banking was not immediately understood; comprehension was hindered by the preoccupation with past institutional structures and problems, e.g., the rigid reserve requirements of the National Banking Act, and, perhaps primarily, by the belief that what was true for an individual bank was true for all banks taken together. The very ideas of fractional reserve banking, the proper role of reserves in such a system, the nature of bank deposits originating out of loans, the credit creation and destruction process and its limits, the difference between primary and derivative deposits, the nature of metal reserves in a fractional reserve system, and finally the relation of the banks to the supply of money, including the character of bank obligations as money and the supply of money as a governmental function in relation to the banks – all these ideas and practices were largely only being worked out during the first decade of this century and most if not all, until the National Monetary Commission had completed its work, were only imprecisely (albeit increasingly) understood within the profession, in industry and finance, and in government. (And even after the commission completed its work, much ignorance remained – for example, concerning financial multipliers.) This is true even though Andrew and others gave considerable attention, for example, to bank clearings and the relation of loans to deposits as business barometers. They understood the quantity theory, Gresham's Law, and the consequences of the specie flow or balance-of-payments mechanism, within the institutions then existing and known to have existed; but gold alone was money, and currency and credit were lesser and only derivative of gold.

The hold of traditional problems and of conventional formulations and conceptions is amply manifest in Andrew's lecture notes; but so also are his groping efforts to transcend the old questions and raise new ones, thereby at least partially eclipsing the burden of his doctoral training in the late 1890s – but also building upon the work of F. W. Taussig, T. N. Carver, G. C. Selden, and others. In notes on paper watermarked 1900, Andrew explored the growth of loans and deposits and their changing relation to each other depending upon circumstances; he included the processes of deposit expansion. In notes entitled 'Defects in the National Banking System', dated 2 May 1900, Andrew, among other things, indicated concern over country bank deposits in city banks counting as reserves (appropriately enough, as this was a major problem under the National Banking System) and stressed the inelasticity of national bank note issue. But bank-issued currency was currency and not money. In notes on paper watermarked 1904, he concluded that 'the essential and distinguishing feature of modern banking is not the receipt and lending of money – but the creating and lending of credit'. Re-education came hard. In notes with a 1900 watermark, deposits are also not considered money, although he did stress that, *ceteris paribus* specie flow and without cash drain, an indefinite multiplication in deposits was possible. *Money*, however, was the reserves. On still other notes, dated 9 April 1900, he posed the question, 'Under what circumstances do checks act as substitutes for money?' and his answer was that cheques substitute for money when deposited in payment of a transaction: 'When they are deposited in the banks by those who receive them – so that payments are effected by them, and transactions settled without any even eventual use of money.' If, however, they are used only to get cash, cheques are not a money substitute, although they would 'much increase' the efficiency of money. Among other things, cash flow is indicated as a 'natural limit' to the extension of 'uncovered deposit liabilities'. Interestingly, on paper also carrying a 1900 watermark, he noted that 'undoubtedly throughout the country at large an *enormous amount of purchases* are made in this way on credit – sometimes by the giving of a promissory note – but more frequently by the mere inscription of the debt on the dealer's books', thereby suggesting that he had not yet made the complete transition from dealer debt to banker debt cum deposit creation. Andrew then queried, '*Does such a use of credit affect prices*? Are prices higher because of the existence of this vast amount of postponed payments? What is the effect upon the general level of prices of purchases made by pledged future payment?' His answer begins with the statement, 'Mill says that they always tend to raise prices', and continues: 'It seems to me that sometimes prices are raised and that sometimes they are not and sometimes *they are even lower than they otherwise would be* because of the existence of this credit'; to which he added: 'It is obvious that credit in these forms does not definitively settle transactions. It only temporarily postpones their settlement.' But, under a line indicating an intended break in the discussion, Andrew proceeds to state the following: 'Speaking broadly, we may say that the value of money at any one time depends upon the quantity of money and its rapidity of circulation, and the quantity of bank deposits and their rate of circulation. Of course on the other side it depends upon the amount of money . . . ' Alas, the last word is undecipherable! The next line simply states: 'Relation between quantity of money and quantity of deposits.' Deposits were not *money* (nor, of course, was currency), but deposits – bank credit – did govern the price level.

In 1900 Andrew was clearly near the beginning of (but already involved in) what was to be a long adventure, eventually to arrive, among very few in the country, at a deeper understanding of the money supply and fractional reserve banking. By the time he began working for Senator Nelson Aldrich in 1908 on what eventually became the Federal Reserve System, he had transcended the question of cheques as a money substitute and saw that the obvious distinctions between cheques and notes and between credit and gold are irrelevant to the fundamental problem of both money supply and banking reform, namely, the mobilization of reserves. More important, with Andrew's realizations, and in part because of his evangelism on their behalf, a new monetary and banking system eventually was adopted. The conservative but policy-oriented economist used his observations and his theory to help mould a major institutional creation.

Notes

1. The salvaged materials relating to Andrew's course in Commercial Crises and Cycles are fairly ample (although not complete) and confirm the accuracy of Hale's notes reported upon in Samuels 1972. Included in the materials not thrown into the harbour is a 254-page typed manuscript treating the history of crises and cycles from the Dutch tulip mania through to the late 1900s.
2. Quotations from notes are given with minor editorial changes. All emphasis is in the original. Some notes appear to be adapted from current textbooks and treatises, including some notes taken by Andrew as a graduate student, but, given the incompleteness of most items, no attempt has been made to track them down. Like Samuels (1972), Fusfeld (pp. 261–63) was able to rely upon sets of students notes, among other sources. No attempt is made to interpret or discuss Andrew's published writing during the period he was teaching at Harvard. See especially Andrew 1905 and the other references listed in the *Index of Economic Journals*, 1961, vol. 1, p. 61.

References

Andrew, A. Piatt (1905) 'Credit and the Value of Money', American Economic Association Publications, 3rd ser., Papers and Proceedings of the Seventeenth Annual Meeting, vol. 6, part I (1905).

Fusfeld, Daniel R. (1956) *The Economic Thought of Franklin D. Roosevelt and the Origins of the New Deal* (New York: Columbia University Press).

Garland, Joseph E. (1971) *Eastern Point* (Peterborough, N. H.; Noone House).

Gray, Andrew (1971) 'Who Killed the Aldrich Plan?' *Bankers Magazine*, vol. 154 (Summer), pp. 67–74.

Index of Economic Journals, 1961.

Samuels, Warren J. (1972) 'The Teaching of Business Cycles in 1905–1906: Insight into the Development of Macroeconomic Theory', *History of Political Economy*, vol. 4 (Spring), pp. 140–62.

——— and Andrew Gray, (1974) '"One Great Tragedy": A Vignette', *History of Political Economy*, vol. 6 (Spring), pp. 114–18.

Tugwell, Rexford G. (1957) *The Democratic Roosevelt* (Garden City, N. Y.: Doubleday).

12 Preface: Friedrich von Wieser in the History of Economic Thought*

Friedrich von Wieser was one of the outstanding practitioners of the discipline of economics. He is not, however, among the recognized giants in the history of economic thought: Adam Smith, David Ricardo, Karl Marx, Alfred Marshall, and John Maynard Keynes. He is, paradoxically, one of those recognized outstanding economists still unfortunately neglected. The fault for this arguably lies not so much with Wieser and his work but with the discipline of economics. The reason for this predicament is that Wieser's work has not always been interpreted in its entirety and also because of the narrow focus of the main interests of the discipline. An intellectual discipline creates his own self-perception from its history and its history from its self-perception. Accordingly, Wieser is honoured for some of what he did but the rest is neglected if not widely forgotten. Ironically, Wieser was himself partially responsible for this predicament. I shall attempt in this chapter to place Wieser in the history of economic thought and to explain the partial recognition and acclaim accorded to him accompanied by the partial failure of collective remembrance of his work.

Wieser was one of the leaders, though not one of the founders, of the Austrian School. He made major contributions to its development of marginal utility theory, especially the ideas of opportunity cost and imputation. From this point of view, economic analysis is principally concerned with the role of subjective utility in the market, in price formation, and thereby in the allocation of resources. Its focus is on the exercise of personal subjective choice from within an individual's opportunity set. As expressed by Wieser's English counterpart and earlier co-founder of the school, William Stanley Jevons, economics is principally the mechanics of marginal utility and self-interest.

The utility point of view has more than narrow technical consequences; it affects the very conception of economics, its fundamental nature and its methodology. From the Austrian point of view, economics is the economics

* Originally published in Friedrich von Wieser, *Gesammelte Abhandlungen* (Vienna: Hermann Bohlaus, 1991).

of the market system, of pure markets *qua* markets. The core of the market system is exchange channelled by price (value); and both exchange and price are governed by the operation of marginal utility. Marginalism here has at least three facets of significance: marginal utility, constrained maximization, and marginal adjustments between economic variables and phenomena both within and between markets, in part through the process of imputation as a means of integrating all markets. On the one hand, marginal utility, in the fundamental view of the Austrians, is not just a theory of the demand side but the all-encompassing operative force on both sides of the market; it is, through imputation, the single explanatory principle. On the other, marginalism is the very nature of economics as a scientific discipline. The distinguishing characteristic, indeed, the characteristic lauded by all devotees of Austrian economics, is its methodological individualism: the view that the best way to understand man in society is to analyse the behaviour of individual economic actors.

The ironic thing about the development of Austrian economics is that while its leading figures defined economics in marginalist and methodological individualist terms, and certainly made permanent contributions to the discipline under that aegis, they also pursued the analysis of man in society in broader terms, focusing on the institutional and power structures of economy and society, and on the impact thereof on individual opportunity sets. This is true of the principal earlier contributors to marginalism: including Jevons, Carl Menger, Leon Walras, Vilfredo Pareto, and Wieser; and of the more recent giants: Friedrich von Hayek, Ludwig von Mises, Joseph Schumpeter and Frank Knight, among others. Whereas in their formal economic analyses, economics was defined in terms of the play of marginal utility in the pure market, in their broader analyses the structure, the social location and the operation of the market itself were central. Whereas methodological individualism characterized their formal economics, methodological collectivism – the analysis of group processes, forces and problems – characterized their broader work. Within Austrian economics, as within mainstream economic in general, there is therefore a fundamental dichotomy: (1) economic theory, narrowly defined to focus on the allocation of resources through markets, and (2) what may be called the theory of economic order (or theory of economic policy, so long as it is recognized to encompass more than the economic role of government), broadly defined to deal with the organization and control of the economy, especially the structure and processes of power.

A parallel irony exists with regard to the normative policy perspective of the Austrian School. The foregoing discussion dealt with positive economics, at least insofar as economics is or can be a positive discipline. There is a parallel dichotomy regarding the normative theory of economic policy, the normative (as distinguished from the methodological) individualism, of the Austrian School. On the one hand, the distinguishing characteristic of the Austrian approach to policy is its libertarian emphasis on the individual, on the freedom of individuals to choose on the basis of their respective subjective preferences. The theories, for example, of consumer sovereignty and of rational economic consequences are governed by this point of view. On the other hand, however, the Austrian economists, writing with regard to their broader concerns, were implicitly or explicitly aware that the problem is not solely that individual preferences are to count but the role of processes and structures within which individual preferences are weighted in the counting process; in other words, the organization and control, and the institutional and power structure, of the economy. Advocacy of *laissez-faire* libertarianism is thus joined with studies of economic order, in which the claims for freedom made by their normative individualism are shown, although perhaps not always seen, to be severely limited by recognition of both the requirements of order and of collective action and the role of power in economic affairs. Their methodological and normative collectivism has often been substantially if not completely eclipsed by their methodological and normative individualism. Notice that this emphasis on methodological collectivism may be seen in either of two ways: as not accompanied by a normative collectivism, or, by virtue of the Austrian affirmation of the entrepreneurial market system, as accompanied by a particular form of normative collectivism, one manifestly not socialist in any traditional, especially pejorative, sense, but one nonetheless collectivist insofar as it postulates and affirms certain notions of social welfare in matters of the organization and control of the economy and of government. That Austrian economists have had their own reformist agendas for government is also, of course, constitutive of normative collectivism.

This concern with collective action, or with what has more recently been designated public choice or social choice, has placed the Austrian School in a complex and somewhat ambiguous relationship to American institutional economics. The institutionalists have generally been advocates of the market economy. While they often have questioned its competitiveness and specific institutional forms, they typically, albeit not uniformly, have affirmed its underlying productiveness and its enhancement of freedom. The institutionalists have generally been methodological collectivists, always focusing on the problem of organization and control, on the structure and processes of power, on institutions, and even on the market itself as such a phenomenon. The institutionalists have generally desired to reform capitalism; to enlarge and diffuse its distribution of power, opportunity and welfare; to render it more competitive or more subject to democratic government control where the former is not possible; and to use government affirmatively for these purposes, while at the same time examining and analysing the fundamental operation of government in the economic system, for example, the legal foundations of capitalism itself.

But the mainstream of economics has focused on the analysis of the operation of markets, indeed, typically on pure markets contemplated independent of the institutions which form and operate through the market. This has meant both that Austrian and not institutional economics has been especially congruent with the mainstream of economics, and that those aspects of Austrian economics which have focused on the market have been more congruent with the mainstream of economics than those, akin to the interests of the institutionalists, which have not so focused. Thus, for example, Menger's seminal contributions to the Austrian School's formulation of marginal utility economics have greater status *qua* economics than his work on the spontaneous development and rational reform of institutions which, while by no means forgotten, have been a part of the methodologically collectivist (not individualist, as is so often claimed) heritage of the Austrian School existing largely outside the mainstream of economics.

To the extent, then, that Wieser contributed to the identification of economics with the analytics of the operation of pure markets, he contributed to the eclipse within economics of both the broader, methodologically collectivist work of Menger's school and of his own work along those lines. The opportunity cost of this separation arguably has been substantial. The work of the Austrian School along these broader dimensions of inquiry is perhaps every bit and possibly infinitely more important than its marginal utility analysis, and for this work to have been excluded from the formal (fortunately not the *de facto*) definition of what economics is all about, and of what economists do, has been to deny to economists both much of what in fact has been their rich and robust heritage and vibrant opportunities for the future advancement of their subject.

Wieser himself cannot accurately be understood solely in terms of his pure theory of value. Wieser was a leading marginal utility theorist who studied the development and operation of modern economic society in its fullest. He envisioned the economy as a unified entity, encompassing more than the processes of utility valuation and resource allocation. In a series of publications, especially his *Theorie der gesellschaftlichen Wiestschaft* (1914) and *Das Gesetz der Macht* (1926), Wieser explored the economy as a system of power. He argued that power was important: for example, that price formation itself was stratified on the basis of power operating in the market; that an unequal distribution of bargaining and other power in the market arose from the class structure of society; and that the existence of power meant inexorable departures from distribution in accordance with marginal productivity, indeed, that marginal productivity was probably the upper limit which workers were likely to receive, even if unionized. Accordingly, he argued that the classical theorem, which equated private and social interests, had to be recognized as having a narrow range once one acknowledged the role of power in economic life. He argued that the legal order is fundamentally important with regard to relative rights and thereby the solution of basic, for example, allocative, economic problems. He affirmed that both law and competition are social regulatory systems, as are also moral rules, all of which restrain or channel self-interest and private coercion. He recognized that state action could, under historically prepared and propitious conditions, both ameliorate the burden of dynamic change hitherto so much shifted to workers, and facilitate the adoption and operation of unions to promote worker interests as workers themselves, and their leaders, envisioned them. He recognized that history was essentially a learning, an educational, process, and that this process channelled and informed the workings of individual choice and thereby the play of marginal utility in the allocation of resources. He affirmed both competition as a process and the role of leadership selection, and recognized the problems ensconced in the relationships between the leaders and the led, the rulers and the ruled. Especially did he recognize that capitalism was essentially a bourgeois phenomenon and that power under capitalism had to be comprehended in that context. As both Robert B. Ekelund and I separately have stressed, one finds in the total corpus of Wieser's work an elaborate, powerful, suggestive, and memorable effort to pursue the recondite and often intractable combination of power and utility.

That Wieser, who is hardly omitted from accounts of the history of economics, is not given even greater prominence and honour therein, is therefore both not his fault and very clearly his fault. It is not his fault in that he made fundamental contributions far beyond and arguably more important than narrow marginal utility analysis. It is his fault in that he contributed to a narrow conception of what economics is all about. A further irony is that Joseph Schumpeter, Wieser's magnificent student and intellectual heir, perpetuated pretty much the same shortcoming. While he recognized economic statistics, economic history and economic sociology along with economic theory as the major compartments of economics, he too tended to concentrate on value or price theory as the core of economics to the formal, but fortunately not totally the substantive, neglect of the other areas. The ultimate opportunity cost is suggested by this: if Wieser had officially recognized his broader interests to be within economics, it is conceivable that he could have written even more on, and have been the founder of, a truly comprehensive and analytically rich social economics, perhaps in the vein of Pareto's 'sociological' work. The highest compliment that one can pay Wieser, then, is that if in the future a seminal figure develops a magisterial economic sociology, Wieser will be one of his or her leading precursors. The pity is that Wieser himself did not do so, for many of the elements thereof are in fact present in his work.

Selected References

Robert B. Ekelund, 'Power and Utility: The Normative Economics of Friedrich von Wieser', *Review of Social Economy*, vol. 28 (September 1970), pp. 179–96.

Friedrich von Hayek, 'Hayek on Wieser', in Henry W. Spiegel, *The Development of Economic Thought* (New York: Wiley, 1952), pp. 555–67.

Warren J. Samuels, 'Introduction', Friedrich von Wieser, *The Law of Power*, W. E. Kuhn, Trans. (Lincoln: Bureau of Business Research, University of Nebraska, 1983), pp. xiii–xxxvi.

Warren J. Samuels, 'The Influence of Friedrich von Wieser on Joseph A. Schumpeter', *History of Economics Society Bulletin*, vol. 4. (Winter 1983), pp. 5–19.

13 Taussig on the Psychology of Economic Policy*

Two generations ago, Frank W. Taussig was a main pillar of the profession. Urbane, conservative, open-minded, a great teacher, Taussig was, in the words of Schumpeter, 'an eminent theorist' to whom nonetheless 'economics always remained political economy' and who was, appropriately, 'the American Marshall'.[1] Although then-contemporary institutionalists could not have agreed[2] – he *was*, after all, with T. N. Carver, the leader of orthodoxy – Schumpeter also felt that Taussig was more of a leader than an opponent of institutionalism: this because of Taussig's interest and productivity in what Schumpeter called 'economic sociology', which included the study of institutions and the study of individual and group behaviour within the institutional setting.[3]

Taussig, it may be said, was not interested solely in the operation of market forces in terms of neoclassical economics – to whose development and growth in this country he was a preeminent contributor. He was also cognizant of and interested in the larger matrix of which market forces are a part. That is to say, Taussig's writings, which included realistic appreciation of the making of tariffs and thus of the relations between government and business, reflect fundamental appreciation of the developing interaction between market and framework (moral and legal) and of the resolution of the dual basic social problems of freedom and control, and continuity and change. More particularly, Taussig had a deep understanding of the fundamental dimensions of the theory of economic policy, two of which will be the focus of this essay: psychology and, to a lesser degree, power.[4]

The objective of this chapter is to examine Taussig's theory of economic policy as it is manifest in the one volume in which he approached being a theoretical institutionalist, his *Inventors and Money-Makers*.[5] In it Taussig investigated the relations between economics and psychology in a context which can be best described as a consideration of the psychological and power dimensions of the theory of economic policy. This chapter is thus not an inquiry into Taussig's theory of policy as a whole. It is rather an exploration into the dimensions of economic policy as manifest in his view in *Inventors and Money-Makers*.

---

* Originally published in *Indian Economic Journal*, vol. 15 (July-September 1967), pp. 1–13.

Taussig's *Inventors and Money-Makers*, with its psychological policy-oriented analysis, was first published in 1915 (as an amplified and annotated version of lectures given at Brown University) and reissued in 1930. The date of its original publication is particularly interesting because it was written during the period in which Vilfredo Pareto was assembling and writing his *Trattato di Sociologi Generale*,[6] with which Taussig's study has no small area of parallel scope and, to a limited extent, agreement. Interesting, too, is that Taussig's and Joslyn's later *American Business Leaders*[7] evidences the interest of Taussig – also shared, independently, with Pareto – 'among those few economists who realize that the method by which a society chooses its leaders, in what, for its particular structure, is the fundamental social function . . . is one of the most important things about a society, most important for its performance as well as for its fate'.[8]

I

From the perspective of the present author, the main thrusts of Taussig's *Inventors and Money-Makers* are: (1) that economic actors are psychologically motivated, (2) that these motivations (whatever utilitarianism and the rationality assumption have had to say about them) are complex and have their genesis deep within the individual personality, and (3) that social policy is at least in part interpretable as the result of the interplay of psychic states or postures.

Taussig quite appropriately qualified his efforts by denying any 'pretense of dealing with all the relations between economics and psychology' (p. v).[9] He was chiefly interested, rather, in arousing 'interest in the important topics that lie on the borderline between economics and psychology and ethics' (p. vi). His main concern was over the use of the term *instinct*. His anxiety was greater in 1930 than in 1915 but he had his reservations earlier. He liked the terms *propensity, impulse, instinct* and *disposition*, but elected to use (and remain with) the term *instinct*. Thus, in the Preface to the second edition, he declared that 'I am still unable to find a term that serves better to direct attention to the play of men's aptitudes, motives, ambitions; and it is the import of these words which I try to consider, not any theory of instinct in the sense which is given to that term in the world of science' (p. vi). In retrospect, his concern can be appreciated, and the use of the term *instinct* can be understood as but designating 'those general human tendencies whose influence as social forces we find so great' (p. 6) without any connotation of a strict instinct theory of psychology.

Taussig maintained that it would be pedantic and superfluous to his purpose to construct a schematic list of the 'social instincts', rather, he wrote, 'It will suffice to mention some of the instincts which on their face appear to be significant in economic inquiry' (p. 7). Within the compass of his inquiry, he found the following as most conspicuous and useful: contrivance (or workmanship), acquistion (or accumulation), domination (or pugnacity or predation), emulation (or imitation or status), sympathy (including altruism and devotion), play (or the chase, or adventure), and curiosity (or ratiocination) (pp. 7, 79, and *passim*). While the two schemata are quite different, what Taussig considered as 'instincts' Pareto differentiated into 'sentiments' and their manifestations, 'residues'. In both cases, they may be considered as psychic states or postures from and in terms of which individuals face the world, interpret or define their indentity, interact, and function as economic actors. Pareto's 'derivations', which are statements, theories, and myths functioning to 'explain' and legitimize behaviour and beliefs, are generally not treated by Taussig, but he was aware of their existence: 'Almost all men', he wrote, 'deceive themselves as well as their associates with conventional phrases, with expressions which, though quite devoid of insincerity, yet are far from genuine' (p. 20).

With respect to the instinctual character of the personality structure, Taussig's interpretation emphasized fluidity or malleability. He maintained that the person has a complex admixture of instincts, that behaviour is a function of a changing blend of instincts so far as any one person is concerned, that there is an uneven distribution of instincts between persons, that the play of instincts for any person is at least in part circumstantially or environmentally conditioned, and that there is but an uncertain possibility of personality modification through deliberate social control. These facets will be examined briefly.

Although Taussig developed the psychology of the inventor in terms of the instinct of contrivance (see Part II, below), he pointed out that 'The case, in truth, is almost invariably one of mixed motives' (p. 18). The inventor is thus dominated by the instinct of contrivance yet he is also influenced by the prospect of pecuniary gain. Taussig's resolution of the problem was that 'the direction in which the contriver turns his bent is immensely affected by the prospect of gain for himself' (p. 50). 'What deserves emphasis is the influence of calculated profit in directing the inventor's activity, spontaneous though it be, into channels of general usefulness' (p. 51). Economic behaviour is thus a function of both deliberative and non-deliberative forces. So also with the businessman: the motivation of the businessman, the desire for additional wealth, 'far from being a simple premise in economics, is highly complex. It is a curious blend of a number of instincts' (p. 121). Thus, in concluding his book, Taussig stressed that the economist 'must be content to face and accept', among other things, 'the complexity of human motivation' and 'the interplay of conflicting instincts' (p. 135).

Taussig also insisted that the instincts are unevenly, or unequally, distributed. The instinct of contrivance, for example, 'is to be discerned in all men, and actuates all in some degree' (p. 55) but not to equal degrees. Thus, 'It is by no means obvious that all men desire to obtain additional wealth' (p. 77). 'What perhaps is true is that a small circle of persons, especially among modern peoples of Western civilization, manifest an insatiable desire for additional wealth. Among them the trait is most of all characteristic of the capitalist business man – the nearest approach to the "economic man" of older literature' (pp. 77–8). Yet even among the business men . . . there is no one simple desire or impulse. The wish for additional wealth, so far as it appears at all, is a most complex psychological phenomenon, the resultant of a number of instincts or dispositions, of which the possessor himself is only half-conscious' (p. 78) and which vary in relative intensity (cf. p. 121). It is at this point that Taussig makes a point retrospectively significant in the light of recent attention to the psychological foundations of economic development:[10] arguing that the modern economist does *not* consider 'the origin and makeup of the desire [for additional wealth] . . . a matter beyond the scope of economic inquiry, and at all events not likely to point to any conclusions of significance for the economist', Taussig maintains that 'The psychological analysis not only gratifies [the economist's] intellectual curiosity, but promises to give aid in understanding economic phenomena and in directing economic policy' (pp. 78–9).

Socioeconomic policy is thus a function of the interplay of psychic postures. But the instincts which comprise one's psychic posture are both independent and dependent variables. They are both given and emergent; something with which policy must cope; at the same time an object of control by policy, conditioned by policy in any event and yet also a determinant of policy. Circumstances may 'foster and strengthen' an instinct but they may also 'tend to push it aside and smother it' (p. 69). Consideration of the role of circumstances led to consideration of the role and effect of social control. Social control is a necessity and is presumed to have effect. Some instincts 'need to be held in check, alike for the individual's well-being and for that of his fellows; some may be given full rein' (p. 56). As for full rein, twice did Taussig state that the instinct of contrivance should be allowed great, but not full, rein: 'Among those to which it seems possible to give wide scope, without danger of satiation or remorse, is this one of contrivance' (p. 56). He even wrote that 'There would seem to be no reason why the instinct of contrivance, for example, should be restrained.' But two sentences later he added the qualification: 'On the other hand, that same instinct needs to be steadied, and its aberrations and idiosyncrasies prevented. It should be guided into the channels of general usefulness. This much the pervasive desire for wealth does tend to bring about' (pp. 123–4).[11] But his main points were, first, recognition that, 'Granted that there is the instinct, the question remains, what are the conditions under which it is evoked, what those under which is made conducive to the general welfare?' (p. 18) and second, that while the 'relative influence' of the instincts 'in directing conduct will be greatly affected by education, the state of public opinion, habituation', nevertheless, 'We are unable to say just how far they are rooted and unchangeable, how far subject to modification through the environment. It is certain that no one among them can be stamped out entirely; it is certain also that all are in some degree subject to deliberate control' (p. 121).[12] He thus concluded with acknowledgement of 'a tantalizing uncertainty concerning the possibilities of modifying their relative strength' (p. 135).

To take a very simple example, Taussig was not the first economist to call attention to the operation of the 'wise legislator and social reformer' in looking to the instinct of play 'for relief from the monotony of our industrial life, for healthful and joyous vent to activity and emulation' (p. 9).[13] To the same effect, Taussig compared the operation of two different institutional complexes as sets of transmutation mechanisms by which the instinct of domination is channelled: 'Can it not be utilized, enlisted, encouraged, turned into channels of general service? Something of this sort has in fact been achieved by our capitalistic institutions, through the very desire for wealth.[14] The instinct of domination is not necessarily ferocious or predatory; it may be satisfied by the achievements of peace as well as by those of war. Not a little has been gained through the mere circumstance that it is so largely shifted from the political and military to the industrial. Better that we should have Napoleons of industry than the blood-guilty Napoleons of history' (p. 129). At another point he wrote that 'The whole structure of private property is built on the foundation of a striving for one's own . . . in the folds of a system which compels them to exercise their powers for their own advantage' (p. 52). Taussig was, it would appear no less shrewd a student of human nature than was Adam Smith. He then acknowledged 'the wider problem of human motivation, which is at the root of the controversy between collectivism and individualism', and pointed out that 'The fact that the instinct of contrivance is at present turned to advantageous exercise by the motives of material gain does not prove that such motives are indispensable to the same sort of usefulness under any and every economic system' (pp. 52–3). Creativity needs the spur of gain, but gain is institutionally defined and institutionally channelled. In addition, democracy and leadership in industry are both *desiderata*, but they must be reconciled (p. 130).

II

The psychology of the inventor was largely (though, as has already been seen, not entirely) specified in terms of the instinct of contrivance. Taussig did not develop the point at any length but he did indicate that inventors are not the only persons manifesting the instinct of contrivance. The psychology of contrivance is apparently characteristic of all those 'whose creative and guiding activity is indispensable for human progress' (p. 53).

Unlike Pareto, Taussig was sensitive about the use of words; in any event, he preferred to stick with McDougall's term, 'contrivance' (p. 11).[15] The instinct in question is literally the instinct to contrive and invent (pp. 12, 21 and *passim*). 'In the average man it perhaps should be called an instinct of construction rather than one of contrivance' (p. 57), or, with Veblen, one of workmanship (pp. 6, 11); in the successful businessman, it is a 'passion for building' or 'building mania' an unrestrained instinct of contrivance (p. 59). The instinct is dramatically manifest in the constant experimentation of inventors and their 'absorbed interest of trial, experiment, novel problems, happy solution' (p. 22). It is a psychological posture and not simply or alone a function of rational (conscious) utilitarian considerations (pp. 17ff.). There is, rather, 'the state of inward happiness which comes from the exercise of the contriving bent' (p. 15), which also may be juxtaposed 'to those of inert mind and tranquil disposition' (p. 62).

Taussig's instinct of contrivance has much in common with Pareto's Class I Residue, the instinct for combinations. Both represent psychic postures tautologically related to behaviour involving creation, rearrangement, and experimentation. Just as Platonism is a theory of knowledge in relation to social policy with a built-in emphasis upon reform, so do the instincts of contrivance and combination manifest a psychic posture characterized by a willingness if not eagerness to change status quo arrangements, whether the person be technological inventor, social reformer, or businessman (for example, in the sense of the Schumpeterian innovator), there is a psychic urge to remake the world (or the relevant part of the world) in the image of the beholder's goals, both conscious and subconscious. As indicated earlier, the inventor, given the scope of Taussig's book, is predominantly under the aegis of the instinct of contrivance (or combination, to Pareto), though the business-like prospect for gain channels the direction of the contriving bent at least to some extent.

Insofar, then, as policy involves the problem of continuity and change, the existence of the instinct of contrivance means that there will be pressure for change from those dissatisfied with the status quo and those with an affinity for novelty and experiment – for both utilitarian and, especially, psychic reasons – and thereby at least potential conflict between them and those whose tautology of personal psychology and behaviour manifest attachment to the status quo, i.e., continuity. But Taussig did not discuss the psychology of continuity (as did Pareto, for example, largely though not exclusively in terms of his Class II Residue, group-persistences or persistence of aggregates).

Taussig did discuss, however, the scope given to the instinct of contrivance in the case of industrial workers. Comparing the relative scope given as between employees and employers, Taussig found a 'clear difference' (p. 61) and is not sanguine about the instinct in the case of the former. Industrial capitalism, he found, seems 'to lessen seriously the possibilities of a life of spontaneous activity and of sustained happiness for the manual workmen who form the great body of employees' (p. 61). The division of labour and mechanization means 'a loss of interest, in possible variety, in the exercise of skill and contrivance' (p. 63). The decline of handicraft 'means less opportunity for individual adaptation and workmanship' (p. 64).

This concern, of course, is to be found in Smith; and it amounts to a serious appreciation that circumstances both strengthen some and inhibit other 'instincts' and thus affect both style of life and personality development. Significant, also, is that one may find here the germ of Perlman's differentiation between opportunity-consciousness and job-consciousness (cf. pp. 61–5).

But whereas Perlman found that workers made unions not a substitute for opportunity but a means of enhancing and expanding their opportunity along lines creative for them, Taussig found that the instinct of contrivance had been further reduced by the 'relations between employers and workmen which have developed from' (p. 64) industrial capitalism. It is in this direction that Taussig finds 'the most serious evil' (p. 64). 'The union', wrote Taussig, 'is inevitable; in the bargainings between employers and hired workmen it conduces alike to the material gain of the workmen and to their self-respect' (p. 66). But sundry policies of unions, he found, 'tend to smother the instinct of construction and the inherent satisfaction from work' (p. 67). With respect to the instinct of contrivance – which was associated by Taussig with the movement to material progress – 'The position of the employer obviously is just the opposite from that of the men. In his case all the surrounding circumstances tend to foster and strengthen the contriving impulse, whereas among the men the accepted methods of bargaining tend to push it aside and smother it' (p. 69). It again will be noticed that the context is circumstantial: the adverse effect on the worker directly and through unionism is a product of circumstances. In particular, 'The wages system in its ordinary form inhibits, in this respect as in others, the normal operation of our instincts and activities' (p. 70). Taussig may not be excused for the valuational judgement and presumption contained in the term 'normal', but his meaning is clear: by the criterion of its contributing to material progress and personal happiness, the instinct of contrivance is beneficial and should be strengthened beyond that (variable) degree already found in all men; but the wages system undermines rather than strengthens it. Taussig was critical of both cooperativism and profit-sharing as solutions, but was favourably disposed towards scientific management. 'But', he pointed out, 'the management must be not only scientific, but human. The familiar schemes have too much of the mechanical and non-human element' (p. 71). Enlightened scientific management is practicable but as to its probability of adoption, he 'would not venture to say. The average employer is a narrow-minded person, well-informed and thoughtful only about the small circle of his routine business operations. Too commonly he thinks of his employees as mere pieces of usable mechanism, not as human beings. The suspicions and prejudices of the workmen, engendered by their own narrowmindedness and strengthened by bitter experiences, contribute in turn to a mechanical relation between masters and men' (p. 74). Clearly Taussig was here writing as both a humanist and an economist: with Smith he looked to the conditions of life of the greater part of humanity, and with the profession in general he looked to the instrumental and circumstantial functioning of psychic states and their part in producing well-being. What is of interest here is not where Taussig's analysis led him, nor his policy implications, but that his analysis was conducted in terms of the interplay and circumstantial manipulation of psychic states in the process through and from which issues society's economic policy.

III

The businessman, whose psychology is that of money-making, is accordingly the cool calculator (p. 33); it is the capitalist businessman who is 'the nearest approach to the "economic man" of older literature'. Moreover, he

> is the figure that dominates modern society, directs its energies, gives the tone to the small controlling set of employers and property owners. Of such a person it may be true that he wants ever more wealth and still more; and he communicates the same state of mind to all who have ambition or hope to enter the charmed circle of the affluent and externally distinguished. (p. 78)

> Yet even among the business men . . . there is no one simple desire or impulse. The wish for additional wealth, so far as it appears at all, is a most complex psychological phenomenon, the resultant of a number of instincts or dispositions, of which the possessor himself is only half-conscious. (p. 78)

Taussig then proceeded to survey the drives that comprise the psychology of money-making. These include the instincts of contrivance, acquisition or accumulation, domination, emulation (status), and 'that of sympathy, altruism, or devotion' (p. 79). Contrivance, Taussig found, is present but 'is not among the more powerful of the impulses that stir the man of affairs' (p. 80). Acquisition 'does not seem to be an outstanding or characteristic trait'. Indeed, Taussig doubted 'whether there is anything in the nature of an all-encircling acquisitive instinct, just as [he doubted] whether there is a real instinct of ownership'. To argue that there is an instinct of acquisition is to assume with Senior, wrote Taussig, 'that all men strive for additional wealth without limit. Why some men seem to do so is precisely the problem which we are trying to solve' (pp. 83–4). This may be open to criticism even within Taussig's own system, but it indicates his tentativeness and that he in any event deprecated the role of acquisition in the psychology of money-making.

Much more important for Taussig is an instinct of domination, or what Sombart would call the conqueror strain in the business leader (p. 86). 'Domination, power, conquest – this plays a great part in the industrial world as well as in the political. It goes with the love of adventure, to which we give in business life the more euphemistic term "enterprise"' (p. 87). The successful businessman may be possessed and held to his industrial activity by the instinct of devotion, 'But that of domination seems here to be the more important' (p. 91). Domination 'plays a considerable part' (p. 92) in the movement for combinations; 'To no small degree, it is the instinct to suffer no opposition to control', 'to a great degree mere manifestations of megalomania' (p. 93). The love of power – the instinct of domination – wrote Taussig, also 'helps to explain the intemperate opposition to trade-unions which is almost invariably shown by the business leader . . . He wants to run his own business' (p. 93). Indeed, 'precisely this same instinct of domination easily takes possession of the strong labor union and especially of its leaders. . . . Alongside the questions of wages, hours, working conditions, is the contest for control'. The game is one of power play, and the power play – for example, the employer's 'desire to crush the union' – is not strictly deliberate and utilitarian: 'unaware of what is working within him, he obeys a primal impulse' (p. 94).

But domination is primarily important 'in the later stages' and then particularly 'among the leaders of the first rank'; in the early stages of his career the 'budding business man' is impelled by 'the wish to swing . . . into the supposedly upper class' (p. 97), i.e., by the instinct of 'emulation, and its concomitant of imitation' (p. 95). 'It is of the essence of emulation that there is never an end to it' (p. 98). Yet the businessman is also impelled by 'non-economic' motivations, which were denoted by Taussig as the instinct of devotion. 'The "strictly economic" doings of the business man, as well as those which are commonly treated as quite outside the economic pale, are often', emphasized Taussig, 'in reality manifestations of a wider and larger self. There is devotion to the business itself', but 'Not money-making alone is the goal and end. There is some expression of the man's personality, something to which he gives himself for its own sake' (p. 115). The 'influence of sympathy, or altruism, or devotion', while often overshadowed by the argument and feeling that 'Business is business' (p. 112), is a motive force or energizer, particularly if one is engaged in 'one's own creation' (p. 117). (Thus like Smith, Taussig found devotion more likely to be found in the sole proprietor or partnership than in the corporation (pp. 115–16).) What Taussig was trying to say, perhaps, was that the businessman derives psychic energy from his identification with the business, with and through which he identifies himself, through realizing (or seeking) the image he in part makes for himself.

IV

In Taussig's view, then, the two dynamic actors in the complex of industrial capitalism are the inventor and the capitalist and both are psychic phenomena. The process of capitalist development thus issues from the activity energized by the instincts of contrivance, domination, and the like, or, that is to say, from the psychic states which these 'instincts' are attempts to define, identify, label, differentiate, and disaggregate. Socioeconomic policy is in part the product of their energy, their realization, and their interaction.

But while the psychological dimension of policy was the focus of Taussig's attention, another, that of power, was also acknowledged. As has already been indicated, the instinct of domination in many ways is one of power and gives rise to power play; this in addition to the fact that conflicting instinctual urges, under conditions of scarcity, will lead to power play. Moreover, 'There cannot be domination without subjugation' (p. 128); as has already been indicated, also, the genius of industrial capitalism is that it tends to transmute potential militarists into industrialists (p. 129). The instinct of domination is itself in part a function of its promotion by 'the present regime of private property' (p. 132); nevertheless, 'Deliberate regard for the general welfare is within the possibilities of private business as well as of public' (p. 133). But while this latter was the closing theme of the book ('Business will not necessarily remain solely business' (p. 134)), Taussig's discussion was replete with comments reducing to at least implicit recognition that the economic decision-making process is a process of mutual coercion or manipulation, that it is one therefore of power play, and that the 'love of power' (p. 93) is an important dimension not only of the problem of freedom and control but of the formation of economic policy. While psychology and power are not always (though hardly never at all) two sides of the same coin, they are two dimensions of policy making. It may be remarked, finally, that Taussig's discussions were in terms readily applicable to both the managerial decision-making process within a particular business (or government agency) and the economy (considered as a decision process) as a whole.

V

From the perspective of a half-century after his original lectures, Taussig's little volume is easily considered unsatisfactory. It is by no means a complete theory of economic behaviour, nor is it a complete psychology of economic policy. Moreover, he wrote of instincts, and in an equivocal and ambiguous manner; and while Taussig was sweet and gentle in comparison with Pareto's abrasiveness and acidity, his analysis seems more than a trifle romantic, this perhaps a manifestation of his own sense of devotion in reaction to what he considered (pp. 109–12) to be the economist's rationalist temperamental bent. In addition, Taussig's analysis is, of course, largely non-operational.

But to one interested in both the history of economic thought and the theory of policy, it is significant that Taussig's traditionalism did not keep him from underscoring both the psychological and power dimensions of economic policy. Taussig's *Inventors and Money-Makers* showed the relevance of psychic states and something of their relevance to the problems of freedom and control, and continuity and change, as well as that they were part of the process through which economic policy was developed. In retrospect and in general, time has proved Taussig not basically wrong in his views which are reducible to the propositions (1) of the limited but emergent character of personality as a product of personal, interpersonal and circumstantial variables in character development and (2) of society's policy (concerning the rate of economic growth, decision-making structure, resource allocation, income distribution, etc.) as a partial product of the interplay of psychic states. Taussig quite perceptively held that an appreciation of the policy process (and the economy as a whole is a policy process, as well as are its interacting parts) requires an understanding of the psychological dimension of policy. For this reason Taussig's book is retrospectively important and suggestive; moreover, it shows additional reason, if more were indeed necessary, for considering Taussig as a great political economist.

Notes

1. Joseph A. Schumpeter, *Ten Great Economists* (New York: Oxford University Press, 1951), pp. 196, 220.
2. Cf. Allan G. Gruchy, *Modern Economic Thought* (New York: Prentice-Hall, 1947), pp. 12–15 and *passim.*
3. Schumpeter, *Ten Great Economists*, pp. 196, 206–7.
4. The concept, 'theory of economic policy', is further developed in the essay, 'The Nature and Scope of Economic Policy', in Warren J. Samuels, *The Classical Theory of Economic Policy* (Cleveland: World Publishing Co., 1966) explicitly in terms of power and implicitly in terms of psychology. The present study is a partial outgrowth of a larger research study on the psychological and knowledge dimensions of economic policy.
5. F. W. Taussig, *Inventors and Money-Makers* (New York: Macmillan, 1930). All page references in the text are to this volume.
6. Vilfredo Pareto, *A Treatise on General Sociology* (formerly published in translation as *The Mind and Society*) (New York: Dover, Two Volumes, 1963).
7. F. W. Taussig and C. S. Joslyn, *American Business Leaders* (New York: Macmillan, 1932).
8. Schumpeter, *Ten Great Economists*, p. 217. Attention to the problem of democratic leadership is also given throughout the writings of Frank H. Knight.
9. See note 5.
10. See, for example, E. E. Hagen, *On the Theory of Social Change* (Homewood:

Irwin, 1962), and D. C. McClelland, *The Achieving Society* (Princeton: Van Nostrand, 1961).

11. 'One thing stands out conspicuously: the race of contrivers and inventors does obey an inborn and irresistible impulse . . . there is increasing interest in new dodges, unceasing trial of new devices' (p. 21).
12. In a brief discussion on 'the sexual instinct' – which 'must be kept within bounds, yet it cannot be eradicated' – Taussig yields an excellent example of both the difficulty of balancing freedom and control and the difficulty of expressing the terms of dimensions of such balance. Wrote Taussig: 'Whatever modification there may be in details of existing law concerning the family, there must be no unbridled scope for the sexual passion, nor yet lack of opportunity for its satisfaction' (p. 122).
13. See, for example, the essay, 'Amusements of the People', originally published by William Stanley Jevons in *Contemporary Review*, vol. 33 (1878), and republished in his *Methods of Social Reforms* (1883) (New York: Kelley, 1965), pp. 1–27.
14. On Adam Smith's view of 'The pleasures of wealth and greatness' as the 'deception which rouses and keeps in continual motion the industry of mankind', see Samuels, *Classical Theory*, p. 37 and *passim*.
15. Cf. Robert Aaron Gordon, *Business Leadership in the Large Corporation* (Berkeley: University of California Press, 1966), p. 307.

14 Introduction, Frank W. Taussig, *Inventors and Money-Makers**

Many economists have for generations typically pursued their analyses upon the notion of 'economic man'. Economists thereby have assumed that individuals know what their interests are and act to achieve those interests. For the most part, economists have meant neither that people always do act as economic men nor that they always should, but that it is a useful and indeed meaningful assumption with which to conduct analysis. Many economists, however, especially the heterodox ones, have severely criticized this assumption for its patent rationalistic hedonism. They, for example, Thorstein Veblen, affirm that much 'economic choice' is actually a matter of custom, habit, and emulation of the behaviour of others. The assumption also has been criticized for being formalist and empty, reducing to the proposition that people demand what they demand; by taking preferences as given and by not pursuing the factors and forces which govern tastes and preferences, it can say very little about extant economic reality. In these respects, of course, the economic-man assumption forces upon the analysis the nature and limitations of a model, which is only an incomplete representation of reality. A further criticism is (like the first) substantive: it objects to the use of economic-man theorizing in the form of utility maximization in such a way that the product of labour is stipulated as pleasure and the labour itself as pain (disutility), preferring in general to believe that labour is a mode of living and of self-realization as well as of self-gratification.

Whatever one may think about the usefulness of the economic-man assumption, it by no means fully exhausts the treatment of human motivation or psychology by economists. Although this aspect of their work has not been as conspicuous (and controversial) as the economic-man assumption, economists have always engaged in speculation and theorizing concerning the springs of human action in general and of economic action in particular. Adam Smith, to whom so many trace the doctrine of self-interested behaviour, also and perhaps paramountly stressed that

---

* Originally published in Frank W. Taussig, *Inventors and Money-Makers* (New Brunswick: Transaction, 1989) pp. xi–xxxiv.

individuals were driven by vanity, by a need or desire to look good in the eyes of others (as well as in their own eyes), and by status emulation. Thorstein Veblen also stressed status emulation, as well as forces which led him to emphasize a distinction between pecuniary and industrial activities, the difference between making goods and making money. Vilfredo Pareto was somewhat more reductionist, identifying six types of psychic propensities, stressing especially two, an instinct for combinations and an instinct of group-persistences (persistence of aggregates), which may be interpreted, respectively, as efforts to rearrange and thereby change the status quo, and as efforts to consolidate or make permanent existing arrangements, that is, propensities making for change and for continuity. Pareto also believed that people's beliefs were governed by their material interests and, perhaps especially, their psychic states. Selig Perlman less ambitiously but nonetheless usefully distinguished between two states of mind which produce quite different belief systems and patterns of behaviour: opportunity consciousness – the sense that one could do almost anything that one reasonably set one's mind to do – and job consciousness – the sense that one was probably going to be in one's present job, or one similar, for the rest of one's life and that one had to focus on and make the best of it and its constraints. In this context Perlman interpreted trade unions. These approaches to the psychology of economics are very suggestive but they only scratch the surface of the history of economists' efforts to penetrate deeper into psychology than is permitted by the economic-man assumption.

One of the great efforts in this genre is Frank William Taussig's *Inventors and Money-Makers*, first published in 1915 and reissued in 1930. In this volume Taussig endeavoured to identify the propensities which seem – both individually and, especially, in combination (a point made by Pareto) – to account for, or least render more meaningful, the economic behavior of individuals in modern society. It is these propensities which drive the economy and render economic behaviour understandable.

Taussig was no heretic. On the contrary, he was a pillar of economic orthodoxy. He wrote, however, during a period when economics as a discipline was more respectful of individual diversity and heterodoxy than in recent decades. In addition, he was both broader and infinitely more candid *qua economist* than most other mainstream economists. Although an advocate of the market economy, he did not consider that economists were its high priests with the task of providing its air-tight explication and rationalization. He believed that economics was or should be more an organon of inquiry than a body of doctrine.

Born in 1859 in St Louis, Taussig was educated at Washington University, the University of Berlin, and Harvard. He earned both a doctorate in economics and a law degree. He served on the Harvard faculty from 1885 to 1935, where he was a magisterial teacher and editor of the *Quarterly Journal of Economics* for forty years. He was also the first chairman of the US Tariff Commission.

Taussig's principal work as an economic theorist was in wage theory and in international trade theory and policy. His other work largely set him off from most other leading orthodox economists. Even in his *Principles of Economics* (1911; 4th edn 1939), he portrayed society and economy as both a structure and struggle for power and privilege, and presented a functional analysis of what Veblen had earlier called the 'leisure class'. In other writings he explored the role of business leadership in the successful operation of the market system. Joseph Schumpeter included Taussig in his *Ten Great Economists* (1951), writing that he was 'among those few economists who realize that the method by which a society chooses its leaders, in what, for its particular structure, is the fundamental social function . . . is one of the most important things about a society, most important for its performance as well as for its fate'.

For Taussig, the power structure and the leadership selection process were not the only important facets of man and society of which economists should take account but typically did not. There was also the complex psychological foundation of economic behaviour, and this he addressed in *Inventors and Money-Makers*.

Taussig identifies a number of 'instincts' which, he believes, drive economic behaviour and choices. As the reader will observe, he was somewhat sensitive to the choice of the term 'instincts', because its reductionist and deterministic nuances were increasingly causing serious doubts about the term in psychology and the social sciences. He wants to use it as a synonym for propensity, impulse, motive, drive, ambition, disposition, and like terms, as a means of expressing the constituent elements of economically relevant psychic states, in order to explore the significance of psychological motivation for the purposes of economic analysis. He does not propose to adopt a rigid schema of instinct psychology. As is evident in the work of other writers, for example, Veblen and Pareto, 'instinct' was a more or less conventionally used term during the early decades of this century.

Taussig is anything but rigid in his identification and classification of instincts. One is an instinct of 'contrivance or workmanship'. Another is an instinct of 'Accumulation, acquisitiveness, collection, ownership'. 'Still others', he says, 'are domination, pugnacity, predation; sympathy or devotion; play, the chase, adventure; curiosity or ratiocination' (p. 7). These, he insists, are the 'direct and obvious springs of industrial activity' (p. 11).

The instinct of contrivance is close to that of Pareto's instinct for combinations. It involves the desire to create, to recombine things with other things and is a source of satisfaction, a psychological end. The contriving instinct, 'like the other instincts . . . is to be discerned in all men, and actuates all in some degree' (p. 55). If this is the case, says Taussig, then 'we are led to question the proposition that progress in the arts depends on an experience or prospect of gain' (p. 17). Men may 'invent anyhow: they obey the instinct and therein take joy' (p. 18). This, however, does not rule out the fact that 'the inventor himself may be spurred directly and immediately by the prospect of pecuniary gain' (p. 42). Men may also believe that they are instruments 'working out the designs of God' (p. 47); they also can show varying 'degrees of public spirit' (p. 50). As Taussig stresses, 'The case, in truth, is almost invariably one of mixed motives' (p. 48).

But a psychological propensity, or instinct, does not just exist; 'the question remains', he argues, 'what are the conditions under which it is evoked, what those under which it is made conducive to the general welfare?' (p. 18). Taussig insists both that 'One thing stands out conspicuously: the race of contrivers and inventors does obey an inborn and irresistible impulse' (p. 21), and that 'the *direction* in which the contriver turns his bent is immensely affected by the prospect of gain for himself' (p. 50). Both 'contrivance for the mere sake of contrivance' and 'the calculation of ulterior gain' are operative (p. 52). In any case, the first two chapters, over half the volume, constitute Taussig's exploration of these matters.

Several points which Taussig makes therein in passing are worth noting. First, Taussig, like Pareto, believes that people invoke rationalizations (Pareto called them 'derivations') in order to put a gloss of rationality and legitimacy upon behaviours and beliefs generated by their psychic propensities: 'Almost all men deceive themselves as well as their associates with conventional phrases, with expressions which, though quite devoid of insincerity, yet are far from genuine' (p. 20).

Second, he stresses the process of selection, in which 'two closely connected factors seem to count: the support and guidance of the cool and calculating business man, and the cool calculations of the inventor himself' (p. 33). The reader should note both (1) the role of the selection process and (2) the process of rational calculation which is not rival to the instinct of contrivance (or, for that matter, the other instincts) but is both a mode through which they are expressed and effectuated and a means of restraining or guiding the instinct of contrivance (p. 60).

Third, Taussig does not restrict his emphasis on the contriving instinct to the inventor or businessman. In a manner akin to Veblen's instinct of workmanship, Taussig argues that 'In the average man it perhaps should be called an instinct of construction rather than one of contrivance. Every one of us is conscious of a satisfaction in doing his work handily and well, in seeing the product grow under his own hands' (p. 57). Taussig's candour extends not only to his recognition of economic classes (the employing and the employed) but that the combination of 'capitalistic organization of industry, large-scale production, hired labor, and the wages system . . . seem[s] to lessen seriously the possibilities of a life of spontaneous activity and of sustained happiness for the manual workmen who form the great body of employees' (p. 61), a view not dissimilar from that of Smith, who also was concerned about the adverse consequences on human beings of labour in the industrial system (pp. 62–3).

Taussig says, however, that 'the most serious evil' arises elsewhere, specifically in the 'relations between employers and workmen' which have developed within the modern industrial system (p. 64). He has a mixed view of unions. On the one hand, he feels that 'The union is inevitable; . . . it conduces alike to the material gain of the workmen and to their self-respect.' On the other, he finds that 'they have been subject to sufficiently scathing criticism; nor is it possible to defend them on any large grounds of social policy'. Indeed, he finds that 'they tend to smother the instinct of construction and the inherent satisfaction from work' (pp. 66–7). Still, he says, 'Group interest and group emulation are psychological factors of no mean interest. The employer himself feels emulation; he is playing the game on his own account; herein lies no small part of the attractiveness of his work' (p. 74). Taussig is obviously more interested in understanding the psychodynamics of labour–management relations than in endeavouring to reach conclusions for labour relations policy. His final words are telling on both sides: 'The average employer is a narrow-minded person, well-informed and thoughtful only about the small circle of his routine business operations. Too commonly he thinks of his employees as mere pieces of usable mechanism, not as human beings. The suspicions and prejudices of the workmen, engendered by their own narrow-mindedness and strengthened by bitter experiences, contribute in turn to a mechanical relation between masters and men' (p. 74).

Chapter III is an exploration of the psychology of money-making, particularly the fact that 'a small circle of persons, especially among modern peoples of Western civilization, manifest an insatiable desire for additional wealth' (p. 77). The more or less conventional assumption that individuals are wealth maximizers is not adopted by Taussig; rather, he maintains that 'It is by no means obvious that all men desire to obtain additional wealth' (p. 77). The trait, he says, 'is most of all characteristic of the capitalist business man – the nearest approach to the "economic man" of older literature' (pp. 77–8). The modern Western economic system is distinctively driven by the money-making psychology of its dominant or leadership group, the money-maker or capitalist business man. But the 'wish for additional wealth, so far as it appears at all, is a most complex psychological phenomenon, the resultant of a number of instincts or dispositions, of which the possessor himself is only half-conscious' (p. 78). Whereas earlier economists believed that 'the origin and make-up of the desire' was 'a matter beyond the scope of economic inquiry, and at all events not likely to point to any conclusions of significance to the economist', the modern economist finds that the 'psychological analysis not only gratifies his intellectual curiosity, but promises to give aid in understanding economic phenomena and in directing economic policy' (pp. 78–9).

The motivation of the business man Taussig traces to the combination of the instincts of contrivance, acquisition, domination, emulation, and sympathy, altruism or devotion, but not in descending order of importance. These are explored in quite some detail in Chapter III. For example, he doubts 'whether there is anything in the nature of an all-encircling acquisitive instinct' or 'whether there is a real instinct of ownership. To say that there is an instinct of acquisition comes to much the same thing as to assume . . . that all men strive for additional wealth without limit. Why *some* men seem to do so is precisely the problem which we are trying to solve' (pp. 83–4).

Perhaps the most distinctive aspect of Taussig's work is his focus on the instinct of domination. Domination, he argues, is of great influence in the social and economic sphere: 'Domination, power, conquest – this plays a great part in the industrial world as well as in the political. It goes with the love of adventure, to which we give in business life the more euphemistic term "enterprise"' (p. 87). Taussig is quite serious: industry is an alternative to politics as an outlet for the desire for power: 'Like Alexander or Napoleon, the captain of industry would rule the world' (p. 89). Whereas the instinct of contrivance 'is not among the more powerful of the impulses that stir the man of affairs; though surely not to be neglected' (p. 80), of all 'the overmastering instincts' (p. 91) which drive the captain of industry, 'that of domination seems here to be the more important' (p. 91). The instinct of domination, he says, 'plays a considerable part . . . in the movement for combination' (p. 92). 'To no small degree, it is the instinct to suffer no opposition to control' (p. 93). It explains, he believes, 'the intemperate opposition to trade-unions which is almost invariably shown by the business leader' (p. 93): 'The strong employer's desire to crush the union is not merely the outcome of cold calculations of profit; unaware of what is working within him, he obeys a primal impulse' (p. 94).

Status emulation is also a major force combining spontaneously with the other instincts. 'The wish to be considered a member of a superior set appears in every organized aggregation of human beings' (p. 96). It is 'the force which more than any other influences the budding business man. During the earlier stages of his career . . . it is this motive above all that impels him. It is only in the later stages – if he be among the leaders of the first rank – that the instinct of domination becomes conspicuous' (p. 97). Interestingly this implies that domination may be in part a strategy defensive of status much more than of profit. Striking also is Taussig's explanation of the basis for the wealth-maximizing assumption: as Smith himself recognized, people seek wealth to impress others and to achieve status, but, says Taussig, 'It is of the essence of emulation that there is never an end to it' (p. 98).

Chapter IV treats the instinct of devotion, or altruism. Here he distinguishes between two types of temperament, the 'tough-minded' and the 'tender-minded'. Of particular interest in this connection is his profound understanding that such psychic propensities deeply influence our way of regarding the universe, that is, our perception or definition of reality. Taussig also notes the view that 'Business is business; it must not be mixed with charity' (p. 112), but also argues that 'The instinct of domination . . . is uppermost during the competitive struggle, and gives way to that of compassion only after the victory is won' (p. 113). More important, I think, to Taussig is the circumstance that 'The "strictly economic" doings of the business man, as well as those which are commonly treated as quite outside the economic pale, are often in reality manifestations of a wider and larger self. . . . Not money-making alone is the goal and end. There is some expression of the man's personality, something to which he gives himself for its own sake' (p. 115).

The perceptive and critical reader will discern that Taussig does not attempt to examine the origins of the instincts. Nor does he investigate how culture reinforces and strengthens some instincts and inhibits and weakens others. Surely he is aware of the importance of the former and the truth of the latter. Apropos of both matters, consider the statement which can serve as a powerful summary of his overall point of view:

> the desire for additional wealth, far from being a simple premise in economics, is highly complex. It is curious blend of a number of instincts. Some of these will have greater strength in one individual, others in another. Their relative influence in directing conduct will be greatly affected by education, the state of public opinion, habituation. We are unable to say just how far they are rooted and unchangeable, how far subject to modification through the environment. It is certain that no one

among them can be stamped out entirely; it is certain also that all are in some degree subject to deliberate control. (p. 121)

Three-quarters of a century after these words were first published, the conflict between nature and nurture remains unresolved. We are still deliberating both the degree to which capitalism generates the motivations which seem so natural under its aegis and the likelihood that alternative systems of economic organization constitute different modes through which the instincts, perhaps especially of domination, are channelled, with the implication that it is the human material and not the system which generates undesired outcomes. At the centre of these debates still resides the psychological subject-matter which Taussig endeavoured to articulate.

Taussig himself saw that the problem involves not only individual psychic structure but, as he expressed it, 'the great problem of private property and socialism'. His approach was practical and reformist. He says that 'The desire for additional wealth is the special psychological appurtenance of the prosperous and property-owning classes. The question how far this complex combination of impulses is modifiable, is part of a whole series of questions on the possibility of modifying the capitalistic regime' (pp. 122–3). Taussig then continues a tradition extending at least as far back as Adam Smith in which individual self-interested behaviour is understood to be channelled by the institutions of social control for the benefit of both the individuals themselves and others, or society. 'Some of the constituent instincts, it would seem', writes Taussig, 'can be enlisted and encouraged almost without reserve. Others, though they are too strong to be entirely suppressed, must in some way be held in check' (p. 123). The instinct of contrivance, he feels, should not be restrained, although it does need 'to be steadied, and its aberrations and idiosyncracies prevented. It should be guided into the channels of general usefulness'. It is of great importance, as we shall see in a moment, that he immediately thereafter says that 'This much the pervasive desire for wealth does tend to bring about' (pp. 123–4).

Taussig considers neither the processes by which the 'aberrations' and the 'idiosyncracies' of the instinct of contrivance are to be identified and distinguished from its more acceptable, 'generally useful' manifestations, nor the significance of the instinct of domination for the complex relations of business men and others to government. Notwithstanding this situation, after considering the social control of other instincts, Taussig does come to the question on which every economist of intellectual depth and social sensitivity has brooded, the significance and status of capitalism.

Taussig accepts that capitalism can reinforce dysfunctional psychological propensities:

> There cannot be domination without subjugation; the elation of victory necessarily brings also the anguish of defeat. So far as a capitalistic and individualistic society fosters this disposition [of domination], it appears incapable of adding to the sum of human happiness. The losses would seem at least to balance the gains. (p. 128)

The matter does not end with this, however. Taussig next presents what may be the most sophisticated case for capitalism:

> Yet the case is by no means simple. The instinct of domination is a phase in the development of leadership. . . . Can it not be utilized, enlisted, encouraged, turned into channels of general service? Something of this sort has in fact been achieved by our capitalistic institutions, through the very desire for wealth. The instinct of domination is not necessarily ferocious or predatory; it may be satisfied by the achievements of peace as well as by those of war. (pp. 128–9)

Thus does Taussig come to the epigram which poignantly expresses his point of view:

> Better that we should have Napoleons of industry than the blood-guilty Napoleons of history. (p. 129)

If we grant that Taussig (along with Pareto, among others) is correct that psychology is the locus of the critical factors which help us to explain economic organization, operation, and performance, then we are left with at least two questions. First, what is the relative significance of the static mechanics of equilibrium economics that warrants so great an allocation of intellectual resources to it and so little to the investigation of the psychodynamics of economic life? And second, if Taussig is correct that, given the specific presence and force of the instinct of domination, it is better to have the Napoleons of industry than the blood-guilty Napoleons of history, what are we to make of the tendency that the blood-guilty Napoleons of history, nourished by the conjunction of nationalism and economic interest, seem to accompany the Napoleons of industry?

Such is the argument of this perceptive little book. There is much more than the argument as such, for Taussig continually explains the ramifications of his argument in contexts close to the details of everyday life in a manner which again and again is laden with revealing *aperçus*. The book is also a reminder of a time when mainstream economists, not alone among social scientists, directly contemplated the institutional and psychological foundations of the economy – and of the unfinished agenda open to the intellect.

15 The Influence of Friedrich von Wieser on Joseph A. Schumpeter*

INTRODUCTION: THE PROBLEM OF INFLUENCE

Within the last year I have been privileged to work on the careers and contributions of Friedrich von Wieser and Joseph A. Schumpeter. I have worked with W. E. Kuhn, of the University of Nebraska–Lincoln, to secure his translation (and forthcoming publication) of Wieser's *Das Gesetz der Macht* (The Law of Power), for which I have written an introduction. In addition, I have written a critique of Schumpeter's *Capitalism, Socialism, and Democracy*, given as two lectures in March 1982 at the University of Notre Dame in a series devoted to a reconsideration of the book on the occasion of its fortieth anniversary.

Schumpeter was Wieser's student and, while I had earlier studied the work of both men, the coincidence was evident. It also gradually became clear to me that Schumpeter may have been influenced by Wieser to a degree and, especially, in ways which were by no means recognized in the literature. As a further coincidence, Schumpeter, one of our foremost historians of economic thought, was himself very much interested in the filiation of ideas. A perusal of the Index of Authors in his *History of Economic Analysis* immediately reveals that for many (but not all) major figures there are citations to indicate filiations of each one's ideas with those of other economists. Schumpeter wrote that 'scientific economics does not lack historical continuity. It is in fact our main purpose to describe what may be called the process of the Filiation of Scientific Ideas – the process by which men's efforts to understand economic phenomena produce, improve, and pull down analytic structures in an unending sequence. And it is one of the main theses to be established in this book that *fundamentally* this process does not differ from the analogous processes in other fields of knowledge. But, for reasons that it is also one of our purposes to make clear, this filiation of ideas has met with more inhibitions in our field

* Presidential address to the History of Economics Society, originally published in *History of Economics Society Bulletin*, vol. 4 (Winter, 1983), pp. 5–19. The author is indebted to Edward A. Carlin and John P. Henderson for comments on an earlier draft of this paper.

than it has in almost all others. . . . Much more than, in say, physics is it true in economics that modern problems, methods, and results cannot be fully understood without some knowledge of how economists have come to reason as they do'.[1]

Schumpeter was one of the most well-read economists of all time. His knowledge of the literature, of the work of other economists, in many languages, was awesome. This is especially evident in the *History of Economic Analysis* but it also shows in his other, indeed his earliest, writings. Although possessed of his own biases and preferences, he believe that there were many ways in which to do good economics, and he was interested in many of them and in most if not all fields of economics. Moreover, Schumpeter not only read widely but also understood and mastered what he read. (If he had a fault in these respects, it was his inability to relate his own broad scope of economics as well as the systemic dynamics of his substantive economics to the work of the institutionalist, although he was familiar with some of their work.)

His wide reading and expertise make it more difficult to establish the sources of Schumpeter's interests, ideas, and analyses than is the case for most other writers. Furthermore, Schumpeter was unique, his own man, not easily categorized as a member of any school. As Gottfried Haberler has written, 'What he said of Menger holds of Schumpeter himself: "He was nobody's pupil."'[2] Theo Suranyi-Unger wrote that a 'chief merit' of Schumpeter's was that he gave 'an individual and partly original shape' to ideas borrowed from others.[3] Schumpeter also was a product of an educational system in which economics was taught alongside – I do not say fully integrated with – history, politics, law, and sociology. Many of Schumpeter's wide range of specific interests can be explained by – at least traced back to – the broad scope of topics regularly discussed by his professors. For all the dominance of Austrian marginal-utility economics, the teaching of economics was more broadly defined. The topics which interested Schumpeter were common to his contemporaries, especially among continental writers.[4]

Nonetheless, it is a task of the historian of economic thought, as Schumpeter himself would have it, to trace the filiation of ideas, to identify the intellectual sources of Schumpeter's ideas, and to gain a sense of perspective on his ideas in the larger scheme of the development of economic thought.

Filiation, it should be noted, is not limited to the adoption by one writer of a particular view or set of views of an earlier writer. Filiation can involve that, but it also can signify reformulation, perhaps to the point of transformation. The influence of one writer on another also can involve negation or rejection: the felt need to create a different and more acceptable alternative explanation or view. Influence can increase or decrease through time. Filiation also can involve the adoption of fundamental substantive interests (although arousal of interest in an area is not necessarily the same as influence)[5] and/or underlying conceptions. The former perhaps includes a certain paradigmatic vision of what is important, and the latter involves certain conceptual tools to be used in exploring and giving substance to that vision. I shall suggest that it is in both these regards that Wieser may have had a profound influence on Schumpeter, an influence which surprisingly has been largely undiscussed if not unknown.

In the case of Schumpeter there has been, not surprisingly, a wide range of attributions of filial origins. It is reasonably well-known that he had been the student of Eugen von Böhm-Bawerk, Eugen von Philippovich (a student of Carl Menger), Karl Theodore von Inama-Sternegg (a specialist in statistics and medieval history), and, of course, Wieser. It also seems to be the general view that Schumpeter was principally if not profoundly influenced by Karl Marx and Léon Walras in addition to his Austrian-School training, principally that of Böhm-Bawerk.

More specifically, most commentators seem to feel that Marx and Walras were the two major intellectual influences of Schumpeter.[6] Several writers have followed Schumpeter's own lead, provided in the preface to the Japanese edition of his *Theory of Economic Development*, that Walras impressed upon him the pure logic of the interdependence between economic quantities; and Marx contributed the process of economic change and how the economic system itself, broadly conceived, generates the forces which incessantly transform it.[7] Terence Hutchison, however, has stressed the influence of Walras,[8] as did Erich Schneider[9] and Ben Seligman, the latter attributing to Marx an influence on scope and a predilection for sociological implications.[10] Arthur Smithies attributed logical structure to Walras and glamour and passion to Marx.[11] Haberler, in contrast, felt that Schumpeter is closer to Marx than to Walras (regarding the mechanism of economic change, the role assigned to social relationships and to institutional framework, and the historical slant and intent of his theory, but not Marx's historical metaphysics and collectivism).[12] Wolfgang Stolper, however, believed that Marx's influence was not particularly important.[13]

The other common filial source is Böhm-Bawerk, whom Schneider has said was the strongest influence on Schumpeter.[14] Haberler, although emphasizing the influence of Walras, noted that 'close personal and scientific relation' between Schumpeter and Böhm-Bawerk,[15] (Böhm-Bawerk, who was born the same year [1851] as Wieser, was married to Wieser's sister.) Leo Rogin also noted the influence of Böhm-Bawerk (along with that of John Bates Clark).[16] But the filial relation between the two clearly was complex. Schumpeter, in emphasizing economic development, not time, as the key to interest, engaged in an important controversy with his former teacher. William M. Johnston perceived a hate–love ambivalence on the part of Schumpeter, involving a resentment at the failure of his former mentor to 'impart basic insights that must be garnered elsewhere'.[17]

There is some confusion as to the direct influence of Menger on Schumpeter. The literature contains several references to Menger as Schumpeter's teacher.[18] It seems, however, that Menger was already emeritus when Schumpeter studied economics (Wieser succeeded Menger in 1903: Schumpeter attended the University of Vienna from 1901 to 1906), and Menger, whom Schumpeter may have met only once or twice, was quite reclusive.[19]

Another frequently cited source is John Bates Clark. Specific mention is made of Clark's theory of entrepreneurial profits in relation to innovation[20] and of his distinction between statics and dynamics, which Suranyi-Unger felt Schumpeter made 'the central idea of his whole system'.[21] Ben Seligman also attributed to Clark, and to Irving Fisher, great influence on Schumpeter's early vision of the capitalist process.[22] Schumpeter wrote of Clark these words, instructive in the light of Schumpeter's work: 'He was the first to strike a novel note by connecting entrepreneurial profits, considered as a surplus over interest (and rent), with the successful introduction into the economic process of technological, commercial, or organizational improvements.'[23]

Several other individuals also have been occasionally cited as having influenced Schumpeter. In addition to Fisher, there is Wesley Mitchell, Max Weber,[24] Vilfredo Pareto,[25] Gustav Schmoller[26] (and other historically and sociologically oriented German economists),[27] and W. G. Lanworth Taylor (who viewed crises, Schumpeter wrote, 'purely as a reaction to the upsets in the static equilibrium of an economy caused by economic development').[28] Schneider also called attention to the influence of Antoine Augustin Cournot and William Stanley Jevons, Francis Y. Edgeworth, and Alfred Marshall.[29] Arthur Marget noticed the Quesnay–Walras concept of the circular flow, extending the Walrasian connection backward in time.[30] Stolper interestingly suggests that Schumpeter's "real ancestors" were St Thomas Aquinas, St Augustine, Plato, and Thucydides, for the 'belief that one could understand Being only by simultaneously understanding its Order and Motion'.[31] Such a view is pregnant, although it carries us into the realm of larger philosophic and intellectual movements, a realm which I consider important but beyond my present purview. Finally, I note Frank William Taussig, whose emphases on power, social structure, and business leadership certainly were congruent with those of Schumpeter, and the two men were close friends for many years. But congruence is the bedevilling factor in ascertaining influence. *If* Schumpeter's vision along those lines were formed quite early (and that seems to be widely agreed upon)[32] and *if*, further, Wieser had earlier influence along those very lines, then apropos of Taussig the judgment must be one principally of congruence and *reinforcement* rather than influence.[33]

We come finally to Wieser. In the Preface to his first book, Schumpeter indicated his 'closest affinity' to both Walras and Wieser.[34] As Haberler has noted, Schumpeter continued subsequently to acknowledge the influence of Walras but hardly so cited Wieser.[35] Other than Machlup and Haberler (see note 34), it seems that only Terence Hutchinson has called serious attention to Wieser. Schumpeter's 'own theoretical analysis', he writes, 'he built mainly on Walras, while the analysis of the historical and sociological background with which he co-ordinated his theoretical system and filled it out, has various points of likeness with that of Wieser, both in the general way in which economic sociology and analysis are combined and mutually illumined, and on some particular points, for example his emphasis on the role of the creative *élite* of innovating leaders as contrasted with the routine-following majority.'[36] (I would stress that the historical and sociological analysis, so-called, is more than background in the cases of both Wieser and Schumpeter.) Hutchison goes on to note that 'Whatever the exact relation between Wieser's and Schumpeter's ideas may have been, the latter has published some of the essential themes of his economic sociology before the appearance of the *Theory of Social Economy* in which Wieser first fully deployed his ideas on this subject.'[37] Schumpeter's *Theory of Economic Development* appeared in 1912; Wieser's *Theory of Social Economy* was published in 1914. Schumpeter himself noted that Wieser's *Das Gesetz der Macht* (1926) had had its fundamental idea already presented in Wieser's *Recht und Macht* in 1910.[38] Apropos of the discussion to follow, in which I attempt to suggest the influence of Wieser on Schumpeter, Bert Hoselitz's statement regarding Schumpeter will be seen to apply to Wieser as well:

> Schumpeter's main contribution to social theory consists then, above all, in having overcome the partial equilibrium analysis of the Austrian school of economics and replacing it by emphasis on general equilibrium; a general equilibrium, moreover, in which due attention is paid not merely to economic factors, but also to political and social forces. In addition it consists in his stressing the essential sterility of the static approach and the need to regard social phenomena as dynamic processes, whose most important dimension is the historical.[39]

There are two points on which I must make my position or intention clear. First, in stressing the possible influence of Wieser on Schumpeter I do not intend to obliterate or diminish the effect which others had, or may have had, on Schumpeter, especially Marx, Walras, and Böhm-Bawerk Apropos of Böhm-Bawerk, for example, Haberler has written me that 'the relations of Schumpeter to Wieser as far as I know were not very close. He was much closer to Böhm-Bawerk than to Wieser who was probably responsible for Schumpeter not being called to the University of Vienna'.[40] This view is seconded by Machlup, who has the 'impression that there was not much of such a relationship. Schumpeter was much more a student of Böhm-Bawerk's than of Wieser's. His early publications reflect much more the stimulations received in Böhm-Bawerk's seminar than those from contacts with Wieser'.[41] I believe that what I have to say on Wieser and Schumpeter is not inconsistent with Haberler's and Machlup's view but does correct the record which, it appears, with the exception of Hutchison, largely neglects the influence of Wieser.

The second point concerns the precise relationship between Wieser and Schumpeter. This involves, in part, the subtle and tricky question of whether Schumpeter influenced Wieser more than Wieser influenced Schumpeter.[42] The dating of their respective major works between 1910 and 1914 (or 1926, when *Das Gesetz der Macht* was published shortly before its author died) precludes neither. It is more than likely that they learned from – influenced – each other; certainly, as we shall see, they shared certain ideas whose mutual possession may well have served to reinforce them in each other's minds. But the question of precise relationship also is one of evidence. In my view, the evidence clearly shows that Wieser and Schumpeter shared certain quite specific and (for economists) heterodox ideas as to paradigmatic vision and conceptual tools. I also think that the evidence suggests that at least a *prima facie* case can be made for certain influence of Wieser on Schumpeter.

Bearing on both questions – the relative importance of Böhm-Bawerk and Wieser to Schumpeter, and the precise relation of Wieser to Schumpeter – is their sharing of certain concerns, analytical elements, and concepts. These concerns, we shall see, are not unique to them; Marx and Pareto, as well as Taussig, among others, come readily to mind, at least with regard to several points. Whatever Schumpeter acquired from Böhm-Bawerk, there was added thereto a vision comprised of certain concerns which Schumpeter shared only and clearly with Wieser in the depth of their respective beliefs and in the precise formulations given them. Schumpeter differs from Marx, in part, largely in terms shared generally only with Wieser. Whatever one thinks of my *prima facie* case for certain influence of Wieser on Schumpeter, my discussion at least will underscore an approach to economic analysis shared by both men, and now largely overlooked.

SHARED PERSPECTIVE

Friedrich von Wieser was, of course, a major contributor to microeconomic theory, and Joseph Schumpeter believed that pure economic theory was the *sine qua non* of economics, a belief correlative with his understanding that one could distinguish more or less coherently between economic and non-economic variables for purposes of pure economic analysis. It is, however, of the utmost importance to recognize that both men understood economics to encompass much more than the pure economics of the market mechanism. It is particularly in the formulation of this broader economics that Wieser and Schumpeter show considerable affinity and it may be suggested that Wieser may well have influenced Schumpeter in a distinctive manner.

If one considers the major works of Wieser – *Natural Value* (1889), *Recht und Macht* (1910), *Social Economics* (1914), and *Das Gesetz der Macht* (1926) – and of Schumpeter – *Das Wesen und der Hauptinhalt der theoretischen Nationalökonomie* (1908), *Theory of Economic Development* (1912), *Imperialism and Social Classes* (1919, 1927), *Business Cycles* (1939), and *Capitalism, Socialism, and Democracy* (1942), as well as other writings – one sees immediately that the two authors were extraordinarily holistic in their conception of the economic system and in the range of variables which each brought to bear in his analyses. Neither paid only lip-service to larger considerations; each explored in considerable depth and with a wide-ranging scope questions of systemic organization and control as well as evolution.

Consider, first, systemic evolution. Neither took the regnant economic order as given. It had evolved and was undergoing continual transformation. Schumpeter's dramatic conception of creative destruction, whose magisterial formulation in *Capitalism, Socialism, and Democracy* was foreshadowed in his *Theory of Economic Development* thirty years earlier, was appreciated by Wieser in *Das Gesetz der Macht*, in which he wrote of capital having 'continued its irresistible work of economic construction, which at the same time is economic upheaval'.[43] Both men had truly secular time perspectives: Wieser's analysis in *Das Gesetz der Macht* is multi-millenial, and in Schumpeter's analysis in *Capitalism, Socialism, and Democracy*, for example, the period of a century figures prominently. Although neither man articulated in Darwinian or Veblenian terms, their evolutionism encompassed the profound ideas of systemic transformation, creative destruction, and the economy as a disequilibrium process, as well as notions constituting what Gunnar Myrdal has called cumulative causation.

Systemic evolution perhaps most fundamentally involves transformation of the organization and control arrangements of society, polity, and economy. Both Wieser and Schumpeter explored the evolution and the operation of society in many of its aspects in terms of power, especially in one form, namely, social or class structure. Neither typically committed the crude naturalistic fallacy of assuming as given the structural, systemic fundamentals of the existing economic order.

Both men understood capitalism as a system of power, specifically a bourgeois power phenomenon. Both understood that economic power structure was necessary to the weighting of individuals' preferences. Both saw the economy as vehicle for the advancement of the interests of those persons with economic, or political–economic, power. Both recognized the struggle for power over the economic order that takes place in society. Both understood that at the centre of the phenomenon of power is government and the mutual dependence of nominally private and public powers: private power is dependent upon the law, and the law is in part a creation of private power; government is a means to the several ends of power. Both men understood and inquired into various aspects of the multiplicity of power relationships and power situations in economy and society, including the psychology of power, the tendency of power to concentrate, the interdependence between legal and economic processes, the mythologies and ideologies of ostensibly widely diffused power in economic and political affairs, and so on. Both contemplated history as involving the adaptive transformation of power. Both recognized the conflicting tendencies in society toward greater hierarchy and greater equality, but both stressed the force of the former. Both considered imperialism a fact of national political and economic life. As Robert Ekelund has written of Wieser,[44] both men attempted to integrate power and utility as twin organizing principles.

Although neither Wieser nor Schumpeter believed that the market economy was, or for that matter ever had been, very competitive, the structure of economic markets was not the structural phenomenon of greatest interest to either of them. Both understood and indeed emphasized that social structure was of analytical and interpretive importance in understanding the organization, operation, and performance of the economy. Moreover, social power is to be understood in terms of class power. The analysis of both Wieser and Schumpeter is developed, not merely couched, in terms of class. The role of law and of education, for example, is, in part, the reproduction of social structure. We shall see shortly that Wieser's formulation and application of social structure considerations may well have had a significant influence on Schumpeter.

Although both men were interested in pure microeconomic theory, and both were able for purposes of analysis to distinguish between so-called economic and non-economic phenomena or variables, each understood that the economic system encompassed variables beyond those narrowly or technically denominated economic. Both recognized the trichotomy of economic history, statistics, and theory as comprising the core of economics but also added sociological variables, what Schumpeter called Economic Sociology in his own case,[45] and Historical Sociology or Sociological History in the case of Wieser.[46] However labelled, both men dealt with political economy, not a much narrower economics, and they did so even in books dealing principally with technical economic theory. In doing so they introduced, often in a theoretical or abstract fashion (*vide* Wieser's 'history without names')[47] the evolution of the structural, or organization and control, or power, dimensions of the economy.

What some others are predisposed to assign to history and sociology, Wieser and Schumpeter located within and at the core of the work of the economist. Especially did both men stress history. What Haberler has written of Schumpeter applies to Wieser as well: neither was a historicist, but both were strong supporters, and practitioners, of 'the historical method of understanding social and economic phenomena'.[48] Indeed, it is important to recognize that Schumpeter, who lauded scientific economic analysis – the economic statics of our discipline – wrote in his *History of Economic Analysis* that of the three fields – economic history, statistics, and theory – 'economic history . . . is by far the most important. I wish', he wrote, 'to state right now that if, starting my work in economics afresh, I were told that I could study only one of the three but could have my choice, it would be economic history that I should choose'.[49] I stress this in part because Wieser's last book, *Das Gesetz der Macht*, is essentially an interpretation of history, centring on the economic and political power developments of the century preceeding the 1920s in the light of trends that had emerged during several thousand years of Western history.

Both Wieser and Schumpeter, then, were interested, as economists, in a set of problems and variables going beyond, and indeed transcending, market pricing and resource allocation. They were not of the opinion that what others relegated to sociology, political science, and history was not fundamentally important in explaining and interpreting 'economic' phenomena. For both men, political–economic, sociological, and historical work constituted a legitimate and important, perhaps the most important, facet of economic study. By pursuing this work they, in part, avoided taking as given and thereby giving effect, in their microeconomic analysis, to the existing structure of power. They implicitly recognized therein the ultimate governing role of exogenous variables in the performance of endogenous variables. In these matters, furthermore, they had much in common. Questions of structure and historicity were considered critical by both men and in much the same manner and to similar effects. I turn now to two respects in which Wieser may well have had an influence on Schumpeter.

TWO AREAS OF POSSIBLE INFLUENCE

In at least two respects Wieser may have influenced Schumpeter.[50] Both are important to Schumpeter's work as well as to Wieser's. Wieser's influence here has been largely neglected. While the importance of one in Schumpeter's work has been recognized, namely (as Hutchison noted), the role of leadership, the other – discipline – has not been.

Leadership and the Leadership Selection Process

Wieser believed that power is hierarchical. Society and all organizations are hierarchical in structure. Stratification in society takes the form of leaders and masses. The basic form of the constitution of society is found in the division between leaders and masses.

The most fundamental of several specific laws of power, to Wieser, is the Law of Small Numbers. He stresses the historic fact of rule, lawmaking, and ownership of the means of production by a few. The universal and inevitable tendency is for power to concentrate (although there are tendencies over the centuries for power to diffuse). Democracy involves leadership and the Law of Small Numbers no less than any other system.

Hierarchical power structures thus provide, at the upper hierarchic levels, leadership. The role of leadership is to guide. The masses follow, either passively or actively, selecting among aspirants to (further) leadership on the basis of their perceived success. The masses also may provide anonymous leaders from their ranks. Success is the principal selection mechanism. Power is reinforced by success, through the attraction of a following, in industry as well as in government. Success confirms and reinforces power.

Much the same understanding was held by Schumpeter. He believed in and accepted the reality of hierarchic leadership structures in particular institutions and in society itself and in both economic and political organization. No less than Wieser, Schumpeter discussed and analysed hierarchic leadership in terms of class.

As for leadership, the role of hierarchism is to provide it. Schumpeter says that the long run interests of society are entrusted to the upper strata of bourgeois society,[51] because in his view therein lies the social leadership which organizes production, engages in saving and investment, and, as we shall see in a moment, controls and disciplines the human labour force of society.

Leadership selection also is critical to Schumpeter. 'The same apparatus which conditions for performance the individuals and families that at any given time form the bourgeois class, *ipso facto* also selects the individuals and families that are to rise into that class or to drop out of it.'[52] The crumbling of the capitalist class's economic power is due in part, in Schumpeter's view, to the failure of that class to reproduce or replenish itself with viable leadership material, that is, to the failure of its leadership selection process. More generally, in my view, Schumpeter's argument in *Capitalism, Socialism, and Democracy* involves a transformation of the leadership strata of society and of the leadership selection process from one centring on the traditional bourgeois family to one centring on the meritocracy of the corporate system.

However one interprets the meaning and significance of Schumpeter's particular argument, in short both Wieser and Schumpeter focused not only on class but also on the social leadership function performed by upper hierarchic classes and on the importance of the leadership selection process in society, polity, and economy. Schumpeter's views in these matters seem to reflect closely those of Wieser. Words which Schumpeter used to describe Frank William Taussig may be applied quite accurately both to Schumpeter and to Wieser, from whom Schumpeter very likely, if not undoubtedly, learned the lesson: 'He was among those few economists who realize that the method by which a society chooses its leaders in what, for its particular structure, is the fundamental social function . . . is one of the most important things about a society, most important for its performance as well as for its fate.'[53]

There are other aspects of Wieser's thought which seem reflected in Schumpeter's in these respects. One of them is central to microeconomics. Both Wieser and Schumpeter understood that prices are coefficients of economic choice (as Schumpeter expressed it) and that realized marginal utilities and prices were stratified on the basis of the distributions of income and wealth and of social structure (as Wieser expressed it).[54]

Discipline and Historical Education

One of the critical but unfortunately most neglected concepts in Schumpeter's analysis is that of discipline. It is a reformulation, in part, of Wieser's concept of historical education, which was no less critical to his analysis.

History, to Wieser, has been a process of education. It comprises training in civic duties and in peaceful, cooperative activity. Education exists in both school and life, the training of successive generations through formal and non-formal education. Through stern historical education the masses have been trained to participate in collective undertakings. Through historical education leadership has been transformed from despotic to liberal leaders. Wieser thus notes the process of maturation of the masses in England, following the spread of the franchise, a process for which the way had been prepared by earlier maturation. He notes that trade unions represent training in historical education, union discipline constituting a form of moral self-education. He notes that the education of politicians requires them to be financially secure individuals engaged in a full-time vocation.

The absence of historical education, or of sufficient maturity, is the core of Wieser's theory of modern dictatorship, including fascism. These dictatorships are due to situations in which the masses, in his view, have power before their historical education (including what he calls their freedom organs) has sufficiently advanced and they have adequately matured. They crave freedom and self-determination but lack the capacity for governance. The function of law-and-order dictatorship is to abet the task of historical education. Wieser is quite cold-blooded about this (and, of course, one is free to disagree with his interpretation). He is fully aware of the possibilities, indeed the ubiquity, of abuse of power.

The civilizing process is not something discussed frequently these days. With Wieser's multi-millenial perspective on European and world history, the process of historical, civilizing education becomes clearer.

Unlike any other major economist after Wieser, Schumpeter stressed the role of historical education, particularly regarding discipline and maturation. A theme pervading *Capitalism, Socialism, and Democracy* is a concern with discipline, a perceived need in every economic system to control and discipline the human labour force. Schumpeter, I think, would have been receptive to Bertrand de Jouvenel's observation that 'Whoever does not wish to render history incomprehensible by departmentalizing it – political, economic, social – would perhaps take the view that it is in essence a battle of dominant wills, fighting in every way they can for the material which is common to everything they construct: the human labor force'.[55] Schumpeter would have agreed and gone farther to emphasize the necessity of disciplining the human labour force by those in control, whatever the economic system.

'As regards discipline', he says, 'there is an obvious relation between the efficiency of the economic engine and the authority over employees which, by means of the institutions of private property and "free" contracting, commercial society vests with the bourgeois employer. This is not simply a privilege conferred upon Haves in order to enable them to exploit Havenots. Behind the private interest immediately concerned there is the social interest in the smooth running of the productive apparatus'.[56] He distinguishes 'authoritarian discipline, which is taken to mean the habit, inculcated by agents other than the disciplined individuals themselves, of obeying orders and of accepting supervision and criticism' from 'self-discipline . . . in part, at least . . . due to previous, even ancestral, exposure to the disciplining influence of authority', and also 'group discipline which is the result of the pressure of group opinion on every member of the group and similarly due, in part, to authoritarian training undergone in the past'.[57] This analysis applies to all economic systems but is introduced by Schumpeter as a prelude to a discussion of the comparative advantage of discipline in a socialist system. Here he argues that socialist society will not be able to dispense with authoritarian discipline although it will be less necessary than in a society of (fettered) capitalism, and authoritative enforcement of discipline will prove an easier task in socialism. Schumpeter stresses that 'we need not project the tendencies inherent . . . very far ahead in order to visualize situations in which *socialism might be the only means of restoring social discipline*' (emphasis in original). He concludes that 'it is clear in any case that the advantages which a socialist management will command in this respect are so considerable as to weigh heavily in the balance of productive efficiencies'[58] – because of the greater force of dismissal, less constraint on the use of authoritarian discipline, greater motivation to uphold authority, no government opposition, and the greater centrality of economic necessities.[59]

Schumpeter's analysis provides only superficially for the aggregation of individual worker preferences such as they are. More deeply, it posits disciplined preferences and motivation, with the discipline undertaken and targeted by the managers, perhaps formerly capitalist managers, afterward socialist managers. 'After all', he says, 'effective management of the socialist economy means dictatorship not *of* but *over* the proletariat in the factory',[60] a situation not, in his view, very different from that in capitalism. Elsewhere, Schumpeter laments that the increased permissiveness of bourgeois society limits the role of discipline.[61] Only Russia has solved the problem of industrial discipline.[62] One advantage of socialist or quasi-socialist parties in Europe after World War II was that 'they were the very people to administer the right dose of social reform, to carry it on the one hand, and to make the masses accept it on the other'.[63] Schumpeter does not generally think highly of those he considers politicians, but he does state that 'there is one very important thing' that the politician 'knows professionally, viz., the handling of men'.[64]

Finally, when it comes to the transition to socialism, it will be facilitated, Schumpeter feels, if capitalist society has matured, that is, if the economic process largely has socialized the human soul and the means of production through concentration of ownership in corporate business; if depersonalization and the wilting away of capitalist motivation and standards have taken place; and so on. Socialization in a state of immaturity is not impossible but is more difficult and likely to be more wild. Maturity requires historical preparation, a process largely (but not entirely) educational in character.[65]

CONCLUSION

In conclusion, let me say that I am here not concerned principally with the accuracy, importance, or normative status of these ideas and arguments regarding leadership, leadership selection, discipline, and maturation. I am intrigued by the parallel treatment given them by Wieser and by Schumpeter, as to both content and importance. My reading of their works suggests to me, at least, that Wieser may have influenced Schumpeter in these respects and therefore in a manner or direction of critical importance to Schumpeter's "system". Wieser, it would seem, needs to be given a more central role in the filiation of Schumpeter's ideas.

It also is clear that Schumpeter was institutionalist in the scope and content of his interests, but, possibly for reasons of ideology, world-view, and career, was loath to admit it. Schumpeter seems to have been ambivalent. He supported the ascendency of economics as the study of "pure" market statics (with a focus on price and resource allocation) but he also practised an economics transported, if not fully transformed, into Economic Sociology. In this he was preceded and possibly, if not quite likely, influenced in certain specifics by Wieser. He wanted to be accepted as orthodox and was sensitive about his broader interests, but underneath was his uninhibited institutionalism.

Notes

1. Joseph A. Schumpeter, *History of Economic Analysis* (New York: Oxford University Press, 1954), p. 6. Apropos of natural science, Schumpeter undoubtedly understated the role of the past in its development, a matter now clearer after the work of Thomas Kuhn.
2. Seymour E. Harris (ed.), *Schumpeter: Social Scientist* (Cambridge: Harvard University Press, 1951), p. 29.
3. Theo Suranyi-Unger, *Economics in the Twentieth Century* (New York: Norton, 1931), p. 319.
4. It also might be mentioned that Schumpeter grew to adulthood during a period of growing scepticism and pessimism regarding the future of European (not merely Austrian or Austro-Hungarian) civilization.
5. See Harris (ed.), *Schumpeter: Social Scientist*, p. 120, regarding Otto Bauer and Rudolf Hilferding.
6. For example, Jacob Oser, *The Evolution of Economic Thought*, 2nd edn: (New York: Harcourt, Brace & World, 1970), p. 413.
7. Arthur Smithies, in Harris (ed.), *Schumpeter: Social Scientist*, p. 18; and Oser, *Economic Thought*, p. 413.
8. T. W. Hutchison, *A Review of Economic Doctrines, 1870–1929* (New York: Oxford University Press, 1953), pp. 191–2.
9. In Harris (ed.), *Schumpeter: Social Scientist*, p. 54.
10. Ben B. Seligman, *Main Currents in Modern Economics* (New York: Free Press, 1962), p. 696.
11. In Harris (ed.), *Schumpeter: Social Scientist*, p. 17.
12. Ibid., p. 41.
13. Ibid., p. 106.
14. Enrich Schneider, *Joseph A. Schumpeter*, W. E. Kuhn, trans. (Lincoln: Bureau of Business Research, University of Nebraska, 1975), p. 1.
15. In Harris (ed.), *Schumpeter: Social Scientist*, p. 40.
16. Leo Rogin, *The Meaning and Validity of Economic Theory* (New York: Harper, 1956), pp. 546–8.
17. William M. Johnston, *The Austrian Mind* (Berkeley: University of California Press, 1972), p. 253.
18. Harris (ed.), *Schumpeter: Social Scientist*, p. ix; and W. E. Kuhn, *The Evolution of Economic Thought*, 2nd edn (Cincinnati: South-Western, 1970), p. 403. Paul Samuelson has written: 'Being the son of Schumpeter, I am the grandson of Böhm-Bawerk and Menger. Being the son of Leontief, I am the grandson of Bortkiewicz and am the great-grandson of Walras' (Paul A. Samuelson, *The Collected Scientific Papers of Paul A. Samuelson*, R. C. Merton (ed.) (Cambridge: MIT Press, 1972), vol. 3, p. 684).
19. Haberler, in Harris (ed.), *Schumpeter: Social Scientist*, pp. 25–6; and Schneider, *Schumpeter*, p. 51, n.3.
20. Joseph Dorfman, *The Economic Mind in American Civilization* (New York: Viking Press, 1959), vol. 4, p. 166; and Harris (ed.), *Schumpeter: Social Scientist*, pp. 56, 102.
21. Suranyi-Unger, *Economics*, p. 319; see also pp. 68–70. Also see Hutchison, *Doctrines*, p. 192.
22. Seligman, *Main Currents*, p. 696.

23. Schumpeter, *History of Economic Analysis*, p. 894.
24. Julian Freund, in Tom Bottomore and Robert Nisbet (eds.), *A History of Sociological Analysis* (New York: Basic Books, 1978), p. 183.
25. Lewis A. Coser, *Masters of Sociological Thought*, 2nd edn (New York: Harcourt Brace Jovanovich, 1977), p. 424.
26. Hutchison, *Doctrines*, p. 191.
27. Allen M. Sievers, *Revolution, Evolution, and the Economic Order* (Englewood Cliffs: Prentice-Hall, 1962), p. 26.
28. Quoted by Schneider, in Harris (ed.), *Schumpeter: Social Scientist*, p. 57.
29. Ibid., pp. 54, 57.
30. Ibid., p. 62.
31. Ibid., p. 108.
32. For the view that much of his important later work is 'either stated or foreshadowed in his early work', see Harris (ed.), *Schumpeter: Social Scientist*, p. ix and also pp. 27, 108, 127 and *passim*.
33. One also can speculate as to the influence of, or interests shared with, Eugen Ehrlich, a principal figure in the sociology of law and Schumpeter's colleague at Czernowitz (1908–11). Schumpeter wrote that Ehrlich's legal realism ('studying the actual legal ideas and habits of the people . . . and in making generalizations from these, rather than the abstractions of jurisprudence') was 'produced in a small Austrian university under the most unfavorable circumstances imaginable' Schumpeter, *History of Economic Analysis*, p. 794. One suspects at least mutual moral reinforcement if not also substantive influence.
34. Fritz Machlup, in Harris (ed.), *Schumpeter: Social Scientist*, p. 95; and Haberler, ibid., p. 29. Joseph A. Schumpeter, *Das Wesen und der Hauptinhalt der theoreticschen Nationalökonomie* (München und Leipzig: Duncker & Humblot, 1908), p. ix.
35. Harris (ed.), *Schumpeter: Social Scientist*, p. 29.
36. Hutchison, *Doctrines*, pp. 191–2.
37. Ibid., p. 192. Of course, one cannot expect affinity to mean identity. Thus, for example, although, as Johnston (*Austrian Mind*, p. 84) notes, both Wieser and Schumpeter shared a 'horror of ideology', the two disagreed as to the significance of the Austrian psychological approach to economics. Suranyi-Unger, *Economics*, p. 69, Emil Kauder, *A History of Marginal Utility Theory* (Princeton: Princeton University Press, 1965), p. 122; see also 'On the Concept of Social Value', in Joseph A. Schumpeter, *Essays*, Richard V. Clemence (ed.) (Cambridge: Addison-Wesley, 1951), pp. 1ff.
38. Schumpeter, *History of Economic Analysis*, p. 795, n.29. The only reference to Wieser in *Capitalism, Socialism, and Democracy*, 3rd edn (New York: Harper, 1950) is a citation that Weiser had hinted at the Barone solution in his *Natural Value*, which first appeared in 1889 (p. 173, n.2).
39. Joseph A. Schumpeter, *Imperialism and Social Classes*, Bert Hoselitz (ed.) (New York: Meridian Books, 1955), pp. ix–x.
40. Gottfried Haberler to Warren J. Samuels, 24 February 1982.
41. Fritz Machlup to Warren J. Samuels, 2 March 1982.
42. Richard S. Howey to Warren J. Samuels, 24 February 1982.
43. Friedrich von Wieser, *Das Gesetz der Macht* (Vienna: Springer, 1926),

translated by W. E. Kuhn, with an Introduction by Warren J. Samuels, as *The Law of Power* (Lincoln: Bureau of Business Research, University of Nebraska, 1983), ch. 12, sec. 5.

44. Robert B. Ekelund, Jr, 'Power and Utility: The Normative Economics of Friedrich von Wieser', *Review of Social Economy*, vol. 28 (September 1970), pp. 179–96.
45. Schumpeter, *History of Economic Analysis*, pp. 20–1.
46. Joseph A. Schumpeter, *Ten Great Economists* (New York: Oxford University Press, 1951), p. 301.
47. Ibid., p. 301; compare Schumpeter, *History of Economic Analysis*, p. 21.
48. Harris (ed.), *Schumpeter: Social Scientist*, p. 44.
49. Schumpeter, *History of Economic Analysis*, p. 12.
50. The following discussion is based in part on my Introduction to the translation of *Das Gesetz der Macht* (n. 43 above) and my 'A Critique of *Capitalism, Socialism, and Democracy*', in Charles Wilber, *Capitalism and Democracy: Schumpeter Revisited* (Notre Dame: University of Notre Dame Press, 1985).
51. Schumpeter, *Capitalism, Socialism, and Democracy*, pp. 145, 160.
52. Ibid., p. 74.
53. Schumpeter, *Ten Great Economists*, p. 217.
54. Friedrich von Wieser, *Natural Value*, William Smart, trans. (London: Macmillan, 1893; first published as *Der Naturliche Werth*, 1889), pp. 58–60, 242, and *passim*. For Schumpeter's view, see his 'On the Concept of Social Value', pp. 2, 4, 6.
55. Bertrand de Jouvenal, *On Power* (Boston: Beacon Press, 1962), p. 177.
56. Schumpeter, *Capitalism, Socialism, and Democracy*, p. 210.
57. Ibid., p. 211.
58. Ibid., p. 215.
59. Ibid., p. 215.
60. Ibid., p. 302.
61. Ibid., pp. 151, 214.
62. Ibid., pp. 216ff., 379, 385–6.
63. Ibid., p. 355.
64. Ibid., p. 289.
65. Ibid., chapter 19.

16 Introduction, William H. Hutt, *Economists and the Public*[*]

William Harold Hutt (1899–1988) published his *Economists and the Public* in 1936, the momentous year which also witnessed the publication of John Maynard Keynes's *General Theory of Employment, Interest, and Money*. Keynes's great book had an enormous influence on Hutt's future work, as he became one of its most outspoken critics. But his own book of 1936 slowly gained a reputation of its own among a diverse group of admirers and now exists as a minor classic in economics.

Hutt was the son of a working-class family in London. He graduated from the University of London in 1924, having studied at the London School of Economics. He taught at the University of Cape Town, South Africa, for almost four decades, after which he was a visiting professor at several universities in the United States, including eleven years at the University of Dallas. Most of his published work was in labour economics, as a critic of strike-enforced collective bargaining, and in macroeconomics, as a critic of Keynesian macroeconomics; all of it in defence of his conception of the free-market economy. Hutt's intellectual pedigree is a mixture of non-Ricardian classical political economy, especially its nineteenth-century liberalism, and Austrian economics. He was associated with economists of a more or less similar orientation, including Edwin Cannan, Arnold Plant, and Lionel Robbins. As somewhat of an Austrian economist his thinking was close to that of Ludwig von Mises and Friedrich von Hayek; and as a nineteenth-century liberal, close to that of Henry C. Simons, Frank H. Knight, and Milton Friedman. His political–economic philosophy was utilitarian rather than natural-rights in orientation. He was a member of the Mont Pelerin Society.

Hutt's defence of capitalism centred on his belief that the competitive market was the institutional arrangement which best assured members of the working class of opportunity to improve their welfare. His criticism of the strike as a collective bargaining weapon was intended by him to protect

* Originally published in William H. Hutt, *Economists and the Public* (New Brunswick: Transaction, 1991)

the interests of the non-unionized from being shut out of jobs and of the mass of consumers from inflation, but was understood by his critics as anti-union. He denied the criticism, emphasizing that unions had important functions to perform. The difference apparently arose from conflicting perceptions of the legitimate role of unions. His advocacy of strong anti-trust enforcement was intended by him to promote competition as a process, but was understood by critics (not the same ones who lamented his treatments of strikes) as a willingness to use government coercion and therefore a lapse from his classical liberalism. As readers of this book will observe, Hutt's views on egalitarianism are complex, perhaps even inconsistent, certainly subtle. In his view, the system of economic freedom which he identified with the market economy was an egalitarian process which yielded temporary non-egalitarian results.

Economists and the Public is noteworthy in several respects. First, it encompasses a defence of English classical political economy and a criticism of what Hutt considered the subsequent corruption of economic thought; indeed, his economic theorizing, like that of so many others with similar views, was driven by his belief that it was the function of economists to both explicate and defend the market system. Second, it seeks a renaissance of the role of authoritative professional economic thought in the formation of public opinion and in public policy. Third, it attempts to legitimize the capitalist system in terms of both impersonal market forces and the doctrine of consumers' sovereignty, a concept with a long history but a term coined by Hutt in this volume. It attempts to deal in a coherent manner with the fundamental question of hierarchy versus equality in economy and society. Finally, it identifies three modes of thinking: rational-thought, custom-thought, and power-thought.

Hutt's identification of different modes of thought is somewhat in the tradition of Vilfredo Pareto's distinction between logico-experimental and non-logico-experimental thinking, and Thorstein Veblen's distinction between teleological and matter-of-fact preconceptions. It is also reminiscent of Pareto's notion of derivations and of James Harvey Robinson's concept of rationalizations. All these approaches to human modes of thought emphasize the distinctions between positive and normative statements and between statements intended strictly to inform and those intended to induce belief, action and policy. Hutt's efforts also seem to be somewhat in the tradition of structuralism, semiotics, deconstruction, and hermeneutics, in that it seeks to identify the deeper social meanings, premises, nuances, and implications (for example, for social structure) resident in ordinary language.

By 'rational-thought' Hutt means objective and, especially, disinterested inquiry, inquiry which can result in the accumulation of undisputed knowledge in the social sciences. He believes that traditional mainstream economics, at least after the vestiges of its corruption by class-interest driven ideology have been removed, is essentially rational-thought and thereby should be the premier basis for understanding our world and especially economic policy. By 'custom-thought' Hutt means modes of thinking which are infused with implicit premises and ideas derived from tradition and customary ways of doing and looking at things, a tradition dominated some times by the interests of upper hierarchic levels and at other times by the wishful thinking romanticism of the masses. By 'power-thought' Hutt means modes of thought and expression which are constructed to have intended effects on power, politics, policy, and whose meaning and significance derives principally if not completely from their service in psycho-political mobilization. Even though possibly sincere, power-thought is interested in consequences, not in truth *per se*. Power-thought may serve to reinforce custom-thought. (The distinction between custom-thought and power-thought, therefore, is not the same as that between continuity-oriented and changed-oriented residues in the Paretian system. But the emphasis on the manipulation of motivation and political psychology seems the same.)

At the very least, Hutt's presentation of the three modes of thought requires that analysts inquire into (1) the systemic and structural preconceptions of their theories and (2) the services which those theories may perform, intentionally or inadvertently, for various socioeconomic or political interests. The problem, of course, is that all language functions to induce persuasion and is in that sense manipulative. It is, therefore, not always clear when statements are to be comprehended, and presumably discounted, as power-thought. Judgement must be exercised – and such judgement may itself be driven by the same preconceptions that characterize the statements in question. Accordingly, Hutt's analysis seems to reduce to two things, first, the need for sensitivity to the presence of preconceptions and surreptitious motivations and consequences; and second, attention to human thought and communication as a *process* rather than comprising absolute truth.

Hutt's classical liberal orientation clearly made him unreceptive to a wide range of modern thought; so much is evident in this book. It also prevented him from appreciating the contributions of Keynes. In a series of books, including *The Theory of Idle Resources* (1939), *Keynesianism – Retrospect and Prospect* (1963), *A Rehabilitation of Say's Law* (1974), and *The Keynesian Episode* (1979), Hutt rejected Keynes's and Keynesian thinking, in part because he failed to appreciate what Keynes had to say about money as the means through which choice could be deferred in the face of either uncertainty or undesirable conditions, and therefore about decisions to spend or not spend in a manner contributory to the realization of new output, income, and employment. (Hutt's belief that all saving is invested fails to recognize that portfolio investment is not analytically the same as real investment. His emphasis that the Keynesian system turns on price rigidity, a view similar to that of Gardiner C. Means, was rejected by Keynes in favour of an emphasis on the failure of certain other assumptions of Say's Law). Even his own supporters fault his lack of clarity as to the role of money in both micro- and macroeconomic discoordination. Some of his lines of reasoning appear close to the contemporary doctrines of the rational expectations and new classical schools of macroeconomic thought, which have raised questions about, among other things, the meaning of 'full employment'. But his rejection also stemmed from his belief that Keynesian thought was power-thought, ideas useful for those who desired to use the state for purposes inconsistent with perceived liberal principles. It is this desire to denigrate the efforts of certain users of the state which motivates so much contemporary conservative (nineteenth-century liberal) economic thought in the United States, and including Hutt's.

Hutt's writing is not always easy to follow. His mind was very wide-ranging, and he often gave vent to a sensed necessity to explore both the many facets of a complex topic and cognate topics, so his argument is often quite complex and his writing sometimes appears unfocused. This predicament relates to his own diagnosis of the problems of liberal society: the failure of many people, including the masses and even many economists, to appreciate the very complex and subtle reasoning which is necessary to understand and appreciate the quality of the market economy.

But that consideration notwithstanding, not every one will concur with all of Hutt's arguments; indeed, there are serious defects. First, he is not completely self-referential: he fails fully to apply his own strictures concerning custom-thought and power-thought to his own thinking, though he is aware of the problem. Second, his model of modes of thought is not one of definite categories with conclusive and unequivocal content: judgements have to be made concerning what is rational-, custom-, and power-thought. Third, his treatment of coercion (and much else) is laden with selective perception: not necessarily wrong, but arguably one-sided, subjective, normative, and inconclusive. Fourth, as even his supporters acknowledge, his analysis is driven by evident biases. Fifth, his view of the canons of classical liberalism may be predicated on circumstances which even he acknowledged no longer exist, for example, the predominance of small, atomistically competitive firms. In other words, individualism is a very complex concept and various facets of it may be elicited by different existential circumstances. This bears, of course, on his treatment of equality and inequality, so that his evident love of individual autonomy must be juxtaposed to the existing structural and social-control conditions of life. This also means, however, that his repudiation of certain modern schools of economic and political thought may have been biased, a product of a particular, perhaps unrealistic, and certainly arguable understanding of modern economic life. His is only one conceptualization of the best ways of achieving increased economic and political welfare for the masses.

Hutt's thought is indeed very complex and subtle. This is particularly true of his treatment of the economic role of government. Instead of a blanket condemnation of government, in the natural-rights oriented tradition, Hutt had a characteristic utilitarian or instrumental view of it: government could be a tool for good or for bad. (At least one friendly critic cannot understand his willingness to use government coercion to promote competition through strong anti-trust enforcement. This person, who is more friend than critic, has no answer to the rebuttal that anti-trust law is a denial that the rights of private property include the right to monopolize and that private property itself is a result of government coercion – ideas which, it seems, Hutt appreciated.) Not the least simple was his explication (in *The Economics of the Colour Bar*, 1964, and elsewhere) of South African apartheid as the result of efforts by white labour unions to suppress competition from non-whites. Hutt opposed both apartheid and the excesses of unions (if not unions *per se*, which he denied doing), and it was easy for him to place blame for the former on the latter (and in retrospect his criticism of apartheid seems oddly muted for such an outspoken advocate of individualism).

Regardless of how much or wherein one agrees and disagrees with what Hutt has to say in this book, there is much of permanent importance to think about – and that is ample justification for reprinting the volume. Consider, for example, his view, discussed early in Chapter IX, that a 'major difficulty' in considering the late eighteenth and early nineteenth centuries 'is the fact that the poor were then merely a problem and not a power in politics'. And consider, in that connection, the situation that Jeremy Bentham, a major thinker during that period, has been called the father of both English individualism and English collectivism. If the masses (not only the poor) were 'a problem', they were a problem for those in power who had to cope with them and their often inarticulate but nonetheless manifest longings. Once the masses received the franchise (in quest of individualism in the sense that *all* individuals were somehow to count in both polity and economy), politicians in search of votes – and therefore politics – inexorably turned to their interests relative to the interests of the already established landed and non-landed propertied. Thus arose the welfare state – collectivism, or the creation of equivalents to private property in the form of legal protections and entitlements not honorifically designated as private property. The key questions here are the structure of power in the socioeconomy, or whose interests are to count; and the economic role of government, especially the legal change of the interests to which government is to give its support. Other questions include the sociology of economics and of the authority of economics in the formation of public opinion and policy; and the significance of the argument that the market is governed by impersonal market forces when the market itself is a product of structural factors which both form and operate through it, not the least in a world of inequality. The issues involved in this situation and in these questions are broad, complex, deep, and subtle; they are, in part, issues of the existence of individualism in a world of power, selective perception, and of language (such that Hutt could write in his 1963 book on Keynes that language can both hinder the perception and the saying of certain things;[1] and such that Murray Rothbard, of similar free-market views, could view Hutt's concept of consumer sovereignty as but a 'metaphorical shibboleth').[2] And they are the issues with which Hutt grapples in this volume.

Notes

1. Hutt readily acknowledged that this could apply to his own thinking as well as to that of others. W. H. Hutt, *Keynesianism – Retrospect and Prospect* (Chicago: Henry Regnery, 1963), p. ix.
2. Murray N. Rothbard, *Man, Economy, and the State* (Los Angeles: Nash Publishing, 1970), p. 561.

Name Index

Andrew, A(bram) Piatt, 8, 9, 176, 204–38
Ashley, William James, 8, 176–84

Bentham, Jeremy, 100–3, 107, 110, 114–15, 120, 172
Blaug, Mark, 3–4
Böhm-Bawerk, Eugen von, 187–8, 190–1, 193–4, 196–7, 269–70, 272

Cairnes, John Elliot, 195–6
Carver, Thomas Nixon, 207, 212–13, 245
Clark, John Bates, 270
Condorcet, Marquis de, 141, 145, 148–9

Edgeworth, Francis Ysidro, 8, 167–75
Ekelund, Robert E., 243, 274

Godwin, William, 141, 144–5, 148–9

Hale, Robert Lee, 8, 203, 205–8, 218n1
Hicks, John R., 169
Hutt, William H., 10, 284–9

Keynes, John Maynard, 8, 162–6, 286–7

Locke, John, 65, 179, 182–3

Malthus, Thomas Robert, 7–8, 118, 140–66, 180
Marshall, Alfred, 157, 167, 185, 187–9, 192, 196
Marx, Karl, 186, 269, 272
McCulloch, John Ramsey, 109–10, 114, 118–20, 192–3
McDougall, William, 250
Mill, John Stuart, 103–6, 108, 110–11, 115–16, 120–1

Quesnay, François, 5, 12, 17–21, 28–9, 32–41, 162

Pareto, Vilfredo, 246, 247, 251, 259, 260, 261, 285
Perlman, Selig, 251
Pigou, Arthur C., 172

Ricardo, David, 99–100, 106–7, 109, 113–14, 117–18, 151–3, 159, 186, 190, 192
Robbins, Lionel, 86–8, 115
Robinson, James Harvey, 285

Samuelson, Paul A., 9, 168
Schumpeter, Joseph A., 10, 267–83
Seldon, George Charles, 207, 212–14
Smith, Adam, 5–7, 47–85, 89–99, 111–13, 116–17, 153, 155–7, 158, 160, 179–80, 183–4, 195, 249–50, 251, 254, 258–9

Taussig, Frank William, 8, 9–10, 176, 184–98, 245–66, 277
Torrens, Robert, 100
Turgot, Anne Robert Jacques, 15–17, 20, 35

Veblen, Thorstein, 198, 259, 260, 261

Walras, Léon, 269
Wieser, Friedrich von, 9, 10, 239–44, 267–83

Subject Index

Austrian school, 239–44

business cycles, 203–22, 228
business cycle theory, 210–15

choice, 1
coercion, 47–64, 71
Colbertism, 31, 33–4
competition, imperfect, 169–70
conflict, 71–9
contract curve, 168
cost, 1
custom, 111–16

determinacy, problem of, 169–70
discipline, historical, 278–80
distribution, 73, 149–50, 159–62
domination, instinct of, 253–4, 263

economic sociology, 244
economics, functions of, 4, 285
education, 74–5, 116–21, 278–80
English Classical Political Economy, 47–166, 284–9
externalist interpretation, 181–4, 194–5

famine relief, 16–17
filiation of ideas, problem of, 267–73
fractional reserve banking, 235–6
freedom, 88–9, 103–4, 117

government, economic role of, 4, 5–7, 12–139

hermeneutic circle, 11
history of economic thought, externalist interpretation of, 181–4, 194–5
history of economic thought, functions of, 79–82, 181
history of economic thought, methodology of, 1–11, 65–7
history of economic thought, presentism in, 1–2
history of economic thought, problem of influence in, 267–73
history of economic thought, rational reconstruction of, 3–4, 11
history of economic thought, teaching of, 8–9, 176, 202

ideology, 192–3
imperfect competition, 169–70
influence, problem of, in history of economic thought, 267–73
injury, 55
instinct theory, 246–57, 260–1, 264–5
institutional school of economics, 241–2, 280
institutions, 72–9
inventors, 250–2, 262–3
invisible hand, 62, 71, 72

labour market, 49–52
laissez-faire, 5, 28–9, 38–43
leadership selection, problem of, 260, 276–7

macroeconomic theory, history of, 162–6, 203–38
market plus framework approach, 87–8
mathematical economics, 8, 167–75
maximization, 168, 170–5
mercantilism, 178–9
methodology, 153–5, 168
monetary economics, 223–38
monetary policy, 223–38
monetary theory, 223–38
money, 226–8
money makers, 252–4
moral restraint, 144–6
morals, as social control, 89–111
mutual coercion, 47–64

non-competing groups, 189–90, 196
non-deliberative social control, 86–139

order, problem of, 67, 70

Physiocrats, 5, 12–46, 195
political economy, 1–11, 65–85
population theory, 140–50, 180
power, 1, 5–6, 47–85, 149, 174, 198, 240, 243, 260, 274
presentism, 1–2

profit theory, 162
property, 12–23, 56–7, 98, 182–3
psychology, 245–66

quantity theory, 233–4

rational reconstruction, 3–4, 11
religion, as social control, 59–62, 89–111, 148–9
rent, 113, 159–61, 188–9

Say's Law, 8, 164, 211–15, 217–18, 234, 287
scarcity, 1–2
self-interest, 59
social change, 29–36
social construction of reality, 4, 32–6
social control, 12–151
stabilization policies, 16–18, 40–1
statistics, 206, 225

taxation, 18–21
thought, modes of, 285–6, 287–8

utilitarianism, 170–4, 288

wage theory, 161–2, 166, 189–90, 196

value theory, 156–9, 185–94